April 15–17, 2014
Berlin, Germany

I0012820

**Association for
Computing Machinery**

Advancing Computing as a Science & Profession

HiCoNS'14

Proceedings of the 3rd International Conference on
**High Confidence Networked Systems
(part of CPS Week)**

Sponsored by:
ACM SIGBED

Supported by:
TRUST - Team for Research in Ubiquitous Secure Technology

**Association for
Computing Machinery**

Advancing Computing as a Science & Profession

The Association for Computing Machinery
2 Penn Plaza, Suite 701
New York, New York 10121-0701

Copyright © 2014 by the Association for Computing Machinery, Inc. (ACM). Permission to make digital or hard copies of portions of this work for personal or classroom use is granted without fee provided that copies are not made or distributed for profit or commercial advantage and that copies bear this notice and the full citation on the first page. Copyright for components of this work owned by others than ACM must be honored. Abstracting with credit is permitted. To copy otherwise, to republish, to post on servers or to redistribute to lists, requires prior specific permission and/or a fee. Request permission to republish from: permissions@acm.org or Fax +1 (212) 869-0481.

For other copying of articles that carry a code at the bottom of the first or last page, copying is permitted provided that the per-copy fee indicated in the code is paid through www.copyright.com.

Notice to Past Authors of ACM-Published Articles
ACM intends to create a complete electronic archive of all articles and/or other material previously published by ACM. If you have written a work that has been previously published by ACM in any journal or conference proceedings prior to 1978, or any SIG Newsletter at any time, and you do NOT want this work to appear in the ACM Digital Library, please inform permissions@acm.org, stating the title of the work, the author(s), and where and when published.

ISBN: 978-1-4503-2652-0

Additional copies may be ordered prepaid from:

ACM Order Department
PO Box 30777
New York, NY 10087-0777, USA

Phone: 1-800-342-6626 (USA and Canada)
+1-212-626-0500 (Global)
Fax: +1-212-944-1318
E-mail: acmhelp@acm.org
Hours of Operation: 8:30 am – 4:30 pm ET

Printed in the USA

General Chairs' Welcome

It is our great pleasure to welcome you to the *2014 3rd ACM International Conference on High Confidence Networked Systems (HiCoNS'14)* as part of CPSWeek 2014. HiCoNS aims to bring together novel concepts and theories that can help in the development of the science of high confidence networked systems, in particular those considered cyber-physical systems (CPS). The conference will focus on system theoretic approaches to address fundamental challenges to increase the confidence of networked CPS by making them more secure, dependable, and trustworthy. An emphasis will be the control and verification challenges arising as a result of complex interdependencies between networked systems, in particular those at the intersection of cyber and physical areas. In doing so, the conference aims to advance the development of principled approaches to high confidence networked CPS.

This year's conference continues as a premier venue for showcasing research focused on improving the confidence of cyber-physical systems, in particular modern control technologies based on embedded computers and networked systems that monitor and control large-scale physical processes.

The conference technical program is exceptionally strong and we were pleased with the interest from so many authors who submitted to the conference as well as well-known subject matter experts presenting invited keynotes, and young researchers who will present research work in progress talks and posters. We would like to thank the Program Committee Co-Chairs Xenofon Koutsoukos and Saurabh Amin for their efforts to produce the conference program and the entire Program Committee who worked very hard in reviewing papers and providing feedback to the authors.

We also received significant support and guidance from the CPSWeek 2014 Steering Committee and we would like to especially thank CPSWeek 2014 General Chair Prof. Jürgen Niehaus and his staff for their assistance with the overall organization, coordination, and local arrangements.

Finally, we would like to thank the ACM Special Interest Group on Embedded Systems (ACM SIGBED) for sponsoring the conference, and the Team for Research in Ubiquitous Secure Technology (TRUST), a National Science Foundation Science & Technology Center, for organizing the conference. Putting together *HiCoNS'14* was truly a team effort!

We hope that you will find this program interesting and thought-provoking and that the conference will provide you with a valuable opportunity to share ideas with other researchers and practitioners from institutions around the world

Linda Bushnell
HiCoNS'14 General Co-Chair
University of Washington
USA

Larry Rohrbough
HiCoNS'14 General Co-Chair
University of California, Berkeley
USA

Program Committee Chairs' Welcome

It is our great pleasure to welcome you to the *2014 3rd ACM International Conference on High Confidence Networked Systems (HiCoNS'14)* as part of CPSWeek 2014. HiCoNS aims to foster collaborations between researchers from the fields of control and systems theory, embedded systems, game theory, software verification, formal methods, and computer security who are addressing various aspects of resilience of cyber-physical systems (CPS). HiCoNS continues after growing interest and enthusiasm that was created by the *First Workshop on Secure Control Systems (SCS)*, the *Workshop on the Foundations of Dependable and Secure Cyber-Physical Systems (FDSCPS)*, *HiCoNS'12,* and *HiCoNS'13*.

CPS govern the operation of critical infrastructures such as power transmission, water distribution, transportation, healthcare, building automation, and process control. At the core of these systems are modern control technologies based on embedded computers and networked systems that monitor and control large-scale physical processes. The use of internet-connected devices and commodity IT solutions and the malicious intents of hackers and cybercriminals have made these control technologies more vulnerable. Despite attempts to develop guidelines for the design and operation of systems via security policies, much remains to be done to achieve a principled, science-based approach to enhance security, trustworthiness, and dependability of networked cyber-physical systems.

HiCoNS'14 aimed to bring together novel concepts and theories that will help in the development of the science of high confidence networked systems, in particular those considered cyber-physical systems (CPS) and their interactions with human decision makers. The conference focused on system theoretic approaches to address fundamental challenges to increase the confidence of networked CPS by making them more secure, dependable, and trustworthy.

The technical program includes sessions focused on Resilient Monitoring and Estimation, Security of Networked and Distributed Control Systems, Verification of Security Properties, and Security of CPS applications. The technical program also includes an invited session on improving CPS Resilience by integrating Robust Control and Theory of Incentives. During these sessions, presentations will cover both recent research results as well as new directions for future research and development. In addition, the program includes two invited talks and a poster session on emerging topics in resilience of CPS.

We would like to thank our colleagues on the Program Committee who expended a significant amount of time and energy in reviewing papers and formulating constructive comments and suggestions to the authors.

We hope conference attendees find the program as informative and engaging as we do and that these proceedings will serve as a valuable reference for security researchers and developers.

Xenofon Koutsoukos
HiCoNS'14 Program Chair
Vanderbilt University, USA

Saurabh Amin
HiCoNS'14 Program Chair
MIT, USA

Table of Contents

Regular Session: Networked and Distributed Control Systems

Invited Talk

Invited Session: On Improving CPS Resilience by Integrating Robust Control and Theory of Incentives

Author Index

HiCoNS 2014 Conference Organization

General Chairs: Linda Bushnell *(University of Washington, USA)*
Larry Rohrbough *(University of California, Berkeley, USA)*

Program Chairs: Saurabh Amin *(Massachusetts Institute of Technology, USA)*
Xenofon Koutsoukos *(Vanderbilt University, USA)*

Publications Chair: Shreyas Sundaram *(University of Waterloo, Canada)*

Publicity Chair: Mark Yampolskiy *(Vanderbilt University, USA)*

Posters Chair: Peter Horvath *(Vanderbilt University, USA)*

Program Committee: Anuradha Annaswamy *(Massachusetts Institute of Technology, USA)*
Hamsa Balakrishnan *(Massachusetts Institute of Technology, USA)*
Alvaro Cárdenas *(University of Texas at Dallas, USA)*
Dieter Gollmann *(Hamburg University of Technology, Germany)*
Sandra Hirche *(Technische Universität München, Germany)*
Himanshu Khurana *(Honeywell Automation and Control Solutions, USA)*
Deepa Kundur *(University of Toronto, Canada)*
Cedric Langbort *(University of Illinois at Urbana-Champaign, USA)*
Jerome Le Ny *(Polytechnique Montréal, Canada)*
Heath LeBlanc *(Ohio Northern University, USA)*
Michael Lemmon *(University of Notre Dame, USA)*
Rahul Mangharam *(University of Pennsylvania, USA)*
Sayan Mitra *(University of Illinois at Urbana-Champaign, USA)*
Miroslav Pajic *(University of Pennsylvania, USA)*
Radha Poovendran *(University of Washington, USA)*
Henrik Sandberg *(Royal Institute of Technology (KTH), Sweden)*
Galina Schwartz *(University of California, Berkeley, USA)*
Bruno Sinopoli *(Carnegie Mellon University, USA)*
Ashish Tiwari *(SRI International, USA)*
Yevgeniy Vorobeychik *(Vanderbilt University, USA)*
Yuan Xue *(Vanderbilt University, USA)*
David K.Y. Yau *(Singapore University of Technology & Design, Singapore)*

HiCoNS 2014 Sponsor & Supporter

Sponsor:

Supporter:

Resilient Multidimensional Sensor Fusion Using Measurement History

Radoslav Ivanov
Computer and Information
Science Department
University of Pennsylvania
Philadelphia, PA 19104
rivanov@seas.upenn.edu

Miroslav Pajic
Department of Electrical and
Systems Engineering
University of Pennsylvania
Philadelphia, PA 19104
pajic@seas.upenn.edu

Insup Lee
Computer and Information
Science Department
University of Pennsylvania
Philadelphia, PA 19104
lee@cis.upenn.edu

ABSTRACT

This work considers the problem of performing resilient sensor fusion using past sensor measurements. In particular, we consider a system with n sensors measuring the same physical variable where some sensors might be attacked or faulty. We consider a setup in which each sensor provides the controller with a set of possible values for the true value. Here, more precise sensors provide smaller sets. Since a lot of modern sensors provide multidimensional measurements (e.g., position in three dimensions), the sets considered in this work are multidimensional polyhedra.

Given the assumption that some sensors can be attacked or faulty, the paper provides a sensor fusion algorithm that obtains a fusion polyhedron which is guaranteed to contain the true value and is minimal in size. A bound on the volume of the fusion polyhedron is also proved based on the number of faulty or attacked sensors. In addition, we incorporate system dynamics in order to utilize past measurements and further reduce the size of the fusion polyhedron. We describe several ways of mapping previous measurements to current time and compare them, under different assumptions, using the volume of the fusion polyhedron. Finally, we illustrate the implementation of the best of these methods and show its effectiveness using a case study with sensor values from a real robot.

Categories and Subject Descriptors

K.6.5 [**Security and Protection**]: Unauthorized access (e.g., hacking, phreaking); C.3 [**Special-purpose and Application-based Systems**]: Process control systems, Real-time and embedded systems

Keywords

CPS security; sensor fusion; fault-tolerance; fault-tolerant algorithms

Permission to make digital or hard copies of all or part of this work for personal or classroom use is granted without fee provided that copies are not made or distributed for profit or commercial advantage and that copies bear this notice and the full citation on the first page. Copyrights for components of this work owned by others than ACM must be honored. Abstracting with credit is permitted. To copy otherwise, or republish, to post on servers or to redistribute to lists, requires prior specific permission and/or a fee. Request permissions from permissions@acm.org.
HiCoNS'14, April 15–17, 2014, Berlin, Germany.
Copyright 2014 ACM 978-1-4503-2652-0/14/04 ...$15.00.
http://dx.doi.org/10.1145/2566468.2566475.

1. INTRODUCTION

With the cost of sensors constantly falling in recent years, modern Cyber Physical Systems (CPS) can now be equipped with multiple sensors measuring the same physical variable (e.g., speed and position in automotive CPS). Their measurements can be fused to obtain an estimate that is more accurate than any individual sensor's, thus improving the system's performance and reliability. Furthermore, having diverse sensors increases the system's robustness to environmental disturbances (e.g., a tunnel or a mountainous region for automotive CPS that heavily rely on GPS navigation) and sensor limitations (e.g., low sampling rate, biased measurement noise).

The increase in sensor diversity naturally leads to different characteristics of the various sensors. In particular, some sensors may have drift (e.g., IMU), others may not be very accurate (e.g., smart phone applications [12]), yet others may be accurate but not always reliable (e.g., GPS). Hence, the goal of any effective sensor fusion algorithm is to account for these limitations and output a measurement that is robust and accurate.

The importance of reliable sensor fusion is further highlighted with the increase of autonomy of modern control systems. In automotive CPS, for instance, a malicious attacker may be able to corrupt the measurements of some sensors, thereby misleading the controller into performing an unsafe action. The consequences of such attacks may range from slight disturbances in performance to life-threatening situations [3, 8]. Resilience to sensor attacks, therefore, is an emerging additional requirement for modern sensor fusion algorithms.

There is significant amount of academic literature devoted to the problem of fault-tolerant sensor fusion. Problems investigated depend first and foremost on the sensor model in consideration. The most popular model is a probabilistic one: a sensor provides the controller with a numeric measurement that is corrupted by noise with a known distribution (e.g., uniform, Gaussian) [5, 13]. In an alternative approach, a set is constructed around the sensor's measurement containing all points that may be the true value [10, 11]. The pivotal work with this viewpoint considers one-dimensional intervals around measurements and assumes an upper bound on the number of sensors whose intervals do not contain the true value; the author then provides worst-case bounds on the size of the fusion interval [9]. An extension of this work considers intervals in d dimensions, i.e., d-rectangles, and obtains similar results [4]. Furthermore, researchers assume a distribution of the true value over the intervals so probabilistic analysis can again be performed [14]. Finally, this model can be used not only to aid control but also for fault detection [7, 9].

This paper considers the problem of attack-resilient and fault-tolerant sensor fusion with multidimensional *abstract sensors*, i.e., a set is constructed around each sensor's measurement that contains all points that may be the true value. The size of the set depends on the sensor's precision – a larger set means less confidence in the sensor's measurement. Since most modern sensors employ internal filtering techniques (e.g., Kalman filters in GPS) these sets are not always as simple as *d*-rectangles; hence, we focus on *d*-dimensional polyhedra. Some camera-based velocity and position estimators used in urban robotics applications, for example, guarantee different position precisions for different robot velocities. Note that this paper extends our previous work in which we considered attack-resilient sensor fusion with one-dimensional intervals and investigated the effects of communication schedules on the size of the fusion interval (without incorporating past measurements) [6].

The sensor model considered in this work is very general as it does not make any assumptions about the distribution of sensor noise; instead, the polyhedron is constructed based on manufacturer specifications (e.g., worst-case guarantees about sampling rate and implementation limitations) and system dynamics. To deal with malicious and faulty sensors in these scenarios, we propose an extension to the sensor fusion algorithm for *d*-rectangles described by Chew and Marzullo [4]. Given this algorithm, we provide worst-case bounds on the size of the fusion polyhedron based on the number of assumed faulty or attacked (see Section 2 for a definition) polyhedra. Note that this approach could be extended to a set membership technique (e.g., [10, 11]) where some of the sensors or state estimators may be corrupted.

In addition, we note that most CPS have known dynamics. Therefore, this knowledge can be utilized to improve sensor fusion (i.e., reduce the size of the obtained region) by incorporating past measurements in the sensor fusion algorithm. To achieve this, we consider discrete-time linear systems with bounded measurement noise. Measurements are collected from sensors at each time step and are used for the remainder of the system's operation to reduce the size of the fused polyhedron. We consider all possible algorithms of using historical measurements (given our weak assumptions) and compare them by means of the volume of the fusion polyhedron. Finally, we provide a case-study with an autonomous vehicle, called the LandShark [1], to illustrate the effectiveness of the best of these methods. In particular, we consider four speed sensors, two of them also measuring position, that provide the controller with two-dimensional polyhedra. We then show the reduction in the volume of the fusion polyhedron when historical measurements are considered.

This paper is organized as follows. Section 2 introduces the problems considered in the paper, namely reliable multidimensional sensor fusion incorporating historical measurements. Section 3 provides a sensor fusion algorithm that meets the requirements outlined in Section 2. Section 4 extends the algorithm in Section 3 by incorporating system dynamics and past measurements. Section 5 presents an implementation of this algorithm and a case study to illustrate its effectiveness. Finally, Section 6 concludes the work.

2. PROBLEM FORMULATION AND PRELIMINARIES

This section describes the two problems considered in this paper. We start by formulating the multidimensional sensor fusion problem in a single time step (i.e., without taking history into account). Given this algorithm, we outline the problem of using system dynamics and past measurements to improve the system's sensor fusion.

2.1 Fusion Algorithm

We consider a system with n sensors measuring the same physical variables. Each sensor provides the controller with a d-dimensional measurement (e.g., position in three dimensions, or estimates of both position and velocity); a polyhedron is constructed around this measurement based on the sensor's precision and implementation guarantees (e.g., sampling jitter). Additionally, the sensor may have an internal filtering algorithm (e.g., Kalman filter) that will further affect the shape of the polyhedron. Thus, the controller will obtain n d-dimensional polyhedra $P_1, \ldots, P_n$ of the form $P_i = \{x \mid B_i x \leq b_i\}$, where $x \in \mathbb{R}^d$, $B_i \in \mathbb{R}^{m \times d}$ and $b_i \in \mathbb{R}^m$.

DEFINITION 1. *A sensor is said to be* correct *if its polyhedron contains the true value and* corrupted *(due to faults or attacks) otherwise.*

We assume an upper bound of f corrupted sensors; since the actual number of corrupted sensors is not known, f will usually be set conservatively high, e.g., $f = \lceil n/2 \rceil - 1$.

With these assumptions, the problem is to obtain an algorithm that, given n polyhedra as input, will output a polyhedron that is guaranteed to contain the true value and will be as small in volume as possible.

2.2 Fusing Past and Current Measurements

We note that most autonomous systems have known dynamics, hence previous measurements (i.e., measurement history) can be used to aid the fusion algorithm. In this paper we assume that sensors monitor a discrete-time linear system of the form:

$$x(t + 1) = Ax(t) + w.$$

Here $x \in \mathbb{R}^d$ is the state of the system (e.g., position), $A \in \mathbb{R}^{d \times d}$, and $w \in \mathbb{R}^d$ is bounded noise such that $\|w\| \leq M$, where $\| \cdot \|$ denotes the L_∞ norm, and M is a constant.

DEFINITION 2. *In this setting, a sensor is* corrupted *if there exists a time step t such that its polyhedron does not contain the true value at t.*

We still use f to denote the upper bound on the number of corrupted sensors. In particular, this means that there are at least $n - f$ sensors that are correct in all time steps. We relax this assumption in Section 5 when discussing which of the proposed methods of using history should be applied in real systems.

Given a sensor fusion algorithm that satisfies the requirements outlined in the previous section, in this scenario the problem is to find an algorithm to use past measurements that satisfies the following criteria:

- the final fusion polyhedron is guaranteed to contain the true value,

---
Algorithm 1 Sensor Fusion Algorithm

Input: An array of polyhedra P of size n and an upper
    bound on the number of corrupted polyhedra f
1: $C \leftarrow combinations\_n\_choose\_n\_minus\_f(P)$
2: $R_{\mathcal{N},f} \leftarrow \emptyset$
3: **for each** K in C **do**
4:     add($R_{\mathcal{N},f}$, intersection(K))
5: **end for**
6: **return** conv($R_{\mathcal{N},f}$)

- the fusion polyhedron is never larger in volume than the fusion polyhedron obtained when no history is used,

- the fusion polyhedron is as small as possible.

2.3 Notation

Let $\mathcal{N}(t)$ denote all n polyhedra at time t. In Section 3 we drop the time notation and write $\mathcal{N}$ since only one time step is considered. We use $S_{\mathcal{N}(t),f}$ to denote the fusion polyhedron given the set $\mathcal{N}(t)$ and a fixed f. Let $|P|$ denote the volume of polyhedron P; in particular, $|S_{\mathcal{N}(t),f}|$ is the volume of the fusion polyhedron. We use $\mathcal{C}(t)$ to denote the (unknown) set of all correct polyhedra.

3. SENSOR FUSION ALGORITHM

In this section, we describe a sensor fusion algorithm that meets the criteria outlined in Section 2 before providing a bound on the size of the fusion polyhedron based on the number of assumed corrupted sensors.

The algorithm is described in Algorithm 1. It is based on the algorithm for d-rectangles described by Chew and Marzullo [4]. It computes the fusion polyhedron by finding all regions contained in $n - f$ polyhedra, denoted by $R_{\mathcal{N},f}$, and then taking their convex hull in order to return a polyhedron, i.e.,

$$S_{\mathcal{N},f} = \text{conv}(R_{\mathcal{N},f}), \qquad (1)$$

where conv($\cdot$) denotes the convex hull. Intuitively, the algorithm is conservative – since there are at least $n - f$ correct polyhedra, any point that is contained in $n - f$ polyhedra may be the true value, and thus it is included in the fusion polyhedron; the convex hull is computed since the output should be in the same format as the inputs (i.e., a polyhedron).

The algorithm is illustrated in Figure 1. The system consists of three sensors, hence three polyhedra are obtained, and is assumed to have at most one corrupted sensor. Therefore, all regions contained in at least two polyhedra are found, and their convex hull is the fusion polyhedron (shaded).

PROPOSITION 1. *The fusion polyhedron computed by Algorithm 1 will always contain the true value.*

PROOF. Since there are at least $n - f$ correct polyhedra, the true value is contained in at least $n - f$ polyhedra, and hence it will be included in the fusion polyhedron. $\square$

PROPOSITION 2. *The fusion polyhedron computed by Algorithm 1 is the smallest convex set that is guaranteed to contain the true value.*

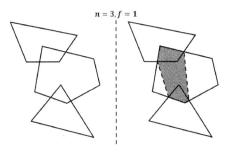

Figure 1: An illustration of the proposed sensor fusion algorithm.

PROOF. We first note that any set that is guaranteed to contain the true value must contain $R_{\mathcal{N},f}$ since any point that is excluded may be the true value. This proves the proposition since conv($R_{\mathcal{N},f}$) is the smallest convex set that contains $R_{\mathcal{N},f}$. $\square$

Having shown the desired properties of the proposed algorithm, we comment on its complexity. There are two subprocedures with exponential complexity. First, finding all combinations of $n - f$ polyhedra is exponential in the number of polyhedra. Second, computing the convex hull of a set of polyhedra requires finding their vertices; this problem, known in the literature as vertex enumeration, is not known to have a polynomial algorithm in the number of hyperplanes defining the polyhedra (hence in their dimension) [2].

To prove a bound on the volume of the fusion polyhedron, for completeness we first prove the following lemma that will be useful in showing the final result.

LEMMA 1. *The vertices of the convex hull of a set of polyhedra are a subset of the union of the vertices of the polyhedra.*

PROOF. Let p be any vertex of the convex hull. Then $p = \sum \theta_i v_i$, where the v_i are the vertices of the polyhedra, $\sum \theta_i = 1$ and $\theta_i \geq 0$ (i.e., p is a convex combination of the v_i's). This means that p lies on a hyperplane defined by some of the v_i's, hence it cannot be a vertex, unless it is one of the v_i's. $\square$

Before formulating the theorem, we introduce the following notation. Let $\min_p \mathcal{B}$ denote the pth smallest number in the set of real numbers $\mathcal{B}$ with size $r = |\mathcal{B}|$. Similarly, we use $\max_p \mathcal{B}$ to denote the pth largest number in $\mathcal{B}$. We note that $\min_p \mathcal{B} = \max_{r-p+1} \mathcal{B}$ (e.g., if $\mathcal{B} = \{14, 15, 16\}, \min_1 \mathcal{B} = 14 = \max_3 \mathcal{B}$). Finally, let v be the number of vertices in the fusion polyhedron.

THEOREM 1. *If $f < n/v$ then*

$$|S_{\mathcal{N},f}| \leq \min_{vf+1}\{|P| : P \in \mathcal{N}\}.$$

PROOF. We use a counting argument. Let $\mathcal{V}$ be the set of vertices of $S_{\mathcal{N},f}$. By Lemma 1, each vertex in $\mathcal{V}$ is a vertex of one of the polyhedra formed by the intersection of $n-f$ of the sensor polyhedra (in step 4 of Algorithm 1). Therefore, it is contained in at least $n-f$ polyhedra. For each $p \in \mathcal{V}$, let P_p denote the number of polyhedra containing p. Consequently, $P_p \geq n - f$. Then

$$v(n - f) \leq \sum_{p \in \mathcal{V}} P_p.$$

3

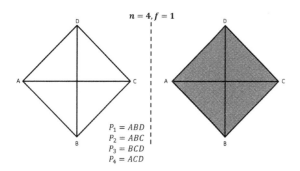

Figure 2: An example showing that the bound specified in Theorem 1 is tight.

The sum in the right-hand side can be split into two sums. One contains the number of polyhedra where each of the polyhedra contains all v vertices (we denote this number by a). Then the number of the remaining polyhedra is $n - a$. The part of the sum due to the polyhedra that contain fewer than v vertices can be bounded from above by $(n-a)(v-1)$ since each of these polyhedra contains at most $v-1$ vertices. We then have

$$v(n - f) \leq av + (n-a)(v-1),$$

which implies that $a \geq n - vf$, i.e., at least $n - vf$ polyhedra contain the v vertices of the fusion polyhedron. Since polyhedra, including the fusion polyhedron, are convex, we conclude that at least $n - vf$ polyhedra contain the fusion polyhedron. This completes the proof, since

$$|S_{\mathcal{N},f}| \leq \max_{n-vf}\{|P| : P \in \mathcal{N}\} = \min_{vf+1}\{|P| : P \in \mathcal{N}\}.$$

$\square$

Theorem 1 suggests that if $f < n/v$ then the volume of the fusion polyhedron is bounded by the volume of some polyhedron. We note that this condition may not always hold as the number of vertices of the fusion polyhedron may be the sum of the number of vertices of the polyhedra. However, the condition is tight in the sense that if it does not hold, then the volume of the fusion polyhedron may be larger than the volume of any of the individual polyhedra. This is illustrated in Figure 2. In this case, each polyhedron (P_1, P_2, P_3 or P_4) is a triangle that is a half of the big square, so $n = 4$, and $f = 1 = n/v$. Hence the fusion polyhedron, i.e., square, is larger in area than any of the triangles. In cases like this one, we resort to the following bound.

THEOREM 2. If $f < \lceil n/2 \rceil$, then $|S_{\mathcal{N},f}|$ is bounded by the volume of $\mathtt{conv}(\mathcal{C})$ (i.e., the convex hull of all correct polyhedra).

PROOF. Assume the opposite – that there exists a point $\mathbf{x}_A \in S_{\mathcal{N},f}$ that is not in $\mathtt{conv}(\mathcal{C})$. Then for any convex combination $\sum \theta_i v_i = \mathbf{x}_A$, where $v_i \in P_j$ for some j, at least one v_i must not be in $\mathcal{C}$, meaning that it is contained in at most f polyhedra, where $f < n - f$. Therefore, there does not exist a convex combination $\sum \theta_i v_i = \mathbf{x}_A$ with all v_i contained in at least $n - f$ polyhedra, and hence $\mathbf{x}_A$ cannot be in $S_{\mathcal{N},f}$. $\square$

In conclusion, three different upper bounds on the volume of the fusion polyhedron exist based on different values of f. If $f > \lceil n/2 \rceil$, then the fusion polyhedron can be arbitrarily large. This is due to the fact that there are now enough corrupted sensors to include points not contained in any correct polyhedra in the fusion polyhedron (as opposed to Theorem 2). On the other hand, if $f \leq \lceil n/2 \rceil$, then $|S_{\mathcal{N},f}| \leq |\mathtt{conv}(\mathcal{C})|$. In addition, if $f < n/v$, then the volume of $S_{\mathcal{N},f}$ is bounded from above by the volume of some polyhedron. Note that either of the last two bounds may be tighter than the other depending on the scenario.

4. FUSING PAST AND CURRENT MEASUREMENTS

Having developed a sensor fusion algorithm that produces a minimal polyhedron from n polyhedra in a given time step, we now consider the problem of incorporating knowledge of system dynamics to improve our resilient sensor fusion by using measurement history. As outlined in Section 2, we assume a discrete-time linear system with bounded noise of the form: $x(t + 1) = Ax(t) + w$. Furthermore, as outlined in Definition 2, the definition of a corrupted sensor is now modified – a sensor s is corrupted if there exists a time t at which s provides a polyhedron that does not contain the true value.

To simplify notation, we use the mapping m defined as

$$m(P(t)) = AP(t) + w,$$

where $P(t)$ is any polyhedron in time t. Then let $m(\mathcal{N}(t)) \cap_p \mathcal{N}(t+1)$ denote the intersection of each sensor s_i's measurement in time $t + 1$ with the mapping of s_i's measurement from time t. Note that this object again contains n polyhedra, some of which may be empty. We will refer to $\cap_p$ as *pairwise intersection*.

It is worth noting here that our assumptions impose a restriction on the number of ways in which history can be used. In particular, we only assume an upper bound on the number of corrupted sensors; thus, it is not possible to map subsets of the polyhedra while guaranteeing that the fusion polyhedron contains the true value. In other words, such mappings would require additional assumptions on the number of corrupted sensors in certain subsets of $\mathcal{N}(t)$; hence, all permitted actions in this work are: a) computing fusion polyhedra for all n polyhedra in a given time step; b) mapping this fusion polyhedron to the next time step; c) or mapping all polyhedra to the next time step, thus doubling both n and f. Formally, following are the ways of using past measurements considered in this work:

1. *map_n*: In this approach we map all polyhedra in $\mathcal{N}(t)$ to time $t+1$, and obtain a total of $2n$ polyhedra in time $t+1$. We then compute their fusion polyhedron with $2f$ as the bound on the number of corrupted polyhedra. This is illustrated in Figure 3a. Formally the fusion polyhedron can be described as

$$S_{m(\mathcal{N}(t)) \cup \mathcal{N}(t+1), 2f}.$$

2. *map_S_and_intersect*: This algorithm computes the fusion polyhedron at time t, maps it to time $t + 1$, and then intersects it with the fusion polyhedron at time $t+1$, as illustrated in Figure 3b. Formally we specify this as

$$m(S_{\mathcal{N}(t),f}) \cap S_{\mathcal{N}(t+1),f}.$$

3. *map_S_and_fuse*: Here the fusion polyhedron from time t is mapped to time $t+1$, thus obtaining a total of $n+1$ polyhedra at time $t+1$, as presented in Figure 3c. Note that f is still the same because $S_{\mathcal{N}(t),f}$ is guaranteed to contain the true value by Proposition 1. Formally this is captured by

$$S_{m(S_{\mathcal{N}(t),f}) \cup \mathcal{N}(t+1),f}.$$

4. *map_R_and_intersect*: This is similar to *map_S_and_intersect*, but instead we map $R_{\mathcal{N}(t),f}$ to time $t+1$, intersect with $R_{\mathcal{N}(t+1),f}$, and compute the convex hull as illustrated in Figure 3d. Formally we describe this as

$$\mathtt{conv}(m(R_{\mathcal{N}(t),f}) \cap R_{\mathcal{N}(t+1),f}).$$

5. *pairwise_intersect*: This algorithm performs pairwise intersection as shown in Figure 3e. Formally we capture this as

$$S_{m(\mathcal{N}(t)) \cap_p \mathcal{N}(t+1),f}.$$

The obvious way to compare these algorithms is through the volume of the fusion polyhedra. We provide below a series of results that relate the sizes of the fusion polyhedra for the aforementioned methods used to incorporate measurement history.

THEOREM 3. *The region obtained using map_R_and_intersect is a subset of the region derived by map_n.*

PROOF. Consider any point $p \in m(R_{\mathcal{N}(t),f}) \cap R_{\mathcal{N}(t+1),f}$. Then p lies in at least $n-f$ polyhedra in $\mathcal{N}(t+1)$, and there exists a q such that $m(q) = p$ that lies in at least $n-f$ polyhedra in $\mathcal{N}(t)$. Thus, p lies in at least $2n-2f$ polyhedra in $m(\mathcal{N}(t)) \cup \mathcal{N}(t+1)$, i.e., $p \in R_{m(\mathcal{N}(t)) \cup \mathcal{N}(t+1),2f}$, implying

$$\mathtt{conv}(m(R_{\mathcal{N}(t),f}) \cap R_{\mathcal{N}(t+1),f}) \subseteq \mathtt{conv}(R_{m(\mathcal{N}(t)) \cup \mathcal{N}(t+1),2f})$$
$$= S_{m(\mathcal{N}(t)) \cup \mathcal{N}(t+1),2f}.$$

□

THEOREM 4. *The polyhedron derived by map_R_and_intersect is a subset of the polyhedron obtained by map_S_and_intersect.*

PROOF. Note that for any sets $\mathcal{A}$ and $\mathcal{B}$, $\mathtt{conv}(\mathcal{A} \cap \mathcal{B}) \subseteq \mathtt{conv}(\mathcal{A})$, and thus

$$\mathtt{conv}(m(R_{\mathcal{N}(t),f}) \cap R_{\mathcal{N}(t+1),f}) \subseteq \mathtt{conv}(R_{\mathcal{N}(t+1),f})$$
$$= S_{\mathcal{N}(t+1),f}.$$

Furthermore, any point $p \in \mathtt{conv}(m(R_{\mathcal{N}(t),f}) \cap R_{\mathcal{N}(t+1),f})$ is a convex combination of points q_i in $m(R_{\mathcal{N}(t),f})$. But $m(R_{\mathcal{N}(t),f}) \subseteq m(S_{\mathcal{N}(t),f})$ (since $R_{\mathcal{N}(t),f} \subseteq S_{\mathcal{N}(t),f}$) and the fact that $m(S_{\mathcal{N}(t),f})$ is convex imply $p \in m(S_{\mathcal{N}(t),f})$. Accordingly,

$$\mathtt{conv}(m(R_{\mathcal{N}(t),f}) \cap R_{\mathcal{N}(t+1),f}) \subseteq S_{\mathcal{N}(t+1),f} \text{ and}$$
$$\mathtt{conv}(m(R_{\mathcal{N}(t),f}) \cap R_{\mathcal{N}(t+1),f}) \subseteq m(S_{\mathcal{N}(t),f})$$

implying

$$\mathtt{conv}(m(R_{\mathcal{N}(t),f}) \cap R_{\mathcal{N}(t+1),f}) \subseteq m(S_{\mathcal{N}(t),f}) \cap S_{\mathcal{N}(t+1),f}.$$

□

THEOREM 5. *The polyhedron obtained by map_R_and_intersect is a subset of the polyhedron derived using map_S_and_fuse.*

PROOF. Note that, since the fusion interval is always guaranteed to contain the true value, the number of corrupted polyhedra in *map_S_and_fuse* is still at most f, but the number of correct ones is now at least $n+1-f$. In addition, note that

$$m(R_{\mathcal{N}(t),f}) \cap R_{\mathcal{N}(t+1),f} \subseteq m(S_{\mathcal{N}(t),f})$$

since $m(R_{\mathcal{N}(t),f}) \subseteq m(S_{\mathcal{N}(t),f})$. Furthermore, any point $p \in R_{\mathcal{N}(t+1),f}$ is contained in $n-f$ polyhedra in $\mathcal{N}(t+1)$. Thus, all points in $m(R_{\mathcal{N}(t),f}) \cap R_{\mathcal{N}(t+1),f}$ are contained in $n+1-f$ polyhedra in $m(S_{\mathcal{N}(t),f}) \cup \mathcal{N}(t+1)$, and hence in $R_{m(S_{\mathcal{N}(t),f}) \cup \mathcal{N}(t+1),f}$. Since the fusion polyhedron is convex,

$$\mathtt{conv}(m(R_{\mathcal{N}(t),f}) \cap R_{\mathcal{N}(t+1),f}) \subseteq S_{m(S_{\mathcal{N}(t),f}) \cup \mathcal{N}(t+1),f}.$$

□

Theorems 3, 4 and 5 suggest that *map_R_and_intersect* is the best of the first four methods enumerated above as can also be seen in Figure 3. This intuitively makes sense since it is only keeping enough information from previous measurements to guarantee that the true value is preserved. In particular, it is not computing the convex hull at time t as *map_S_and_intersect* and *map_S_and_fuse* do (and potentially introduce additional points to the fused region), nor is it mapping potentially corrupted polyhedra as does *map_n*.

We note, however, that without additional assumptions about the rank of A, *map_R_and_intersect* and *pairwise_intersect* are not subsets of each other. Counter-examples are presented in Figure 4. In Figure 4a, $R_{\mathcal{N}(t),f}$ is a single point that is projected onto the x axis. Hence *map_R_and_intersect* is a subset of *pairwise_intersect*, which produces an interval of points. Conversely, Figure 4b shows an example where *pairwise_intersect* is a point, and *map_R_and_intersect* is an interval containing that point. It is worth noting, however, that regardless of which of the two approaches is used, *pairwise_intersect* can be used as a preliminary step to detect corrupted sensors – if the two polyhedra of a certain sensor have an empty intersection, then the sensor must be corrupted (faulty or tampered with) in one of the rounds; thus, it can be discarded from both, effectively reducing n and f by one.

Finally, we note that if A is a full rank matrix and $w = 0$, then *pairwise_intersect* is the best of all five methods, as shown in the following theorem.

THEOREM 6. *If A is full rank and $w = 0$, the polyhedron obtained by pairwise_intersect is a subset of the polyhedron derived using map_R_and_intersect.*

PROOF. Let p be any point in $R_{m(\mathcal{N}(t)) \cap_p \mathcal{N}(t+1),f}$. Then p lies in at least $n-f$ polyhedra in $m(\mathcal{N}(t))$ and at least $n-f$ polyhedra in $\mathcal{N}(t+1)$. Hence,

$$R_{m(\mathcal{N}(t)) \cap_p \mathcal{N}(t+1),f} \subseteq R_{\mathcal{N}(t+1),f}.$$

Furthermore, there exists a point $q = A^{-1}p$ that is contained in $n-f$ intervals in $\mathcal{N}(t)$. Therefore, p is also contained in $m(R_{\mathcal{N}(t),f})$. Then

$$R_{m(\mathcal{N}(t)) \cap_p \mathcal{N}(t+1),f} \subseteq m(R_{\mathcal{N}(t),f}) \cap R_{\mathcal{N}(t+1),f}, \text{ i.e.,}$$
$$S_{m(\mathcal{N}(t)) \cap_p \mathcal{N}(t+1),f} \subseteq \mathtt{conv}(m(R_{\mathcal{N}(t),f}) \cap R_{\mathcal{N}(t+1),f}).$$

□

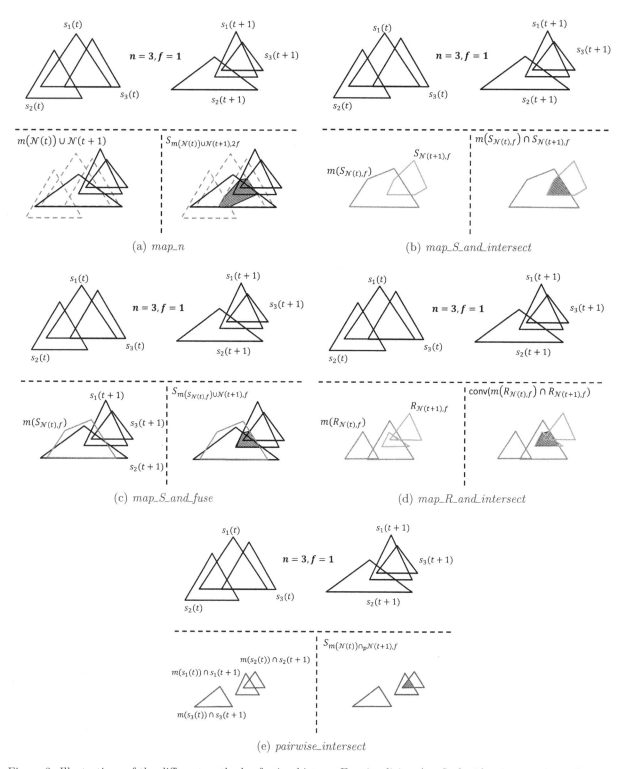

Figure 3: Illustrations of the different methods of using history. For simplicity $A = I$, the identity matrix, and $w = 0$.

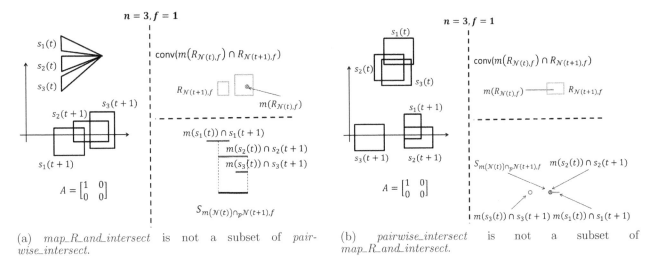

(a) *map_R_and_intersect* is not a subset of *pairwise_intersect*.

(b) *pairwise_intersect* is not a subset of *map_R_and_intersect*.

Figure 4: Examples showing that, in general, polyhedra obtained using *map_R_and_intersect* and *pairwise_intersect* are not subsets of each other if A is not full rank.

The conditions in Theorem 6 may seem too strong at a first glance. In reality, however, the difference between a singular and a nonsingular matrix is almost negligible. In particular, if A is singular, where λ_{min} is its smallest (in magnitude) nonzero eigenvalue, then $A + \varepsilon I$ is nonsingular, where $0 < \varepsilon < |\lambda_{min}|$. Therefore, systems with small noise in their dynamics will closely approximate the above requirements.

Therefore, we argue that systems that incorporate past measurements in their sensor fusion algorithms should use the *pairwise_intersect* method. We now show that it satisfies the requirements outlined in Section 2.

PROPOSITION 3. *The fusion polyhedron computed using* pairwise_intersect *will always contain the true value.*

PROOF. Note that pairwise intersection does not increase the number of corrupted polyhedra. If a sensor is correct, then both of its polyhedra (in time t and $t + 1$) contain the true value; in addition, the map m preserves the correctness of polyhedra, hence any pairwise intersection will also contain the true value. Thus, the number of corrupted and correct sensors is the same, therefore Proposition 1 implies that the fusion polyhedron contains the true value. □

PROPOSITION 4. *The fusion polyhedron computed using* pairwise_intersect *is never larger than the fusion polyhedron computed without using history.*

PROOF. Each of the polyhedra (e.g., $m(P_1(t)) \cap P_1(t+1)$) computed after pairwise intersection is a subset of the corresponding polyhedron when no history is used (e.g., $P_1(t+1)$). Consequently, the fusion polyhedron will always be a subset of the fusion polyhedron obtained when no history is used. □

Note that *pairwise_intersect* and *map_R_and_intersect* do not add significant computational complexity to the sensor fusion algorithm described in Section 3. While they still suffer from the exponential procedure of computing the fusion polyhedron at each time, each of the two methods requires storing at most n polyhedra to represent historical measurements - intuitively they are the "intersection" of all past

measurements. Thus, implementing any of these methods will not add substantial computational or memory cost for the system. The algorithm's implementation is discussed in greater detail in the following section.

5. APPLICATIONS

Given our results in Section 4, we argue that systems with linear dynamics should use the *pairwise_intersect* method. This section provides an algorithm that implements this method and a case study to illustrate its usefulness.

5.1 Implementation

The implementation is shown in Algorithm 2. In essence, at each point in time n polyhedra (the pairwise intersections) are stored. Thus, *past_meas* represents the "pairwise intersection" of all previous measurements of each sensor. In addition to being more efficient in terms of the size of the fusion polyhedron, the algorithm also needs very little memory – the required memory is linear in the number of sensors irrespective of how long the system runs.

An important detail that is hidden behind the `pair_inter` function is how corrupted sensors are dealt with. If a sensor s_i's two polyhedra have an empty intersection then that sensor must be corrupted. This is where we use the assumption about the same set of polyhedra that are corrupted over time. In particular, if we relax this assumption, then *pairwise_intersect* does not guarantee that the true value is contained in the fusion polyhedron. If this is the case, then we revert to *map_R_and_intersect*, the best of the methods that do not rely on this assumption.

On the other hand, if that assumption is satisfied, both polyhedra are discarded and n and f are reduced by one. Furthermore, the system has the option of discarding all future measurements provided by the sensor s_i; alternatively, the system may update *past_meas* with s_i's measurement in the next round. Which choice is made depends on the system's trust in the sensor – if it is believed to be often faulty or under attack, then discarding all or some of its future measurements is the better option. However, if it is faulty rarely, then its future measurements should be kept

Algorithm 2 Implementation of the *pairwise_intersect* algorithm

Input: f, the number of corrupted sensors
1: $past\_meas \leftarrow \emptyset$
2: **for each** step t **do**
3:     $cur\_meas \leftarrow \texttt{get\_meas}(t)$
4:     **if** $past\_meas == \emptyset$ **then**
5:         $past\_meas \leftarrow cur\_meas$
6:     **else**
7:         $past\_meas = \texttt{pair\_inter}(cur\_meas, past\_meas)$
8:     **end if**
9:     $S \leftarrow \texttt{fuse\_polyhedra}(past\_meas, f)$
10:     $\texttt{send\_polyhedron\_to\_controller}(S)$
11: **end for**

Figure 5: LandShark vehicle [1].

and incorporated in the algorithm. Quantification of sensor trust, however, is not within the scope of this paper, hence we take this choice as a design-time decision (input) and leave its analysis for future work.

5.2 Case Study

To show the effectiveness of the *pairwise_intersect* approach we use the sensors on a real autonomous vehicle, called the LandShark [1] (the robot is shown in Figure 5). The LandShark is capable of moving at a high speed on different surfaces and is usually used to carry humans or other cargo in hostile environments.

The LandShark has four sensors that can be used to estimate velocity – GPS, camera and two encoders. In addition, GPS and the camera can be used to estimate the vehicle's position. Therefore, the encoders provide the controller with interval estimations of the vehicle's velocity only, whereas GPS and the camera send two-dimensional polyhedra as estimates of the velocity and position.[1] The sizes of the encoders' intervals were obtained based on the manufacturer's specification, whereas the shapes and sizes of GPS and camera's polyhedra were determined empirically – the LandShark was driven in the open, and largest deviations from the true values (as measured by a high-precision laser tachometer) were collected.

Given this information, the following three scenarios were simulated. The LandShark is moving in a straight line at a constant speed of 10 mph. In each scenario, a different

---

[1] For this case study we only require one-dimensional position as will become clear in the next paragraph. However, our approach could easily be applied to multidimensional measurements.

sensor was attacked such that a constant offset of 1 mph was introduced to the sensor's speed estimate. The sensors' speed tolerances were as follows: 0.2 mph for the encoders, 1 mph for GPS and 2 mph for the camera. GPS's tolerance for position was 30 feet, whereas the camera's tolerance varies with speed (hence its polyhedron is a trapezoid) and was 100 feet at 10 mph. At each point in time, we compute the fusion polyhedron in two ways – using only current measurements and using the *pairwise_intersect* method. Finally, we record the differences and the improvement achieved by using history.

To illustrate consistence with earlier one-dimensional works (e.g., [9]), for each of the three scenarios we first computed the size of the fusion interval in one dimension. Figure 6 presents the results. For each scenario, the size of the fusion interval was never larger when using *pairwise_intersect*, while the gain was significant at certain times. This is particularly apparent when the encoder was under attack. The reason for this, as we have shown in our recent work, is that it is in general beneficial for the attacker to corrupt the most precise sensors [6].

Figure 7 presents the results when two-dimensional polyhedra are considered. Note that in this case there are only two sensors estimating the robot's position – when one is corrupted, the size of the fusion polyhedron can grow dramatically. Consequently, *pairwise_intersect* is greatly beneficial for the system as it identifies the corrupted sensors and discards their measurements when their polyhedra do not intersect. It is worth noting here that in all simulated scenarios if a sensor is found corrupted in any step we do not disregard its measurement in the next step. Note also that the volumes in Figure 7 are much larger than those in Figure 6 – this is a result of the fact that position tolerances are measured in feet and are larger than 10. (i.e., 30 feet for GPS). Finally, as consistent with Proposition 3, all fusion polyhedra contained the actual value of velocity (i.e., 10 mph).

6. CONCLUSION

This paper considered the problem of resilient multidimensional sensor fusion using measurement history. We focused on the setup where each sensor provides a multidimensional polyhedron as a measurement of the plant's state. We presented a fusion algorithm for this case and gave bounds on the volume of the fusion polyhedron based on the number of corrupted sensors. In addition, we investigated several methods of using history to improve sensor fusion and identified the best ones depending on what conditions the system in consideration satisfies. Finally, we presented a case study to illustrate the improvement in sensor fusion that can be obtained when history-based fusion is employed.

There are two main avenues that we plan to explore in the future. Firstly, one could consider extending this approach to nonlinear systems; in this scenario polyhedra may no longer be mapped into polyhedra. Thus, one can utilize a set membership technique in order to compute the set of possible true values [10, 11]. Secondly, one could take into consideration sensor trust, i.e., how often a sensor has been faulty over time, and incorporate this information in the mapping algorithm.

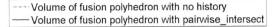

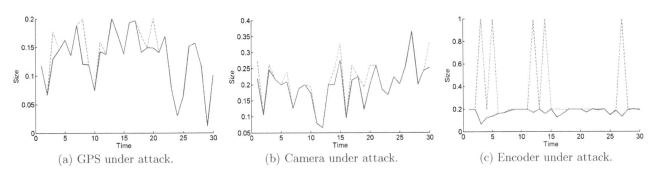

Figure 6: Sizes of velocity (ONLY) fusion intervals for each of the three simulated scenarios; Dashed line – volume of the fusion polyhedra when measurement history is not considered, Solid line – volume of the fusion polyhedra obtained using *pairwise_intersect*.

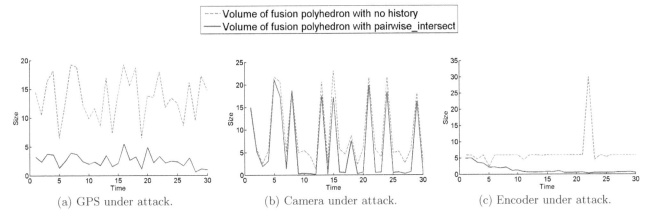

Figure 7: Sizes of fusion polyhedra of velocity and position for each of the three scenarios simulated; Dashed line – volume of the fusion polyhedra when measurement history is not considered, Solid line – volume of the fusion polyhedra obtained using *pairwise_intersect*.

7. ACKNOWLEDGEMENTS

This material is based on research sponsored by DARPA under agreement number FA8750-12-2-0247. The U.S. Government is authorized to reproduce and distribute reprints for Governmental purposes notwithstanding any copyright notation thereon. The views and conclusions contained herein are those of the authors and should not be interpreted as necessarily representing the official policies or endorsements, either expressed or implied, of DARPA or the U.S. Government.

8. REFERENCES

[1] The LandShark.
http://blackirobotics.com/LandShark_UGV_UC0M.html.

[2] D. Avis and K. Fukuda. A pivoting algorithm for convex hulls and vertex enumeration of arrangements and polyhedra. *Discrete and Computational Geometry*, 8(1):295–313, 1992.

[3] S. Checkoway, D. McCoy, B. Kantor, D. Anderson, H. Shacham, S. Savage, K. Koscher, A. Czeskis, F. Roesner, and T. Kohno. Comprehensive experimental analyses of automotive attack surfaces. In *SEC'11: Proc. 20th USENIX conference on Security*, pages 6–6, 2011.

[4] P. Chew and K. Marzullo. Masking failures of multidimensional sensors. In *SRDS'91: Proc. 10th Symposium on Reliable Distributed Systems*, pages 32–41, 1991.

[5] V. Delouille, R. Neelamani, and R. Baraniuk. Robust distributed estimation in sensor networks using the embedded polygons algorithm. In *IPSN'04: Proc. 3rd International Symposium on Information Processing in Sensor Networks*, pages 405–413, 2004.

[6] R. Ivanov, M. Pajic, and I. Lee. Attack-resilient sensor fusion. In *DATE'14: Design, Automation and Test in Europe*, 2014.

[7] D. N. Jayasimha. Fault tolerance in a multisensor environment. In *SRDS'94: Proc. 13th Symposium on Reliable Distributed Systems*, pages 2–11, 1994.

[8] K. Koscher, A. Czeskis, F. Roesner, S. Patel, T. Kohno, S. Checkoway, D. McCoy, B. Kantor, D. Anderson, H. Shacham, and S. Savage. Experimental security analysis of a modern automobile. In *SP'10: IEEE Symposium on Security and Privacy*, pages 447–462, 2010.

[9] K. Marzullo. Tolerating failures of continuous-valued sensors. *ACM Trans. Comput. Syst.*, 8(4):284–304, 1990.

[10] M. Milanese and C. Novara. Set Membership identification of nonlinear systems. *Automatica*, 40(6):957–975, 2004.

[11] M. Milanese and C. Novara. Unified set membership theory for identification, prediction and filtering of nonlinear systems. *Automatica*, 47(10):2141–2151, 2011.

[12] X. Niu, Q. Zhang, Y. Li, Y. Cheng, and C. Shi. Using inertial sensors of iPhone 4 for car navigation. In *Position Location and Navigation Symposium (PLANS), 2012 IEEE/ION*, pages 555–561, 2012.

[13] L. Xiao, S. Boyd, and S. Lall. A scheme for robust distributed sensor fusion based on average consensus. In *IPSN'05: Proc. 4th International Symposium on Information Processing in Sensor Networks*, pages 63–70, 2005.

[14] Y. Zhu and B. Li. Optimal interval estimation fusion based on sensor interval estimates with confidence degrees. *Automatica*, 42(1):101–108, 2006.

Fundamental Limits of Nonintrusive Load Monitoring[*]

Roy Dong, Lillian Ratliff, Henrik Ohlsson, and S. Shankar Sastry
Dept. of Electrical Engineering and Computer Sciences
UC Berkeley
Berkeley, CA, USA
roydong@eecs.berkeley.edu, ratliffl@eecs.berkeley.edu, ohlsson@eecs.berkeley.edu,
sastry@eecs.berkeley.edu

ABSTRACT

Provided an arbitrary nonintrusive load monitoring (NILM) algorithm, we seek bounds on the probability of distinguishing between scenarios, given an aggregate power consumption signal. We introduce a framework for studying a general NILM algorithm, and analyze the theory in the general case. Then, we specialize to the case where the error is Gaussian. In both cases, we are able to derive upper bounds on the probability of distinguishing scenarios. Finally, we apply the results to real data to derive bounds on the probability of distinguishing between scenarios as a function of the measurement noise, the sampling rate, and the device usage.

Categories and Subject Descriptors

H.1.1 [**Information Systems**]: Models and Principles—*energy disaggregation; nonintrusive load monitoring (NILM); performance bounds*

[*]The work presented is supported by the NSF Graduate Research Fellowship under grant DGE 1106400, NSF CPS:Large:ActionWebs award number 0931843, TRUST (Team for Research in Ubiquitous Secure Technology) which receives support from NSF (award number CCF-0424422), and FORCES (Foundations Of Resilient CybEr-physical Systems), the European Research Council under the advanced grant LEARN, contract 267381, a postdoctoral grant from the Sweden-America Foundation, donated by ASEA's Fellowship Fund, and by a postdoctoral grant from the Swedish Research Council.

Permission to make digital or hard copies of part or all of this work for personal or classroom use is granted without fee provided that copies are not made or distributed for profit or commercial advantage, and that copies bear this notice and the full citation on the first page. Copyrights for third-party components of this work must be honored. For all other uses, contact the owner/author(s). Copyright is held by the author/owner(s).
HiCoNS April 15-17, 2014, Berlin, Germany
ACM 978-1-4503-2652-0/14/04.http://dx.doi.org/10.1145/2566468.2576849.

1. INTRODUCTION

Nonintrusive load monitoring (NILM) is a general term which refers to determining the energy consumption of individual devices, or statistics of the energy consumption signal, without installing individual sensors at the plug level. The goals of different NILM algorithms include event detection, i.e. determine when certain devices switch states, and energy disaggregation, i.e. recovering the power consumption signals of each device in its entirety from the aggregate signal. In many cases, we would like to have the latter for many households, but installing sensors on every plug in each house is prohibitively expensive and intrusive. For example, studies have shown that merely providing users feedback on their energy consumption patterns is sufficient to improve their consumption behaviors [12, 17, 1]. Forecasts predict that 20% savings in residential buildings are attainable with the use of personalized recommendations based on disaggregated data. Additionally, these savings are sustainable over long time periods, and are not transient effects of introducing new interfaces to users. These device-level measurements can further be used for strategic marketing of energy-saving programs and rebates, both improving efficacy of the programs and reducing costs.

NILM algorithms can help guide regulation for privacy policies in advanced metering infrastructures (AMIs) [4]. Analyzing NILM algorithms is a way to determine how much device-level information is contained in an aggregate signal. This information is critical to understanding the privacy concerns in AMIs and which parties should have access to aggregate power consumption data. Further, NILM algorithms can provide a good benchmark for defining privacy risk; the state–of–the–art NILM algorithm may be a reasonably conservative model for an adversary. For example, if we use the framework defined in [8, 9], we can analyze how much energy disaggregation an adversary can achieve with a prior on the device usage patterns and models for individual devices.

Technologies and algorithms are constantly evolving, and to the best of our knowledge, there has not yet been an attempt to analyze the fundamental limits of NILM algorithms. An understanding of the fundamental limits can provide a theoretical guarantee of privacy, if we conclude that disaggregation is impossible in a certain scenario. It can be used in the design of AMIs, by determining a minimum sampling rate, sensor accuracy, and network capacity to achieve a desired goal. Further, it may allow us to determine how many measurements actually need to be stored and transmitted.

In this paper, we study the fundamental limits of NILM algorithms. We consider a building containing a number of devices. Given the aggregate power consumption of these devices, we would like to distinguish between two scenarios, e.g. whether or not a light turns on, or whether it was a toaster or kettle that turned on. In particular, provided an arbitrary NILM algorithm, we seek bounds on the probability of distinguishing two scenarios given an aggregate power consumption signal. Additionally, once we have this theory developed for two scenarios, we generalize to find an upper bound on the probability of distinguishing between a finite number of scenarios. With this theory of the fundamental limits of NILM in hand, we address questions about the possibility of NILM in the context of AMIs. Further, using high-frequency, high-resolution measurements of power consumption signals of common household devices as the ground truth, we analyze the probability of successfully identifying common scenarios in a household. We also analyze the tradeoff between successful NILM and sensor/model accuracy, as well as sampling rate.

This paper is organized as follows. In Section 2, we review the relevant literature. We formulate the NILM problem and the model of NILM algorithms in Sections 3 and 4 respectively. In Section 5, we discuss the fundamental limits of NILM algorithms. We derive bounds on distinguishing a finite number of scenarios using a classical hypothesis testing framework. In Section 6, we focus on the case where the NILM model is deterministic with additive Gaussian noise. We derive analytical expressions for bounds on the probability of distinguishing scenarios. We apply the theory to real–data gathered on a number of household appliances in Section 7. Finally, in Section 8, we make concluding remarks.

2. BACKGROUND

The problem of NILM is essentially a single-channel source separation problem: determine the power consumption of individual devices given their aggregated power consumption. The source separation problem has a long history in information theory and signal processing and well known methods include the infomax principle [2], which tries to maximize some output entropy, the maximum likelihood principle [5], which uses a contrast function on some distribution on the source signals, and a time-coherence principle [3], which assumes time-coherence of the underlying source signals. These often lead to formulations which use some variation of a principle components analysis (PCA) or independent component analysis (ICA).

The most common applications of the source separation theory is to audio signals and biomedical signals. For these applications, it is often assumed that source signals are i.i.d. stationary processes. We note that power consumption signals are very different from these types of signals. The power consumption of a device has strong temporal correlations and are not stationary, e.g. whether or not a device is on at a given time is correlated with whether or not it was on an instant ago, and the mean power consumption signal changes with the state of the device. The algorithmic and theoretical development in source separation have therefore not been successfully applied to NILM and most methods for NILM are rather different to those developed for classical source separation.

The field of NILM is much younger than source separation and most development has focused on algorithms. We briefly outline a few approaches here. One approach has focused on the design of hardware to best detect the signatures of distinct devices [18, 13, 11], but algorithms to handle the hardware's measurements are still an open problem. Another approach which has been taken by much of the machine learning community is to use hidden Markov models (HMMs), or some variation, to model individual devices [16, 15, 20]; energy disaggregation can be done with an expectation maximization (EM) algorithm. In recent publications [8, 9], we model individual devices as dynamical systems and use adaptive filtering. These are a few examples of concrete algorithms for NILM. For a more comprehensive review, we refer the reader to [1].

The discussion presented in this paper focus on the theoretical limitations of an arbitrary NILM algorithm. To the best of our knowledge, there has not been any previous work attempting to model the NILM problem in its full generality and derive theoretical bounds. The work is inspired by recent work in differential privacy [10, 6, 19, 14]. The underlying goal of differential privacy is to model privacy in a fashion that encapsulates arbitrary prior information on the part of the adversary and an arbitrary definition of what constitutes a privacy breach. The theory of differential privacy can be extended to give similar, but weaker, bounds to those derived in this paper.

3. THE PROBLEM OF NILM

As mentioned in Section 1, NILM has a variety of end uses. For each of these potential applications, the statistics of interest may be different. Thus, when we state the problem of NILM, we remain as general as possible to accommodate all these applications.

We are given an aggregate power consumption signal for a building. Let $y[t] \in \mathbb{R}$ denote the value of the aggregate power consumption signal at time t for $t = 1, \ldots, T$, and let $y \in \mathbb{R}^T$ refer to the entire signal. This signal is the aggregate of the power consumption signal of several individual devices:

$$y[t] = \sum_{i=1}^{D} y_i[t] \text{ for } t = 1, \ldots, T \tag{1}$$

where D is the number of devices in the building and $y_i[t]$ is the power consumption of device i at time t.

There are many possible goals of NILM. For example, the energy disaggregation problem is to recover y_i for $i = 1, 2, \ldots, D$ from y. Another goal commonly studied is to recover information about the y_i from y, such as when lights turn on or the power consumption of the fridge over a week.

Generally, we will refer to the phenomena we wish to distinguish as scenarios throughout this paper.

4. MODEL OF NILM ALGORITHMS

In this section, we outline a general framework for analyzing the problem outlined in Section 3. At a high level, the framework can be summarized as follows. First, any NILM method must choose some representation for individual devices; these can be seen as functions from some input space to $\mathbb{R}^T$. Depending on the purpose of the NILM algorithm, the input space will vary; essentially, scenarios we wish to distinguish should correspond to different inputs in the input space. Then, we describe NILM algorithms as functions on the observed aggregate signal. The definition is meant to be general and hold across both generative and discriminative techniques.

4.1 Aggregate device model

Formally, let $(\Omega, \mathcal{F}, P)$ denote our probability space. As in Section 3, D denotes the number of devices and T denotes the length of our observed power signal.

Let $\mathcal{U}_i$ denote the input space for for the ith device. Inputs represent scenarios we wish to distinguish. The output space, representing the power consumption signal of an individual device, is $\mathbb{R}^T$ for every device. Then, the model associated with the ith device can be denoted as $G_i : \mathcal{U}_i \times \Omega \to \mathbb{R}^T$. Here, we have the condition that, for any $u_i \in \mathcal{U}_i$, $G_i(u_i, \cdot)$ is a random variable. Finally, let $\mathcal{U} = \mathcal{U}_1 \times \mathcal{U}_2 \times \ldots \times \mathcal{U}_D$, and let $G : \mathcal{U} \times \Omega \to \mathbb{R}^T$ be defined as $G((u_1, u_2, \ldots, u_D), \omega) = \sum_{i=1}^{D} G_i(u_i, \omega)$. Here, G denotes our aggregated system, i.e. the model of our building.

Assumption 1. Given that the input is $u \in \mathcal{U}$, the distribution of the power consumption is $G(u, \cdot)$.

We emphasize the generality of this framework. Many state-of-the-art methods can be formulated in this framework. For example, factorial hidden Markov model methods [16, 15, 20] can be thought of as single-input, single-output systems where the input is the state of the underlying Markov chains. The Markov transition probabilities become a prior on the input signal. In previous work [8, 9], we formulated the models as dynamical systems whose inputs are real-valued and correspond to the device usage. Thus, we now have a general way of expressing different models of devices in a NILM problem.

4.2 NILM algorithms

An algorithm for NILM will be a function of our observed aggregate power consumption signal. Its result will depend on the goal of the algorithm, and the end use of the algorithm output. For example, it could be the set of possible estimated disaggregated energy signals, $\{\widehat{y}_i\}_{i=1}^{D}$, or the set of possible discrete event-labels on our time-series data, or a set of statistics on the disaggregated data.

More formally, let S represent some NILM algorithm and $\mathcal{Z}$ represent its output space, discussed above. Then, the algorithm could be thought of as a function $S : \mathbb{R}^T \to \mathcal{Z}$. We will analyze a general S in the following section.

5. FUNDAMENTAL LIMITS OF NILM

In this section, we derive an upper bound on the probability of successfully distinguishing two scenarios with any NILM algorithm. Then, we extend these results to handle the case where we wish to upper bound the probabilities of distinguishing a finite set of scenarios, as well as two collections of scenarios. Note that in our framework, scenarios correspond to inputs to our device models, and we will use the two terms interchangeably.

5.1 Distinguishing two scenarios

First, fix any two inputs $v_0, v_1 \in \mathcal{U}$ which we wish to distinguish. For example, we may pick v_0 and v_1 so that they differ only in the usage of one device. In that case, we are analyzing the difference in observed output caused by whether or not, say, a microwave turns on in the morning. Alternatively, we may choose inputs that correspond to more dissimilar scenarios, such as whether or not a household uses an air conditioner at all. The choice of v_0, v_1 depends on which scenarios we wish to distinguish in our NILM algorithm.

As mentioned previously, let $S : \mathbb{R}^T \to \mathcal{Z}$ denote any NILM algorithm. Then, let $I : \mathcal{Z} \to \{0, 1\}$ be an indicator for whether or not an algorithm output satisfies some condition. For example, I could output 1 if a particular discrete phenomena, e.g. a light turning on, is detected in the algorithm output, and 0 otherwise. Or, I could output 1 if the estimated power consumption signals of individual devices lies in a certain set.

Suppose that this indicator is supposed to capture whether our algorithm believes the input is v_0 or v_1. That is, $(I \circ S)$ should output 1 if the NILM algorithm believes the input is v_1 and 0 if it believes the input is v_0. For this reason, from this point forward we will refer to I as our discriminator.

Assumption 2. $(I \circ S)$ is measurable, i.e. $(I \circ S)^{-1}(\{1\})$ is a measurable set in $\mathbb{R}^T$, with respect to the Borel field on $\mathbb{R}^T$.

We note that this is a reasonable assumption, as most, if not all, NILM algorithms in practice will be a finite composition of measurable functions.

Additionally, we note that this is a very conservative understanding of an NILM algorithm. In general, these algorithms are not be designed simply to distinguish between v_0 and v_1, and are likely not to be optimal in this regard. Thus, by analyzing an optimal $(I \circ S)$, we have a conservative upper bound on the probability of distinguishing v_0 and v_1. In particular, the scenarios v_0 and v_1 may contain additional information, so our optimal separator is allowed to use side information, such as the switching times of devices, when doing inference, making our bound more conservative.

Furthermore, we can contrast our contribution with existing work in differential privacy. Whereas differential privacy would consider any v_0 and v_1 that are adjacent, and bound the change in distributions for a fixed mechanism, here we fix a particular v_0 and v_1 and consider a bound on the performance of any mechanism.

Thus, we can formulate this in classical hypothesis testing frameworks seen in the statistics literature [7]. Our main contribution is the abstraction of the task of NILM that allows us to use well-known results in detection theory.

Let y denote our observed signal. Suppose that $G(v_0, \cdot)$ has a probability density function (pdf) f_0 and similarly $G(v_1, \cdot)$ with f_1. Let our likelihood ratio be defined as:

$$L(y) = \frac{f_1(y)}{f_0(y)} \tag{2}$$

The maximum likelihood estimator (MLE) finds the input that maximizes the likelihood of our observations. The MLE is given by:

$$\widehat{u}_{\text{MLE}}(y) = \begin{cases} v_1 & \text{if } L(y) \geq 1 \\ v_0 & \text{otherwise} \end{cases} \tag{3}$$

If we have a prior p on the probability of v_0 or v_1 as inputs, we can find the maximum a posteriori (MAP) estimate. This finds the input that is most likely given our observations and prior. The MAP is:

$$\widehat{u}_{\text{MAP}}(y) = \begin{cases} v_1 \text{ if } L(y) \geq \frac{p(v_0)}{p(v_1)} \\ v_0 \text{ otherwise} \end{cases} \quad (4)$$

Note that this prior can be a discrete distribution or a density. However, for simplicity, we'll treat the prior as a discrete distribution throughout this paper; small notational changes are required for the prior to be a density.

Now, suppose we have a maximum acceptable probability of mislabeling the input v_1; let this parameter be denoted $\beta > 0$. Also, let u denote the true input. The optimal estimator with this constraint is:

$$\begin{aligned} \min_{\widehat{u}} \quad & P(\widehat{u} = v_1 | u = v_0) \\ \text{subject to} \quad & P(\widehat{u} = v_0 | u = v_1) \leq \beta \end{aligned} \quad (5)$$

By the Neyman-Pearson lemma, the non-Bayesian detection problem in Equation 5 has the following solution:

$$\widehat{u}_{\text{NB}}(y) = \begin{cases} v_1 \text{ if } L(y) \geq \lambda \\ v_0 \text{ otherwise} \end{cases} \quad (6)$$

where λ is chosen such that $P(\widehat{u}_{\text{NB}} = v_0 | u = v_1) = \beta$.

Throughout the rest of this paper, we will consider the MAP, but these can be extended to the other two cases. The probability of interest is the probability of successful NILM:

Definition 1. For the two-input case, the *probability of successful NILM* for an estimator $\widehat{u}$ is:

$$\sum_{i=0}^{1} P(\widehat{u}(y) = v_i | u = v_i) p(u = v_i) \quad (7)$$

This can be explicitly calculated given the densities and the prior. Additionally, any algorithm and discriminator ($I \circ S$) will perform worse than $\widehat{u}_{\text{MAP}}$, so the MAP estimate provides an upper bound on any algorithm's probability of successful NILM.

Proposition 1. Any estimator $\widehat{u}$ will have a probability of successful NILM bounded by:

$$\sum_{i=0}^{1} P(\widehat{u}_{\text{MAP}}(y) = v_i | u = v_i) p(u = v_i) \quad (8)$$

5.2 Distinguishing a finite number of scenarios

This easily extends to distinguishing between a finite number of scenarios. Let V denote a finite set of inputs. Then:

Definition 2. For the N-input case, the *probability of successful NILM* for an estimator $\widehat{u}$ is:

$$\sum_{i=1}^{N} P(\widehat{u}(y) = v_i | u = v_i) p(u = v_i) \quad (9)$$

The MAP is given by:

$$\widehat{u}_{\text{MAP}}(y) = \arg\max_{v \in V} P(G(u, \cdot) = y | u = v) p(u = v) \quad (10)$$

Proposition 2. There is an upper bound to the probability of successful NILM provided by the MAP:

$$\sum_{i=1}^{N} P(\widehat{u}_{\text{MAP}}(y) = v_i | u = v_i) p(u = v_i) \quad (11)$$

5.3 Distinguishing two collections of scenarios

This philosophy of deriving an upper bound extends nicely to whenever we wish to distinguish two collections of scenarios. This corresponds to distinguishing two sets of inputs.

Now, suppose we have two sets of inputs: V_0 and V_1. We can still define the probability of successful NILM in this context:

Definition 3. For the case where we wish to distinguish two sets of inputs, the *probability of successful NILM* for an estimator $\widehat{u}$ is:

$$\sum_{i=0}^{1} P(\widehat{u}(y) \in V_i | u \in V_i) p(u \in V_i) \quad (12)$$

Depending on the context, this quantity may be calculable. In other cases, it may be possible to find good approximations or upper bounds. We will see this arise in Section 6.

6. GAUSSIAN CASE

In this section, we instantiate our theory on the special case where our model is a deterministic function with additive Gaussian noise.

6.1 Two scenarios

Suppose our system takes the following form:

$$G(u, \omega) = h(u) + w(\omega) \quad (13)$$

where $h : \mathcal{U} \to \mathbb{R}^T$ is a deterministic function and w is a random variable. Furthermore, fix any two inputs v_0, v_1 which we wish to distinguish, and suppose that w is a zero-mean Gaussian random variable with covariance Σ. Furthermore, suppose our prior is $p(u = v_0) = p(u = v_1) = 0.5$.

This can encapsulate the case where the uncertainty arises from measurement noise and model error. Referring to our motivating example, suppose that the only difference between v_0 and v_1 is the presence of a toaster turning on once in v_1. The question we are asking is: can we detect the toaster turning on?

Then, let f_0 denote the Normal pdf with mean $h(v_0)$ and covariance Σ, and similarly let f_1 be the Normal pdf with mean $h(v_1)$ and the same covariance Σ. For shorthand, let $\mu_0 = h(v_0)$ and $\mu_1 = h(v_1)$.

Since the covariance matrix Σ is the same for both random variables, $\widehat{u}_{\text{MAP}}$ is determined by a hyperplane. Let $a^\top = (\mu_0 - \mu_1)^\top \Sigma^{-1}$ and $b = \frac{1}{2} \left(\mu_1^\top \Sigma^{-1} \mu_1 - \mu_0^\top \Sigma^{-1} \mu_0 \right)$. Then:

$$\widehat{u}_{\text{MAP}}(y) = \begin{cases} v_1 & \text{if } a^\top y + b \leq 0 \\ v_0 & \text{otherwise} \end{cases} \quad (14)$$

Now, suppose the input is actually v_0. That is, y is distributed according to f_0. Then, the signed distance from y to the boundary of the hyperplane is given by $\frac{1}{\|a\|_2}(a^\top y + b)$. This is a linear function of Gaussian random variable, and is thus also a Gaussian random variable. Furthermore, the mean of this random variable will be $\frac{1}{\|a\|_2}(a^\top \mu_0 + b)$, and

14

the variance will be:

$$\sigma^2 = \frac{1}{\|a\|_2^2} a^\top \Sigma a = \frac{(\mu_0 - \mu_1)^\top \Sigma^{-1}(\mu_0 - \mu_1)}{(\mu_0 - \mu_1)^\top \Sigma^{-2}(\mu_0 - \mu_1)} \quad (15)$$

Thus, given that the input is actually v_0, the probability that $\widehat{u}_{\mathrm{MAP}}(y) = v_0$ is:

$$P(\widehat{u}_{\mathrm{MAP}}(y) = v_0 | u = v_0)$$

$$= \frac{1}{2}\left(1 - \mathrm{erf}\left(\frac{-\frac{1}{\|a\|_2}(a^\top \mu_0 + b)}{\sqrt{2\sigma^2}}\right)\right) \quad (16)$$

where erf is the Gauss error function and Equation 16 is simply the 1 minus the cumulative distribution function (cdf) of the distance to the hyperplane evaluated at 0, i.e. the probability that the signed distance is positive.

The computations are exactly the same for the case where the input is v_1. Thus:

Proposition 3. By Equation 8, the probability of successfully distinguishing v_0 and v_1 with the MAP is given by:

$$\frac{1}{2}\left(1 - \mathrm{erf}\left(\frac{-\frac{1}{\|a\|_2}(a^\top \mu_0 + b)}{\sqrt{2\sigma^2}}\right)\right) \quad (17)$$

Note that, in general, disaggregation algorithms would not be designed simply to distinguish between v_0 and v_1, and are likely not to be optimal in this regard. That is, Equation 17 provides a theoretical upper bound on how good any possible disaggregation algorithm could perform in distinguishing v_0 and v_1. Also, note that $\frac{1}{\|a\|_2}(a^\top \mu_0 + b)$ will be positive if $\mu_0 \neq \mu_1$. It follows that the upper bound is always greater than 0.5 if $\mu_0 \neq \mu_1$, and the MAP achieves this upper bound. Thus, if the inputs cause different outputs from the system, there will always exist an algorithm that improves the discrimination between v_0 and v_1 over blind guessing.

6.2 N scenarios

In this subsection, we build on the development in Section 6.1 to handle the case where we wish to distinguish several inputs.

Suppose now that we have a finite set of inputs that we wish to distinguish. Consider the set $\{u_i\}_{i=1}^N$, where $u_i \in \mathcal{U}$ for each i. Again, suppose all these inputs are equally likely, i.e. $p(u = v_i) = \frac{1}{N}$ for all i. We wish to find the MAP. We carry over the assumption of Gaussian noise with variance Σ. The MAP will partition $\mathbb{R}^T$ with hyperplanes of the form given in Section 6.1.

So, suppose the actual input is u_1. We wish to ask: what is the probability the MAP will accurately identify u_1 from the other $N-1$ inputs? Let $\mu_i = h(u_i)$ for $i = 1, \ldots, N$. Then, let $a_i^T = (\mu_1 - \mu_i)^T \Sigma^{-1}$ and $b_i = \frac{1}{2}(\mu_i^T \Sigma^{-1}\mu_i - \mu_1^T \Sigma^{-1}\mu_1)$. Given our observation $y \in \mathbb{R}^T$, we wish to ask the probability that $\frac{1}{\|a_i\|_2}(a_i^T y + b_i) > 0$ for $i = 2, \ldots, N$, i.e. that the input u_1 is more likely than any of the other inputs. More succinctly, define:

$$A = \begin{bmatrix} a_2^T/\|a_2\|_2 \\ a_3^T/\|a_3\|_2 \\ \vdots \\ a_N^T/\|a_N\|_2 \end{bmatrix} \quad b = \begin{bmatrix} b_2/\|a_2\|_2 \\ b_3/\|a_3\|_2 \\ \vdots \\ b_N/\|a_N\|_2 \end{bmatrix} \quad (18)$$

We wish to ask the probability that $Ay + b$ is in the positive orthant of $\mathbb{R}^N$. Recall that y is distributed according to

mean μ_1 and covariance Σ. Thus, the random variable $Ay+b$ has mean $A\mu_1 + b$ with covariance $A\Sigma A^T$. The probability that this random variable is in the positive orthant cannot be analytically calculated, but can be approximated with high accuracy.

This can be done for $i = 2, \ldots, N$ as well, and provide an upper bound on the probability of successful NILM. An example based on real data will be explicated in Section 7.

6.3 Linear systems

In this subsection, we specialize the previous theory to the case where all our devices are linear systems. Suppose that the dynamics of our household are of the form $y = Au + e$, and our noise e has covariance $\widehat{\sigma}^2 I$. Note that σ^2 as defined in Equation 15 is equal to $\widehat{\sigma}^2$.

Now, suppose the sets that we wish to distinguish are $V_0 = \{0\}$ and $V_1 = \{v : L \leq \|v\|_2 \leq U\}$, for some constants $0 < L \leq U$. That is, can we detect an input with magnitude in the range $[L, U]$? By Equation 12, we have the probability of successful NILM for an estimator $\widehat{u}$ is:

$$P(\widehat{u}(y) = 0 | u = 0)p(u = 0) + P(\widehat{u}(y) \in V_1 | u \in V_1)p(u \in V_1) \quad (19)$$

First, consider a fixed input $v \in V_1$. If we suppose that $u = v$, then the probability of an estimator $\widehat{u}$ distinguishing v from 0 is bounded by:

$$P(\widehat{u}(y) \neq 0 | u = v) \leq \frac{1}{2}\left(1 + \mathrm{erf}\left(\frac{\|Av\|_2}{2\sqrt{2\sigma^2}}\right)\right) \quad (20)$$

This can be seen by noting that, after a projection into one-dimension, the separating hyperplane is the point $\pm\|Av\|_2/2$. Without loss of generality, let us suppose the separating point is $\|Av\|_2/2$.

Note that this equation is an increasing function of $\|Av\|_2$. This gives us:

$$\frac{1}{2}\left(1 + \mathrm{erf}\left(\frac{\|Av\|_2}{2\sqrt{2\sigma^2}}\right)\right) \leq \frac{1}{2}\left(1 + \mathrm{erf}\left(\frac{\sigma_{\max}(A)U}{2\sqrt{2\sigma^2}}\right)\right) \quad (21)$$

where $\sigma_{\max}(A)$ is the largest singular value of A. This held for any $v \in V_1$, so measure-theoretic properties give us:

$$P(\widehat{u}(y) \in V_1 | u \in V_1) \leq \frac{1}{2}\left(1 + \mathrm{erf}\left(\frac{\sigma_{\max}(A)U}{2\sqrt{2\sigma^2}}\right)\right) \quad (22)$$

Proposition 4. In the linear system case, the probability of successful NILM is bounded above by:

$$p(u = 0) + \frac{1}{2}\left(1 + \mathrm{erf}\left(\frac{\sigma_{\max}(A)U}{2\sqrt{2\sigma^2}}\right)\right)p(u \in V_1) \quad (23)$$

These are bounds which do not depend explicitly on a model, but rather only on the sensitivity of the model. Thus, even with just knowledge of the variance of the noise and the sensitivity of our linear systems, we can still find an upper bound on the probability of successful NILM.

7. REAL DATA ANALYSIS

In this section, we take the theory from Sections 5 and 6 and use them on real data to address several different problems. We used the emonTx wireless open-source energy monitoring node from OpenEnergyMonitor[1] from several devices at 12Hz. We used current transformer sensors

---

[1] http://openenergymonitor.org/emon/emontx

and an alternating current (AC) to AC power adapter to measure the current and voltage respectively of the devices that we monitored. For each device we measured the root-mean-square (RMS) current, RMS voltage, apparent power, real power, power factor, and a UTC time stamp.

Data was recorded in a laboratory setting for a microwave, a toaster, a kettle, an LCD computer monitor, a projector, and an oscilloscope. As our sensors are highly accurate, we treat the measurements as noise free.

Problem 1. What is an upper bound for the probability of successfully detecting a toaster turning on, as a function of the modeling and measurement error?

We took measurements from a toaster. The basic signal is shown in Figure 1. We use the assumptions outlined in

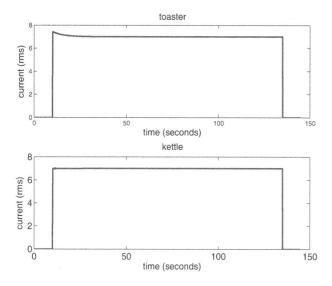

Figure 1: *Top:* The measured RMS current signal for a toaster. *Bottom:* The measured RMS current signal for a kettle.

Section 6.1. Additionally, we assumed that the covariance of the Gaussian noise was $\sigma^2 I$, i.e. the noise was uncorrelated at each time step. Following the analysis in Section 6.1, the probability of distinguishing the toaster turning on is shown in Figure 2.

Note that σ^2 has to grow considerably large before the optimal algorithm starts to fail to distinguish the toaster from nothingness. This is unsurprising, as the optimal algorithm would have several samples to distinguish quite separate means.

Problem 2. What is an upper bound for the probability of successfully distinguishing a toaster turning on and a kettle turning on, as a function of the modeling and measurement error?

We repeated this analysis with both a toaster and a kettle signal, depicted in Figure 1. The devices are on for exactly the same time window. The results are shown in Figure 3. As we can see, the variance on the error is orders of magnitude smaller when the probability drops to near 0.5. However, the σ^2 value is still quite large, and we likely can distinguish the two devices at 12Hz.

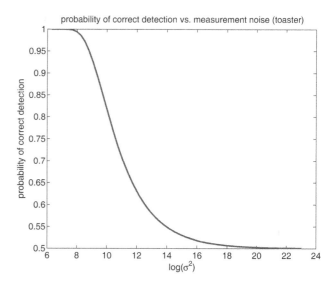

Figure 2: **The probability of successful identification of a toaster as a function of modeling and measurement error.**

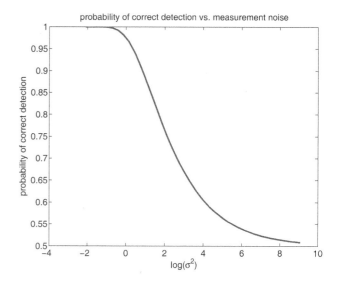

Figure 3: **The probability of successfully discriminating of a toaster and a kettle as a function of modeling and measurement error.**

Problem 3. What is an upper bound for the probability of successfully distinguishing a toaster turning on and a kettle turning on, as a function of the sampling rate?

The results to Problem 2 are promising, as they tell us it is very possible to distinguish two rather similar devices. However, the sampling rate of 12Hz is very high. Now, we analyze how likely we are to distinguish the two devices as the sampling rate changes. This is shown in Figure 4. We down-sampled the 12Hz signal. Additionally, if we down-sampled with rate K, we assumed it was equally likely that the signal would begin on any of the first K time-steps.

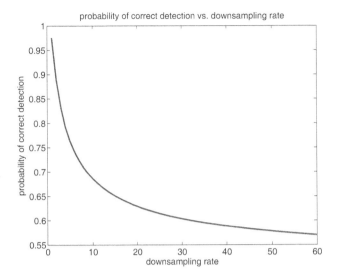

Figure 4: The probability of successfully discriminating a toaster and a kettle as a function of the sampling rate. We fixed $\sigma^2 = 1$.

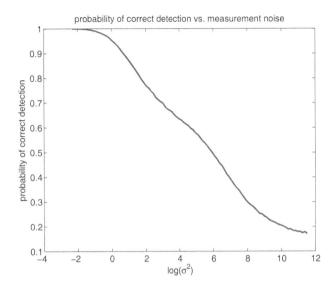

Figure 5: The probability of successfully discriminating one device from the $N-1$ other devices as a function of the measurement and modeling error.

It should be noted that a downsampling rate of K implies that we only receive $1/K$ as many measurements. Thus, if we sample for 1 second, our original problem would be a separation problem in $\mathbb{R}^{12000}$, whereas the downsampled problem is a separation problem in $\mathbb{R}^{\lfloor 12000/K \rfloor}$.

As expected, the probability of successful NILM decreases with the sampling rate. Additionally, the performance degrades quite quickly, and we barely perform better than guessing when the downsampling rate is 60, i.e. we sample every 5 seconds. This result allows us to determine a lower bound on the sampling rate necessary to achieve a certain effectiveness of NILM. It gives prescriptions on what hardware specifications and network capacity is needed in AMIs to achieve a certain goal.

Problem 4. What is an upper bound for the probability of successfully distinguishing several devices, as a function of measurement and modeling error?

Here, we use the results in Section 6.2. The devices in question are a microwave, a toaster, a kettle, an LCD computer monitor, a projector, and a digital oscilloscope. As before, we have one signal for each device, which is activated for the same time window for each device. That is, for each device, we have a *fixed* input. If each device is equally likely to turn on, we have the results shown in Figure 5.

Problem 5. What is an upper bound for the probability of successfully distinguishing several linear systems, as a function of the input magnitude?

Suppose we have the same 6 devices as in the previous problem. Furthermore, suppose they are linear systems, and the observed signals were a result of an input which was a pulse of magnitude 1. Then, we can use results from Section 6.3.

Suppose we wish to determine whether or not a device turned on. The input to our device is nonzero and bounded by U. We plot the upper bound from Section 6.3 on the probability of successful NILM as a function of U. The results are in Figure 6.

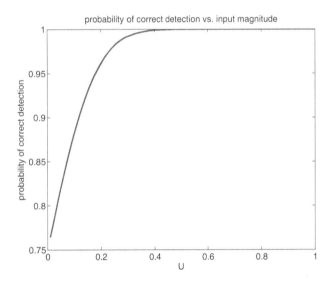

Figure 6: The probability of successfully discriminating a device turning on from the null hypothesis as a function of the input magnitude U. We fix $\sigma^2 = 1$.

8. CONCLUSION

In this paper, we explore the fundamental limits of NILM algorithms. More specifically, we derive an upper bound on the probability of distinguishing scenarios for an arbitrary NILM algorithm. First, we present the theory in its general case, and then we instantiate the theory on the case where the error is additive Gaussian noise independent of the underlying scenario. With this upper bound in hand, and our Gaussian assumption, we interpret real data we collected and discuss how the probability of successful NILM depends on the modeling and measurement error, the sampling rate, and the magnitude of the device usage.

To the best of our knowledge, this is the first paper investigating the fundamental limits of NILM. These fundamental limits are useful for several reasons. They can provide a guarantee on when NILM is impossible, which has implications for the design of privacy-aware AMIs, as well as privacy policies in AMIs. These limits are algorithm-independent, so they will hold regardless of changing technologies. These limits also can provide prescriptions for the design of AMIs, if NILM of a certain sort is desired, in terms of network capacity and sensor accuracy. Finally, it also provides a unified framework for understanding the problem of NILM.

9. ACKNOWLEDGMENTS

The authors would like to thank Alvaro Cárdenas for his helpful comments on an early draft of this document, as well as Aaron Bestick for stimulating conversations and assistance with our experimental setup.

10. REFERENCES

[1] K. C. Armel, A. Gupta, G. Shrimali, and A. Albert. Is disaggregation the holy grail of energy efficiency? The case of electricity. *Energy Policy*, 52:213–234, 2013.

[2] A. J. Bell and T. J. Sejnowski. An information-maximization approach to blind separation and blind deconvolution. *Neural Computation*, 1995.

[3] A. Belouchrani, K. Abed-Meraim, J.-F. Cardoso, and E. Moulines. A blind source separation technique using second-order statistics. *IEEE Transactions on Signal Processing*, 45(2):434–444, 1997.

[4] A. A. Cárdenas, S. Amin, G. Schwartz, R. Dong, and S. S. Sastry. A game theory model for electricity theft detection and privacy-aware control in AMI systems. In *Proceedings of the 50th Allerton Conference on Communication, Control, and Computing*, pages 1830–1837, 2012.

[5] J. Cardoso. Infomax and maximum likelihood for blind source separation. *IEEE Signal Processing Letters*, 4(4):112–114, 1997.

[6] K. Chaudhuri and D. Hsu. Sample complexity bounds for differentially private learning. In *COLT*, pages 155–186, 2011.

[7] T. M. Cover and J. A. Thomas. *Elements of Information Theory*. Wiley-Interscience, 1991.

[8] R. Dong, L. Ratliff, H. Ohlsson, and S. S. Sastry. A dynamical systems approach to energy disaggregation. In *Proceedings of the 52nd IEEE Conference on Decision and Control (CDC)*, 2013.

[9] R. Dong, L. Ratliff, H. Ohlsson, and S. S. Sastry. Energy disaggregation via adaptive filtering. In *Proceedings of the 51th Allerton Conference on Communication, Control, and Computing*, 2013.

[10] C. Dwork. Differential privacy. In *Proceedings of the International Colloquium on Automata, Languages and Programming*, pages 1–12. Springer, 2006.

[11] J. Froehlich, E. Larson, S. Gupta, G. Cohn, M. Reynolds, and S. Patel. Disaggregated end-use energy sensing for the smart grid. *IEEE Pervasive Computing*, 10(1):28–39, 2011.

[12] G. T. Gardner and P. C. Stern. The short list: The most effective actions U.S. households can take to curb climate change. In *Environment: Science and Policy for Sustainable Development*, 2008.

[13] S. Gupta, M. S. Reynolds, and S. N. Patel. Electrisense: single-point sensing using EMI for electrical event detection and classification in the home. In *Proceedings of the 12th ACM international conference on Ubiquitous computing*, Ubicomp '10, pages 139–148, New York, NY, USA, 2010. ACM.

[14] Z. Huang, S. Mitra, and G. Dullerud. Differentially private iterative synchronous consensus. In *Proceedings of the 2012 ACM Workshop on Privacy in the Electronic Society*, WPES '12, pages 81–90, New York, NY, USA, 2012. ACM.

[15] J. Z. Kolter and T. Jaakkola. Approximate inference in additive factorial HMMs with application to energy disaggregation. In *Proceedings of the International Conference on Artificial Intelligence and Statistics*, 2012.

[16] J. Z. Kolter and M. J. Johnson. REDD: A public data set for energy disaggregation research. In *Proceedings of the SustKDD Workshop on Data Mining Appliations in Sustainbility*, 2011.

[17] J. A. Laitner, K. Ehrhardt-Martinez, and V. McKinney. Examining the scale of the behaviour energy efficiency continuum. In *European Council for an Energy Efficient Economy*, 2009.

[18] S. Leeb, S. Shaw, and J. Kirtley, J.L. Transient event detection in spectral envelope estimates for nonintrusive load monitoring. *IEEE Transactions on Power Delivery*, 10(3):1200–1210, 1995.

[19] J. L. Ny and G. J. Pappas. Differentially private filtering. *arXiv:1207.4305*, July 2012.

[20] O. Parson, S. Ghosh, M. Weal, and A. Rogers. Nonintrusive load monitoring using prior models of general appliance types. In *Proceedings of the 26th AAAI Conference on Artificial Intelligence*, 2012.

Resilient Distributed Parameter Estimation in Heterogeneous Time-Varying Networks

Heath J. LeBlanc
Department of Electrical & Computer
Engineering and Computer Science
Ohio Northern University
Ada, OH, USA
h-leblanc@onu.edu

Firas Hassan
Department of Electrical & Computer
Engineering and Computer Science
Ohio Northern University
Ada, OH, USA
f-hassan@onu.edu

ABSTRACT

In this paper, we study a lightweight algorithm for distributed parameter estimation in a heterogeneous network in the presence of adversary nodes. All nodes interact under a local broadcast model of communication in a time-varying network comprised of many inexpensive *normal* nodes, along with several more expensive, *reliable* nodes. Either the normal or reliable nodes may be tampered with and overtaken by an adversary, thus becoming an *adversary* node. The reliable nodes have an accurate estimate of their true parameters, whereas the inexpensive normal nodes communicate and take difference measurements with neighbors in the network in order to better estimate their parameters. The normal nodes are unsure, a priori, about which of their neighbors are normal, reliable, or adversary nodes. However, by sharing information on their local estimates with neighbors, we prove that the resilient iterative distributed estimation (RIDE) algorithm, which utilizes redundancy by removing extreme information, is able to drive the local estimates to their true parameters as long as each normal node is able to interact with a sufficient number of reliable nodes often enough and is not directly influenced by too many adversary nodes.

Categories and Subject Descriptors

C.2.4 [**Computer-Communication Networks**]: Distributed Systems; C.4 [**Performance of Systems**]: Fault tolerance

General Terms

Algorithms, Security, Theory

Keywords

Resilient Systems; Distributed Algorithm; Distributed Parameter Estimation; Clock Synchronization; Localization; Adversary

1. INTRODUCTION

Distributed parameter estimation is a fundamental problem in complex distributed systems including Cyber-Physical Systems [12],

Permission to make digital or hard copies of all or part of this work for personal or classroom use is granted without fee provided that copies are not made or distributed for profit or commercial advantage and that copies bear this notice and the full citation on the first page. Copyrights for components of this work owned by others than ACM must be honored. Abstracting with credit is permitted. To copy otherwise, or republish, to post on servers or to redistribute to lists, requires prior specific permission and/or a fee. Request permissions from permissions@acm.org.
HiCoNS'14, April 15–17, 2014, Berlin, Germany.
Copyright 2014 ACM 978-1-4503-2652-0/14/04 ...$15.00.
http://dx.doi.org/10.1145/2566468.2566476.

sensor networks [7], and even social and economic networks. In certain applications, individual nodes in a network only have accurate *relative* (difference) measurements of parameters rather than *absolute* parameter measurements. For example, clock synchronization in sensor networks requires nodes to communicate to determine relative measurements of their clock parameters including offset and skew [13, 15, 22]. Also, relative position measurements using range sensors or GPS can lead to localization of a network of mobile sensor nodes [1, 14]. For example, GPS coordinates are much more accurate for relative position measurements rather than absolute position measurements due to the fact that measurement errors of different GPS nodes are highly correlated [25]. Even in social networks it is postulated that people use relative opinions of acquaintances to make decisions about consumer products and adoption of new technologies [5, 8]. Although oftentimes relative measurements alone are sufficient for the application, e.g., when measuring velocity using GPS or relative positions for collision avoidance, in other applications accurate absolute estimates are needed. Some applications include TDMA-based communication schemes [21] and autonomous vehicle navigation [2].

A common paradigm in distributed parameter estimation is to facilitate the estimation process by diffusing information throughout the network [18]. The goal is for each node to utilize communication with neighboring nodes to obtain more information than what is immediately available to it in order to compute a more accurate estimate of its true parameters. However, without at least one reliable node that has an accurate estimate of its parameter, the problem of distributed parameter estimation using relative measurements is indeterminate up to a constant error [11]. Therefore, it is insufficient for the network to be entirely *homogeneous*, i.e., comprised of inexpensive *normal* nodes capable of obtaining only accurate relative measurements. Instead it is better to have a *heterogeneous* network, which consists of many normal nodes and a few, more expensive, *reliable* nodes that are able to take an accurate absolute measurement of the desired parameter. For clock synchronization, reliable nodes amount to nodes with access to the Coordinate Universal Time (UTC). For GPS positioning, a reliable node might be a node close to its base station with a differential GPS. For social or economic networks, a domain expert would serve as a reliable node.

In large-scale distributed systems, there are many entry points for malicious attacks or intrusions. If one or more of the nodes are overtaken by an adversary, it is crucial for the networked system to continue operating with minimal degradation in performance. A system that is able to maintain state awareness and an acceptable level of operational normalcy in response to threats of an unexpected and malicious nature is referred to as *resilient* [23].

In this paper, we propose a resilient iterative distributed estimation (RIDE) algorithm. The RIDE algorithm determines accurate absolute estimates of each node's parameter using relative parameter measurements and parameter estimates from its neighbors. By removing extreme information from each node's neighborhood, RIDE is able to maintain resilience in the presence of a bounded number of adversaries in each node's neighborhood. More specifically, we prove that RIDE is resilient in time-varying heterogeneous networks under the assumption that each normal node interacts sufficiently often with reliable nodes and there is a specific bound on the number of adversaries in each node's neighborhood.

The rest of the paper is organized as follows. Section 2 describes the network, execution, and adversary models along with the problem formulation. Section 3 introduces the resilient iterative distributed estimation (RIDE) algorithm. The main theoretical results are given in Section 4. Simulations illustrating the results and exploring the behaviors of the adversaries are given in Section 5. Finally, concluding remarks and discussion of future work is given in Section 6.

2. SYSTEM MODEL AND PROBLEM

Consider a time-varying network modeled by the finite, simple *digraph* $\mathcal{D}(r) = (\mathcal{V}, \mathcal{E}(r))$, where $\mathcal{V} = \{1, ..., n\}$ is the *node set* and $\mathcal{E}(r) \subset \mathcal{V} \times \mathcal{V}$ is the *directed edge set* at round $r \in \mathbb{Z}_{\geq 0}$. The node set is partitioned into a set of *normal* cooperative nodes $\mathcal{N}$, a set of *reliable* cooperative nodes $\mathcal{R}$, and a set of *adversary nodes* $\mathcal{A}$.[1] The classification of each node is unknown a priori to the cooperative nodes. Each directed edge $(j, i) \in \mathcal{E}(r)$ indicates that node i receives information from node j during round r. The set of *in-neighbors*, or just *neighbors*, of node i in round r is defined as $\mathcal{N}_i^{\text{in}}(r) = \{j \in \mathcal{V} : (j, i) \in \mathcal{E}(r)\}$ and the (in-)degree of i is denoted $d_i^{\text{in}}(r) = |\mathcal{N}_i^{\text{in}}(r)|$. Similarly, the set of *out-neighbors* of node i in round r is defined as $\mathcal{N}_i^{\text{out}}(r) = \{j \in \mathcal{V} : (i, j) \in \mathcal{E}(r)\}$. Because each node has access to its own information, we also consider the *inclusive neighbors* of node i during round r, denoted $\mathcal{J}_i^{\text{in}}(r) = \mathcal{N}_i^{\text{in}}(r) \cup \{i\}$.

The time-varying digraph $\mathcal{D}(r) = (\mathcal{V}, \mathcal{E}(r))$ models the communication of the networked system. The nodes communicate under a *local broadcast model*, in which the out-neighbors of each node i in $\mathcal{D}(r)$ are precisely those nodes capable of receiving messages from i during round r. It is assumed that the sender of each message is identifiable by the receiver through a unique identifier; however, the classification of the node (as either normal, reliable, or adversary) is unknown.

2.1 Execution Model

The networked system is *partially synchronous*, meaning the nodes are not tightly synchronized, but there are known bounds on the skew and offsets of the clocks of the nodes such that an *iteration schedule* for the rounds may be formed a priori [11]. It is further assumed that the clock frequencies are stable, so there is effectively zero drift. For the class of algorithms studied in this work, the execution of each node proceeds in a sequence of rounds $r \in \mathbb{Z}_{\geq 0}$ that consists of *communicate*, *measure*, and *update stages*.

Associated with each node $i \in \mathcal{V}$ is a *parameter* of interest, denoted $p_i \in \mathbb{R}$, along with an *initial estimate* of that parameter, $x_i(0) \in \mathbb{R}$. At the beginning of each round $r \in \mathbb{Z}_{\geq 0}$, each cooperative node i broadcasts its estimate $x_i(r)$ to its out-neighbors

in the network and receives estimates $\{x_j(r)\}$, $j \in \mathcal{N}_i^{\text{in}}(r)$, from in-neighbors (communicate stage).

Each normal node i then obtains a *relative parameter measurement*, $\xi_{ji}(r) = p_j - p_i$, for each in-neighbor $j \in \mathcal{N}_i^{\text{in}}(r)$ (measure stage). Here, it is assumed that the relative measurement $\xi_{ji}(r)$ is either obtained from the message sent by in-neighbor j or that node i is able to take the relative measurement directly. For our model, this distinction is mostly important because in the former case, the adversary could provide both a false estimate and false relative measurement to each normal out-neighbor. It is assumed that the normal node $i \in \mathcal{N}$ *does not* have the equipment (e.g., sensors) to take a direct measurement of its parameter p_i, so false information on relative measurements are particularly detrimental to a normal node. Alternatively, the reliable node $j \in \mathcal{R}$ *does* have the equipment to take an accurate measurement of its parameter p_j.

2.1.1 Reliable Node Update Stage

Because each reliable node has an accurate measurement of its parameter, the reliable nodes do not need to participate in the update stage of the algorithm. Therefore, the estimate update is trivially

$$x_j(r+1) = x_j(r) = p_j, \quad \forall j \in \mathcal{R}, \ \forall r \in \mathbb{Z}_{\geq 0}.$$

2.1.2 Normal Node Update Stage

On the other hand, each normal node $i \in \mathcal{N}$ uses its own estimate $x_i(r)$, the estimates of the parameters of each of its neighbors $\{x_j(r)\}$, $j \in \mathcal{N}_i^{\text{in}}(r)$, and the difference measurement $\{\xi_{ji}(r)\}$, $j \in \mathcal{N}_i^{\text{in}}(r)$, to update its estimate as (update stage)

$$x_i(r+1) = f_i(x_i(r), \{x_j(r)\}, \{\xi_{ji}(r)\}), \quad j \in \mathcal{N}_i^{\text{in}}(r), i \in \mathcal{N}.$$

The update rule $f_i(\cdot)$ should be designed so that the normal node i is able to make use of the information shared by its neighbors in order to obtain a better estimate of its parameter. However, the adversary nodes may not follow the prescribed strategy, and may try to deceive normal node i by providing false or erroneous information. The adversary nodes therefore threaten the group objective, and it is important to design the $f_i(\cdot)$'s in such a way that the influence of such nodes can be eliminated or reduced without prior knowledge about their identities.

2.2 Adversary Model

The adversary nodes participate in the communicate, measure, and update stages during each round. If an adversary did not participate in the communicate stage, then no normal node would receive the potentially harmful information from the adversary. Similarly, because a node obtains the difference measurements from neighbors during the measure stage, the adversary would miss potentially useful information by not participating in the measure stage. Finally, the update stage simply indicates the manner in which the adversaries update their (false) estimates, so no update is still a trivial update. Overall, the behaviors in the update stage is described by the threat model and the scope of influence of the adversaries on the cooperative nodes is described by the scope of threat model.

2.2.1 Threat Model

The threat model studied in this paper is that of a Byzantine adversary under a local broadcast model of communication, which is referred to as a *malicious adversary*.

DEFINITION 1. *A node $i \in \mathcal{A}$ is said to be **malicious** if it sends $x_i(r)$ to all of its out-neighbors in each round, but applies some other function $f_i'(\cdot)$ during at least one round. Furthermore, a malicious node may be able to deceive its neighbors in the relative measurements $\{\xi_{ij}(r)\}$.*

---

[1] We use the term "cooperative nodes" to refer to both the normal cooperative nodes and reliable cooperative nodes. Further we interchange the terms "normal cooperative" and "normal" as well as "reliable cooperative" and "reliable".

Malicious nodes are able to update their estimates arbitrarily. If the relative measurements are sent by the in-neighbor of a node, then a malicious node can send a false relative measurement. However, if the relative measurements are obtained directly by each node, then there is no obvious means for the malicious node to deceive the normal node in the relative measurement.

2.2.2 Scope of Threat Model

Given the duplicitous and malicious nature of the adversaries considered, it is clear that their ability to interact with normal nodes must be limited for the normal nodes to have any chance at succeeding. It is a reasonable assumption that the attacker has limited resources and is only able to obtain control over a small subset of the normal nodes (so that these nodes controlled by the attacker are the adversary nodes). To capture this notion, we consider an upper bound on the number of adversary nodes in each normal node's neighborhood (F-local model).

DEFINITION 2 (F-LOCAL MODEL). *A set $\mathcal{S} \subset \mathcal{V}$ is F-**local** if and only if it contains at most F nodes in the neighborhood of the other nodes for all rounds $r \in \mathbb{Z}_{\geq 0}$, i.e., $|\mathcal{N}_i^{in}(r) \bigcap \mathcal{S}| \leq F$, $\forall i \in \mathcal{V} \setminus \mathcal{S}$, $F \in \mathbb{Z}_{\geq 0}$. The F-**local model** refers to the case when the set of adversaries is an F-local set.*

It should be noted that the local properties defining an F-local set must hold for *all* rounds. The F-local scope of threat model has been studied in the context of fault-tolerant (or resilient) broadcasting [4,17,27] and resilient consensus [9,10,27].

2.3 Resilient Distributed Estimation

Given the threat model and scope of threats, we formally define resilient distributed estimation.

DEFINITION 3. *The normal nodes achieve the resilient distributed estimation objective in the presence of adversary nodes (given a particular adversary model) if*

$$x_i(r) \to p_i \text{ as } r \to \infty, \forall i \in \mathcal{N},$$

for any set of parameter values $\{p_i\}$, $i \in \mathcal{N}$, and any choice of initial values $\{x_i(0)\}$, $i \in \mathcal{N}$.

Recall that each reliable node has an accurate measurement of its own parameter, so there is no need to include reliable nodes in the problem formulation.

3. ESTIMATION ALGORITHM

In this paper, we study a resilient form of a linear iterative algorithm that is amenable to distributed parameter estimation [11]. For now, let us assume that all the nodes are normal cooperative nodes (i.e., $\mathcal{V} = \mathcal{N}$). Then, in each round r, each node i receives the estimates $\{x_j(r)\}$, $j \in \mathcal{N}_i^{in}(r)$, from its in-neighbors along with the relative parameter measurements $\{\xi_{ji}(r)\} = \{p_j - p_i\}$, $j \in \mathcal{N}_i^{in}(r)$, and updates its estimate according to the Linear Iterative (LI) algorithm

$$x_i(r+1) = x_i(r) + \sum_{j \in \mathcal{N}_i^{in}(r)} w_{ij}(r) \left[(x_j(r) - x_i(r)) - \xi_{ji} \right], \quad (1)$$

where $w_{ij}(r)$ is a weight assigned to the information from node j in round r, and the weights should satisfy the following conditions:

- $w_{ij}(r) = 0$ whenever $j \notin \mathcal{N}_i^{in}(r)$, $i \in \mathcal{N}$, $r \in \mathbb{Z}_{\geq 0}$;

- $w_{ij}(r) \geq \epsilon > 0$, $\forall j \in \mathcal{N}_i^{in}(r)$, $i \in \mathcal{N}$, $r \in \mathbb{Z}_{\geq 0}$;

- $\sum_{j \in \mathcal{N}_i^{in}(r)} w_{ij}(r) \leq 1 - \epsilon$, $\forall i \in \mathcal{N}$, $r \in \mathbb{Z}_{\geq 0}$.

Each term $s_{ji}(r) = [(x_j(r) - x_i(r)) - \xi_{ji}]$ in the sum represents a step determined by information from node j that moves node i's next estimate away from its current estimate. These steps are either positive or negative, depending on whether the *relative estimate* $x_j(r) - x_i(r)$ is greater or less than the relative parameter measurement ξ_{ji}, respectively.

Given this viewpoint of the algorithm in (1) it is intuitive that without proper guidance on the correct steps to take, distributed estimation will not be achieved. Specifically, without any reliable nodes in the network, the algorithm in (1) will not enable the estimate x_i to converge to its true parameter p_i. To formalize this discussion, consider the estimate error

$$e_i(r) = x_i(r) - p_i, \quad \forall i \in \mathcal{V}. \quad (2)$$

Then, the estimate error dynamics take the form

$$e_i(r+1) = e_i(r) + \sum_{j \in \mathcal{N}_i^{in}(r)} w_{ij}(r) (e_j(r) - e_i(r))$$

$$= \sum_{j \in \mathcal{J}_i^{in}(r)} w_{ij}(r) e_j(r), \quad (3)$$

where the self-weight $w_{ii}(r)$ is given by

$$w_{ii}(r) = 1 - \sum_{j \in \mathcal{N}_i^{in}(r)} w_{ij}(r) \geq \epsilon$$

The conditions on the weights in the error dynamics in (3) can be summarized as

- $w_{ij}(r) = 0$ whenever $j \notin \mathcal{J}_i^{in}(r)$, $i \in \mathcal{N}$, $r \in \mathbb{Z}_{\geq 0}$;

- $w_{ij}(r) \geq \epsilon > 0$, $\forall j \in \mathcal{J}_i^{in}(r)$, $i \in \mathcal{N}$, $r \in \mathbb{Z}_{\geq 0}$;

- $\sum_{j=1}^n w_{ij}(r) = 1$, $\forall i \in \mathcal{N}$, $r \in \mathbb{Z}_{\geq 0}$.

With these conditions on the weights, the error dynamics in (3) are in fact linear, iterative consensus dynamics [16]. If information is able to be diffused throughout the network sufficiently often over time, then the errors will reach a consensus [20]. Technically, under the conditions stated above, a sufficient condition for reaching asymptotic consensus is that there exists a uniformly bounded sequence of contiguous time intervals such that the union of digraphs across each interval has a rooted out-branching [19]. A more general condition on the time-varying network is referred to as the *infinite flow property*, which has been shown to be both necessary and sufficient for asymptotic consensus for a class of discrete-time stochastic models [26]. In any case, the consensus value will (most likely) be a nonzero value within the range of initial estimate errors.[2]

However, if there is a reliable node in the network with an accurate measurement of its true parameter, then the reliable node's estimate is equal to its true parameter, and its estimation error is zero. If that reliable node has enough influence – i.e., is the root of a directed spanning tree often enough over time – then its zero error will drive the other nodes' errors to zero, achieving the distributed estimation objective. Put another way, the reliable node becomes

---

[2]There is the possibility, for example, that the network is always balanced and the average of the initial estimate error is zero, in which case the consensus value is in fact zero [16]. However, in any situation in which consensus to zero error occurs, there exists a different set of initial values that would produce consensus to a nonzero error.

a leader in the estimation error consensus dynamics, driving them toward its value of zero [6].

A problem arises in the case where some of the nodes are adversaries. It has been shown in [3] that if there are adversary nodes insinuated in a network of normal nodes and the adversaries have enough influence in the network topology over time, then they can cause all normal nodes to reach consensus on an arbitrary value of their choosing. In a heterogeneous network, with both reliable and normal cooperative nodes, the adversary nodes can still disrupt the consensus process. Of course, disrupting the consensus process in the estimation error dynamics is equivalent to disrupting the distributed estimation objective. This scenario is illustrated in the example of Section 5.1.3.

3.1 The RIDE Algorithm

A simple modification can be made to the iterative algorithm of (1) that enables resilience against adversary nodes, which we refer to as the Resilient Iterative Distributed Estimation (RIDE) algorithm. Before describing RIDE, it is important to emphasize that an adversary model – i.e., threat model and scope of threat assumption – should be selected at *design time* so that certain theoretical guarantees concerning resilience are met during *run time*, as long as the assumptions of the adversary model hold. In this work, we tailor the modifications to the malicious threat model under the F-local scope of threat assumption, where the value of $F \in \mathbb{Z}_{\geq 0}$ is selected at *design time*. Recall that under this assumption there will be at most F adversary nodes in the neighborhood of any normal node i during every round.

The idea of the modification is to sort the steps attained from each neighbor, $s_{ji}(r) = [(x_j(r) - x_i(r)) - \xi_{ji}]$, which provides information on the range of steps away from its current estimate that each neighbor offers. By removing the F largest positive steps (a step to the right along the real line) and the F smallest negative steps (a step to the left along the real line), then the normal node is guaranteed not to be influenced by an adversary to move further away from its current estimate than another cooperative node would potentially lead it. More specifically, in each round $r \in \mathbb{Z}_{\geq 0}$:

1. Each normal cooperative node i receives estimates from each of its in-neighbors $x_j(r)$, $j \in \mathcal{N}_i^{\text{in}}(r)$, and obtains relative measurements $\xi_{ji}(r) = p_j - p_i$, $j \in \mathcal{N}_i^{\text{in}}(r)$. From these, it forms the steps $s_{ji}(r) = [(x_j(r) - x_i(r)) - \xi_{ji}(r)]$, $j \in \mathcal{N}_i^{\text{in}}(r)$, and forms a sorted list.

2. If there are less than F positive steps $s_{ji}(r) > 0$, then normal node i removes all positive steps. Otherwise, it removes precisely the largest F positive steps in the sorted list (breaking ties arbitrarily). Likewise, if there are less than F negative steps $s_{ji}(r) < 0$, then node i removes all negative steps. Otherwise, it removes precisely the smallest F negative steps.

3. Let $\mathcal{T}_i(r)$ denote the set of nodes whose steps were removed by normal node i during round r. Each normal cooperative node i applies the update

$$x_i(r+1) = x_i(r) + \sum_{j \in \mathcal{N}_i^{\text{in}}(r) \setminus \mathcal{T}_i(r)} w_{ij}(r)[(x_j(r) - x_i(r)) - \xi_{ji}(r)],$$

(4)

where the weights $w_{ij}(r)$ satisfy the conditions stated above, but with $\mathcal{N}_i^{\text{in}}(r)$ replaced by $\mathcal{N}_i^{\text{in}}(r) \setminus \mathcal{T}_i(r)$.[3]

---

[3]In this case, a simple choice for the weights is to let $w_{ij}(r) = 1/(1 + d_i^{\text{in}}(r) - |\mathcal{T}_i(r)|)$ for $j \in \mathcal{N}_i^{\text{in}}(r) \setminus \mathcal{T}_i(r)$.

As a matter of terminology, we refer to F as the *parameter* of the algorithm, which is selected at design time to provide resilience against F-local malicious adversaries. This algorithm is very lightweight in terms of computation, and does not require any cooperative node to have any knowledge of the network topology nor of the classification of the other nodes (i.e., normal, reliable, or adversary). Given these highly desirable properties, the question we pose in this paper is: under what conditions on the interactions between the different nodes will this algorithm facilitate resilient distributed estimation?

4. RESULTS

A first step toward answering the underlying question of this paper is to consider the estimate error dynamics of the resilient algorithm as we did in the discussion of the algorithm in (1) in the previous section. Under the change of variables in (2), the resilient estimate error dynamics are given by

$$e_i(r+1) = \sum_{j \in \mathcal{J}_i^{\text{in}}(r) \setminus \mathcal{T}_i(r)} w_{ij}(r) e_j(r), \quad i \in \mathcal{N} \quad (5)$$

with the conditions on the weights given by

- $w_{ij}(r) = 0$ whenever $j \notin \mathcal{J}_i^{\text{in}}(r) \setminus \mathcal{T}_i(r)$, $i \in \mathcal{N}$, $r \in \mathbb{Z}_{\geq 0}$;

- $w_{ij}(r) \geq \epsilon > 0$, $\forall j \in \mathcal{J}_i^{\text{in}}(r) \setminus \mathcal{T}_i(r)$, $i \in \mathcal{N}$, $r \in \mathbb{Z}_{\geq 0}$;

- $\sum_{j=1}^n w_{ij}(r) = 1$, $\forall i \in \mathcal{N}$, $r \in \mathbb{Z}_{\geq 0}$.

Hence, the estimate error dynamics take the form of the resilient consensus algorithm referred to as the Weighted Mean Subsequence Reduced (W-MSR) algorithm [9]. It follows immediately that all of the results of [9] in terms of resilient consensus apply as well to the estimate error dynamics of (5). While these results provide immediate insight into the behavior of both the estimate error dynamics and, in turn, the RIDE algorithm, they *only apply to the case of a homogeneous network of normal cooperative nodes interacting with malicious nodes*. In fact, we have already shown in the previous section that without reliable nodes that have sufficient influence in the network, the distributed estimation algorithm studied in this paper will not achieve distributed estimation, even with no adversaries. Therefore, the resilient distributed estimation problem studied in this paper is more challenging than the resilient distributed consensus problem. More specifically, the resilient distributed consensus algorithm guarantees that the estimate errors will reach a consensus under the topological conditions described in [9]. However, that consensus value may be *anywhere* within the range of initial estimate errors of the cooperative nodes. For resilient distributed estimation, we need the estimate errors to all converge to the *specific* value of zero.

In order to facilitate the analysis, we define the *maximum estimate error*, *minimum estimate error*, and *estimate error range* of the cooperative nodes during round r by

$$m_e(r) = \min_{k \in \mathcal{N} \cup \mathcal{R}} \{e_k(r)\}, \quad M_e(r) = \max_{j \in \mathcal{N} \cup \mathcal{R}} \{e_j(r)\},$$

and

$$\mathcal{I}_r = [m_e(r), M_e(r)].$$

Since reliable nodes are included in these definitions, it follows that $0 \in \mathcal{I}_r$, for all $r \in \mathbb{Z}_{\geq 0}$. Therefore, the normal nodes achieve resilient distributed estimation if and only if the function

$$V_e(r) = M_e(r) - m_e(r) \quad (6)$$

approaches zero asymptotically. Over the $|\mathcal{N}|$-dimensional space defined by the estimate errors of the normal nodes along with the fixed zero estimate errors of the reliable nodes, the function V_e is positive definite and radially unbounded. Hence, V_e is a Lyapunov candidate for the estimate error dynamics.

Before we analyze the convergence properties of the estimate error dynamics, we first consider what sort of *invariance* (or *safety*) properties are guaranteed by the resilient distributed estimation algorithm under the F-local malicious adversary model. The following result shows that the estimate errors are *bounded functions* and $\mathcal{I}_0$, the initial estimate error range of the cooperative nodes, is an invariant set for the error dynamics.

THEOREM 1. *If the normal nodes execute the RIDE algorithm with parameter F and the F-local malicious adversary assumption holds, then*

$$e_i(r+1) \in \mathcal{I}_r, \ \forall i \in \mathcal{N} \cup \mathcal{R}$$

which implies that the initial estimate error range $\mathcal{I}_0$ is an invariant set, $M_e(r)$ is a non-increasing function over the rounds, and $m_e(r)$ is a non-decreasing function over the rounds.

PROOF. All reliable nodes always have estimate error zero; therefore, we concentrate on normal nodes. Suppose there is a normal node i and round r such that an estimate error $e_j(r) > M_e(r)$ is used in the update of (5). By the definition of $M_e(r)$, the node j must be an adversary. Further, since $e_j(r)$ remains in the sum of (5), it follows that $j \notin \mathcal{T}_i(r)$ and $s_{ji}(r)$ remains in the sum of (4). Since $s_{ji}(r) = e_j(r) - e_i(r) > 0$, there must be at least F other nodes $j_1, j_2, \ldots, j_F$ in i's neighborhood satisfying $s_{j_k i}(r) \geq s_{ji}(r)$, or, equivalently, $e_{j_k}(r) \geq e_j(r)$, for $k = 1, \ldots, F$. Hence, $j_1, j_2, \ldots, j_F$ must also be adversaries, which contradicts the F-local assumption. Therefore, it must be the case that $e_j(r) \leq M_e(r)$ for all $i \in \mathcal{N}$ and $r \in \mathbb{Z}_{\geq 0}$. A similar argument can be made for the case $e_j(r) < m_e(r)$. Since $e_i(r+1)$, is a convex combination of values in $\mathcal{I}_r$ it follows that $e_i(k+1) \in \mathcal{I}_r$. □

Theorem 1 guarantees that any set of malicious adversaries that satisfies the F-local model has limited influence on the estimate errors of the normal nodes whenever the RIDE algorithm is used. This result, by itself, indicates a level of resilience of the algorithm to adversaries. However, it says nothing about convergence of each normal node's estimate to the true parameter, which is the ultimate goal of the algorithm. The following result shows that as long as each normal node receives more reliable information (specifically from $F+1$ reliable nodes) than false information from adversaries, periodically over time, then the range of estimate errors converges to zero.

THEOREM 2. *Suppose the normal cooperative nodes execute the RIDE algorithm with parameter F and the F-local malicious adversary model holds. If for each normal node $i \in \mathcal{N}$ there exists $q_i \in \mathbb{Z}_{>0}$ and a sequence of rounds $\mathcal{S}_i = \{r_{i_1}, r_{i_2}, \ldots\}$ with $r_{i_{k+1}} - r_{i_k} \leq q_i$ for $k \in \mathbb{Z}_{>0}$, such that $|\mathcal{N}_i(r_{i_k}) \cap R| \geq F+1$ for all $r_{i_k} \in \mathcal{S}_i$, then resilient distributed estimation is achieved.*

PROOF. Fix $r \in \mathbb{Z}_{\geq 0}$ and let $q = \max_{i \in \mathcal{N}}\{q_i\}$. By hypothesis, there exists integer $0 \leq k \leq q-1$ such that there is a normal node $i \in \mathcal{N}$ with at least $F+1$ reliable nodes as neighbors in round $r+k$. This, in turn, implies that at least one zero error will be used in the estimate error update (5). The weight on each error used is no less than $\epsilon > 0$ and $M_e(r) > 0$ for all r. According to Theorem 1, no estimate error greater than $M_e(r)$ will be used in the estimate

error update of (5), so we have

$$e_i(r+k+1) = \sum_{j \in \mathcal{J}_i^{\text{in}}(r+k) \setminus \mathcal{T}_i(r+k)} w_{ij}(r+k)e_j(r+k)$$

$$= \sum_{j \in \mathcal{J}_i^{\text{in}}(r+k) \setminus (\mathcal{T}_i(r+k) \cup R)} w_{ij}(r+k)e_j(r+k)$$

$$\leq (1-\epsilon)M_e(r+k)$$

$$\leq (1-\epsilon)M_e(r).$$

The last step uses the fact that $M_e(r)$ is a non-increasing function, which is a consequence of Theorem 1. For the next round, we use the fact that $e_i(r+k+1) \leq (1-\epsilon)M_e(r)$ to show

$$e_i(r+k+2) = \sum_{j \in \mathcal{J}_i^{\text{in}}(r+k+1) \setminus \mathcal{T}_i(r+k+1)} w_{ij}(r+k+1)e_j(r+k+1)$$

$$\leq \epsilon(1-\epsilon)M_e(r) + (1-\epsilon)M_e(r+k+1)$$

$$\leq (1-\epsilon^2)M_e(r).$$

In general, if $e_i(r+k+l) \leq (1-\gamma)M_e(r)$, for $0 < \gamma < 1$ and $l \in \mathbb{Z}_{>0}$, then

$$e_i(r+k+l+1) = \sum_{j \in \mathcal{J}_i^{\text{in}}(r+k+l) \setminus \mathcal{T}_i(r+k+l)} w_{ij}(r+k+l)e_j(r+k+l)$$

$$\leq \epsilon(1-\gamma)M_e(r) + (1-\epsilon)M_e(r+k+l)$$

$$\leq (1-\epsilon\gamma)M_e(r).$$

Therefore, by induction,

$$e_i(r+k+q) \leq (1-\epsilon^q)M_e(r).$$

By hypothesis, in the q rounds (inclusively) between $r+k$ and $r+k+q-1$ there is at least one round r_j for each other normal node $j \in \mathcal{N}$ in which j has at least $F+1$ reliable nodes as neighbors. Hence, using the same argument as above

$$e_j(r+k+q) \leq (1-\epsilon^{(r+k+q-r_j)})M_e(r)$$

$$\leq (1-\epsilon^q)M_e(r), \ \forall j \in \mathcal{N}.$$

Likewise, using a similar argument, we can show

$$e_j(r+k+q) \geq (1-\epsilon^q)m_e(r), \ \forall j \in \mathcal{N}.$$

Since these inequalities hold for all $j \in \mathcal{N}$, we obtain

$$M_e(r+k+q) \leq (1-\epsilon^q)M_e(r)$$

and

$$m_e(r+k+q) \geq (1-\epsilon^q)m_e(r).$$

Finally, to reach inequalities that are independent of the fixed value of r, we apply Theorem 1 once more, along with the fact that $k \leq q-1$ to get

$$V_e(r+2q) \leq (1-\epsilon^q)V_e(r),$$

which holds for all $r \in \mathbb{Z}_{\geq 0}$. Therefore, every $2q$ rounds the Lyapunov candidate attenuates by a factor no larger than $(1-\epsilon^q) < 1$ and $V_e(r) \to 0$ as $r \to \infty$. □

Theorem 2 provides a sufficient condition for the RIDE algorithm to achieve resilient distributed estimation in time-varying networks. The conditions in Theorem 2 are requirements on both the periodicity and number of interactions between reliable nodes and normal nodes. This condition would be satisfied, for example, if there are clusters of at least $F+1$ reliable nodes spatially distributed and mobile such that each of the normal nodes are able to

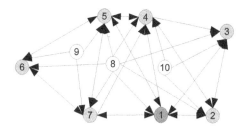

Figure 1: Ten node network with 1 adversary, 2 reliable nodes, and 7 normal nodes.

periodically interact with a sufficient number of reliable nodes. Of course, the condition of Theorem 2 is not a necessary condition, which will be illustrated in the following section through simulations.

5. SIMULATIONS

The Resilient Iterative Distributed Estimation (RIDE) algorithm, described in Section 3, has been implemented in Matlab and used to simulate different network topologies for different adversary modes. The first few simulation examples emphasize fixed network topology in order to focus on specific attributes of the topology on the behavior of RIDE and the adversaries. These fixed network topologies are shown in Figures 1, 6, and 8. In these figures, the dark gray nodes are adversaries, the light gray nodes are normal, and the white nodes are reliable. For all of these simulations, the normal nodes have initial estimates of zero and the goal is for them to converge to their true parameters. The parameters are set randomly between -5 and 5. After illustrating several fixed network examples, we show examples on time-varying Bernoulli networks. The weights $w_{ij}(r)$, for $j \in \mathcal{N}_i^{\text{in}}(r)$, are set as $\frac{1}{\mathcal{N}_i^{\text{in}}(r)+1}$ for both fixed and time-varying networks. This choice of weights satisfies the conditions following (1) and only requires local information. Furthermore, for time-varying network topologies, the weights also vary with time.

Throughout the simulations we assume that the measurements are sent through communication to out-neighbors so that adversary nodes are able to disturb the convergence of the network by providing false estimates as well as false measurements. To simulate false relative measurements, the parameter of the adversary node is the only thing changed so that it is unnecessary to plot each of the relative measurements. Instead, the false parameter of the adversary node is plotted.

5.1 Simulation Examples

5.1.1 Fixed Network with Different Adversary Modes

The first fixed network topology, shown in Figure 1, is created out of ten nodes where node 1 is an adversary, nodes 2 to 7 are normal, and nodes 8 to 10 are reliable. This topology satisfies Theorem 2 with $q = 1$ under the 1-local model (i.e., all normal nodes have more reliable nodes than adversary nodes). Hence, no matter what the strategy of the adversary is, all normal nodes should be able to estimate their parameters and the Mean Square Error (MSE) of the parameter estimation should converge to zero in a few iterations whenever RIDE with parameter $F = 1$ is used. This network is simulated using two different adversary modes: ramp and bounded random motion. The results of the simulations for RIDE with parameter $F - 1$ and the two different adversary modes are shown in Figures 2 and 3, respectively. Based on simulation,

all normal nodes are able to estimate their parameters with a MSE of zero in around 20 rounds.

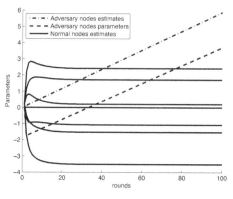

(a) Parameter Estimates.

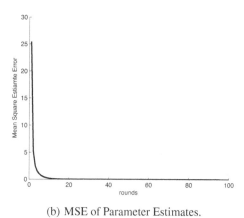

(b) MSE of Parameter Estimates.

Figure 2: RIDE in fixed network of Figure 1 with ramp adversary.

5.1.2 Fixed Network with Time-Varying Parameters

The RIDE algorithm should be able to track slowly varying parameters. To test this hypothesis, a simulation is done on the network topology in Figure 1 with the parameters of the nodes set to sinusoids of different frequencies and amplitudes. The result of this simulation is shown in Figure 4. A crash adversary mode is considered in this simulation. Based on the results, all normal nodes are able to track their slowly varying parameters with the MSE converging to zero in around 20 rounds.

5.1.3 LI Algorithm with 1 Adversary

The RIDE algorithm involves sorting the step values and ignoring the extreme step values. To verify the importance of this stage, this simulation illustrates the RIDE algorithm with parameter $F = 0$ (which is equivalent to the LI algorithm in (1)) on the fixed topology of Figure 1. A crash adversary is used in this simulation, and the results are shown in Figure 5. Clearly the estimates of the normal nodes fail to converge to their true parameters because the adversary node is able to disturb the consensus process even though there are more reliable nodes than adversary nodes communicating with each normal node. This example also illustrates how the RIDE algorithm can fail if the F-local malicious adversary assumption does not hold.

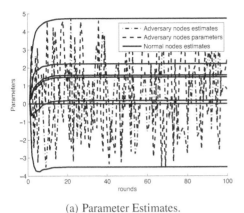

(a) Parameter Estimates.

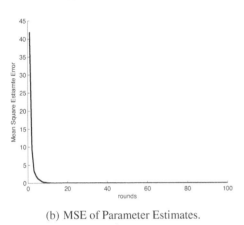

(b) MSE of Parameter Estimates.

Figure 3: RIDE in fixed network of Figure 1 with bounded random adversary.

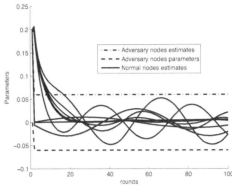

(a) Parameter Estimates.

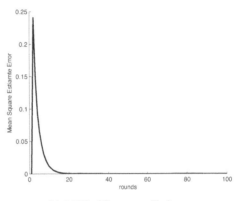

(b) MSE of Parameter Estimates.

Figure 4: RIDE in fixed network of Figure 1 with time-varying parameters and crash adversary.

5.1.4 Fixed Topology in which RIDE does not Converge

A sufficient condition for the RIDE algorithm to converge to a MSE of zero is to have more reliable nodes than adversary nodes around each normal node (with at least $F + 1$ reliable nodes). The second fixed topology, shown in Figure 6, does not satisfy this condition. This network is created out of eleven nodes, where node 1 is adversary, nodes 2 to 9 are normal, and nodes 10 and 11 are reliable. Although most of the network is well connected, the reliable nodes are only communicating with node 2. Because node 2 has no out-neighbors, the reliable information from the reliable nodes is not propagated through the network. On the other hand, the adversary node, which is connected to nodes 2, 3, 4, 5 and 6, has much stronger control over the network. Unsurprisingly, the results of simulation with a crash adversary, shown in Figure 7, acknowledge this fact. The estimates of the normal nodes converge, but with a finite MSE larger than zero.

5.1.5 Fixed Network not Covered by Theorem 2

The final fixed topology, shown in Figure 8, is simulated to show that the convergence condition of Theorem 2 is sufficient but not necessary. The network of Figure 8 has eleven nodes, where nodes 3 and 9 are adversaries, 8, 10 and 11 are reliable, and the rest of the nodes are normal. This network satisfies the 1-local model, so a parameter of $F = 1$ may be used and Theorem 1 is satisfied. In this topology, only nodes 5 and 6 have more reliable than ad-

versary nodes in their neighborhood. However, unlike the previous topology the information from the reliable nodes can easily propagate through the network. Based on the simulation results, shown in Figure 9 with two crash adversaries, the estimates of the normal nodes in this network converge to their true parameters with a MSE approaching zero after around 200 rounds.

5.1.6 Bernoulli Time-Varying Random Networks

To investigate the speed of convergence in time-varying networks, we consider a Bernoulli random network where every directed edge follows a Bernoulli trial with probability of existence p for every round. Bernoulli random networks are often used to model lossy packet-switched networks [24]. For $0 < p < 1$ there is a finite probability that the conditions of Theorem 2 hold for a sufficient number of rounds to achieve convergence. However, this probability approaches zero as p decreases, which is illustrated in our simulations. We define that convergence is achieved in round r_0 if r_0 is the first round in which the MSE is less than 0.1% of the initial MSE (i.e., at round $r = 0$). In the following simulations we fix all but one of the following variables to explore how each variable affects the speed of convergence: probability of directed edge existence p, total number of nodes n, and percentage of adversary nodes (with reliable nodes fixed to 1.5 times the number of adversary nodes). The initial estimates and parameters of the normal nodes are set randomly between -5 and 5. Each data point in the simulation plots is the average over twenty different simulations.

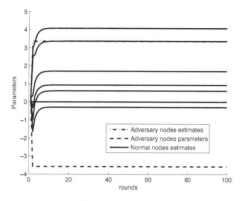

(a) Parameter Estimates.

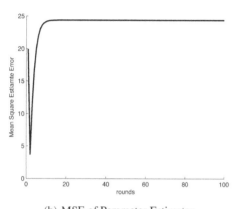

(b) MSE of Parameter Estimates.

Figure 5: RIDE with $F = 0$ in fixed network of Figure 1 with 3 reliable nodes and 1 crash adversary.

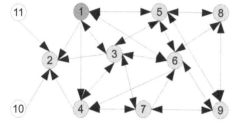

Figure 6: Eleven node network with 1 adversary, 2 reliable nodes, and 8 normal nodes.

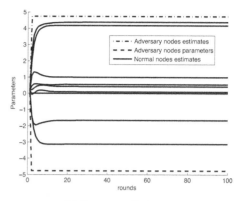

(a) Parameter Estimates.

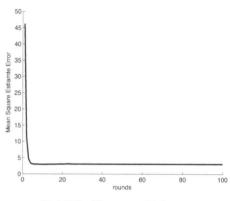

(b) MSE of Parameter Estimates.

Figure 7: RIDE algorithm in fixed network of Figure 6 with 2 reliable nodes and 1 crash adversary.

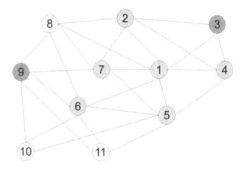

Figure 8: Eleven node network with 2 adversary, 2 reliable nodes, and 7 normal nodes.

Figure 10 shows simulation results varying the total number of nodes n from 8 to 1024 in powers of 2, with the value of $p = 0.4$, the percentage of adversary nodes set to 20% (using the floor operation) and the percentage of reliable nodes set to 30% (using the ceiling operation). Other than the first increment from 8 to 16 nodes, the trend is increasing n increases the speed of convergence. The reason for the anomalous increment from 8 to 16 is the floor and ceiling operations on the small number of n provides a large difference in the actual numbers of adversary and reliable nodes.

Figure 11 shows simulation results varying the Bernoulli probability p from 0.25 to 1 in increments of 0.0625, with the total number of nodes $n = 50$, 10 adversaries (i.e., 20%), and 15 reliable nodes (i.e., 30%). The parameter of the RIDE algorithm is set to $F = 10$, and the algorithm may remove up to $2F = 20$ nodes in

the removal process. Therefore, whenever the expected number of neighbors approaches the value of $2F = 20$, which occurs in this example at $p = 0.4$, it is reasonable to expect a significant decrease in the rate of convergence. As can be seen in Figure 11, the number of rounds to achieve convergence begins to sharply increase at this value, as expected.

Figure 12 shows simulation results varying the number of adversary nodes, with 50% more reliable nodes, total number of nodes $n = 100$, and Bernoulli probability $p = 0.4$. The parameter F of the RIDE algorithm is set to vary with the number of adversary nodes so that it is always sufficiently resilient. Because $p = 0.4$, the expected number of neighbors is approximately 40. In this case,

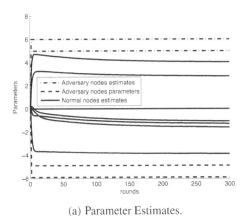

(a) Parameter Estimates.

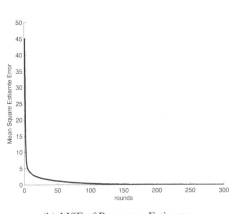

(b) MSE of Parameter Estimates.

Figure 9: RIDE algorithm in fixed network of Figure 8 which does not satisfy Theorem 2 yet still converges with zero error.

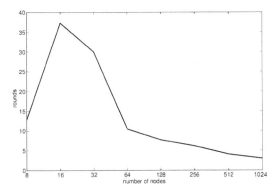

Figure 10: Number of rounds for convergence of a Bernoulli random network with $p = 0.4$, 20% crash adversaries, 30% reliable nodes, and varying the total number of nodes.

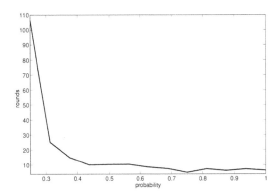

Figure 11: Number of rounds for convergence of a Bernoulli random network with $n = 50$ nodes, 20% crash adversaries, 30% reliable nodes, and varying p.

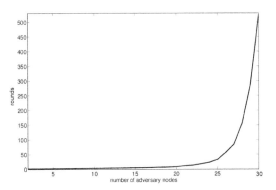

Figure 12: Number of rounds for convergence of a Bernoulli random network with $p = 0.4$, 100 nodes, and varying percentage of adversary nodes (with 50% more reliable nodes).

we expect a dramatic increase in the number of rounds needed to converge whenever $2F = 40$, or $F = 20$. As seen in Figure 12, 20 adversaries is the point of inflection where the number of rounds required for convergence begins to spike, as expected.

6. CONCLUSIONS

In this paper, we have proposed a Resilient Iterative Distributed Estimation (RIDE) algorithm that enables each normal node in the network to obtain an accurate estimate of its true parameter using relative parameter measurements and estimates from neighbors. Through these interactions with reliable and adversary nodes in a time-varying heterogeneous network, we prove that under the condition that each normal node receives information directly from enough reliable nodes often enough and from not too many adversary nodes, then the distributed estimation objective is achieved.

Our simulations indicate that this sufficient condition is not necessary. It is clear from the simulation results that as long as information from reliable nodes is able to propagate to all normal nodes often enough over time, then estimation of the parameters is achieved. Therefore, based on these simulation examples, we hypothesize that the necessary condition should be a condition similar to the *infinite flow property* [26], but with a notion of redundancy in flows to take into account the removal of extreme information from neighbors that is done in the RIDE algorithm.

We have shown that the RIDE algorithm reduces the parameter estimation problem to a first order consensus problem. Typically, first order consensus algorithms have a tendency to drift under noisy disturbances; however, the reliable nodes mitigate this factor to keep the error low. Furthermore, first order consensus algorithms are self stabilizing.

Although stochastic variations in the parameters are not taken into consideration in the theoretical results, we have shown through simulation that the RIDE algorithm is able to track varying parameters (c.f., Figure 4). In future work we plan to incorporate different noise models into the relative measurements of the normal nodes and absolute measurements of the reliable nodes. Including noise will better model the distributed parameter problem dealt with in clock synchronization and position estimation dealt with in localization. We also plan to explore the idea of redundancy of infinite flow to try to obtain necessary conditions on the time-varying network topology. Finally, we plan to implement RIDE on an experimental platform of mobile robots to use for both clock synchronization and localization in the presence of adversary robots. For the relative measurements needed for clock synchronization, we plan to use a pairwise synchronization technique to compute the relative skew and offset such as in [15]. Since RIDE tracks slow varying parameters well, we hope that small amounts of clock drift will not be an issue. For localization, any range sensor may be used to determine the relative position measurements; however, matching these measurements to the correct corresponding neighbors is more easily done by using GPS coordinates as a relative measurement shared via wireless communication.

7. REFERENCES

[1] P. Barooah, N. M. da Silva, and J. P. Hespanha. Distributed optimal estimation from relative measurements for localization and time synchronization. In *Distributed Computing in Sensor Systems*, pages 266–281. Springer, 2006.

[2] I. J. Cox. Blanche-an experiment in guidance and navigation of an autonomous robot vehicle. *IEEE Transactions on Robotics and Automation*, 7(2):193–204, 1991.

[3] V. Gupta, C. Langbort, and R. M. Murray. On the robustness of distributed algorithms. In *IEEE Conference on Decision and Control*, pages 3473–3478, San Diego, California, Dec. 2006.

[4] A. Ichimura and M. Shigeno. A new parameter for a broadcast algorithm with locally bounded Byzantine faults. *Information Processing Letters*, 110:514–517, 2010.

[5] Y. M. Ioannides and L. D. Loury. Job information networks, neighborhood effects, and inequality. *Journal of Economic Literature*, 42(4):1056–1093, 2004.

[6] A. Jadbabaie, J. Lin, and A. S. Morse. Coordination of groups of mobile autonomous agents using nearest neighbor rules. *IEEE Transactions on Automatic Control*, 48(6):988–1001, June 2003.

[7] S. Kar, J. Moura, and K. Ramanan. Distributed parameter estimation in sensor networks: Nonlinear observation models and imperfect communication. *IEEE Transactions on Information Theory*, 58(6):3575–3605, 2012.

[8] P. J. Kotler and G. M. Armstrong. *Principles of marketing*. Pearson Education, 2010.

[9] H. J. LeBlanc, H. Zhang, X. D. Koutsoukos, and S. Sundaram. Resilient asymptotic consensus in robust networks. *IEEE Journal on Selected Areas in Communications*, 31(4):766–781, 2013.

[10] H. J. LeBlanc, H. Zhang, S. Sundaram, and X. Koutsoukos. Consensus of multi-agent networks in the presence of adversaries using only local information. In *Proceedings of the 1st International Conference on High Confidence Networked Systems (HiCoNS)*, pages 1–10, Beijing, China, 2012.

[11] C. Liao and P. Barooah. Disync: Accurate distributed clock synchronization in mobile ad-hoc networks from noisy difference measurements. In *Proceedings of the American*

Control Conference, pages 3332–3337, Washington, D.C., June 2013.

[12] Y. Liu, P. Ning, and M. K. Reiter. False data injection attacks against state estimation in electric power grids. *ACM Transactions on Information and System Security (TISSEC)*, 14(1):13, 2011.

[13] M. Maróti, B. Kusy, G. Simon, and A. Lédeczi. The flooding time synchronization protocol. In *Proceedings of the 2nd international conference on Embedded networked sensor systems*, pages 39–49. ACM, 2004.

[14] D. Moore, J. Leonard, D. Rus, and S. Teller. Robust distributed network localization with noisy range measurements. In *Proceedings of the 2nd international conference on Embedded networked sensor systems*, pages 50–61, 2004.

[15] K.-L. Noh, Q. M. Chaudhari, E. Serpedin, and B. W. Suter. Novel clock phase offset and skew estimation using two-way timing message exchanges for wireless sensor networks. *IEEE Transactions on Communications*, 55(4):766–777, 2007.

[16] R. Olfati-Saber, J. A. Fax, and R. M. Murray. Consensus and cooperation in networked multi-agent systems. *Proceedings of the IEEE*, 95(1):215–233, 2007.

[17] A. Pelc and D. Peleg. Broadcasting with locally bounded Byzantine faults. In *Information Processing Letters*, pages 109–115, 2005.

[18] K. R. Rad and A. Tahbaz-Salehi. Distributed parameter estimation in networks. In *49th IEEE Conference on Decision and Control (CDC)*, pages 5050–5055, Atlanta, GA, 2010.

[19] W. Ren and R. W. Beard. Consensus seeking in multiagent systems under dynamically changing interaction topologies. *IEEE Transactions on Automatic Control*, 50(5):655–661, May 2005.

[20] W. Ren, R. W. Beard, and E. M. Atkins. Information consensus in multivehicle cooperative control. *IEEE Control Systems Magazine*, 27(2):71–82, April 2007.

[21] I. Rhee, A. Warrier, J. Min, and L. Xu. DRAND: distributed randomized tdma scheduling for wireless ad-hoc networks. In *Proceedings of the 7th ACM international symposium on Mobile ad hoc networking and computing*, pages 190–201, 2006.

[22] I.-K. Rhee, J. Lee, J. Kim, E. Serpedin, and Y.-C. Wu. Clock synchronization in wireless sensor networks: An overview. *Sensors*, 9(1):56–85, 2009.

[23] C. Rieger, K. Moore, and T. Baldwin. Resilient control systems: A multi-agent dynamic systems perspective. In *IEEE International Conference on Electro/Information Technology (EIT)*, pages 1–16, 2013.

[24] L. Schenato, B. Sinopoli, M. Franceschetti, K. Poolla, and S. Sastry. Foundations of control and estimation over lossy networks. *Proceedings of the IEEE*, 95(1):163–187, 2007.

[25] G. Seeber. *Satellite geodesy: foundations, methods, and applications*. Walter de Gruyter, 2003.

[26] B. Touri and A. Nedić. On ergodicity, infinite flow, and consensus in random models. *IEEE Transactions on Automatic Control*, 56(7):1593–1605, July 2011.

[27] H. Zhang and S. Sundaram. Robustness of information diffusion algorithms to locally bounded adversaries. In *Proceedings of the American Control Conference*, pages 5855–5861, Montréal, Canada, 2012.

Passivity Framework for Modeling, Mitigating, and Composing Attacks on Networked Systems

Radha Poovendran
Network Security Lab (NSL@UW)
EE Department, University of
Washington
Seattle, WA 98195-2500
rp3@uw.edu

ABSTRACT

Cyber-physical systems (CPS) consist of a tight coupling between cyber (sensing and computation) and physical (actuation and control) components. As a result of this coupling, CPS are vulnerable to both known and emerging cyber attacks, which can degrade the safety, availability, and reliability of the system. A key step towards guaranteeing CPS operation in the presence of threats is developing quantitative models of attacks and their impact on the system and express them in the language of CPS. Traditionally, such models have been introduced within the framework of formal methods and verification. In this talk, we present a control-theoretic modeling framework. We demonstrate that the control-theoretic approach can capture the adaptive and time-varying strategic interaction between the adversary and the targeted system. Furthermore, control theory provides a common language in which to describe both the physical dynamics of the system, as well as the impact of the attack and defense. In particular, we provide a passivity-based approach for modeling and mitigating jamming and wormhole attacks. We demonstrate that passivity enables composition of multiple attack and defense mechanisms, allowing characterization of the overall performance of the system under attack. Our view is that the formal methods and the control-based approaches are complementary.

Categories and Subject Descriptors: C.2.0 [**Computer Systems Organization**]: Commputer-Communication Networks– *Security and protection (e.g., firewalls)*

Keywords: Cyber Physical Systems; Network Security; Passivity

Permission to make digital or hard copies of part or all of this work for personal or classroom use is granted without fee provided that copies are not made or distributed for profit or commercial advantage, and that copies bear this notice and the full citation on the first page. Copyrights for third-party components of this work must be honored. For all other uses, contact the owner/author(s). Copyright is held by the author/owner(s).

HiCoNS'14, April 15–17, 2014, Berlin, Germany.
ACM 978-1-4503-2652-0/14/04.
http://dx.doi.org/10.1145/2566468.2566470

Understanding the Security of Interoperable Medical Devices using Attack Graphs

Curtis R. Taylor, Krishna Venkatasubramanian, Craig A. Shue
Department of Computer Science,
Worcester Polytechnic Institute
Worcester, MA, 01609
crtaylor@cs.wpi.edu, kven@wpi.edu, cshue@cs.wpi.edu

ABSTRACT

Medical device interoperability is an increasingly prevalent example of how computing and information technology will revolutionize and streamline medical care. The overarching goal of interoperable medical devices (IMDs) is increased safety, usability, decision support, and a decrease in false alarms and clinician cognitive workload. One aspect that has not been considered thus far is ensuring IMDs do not inadvertently harm patients in the presence of malicious adversaries. Security for medical devices has gained some traction in the recent years following some well-publicized attacks on individual devices, such as pacemakers and insulin pumps. This has resulted in solutions being proposed for securing these devices, usually in stand-alone mode. However, the introduction of interoperability makes medical devices increasingly connected and dependent on each other. Therefore, security attacks on IMDs becomes easier to mount in a stealthy manner with potentially devastating consequences.

This work outlines our effort in understanding the threats faced by IMDs, an important first step in eventually designing secure interoperability architectures. In this regard, we present: (1) a detailed attack graph-based analysis of threats on a specific interoperability environment based on providing a patient pain medication (PCA), under various levels of interoperability from simple data aggregation to fully closed-loop control; (2) a description of the mitigation approaches possible for each of class of attack vectors identified; and (3) lessons learned from this experience which can be leveraged for improving existing IMD architectures from a security point-of-view. Our analysis demonstrates that *even if we use provably safe medical systems in an interoperable setting with a safe interoperability engine, the presence of malicious behavior may render the entire setup unsafe for the patients, unless security is explicitly considered.*

Categories and Subject Descriptors

C.2.0 [**Computer-Communication Networks**]: General - Data communications, Security and protection; K.6.5

Permission to make digital or hard copies of all or part of this work for personal or classroom use is granted without fee provided that copies are not made or distributed for profit or commercial advantage and that copies bear this notice and the full citation on the first page. Copyrights for components of this work owned by others than ACM must be honored. Abstracting with credit is permitted. To copy otherwise, or republish, to post on servers or to redistribute to lists, requires prior specific permission and/or a fee. Request permissions from permissions@acm.org.
HiCoNS'14, April 15–17, 2014, Berlin, Germany.
Copyright 2014 ACM 978-1-4503-2652-0/14/04 ...$15.00.
http://dx.doi.org/10.1145/2566468.2566482 .

[**Computing Milieux**]: Security and Protection - Authentication, Unauthorized access; J.3 [**Computer Applications**]: Life and Medical Sciences - Medical information systems

General Terms

Security, Interoperability, Medical Device Systems

Keywords

Interoperable Medical Devices, Security, PCA, Infusion Pump

1. INTRODUCTION

Medical systems are increasingly being connected to each other as a way to improve patient safety [26]. The ability of medical devices to interoperate with one another has the potential to yield better performance, from reduced false alarms to automatic decision/diagnosis support and medication interaction checking in real-time [1]. Not surprisingly, interoperability has been predicted to improve patient outcomes by reducing the 95K - 195K errors committed in U.S. hospitals [12].

While there may be impediments to device manufacturers providing interoperability with their competitors' medical devices, such as a lack of data standards, alternative mechanisms are possible. In particular, a communication/middleware standard would allow heterogenous devices to communicate with one another. The *Medical Device Plug-n-Play Integrated Clinical Architecture* (ICE) is a result of such standardizing efforts [2]. Although there can be interoperability at many different granularities from technical (being able to exchange bytes) to conceptual (shared assumptions about the reality at a meaningful abstraction) [28, 31], the interoperability in the ICE standard is somewhere in between syntactic (data format of communication is standard) and semantic (the meaning of the data being exchanged is unambiguously defined) interoperability.

The goal of ICE is to enable *safe interoperability* between medical devices. Specifically, safety in this context is defined as ensuring the patient's health is not harmed in anyway by the use of the medical devices in an interoperable fashion. One important issue that is not addressed in this standard is security. Considering security for IMDs is necessary because: (1) they deal with sensitive patient information, (2) laws such as the Health Insurance Portability and Accountability Act (HIPAA) [14], mandate it, and (3) security attacks can have serious safety consequences for the patients. In particular, a malicious entity can now easily suppress legitimate information and introduce bogus information between the devices and the middleware, leading to untimely or unwanted actuation or loss of privacy. *Therefore, we contend that both security and safety need to be enforced in IMDs to ensure that the patient's health outcomes are not worsened under any circumstances.* Recent years have brought increased attention to security vulnerabilities in standalone medical devices [7,8,15,17]. However, the introduction of interoperability makes medical devices increasingly connected and dependent on each other. Therefore, security attacks on IMDs becomes easier to mount, and in a stealthy manner.

There has been growing interest in security issues pertaining to medical data collection, data transfer and processing, and electronic medical health records [5,13,30]. Standardization efforts are also underway [6,20,21]. In [11], the authors performed a detailed survey of existing communication and data standards in the medical domain and the techniques they deploy for security purposes which can be used for medical device interoperability purposes. It was found that significant gaps existed in the today's standards in terms of security particularly relating to communication security. This myopic focus on safety without considering the whole spectrum of security issues makes these standardization efforts essentially incomplete. The proper development of strong security solutions for IMDs is still an open research question.

To develop security solutions for IMDs, we need a good understanding of the various threats to an IMD setup. Instead of analyzing the security requirements of IMDs as a whole as done by earlier efforts [35] [32], which forces one to abstract out situation specific details and therefore make very broad conclusions, we take bottom-up approach in this paper. We present a detailed description of attacks on a specific interoperability scenario for patient controlled analgesia (PCA). This *PCA-IMD* setup consists of a PCA pump, and pulse-oximeter (measures O_2 levels in the blood) and a capnograph (measures CO_2 levels in the blood) and the goal is to allow patents to infuse pain medication as needed without over-infusing indicated by onset of respiratory depression. We further consider various levels of interoperability for this PCA-IMD scenario from simple-cases where interoperability promotes data aggregation to fully-closed-loop control of all three medical devices. The *principal contributions* of this paper therefore are:

- An attack graph-based description of attacks on IMDs when considering the PCA-IMD interoperability scenario.

- A description of the general mitigation strategies for each class of the attacks that are possible on the IMDs.

- A description of lessons learned from our experience, which can be used to design the interoperability architecture in a security-conscious manner.

We chose this PCA scenario for our IMD case-study because it is responsible for a very large number of treatment errors in the hospital setting. One study estimated that there are anywhere between 600,000 to 2 million adverse events in U.S. hospitals every year related to PCA [27]. Our analysis demonstrates that even if we use provably safe medical systems in an interoperable setting with a safe inter-

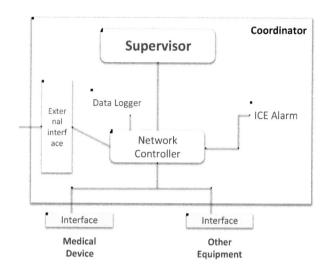

Figure 1: Interoperability architecture of MD PnP ICE standard

operability middleware, the presence of malicious behavior renders the entire setup unsafe — potentially harm inducing — for the patients.

To the best of our knowledge this is the first systematic attack description for a common treatment scenario (i.e., pain management), which can be implemented with IMDs in a realistic setting. Our work demonstrates that security has profound consequences to the safety of medical device interoperability and the patients they are serving. It is not just enough to design IMDs to be able to handle device failures and communication and software errors in order to be safe. They have to be secured from a variety of malicious behavior as well to be truly safe.

The paper is organized as follows: Section 2 presents background information on interoperability architecture standards and potential deployment approaches. Section 3 presents our problem statement along with the system and trust model. Section 4 illustrates attacks on the system. Section 5 presents the lessons learned and Section 6 presents the related work. Finally, Section 7 concludes the paper and presents the future work.

2. BACKGROUND

Rather than wait for the medical devices from different manufacturers to organically evolve interoperability capabilities, the *Integrated Clinical Architecture* (ICE) was created to enable diverse devices to talk to one another [2]. ICE was designed to act as a middleware to enable interaction of legacy, stand-alone medical devices and the applications using the medical devices. It has the potential to provide anything from data aggregation to closed-loop control over the patient's health. The architecture of ICE typically consists of three entities (see Figure 1):

- A collection of *Medical Devices* on or around a single patient that can perform monitoring and actuation.

- The *Supervisor* receives data from the various medical devices, processes it, and initiates action from the medical devices. The Supervisor runs clinical applications (referred to as *apps* from now on) that use the connected devices to support a clinical scenario selected by the caregiver.

- The *Network Controller* interfaces with one or more medical devices and the supervisor. It is responsible for collecting data from the individual devices. It also connects the entire setup to an external network, such as the Healthcare Information System (HIS). The network controller also records all the actions of the entire system in a data logger for future analysis.

IMDs are configured for each patient according to their individual needs. The caregiver is responsible for configuring the IMDs, which means: (1) identifying the medial devices that are needed to monitor or treat the patient, (2) connecting the devices to the network controller and the supervisor, (3) selecting an appropriate app on the Supervisor for enabling interoperability, and (4) monitoring the patient's well-being through the Supervisor. The caregiver can control various parameters of the system, such as alarm thresholds or algorithms for performing closed-loop control of patients, all through the apps running on the supervisor.

3. PROBLEM STATEMENT

Solutions for building safe IMDs only considers "naturally-occurring" faults within the system. These do not include faults introduced into the system by adversaries, which may not follow the models of "naturally-occurring" faults, but instead act in unexpected ways. Hence, analyzing the security threats for interoperable medical devices is very important for ensuring that the IMDs are safe and do not harm the patient.

In this paper, we investigate the various ways in which a specific instantiation of interoperable medical devices can be attacked, in a systematic manner. We specifically consider cases where the individual devices are themselves "correct-by-design" and therefore are considered "safe" when they are operating in stand-alone fashion [22] . However, when malicious behavior is allowed, even such provably-safe devices working in conjunction with a safe and trusted coordinator in an interoperable environment, are inherently unsafe. We consider this analysis as a step towards building an effective architecture for secure interoperable medical devices that expands on the ICE standard. Before delving into the details of our security analysis, we present our system model and trust/threat model for this work.

3.1 System Model

The ICE standard for interoperability between medical devices can support any combination of medical devices, provided they can be coordinated in a meaningful way to provide effective care for patients [2]. The IMD configuration will vary to account for each patient's specific situation. In order to understand the security threats on IMDs, we consider a small IMD system, consisting of three devices, for a single patient needing pain management. As we will see, even in this very limited scenario, the avenues of attack are large and we can draw broad conclusions about security threats to IMDs in general.

Our scenario, referred to as *PCA-IMD*, consists of an infusion pump programmed to infuse pain medication (e.g., morphine) to the patient at a specific (basal) rate in a hospital or care-facility. As pain medications tend to suppress respiration, we also have a pulse-oximeter (measures level of O_2 in the blood) and a capnograph (measures level of CO_2 in the blood) to determine how the patient is responding to the pain medication. The pulse-oximeter and the capnograph are collectively referred to as *sensors*, in the rest of the paper. The infusion pump also allows the patient to press a bolus button to receive a single, large dose of the medication as needed. Obviously, frequent boluses should only be allowed for a patient if it is not suppressing their respiration to unhealthy levels.

All the medical devices in our setup interact with the coordinator. The details of the coordinator entity are abstracted out as our focus is primarily on its interaction with the medical devices. The coordinator is programmed by the caregiver by loading *medical applications* on it that perform specific tasks such as alarming or providing closed-loop control. In many instances, the coordinator can be used to control the individual medical devices. The coordinator has an internal alarm and logging capability and is connected to a patient display, which displays the patient's status in terms of physiological signals (O_2 and CO_2 in our case) trends. The caregiver essentially monitors the patient through the patient display (dashed arrow in Figure 2). The coordinator also interfaces with the hospital electronic health record (EHR) system. It can update and query the EHR when needed. For example, a medical application running on the coordinator can be used to perform a sanity check on the nurse's programming of the infusion pump based on medication orders in the EHR.

Our interoperability setup can be classified into four *configurations* based on the level of control associated with the coordinator:

- *Simple (SC):* With a simple coordinator, the infusion pump and the sensors are programmed directly by the caregiver and then connected to the coordinator. The coordinator receives status updates from the individual medical devices, and it displays the information to the caregiver via the patient display. If the blood oxygen level of the patient goes below a certain threshold, a medical application on the coordinator will raise an alarm to the caregivers.

- *Alarming (AC):* In this scenario, the coordinator has the capability to program the devices as specified by the caregiver and monitor the patient's condition. If the blood oxygen level goes below a certain threshold, the coordinator (through a medical application executing on it) raises an alarm for the caregivers to react.

- *Bolus-controlling (BC):* In this scenario, the coordinator has the capability to program the devices as specified by the caregiver, raise an alarm if the patient's condition deteriorates, and control the frequency with which the patient can give themselves bolus doses.

- *Fully-closed Loop (FC):* In this scenario, the coordinator, after the initial medical device programming by the caregiver, monitors the patient's condition, and if it deteriorates, automatically modifies the programming in place to reduce the safety risk, such as over-infusion, to the patient. Further, it can raise an alarm for the caregivers and also control the bolus volume and frequency for the patients.

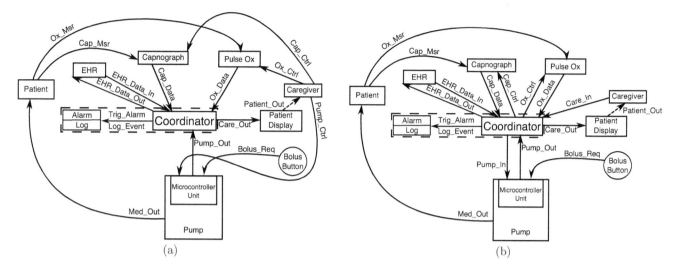

Figure 2: System Model for Interoperability Threat Analysis (a) Simple Case (SC), (b) Other cases (AC,BC, and FC)

Figure 2 (a), (b) shows the assumed interoperability setup for SC and the other modes (AC, BC and FC), respectively. The edges are labeled to indicate the information exchanged between the entities that the edge connects.

3.2 Trust Model

In our interoperability scenario, we consider the coordinator and the associated logging and alarms to be the only members of the trusted computing base (TCB). These components are trusted (they do not have malicious intent) and trustworthy (they will operate as expected). The dashed box in Figure 2 (a) and (b) signifies the TCB in our system model. Further, we assume that the caregiver is not necessarily trustworthy, in that the caregiver can make mistakes in programming the devices, but does not have malicious intent. We further assume that the infusion pump in our system model is verifiably safe as described in [22].

For our work, we essentially consider active adversaries (also called "attackers" interchangeably) who may interfere with communication links, as per the Yao-Dolev model of an adversary [9]. In addition, the adversary may also physically alter the infusion pump or the line from the infusion pump to the patient, the coordinator, the pulse oximeter and capnograph. We assume that adversaries cannot modify the firmware of the devices, but they can mount limited physical attacks on the IMD setup. For example, the attacker can induce readings in the sensor and cut the infusion line to the patient. Note that, while adversaries may simply inject the patient directly and induce a medical emergency, we consider such attacks outside the scope of interoperable medical device security.

Finally, we only consider adversaries that induce over-infusion (for pain medication under-infusion does not hamper patient safety) through the infusion pump. In other types of interoperability scenarios, both under-infusion and over-infusion can be problematic, such as with insulin infusion. This essentially doubles the threat surface.

4. ANALYSIS OF ATTACKS ON PCA-IMD SCENARIO

Before we can understand the security of IMDs, we must first examine their attack surfaces and the associated vulnerabilities. Importantly, by focusing on the assets to be protected and their associated vulnerabilities, we can determine remediation opportunities without having to anticipate an attacker's actions. In the context of medical devices, safety and security have a special relationship. The high-level patient safety goals vary dramatically based on a given patient scenario and set of devices. We therefore take a common treatment option in a hospital which can be improved using IMDs, evaluate its security in a systematic manner, and develop generalizable requirements for improving the safe operation of IMDs.

We consider an IMD scenario for patient-controlled analgesia (PCA), involving a PCA infusion pump, a pulse oximeter, and a capnograph, as a motivating example. In our scenario, there is one simple safety goal for the PCA pump: it must *not* administer an excessive quantity of pain medication (i.e., *over-infusion*). If this safety goal is violated, the patient's respiration may be suppressed and if not remediated, this may lead to patient mortality. In the remainder of this section, we focus on the attack vectors adversaries can use to subvert patient safety and harm the patient. We then discuss some viable countermeasures for these attacks.

4.1 Attack Graphs

The goal of the attack for the PCA-IMD scenario is to harm the patient by infusing excessive pain medication. Therefore over-infusion at the PCA pump is the only "unsafe" state for our case-study. If the infusion pump in our setup fails to infuse a sufficient quantity of analgesia, it is unlikely to cause a life-threatening event. Instead, the patient will experience pain and will alert a caregiver manually. When considering the safety and security of IMDs, each unsafe state must be identified and the paths to that unsafe state enumerated. In Figures 3, 4, 5 we depict the *attack graphs* that describe various *attack vectors* that can lead to the over-infusion state for our setup. *Each of these figures can be thought of as sub-branches of a larger attack graph for*

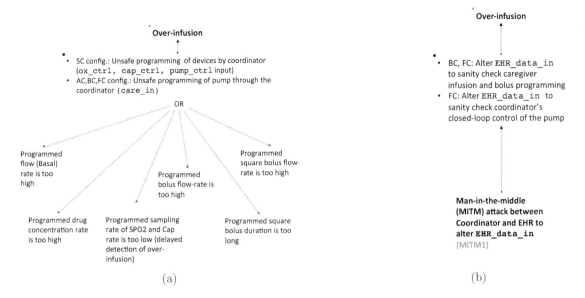

(a)

(b)

Figure 3: Attack Graphs representing attack vectors due to: (a) IMD initialization attacks, (b) EHR access attacks. Step 2 is referenced in the example attack in Section 4.2.1.

PCA-IMD. The figures are representing the following attack scenarios:

- *Initialization Attacks:* Represented in Figure 3 (a), these attacks represent the situations where the caregiver programs the devices (using `cap_ctrl`, `ox_ctrl`, `pump_ctrl` in the SC case, and using `care_in` through the coordinator in the AC, BC, and FC cases) incorrectly.

- *EHR Access Attacks:* Represented in Figure 3 (b), this attack represents the situations where the communication link between the coordinator and the EHR is compromised primarily through a man-in-the-middle attack.

- *Partial Feedback Attacks:* Represented in Figure 4 (a), these attacks represent the situations where the some of feedback channels to the coordinator (e.g, `pump_out`, `ox_data`, etc.) are rendered non-functional. Given that partial or lack of information from the devices, these attacks are probably the easiest to detect and raise alarms for. However, incomplete information at the coordinator may lead to incorrect decisions, especially in emergency situations where action needs to be taken in a time-sensitive manner.

- *Incorrect Feedback Attacks:* Represented in Figure 4 (b), these attacks represent the cases where the feedback received at the coordinator has incorrect information as a result of an adversary tampering with it. This can lead to wrong diagnosis, missed alarms and, in the FC configuration, incorrect actuation leading to over infusion.

- *Delayed Feedback Attacks:* Represented in Figure 5, these attacks include the cases where the feedback received at the coordinator is delayed as a result of an adversary. Such delayed feedback information may be interpreted as a current reading, causing over-infusion.

In last four attack graphs (involving feedback), we only show the avenues for attacks that can cause manipulation of the feedback to the coordinator. We do not attempt to describe the mechanisms for an attacker to perform such manipulation, since attempts to predict adversary behavior often lead to inadequate defenses. Instead, we focus on the broad outcomes of these attacks. Fortunately, many of the attacks can be thwarted with known countermeasures obtained from best practices in network security, software validation, and operating system security to ensure the attack cannot occur. However, one must be aware that attack vectors can be activated simultaneously by the attackers.

Broadly speaking all these attacks are manifestations of the *confused deputy* attack [18]. In a confused deputy attack, a privileged entity (the "deputy") is manipulated by an attacker to perform an unsafe act. Depending on the attack scenario, the caregiver, the coordinator, and the pump can be victims of a confused deputy attack. While the exact details vary for each entity, the general pattern is the same: the attacker would block, alter, or delay the information the deputy requires for proper operation. This would cause the deputy to make a medical decision with inaccurate or limited information. As an example, we consider a confused deputy attack on the caregiver. If the attacker wants to manipulate the caregiver into over-infusing the patient with pain medication, the attacker may alter the sensor readings from the pulse oximeter and the capnograph. In particular, the attacker may alter both sensor readings to indicate the patient's respiration is normal or elevated, regardless of the patient's actual respiration behavior. Accordingly, the caregiver may believe it is safe to administer a greater quantity of medication than what the patient can handle. If the attacker continues to report healthy readings, despite suppressed respiration, the attacker may manipulate the caregiver into programming a larger dose of medication when it is unsafe to do so.

As the model changes to have greater coordinator involvement, the attack vectors shift. Once the coordinator has the

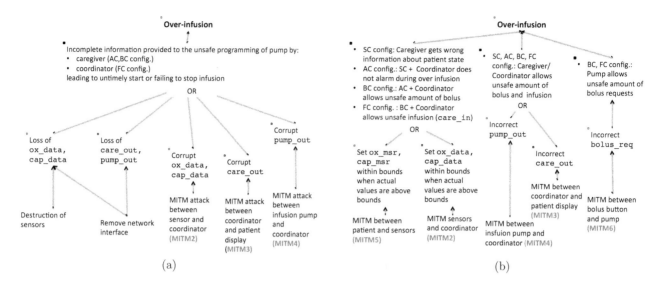

(a)   (b)

Figure 4: Attack Graphs representing: (a) partial feedback attacks, (b) incorrect feedback attacks. Steps 1 and 2 are referenced in the example attack in Section 4.2.1.

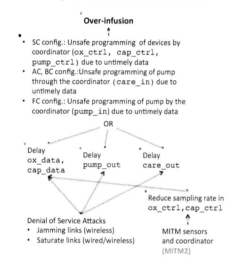

Figure 5: Attack Graphs representing delayed feedback attacks

responsibility of controlling boluses, an attacker can begin to manipulate the inputs to the coordinator with the goal of encouraging the coordinator to allow a bolus that it should prevent. In the FC configuration, the role of the caregiver is completely removed, placing these responsibilities on the coordinator. The essential issue in the FC configuration is to design closed-loop control of the coordinator application to be safe from causing the patient harm. While the change in the FC configuration may seem to introduce a security risk, the attack vectors remain largely the same. The only difference is that the attacker must focus on manipulating the coordinator instead of the caregiver.

4.2 Man-in-the-Middle Attack

The attack graphs shown in Figures 3(b), 4, and 5 demonstrate that one of the most common strategies for an attacker is to insert itself between two legitimate entities in the interoperability setup, i.e., cause Man-in-the-middle (MITM) attacks. The MITM attack can, in theory, be mounted between any two legitimate entities in the PCA-

IMD. As shown in the Figures 3(b), 4, and 5, there are six such MITM scenarios ($MITM_1,...,MITM_6$). Note that we use MITM attacks as a way to illustrate the most general form of spoofing attacks (either through communication of physical compromise) in our system. The rest of this section is dedicated to showing how an attacker could go about mounting an MITM on PCA-IMD in a care-facility setting.

Figure 2 shows an example medical device interoperability setup within (a partial view of) a modern care facility. In this setup, each patient has a set of a PCA-IMD *apparatus* for regular monitoring and actuating treatment for pain management. All three of the medical devices in the PCA-IMD apparatus are connected to the hospital network. The pump through the wired network over $Switch_3$ and the pulse-ox and capnograph over the wireless network through the local access point. In addition, the apparatus has a wireless patient display, which is used by caregivers to view the patient's current health status, as well as access the EHR. The wireless network within the hospital may be used by the caregivers and visitors to access the various systems within the care facility network or access the Internet.

For simplicity of management, we assume each PCA-IMD apparatus has an individual coordinator, which is managed centrally within the care facility. When a patient is brought into the facility, the initial interoperability configuration information is then passed to a dynamically instantiated coordinator. This instantiation occurs on a per patient basis. Figure 6 shows the coordinator is connected to the network over $Switch_2$. For brevity, only one coordinator and simple network paths are shown. In an actual deployment, redundant network paths as well as multiple coordinators may be required.

Example 1: This pertains to the $MITM_2$ and the $MITM_3$ cases. The adversary broadcasts an SSID the same as that of the hospitals AP [4]. This will cause the wireless entities (pulse-ox and the capnograph in $MITM_2$ and patient display in $MITM_3$) in the interoperability apparatus to reassociate to the faux AP due to a higher RSSI value. The attacker then intercepts and forwards all communication from wireless entities to the hospital's AP, effectively becoming the man-in-the-middle. In the SC and AC configuration,

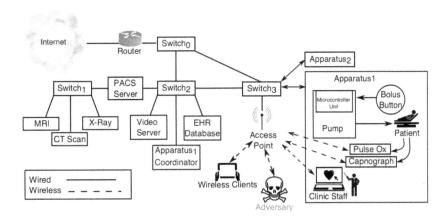

Figure 6: An example interoperable scenario in a care facility. Each patient's apparatus is given an individual coordinator. Some devices within the patient's room connect wirelessly while others are hardwired. The clinic staff uses the patient display to configure the coordinator and retrieve or update EHR records.

such an attack can be mounted to suppress local device alarms and coordinator alarms respectively.

Example 2: This pertains to the $MITM_1$ and the $MITM_4$ cases and requires the adversary to mount MITM on wired links between the EHR and the coordinator and the infusion pump and the coordinator, respectively. This is considerably more difficult as it requires physical access to the care facility's networking infrastructure, such as $Switch_2$. However, once such an access is available, then enabling MITM may be as simple as mounting an ARP poisoning attack [16], where the physical (LAN) address of the communicating entities is modified to that of the attacker during initial discovery using the Address Resolution Protocol (ARP).

Example 3: This pertains to the the $MITM_5$ and the $MITM_6$ cases, where MITM is mounted through physical compromise rather than by manipulating the communication between the entities. $MITM_5$ requires the modification of the physical sensor itself so that the actual patient state is not captured accurately. Similarly, $MITM_6$ requires physical modification of the infusion pump to be able to tamper with the bolus request information being sent from the bolus button.

Note that in the above analysis, we have assumed the infusion pump to be implemented correctly without interface or software defects. The attack example above is being described in a relatively error-free scenario. In reality, adverse events as a result of user interface issues and software defects occurred over 56,000 times from 2005-2009 [10]. Most of these were eventually detected after the devices monitoring the patient start reading irregular values. With MITM attacks, however, these devices cannot be trusted to be accurately relaying readings the coordinator. As a result, the actual scale of the security issue described in the paper is quite a bit larger.

4.3 Mitigating the Attacks

For over-infusion to occur, the infusion pump has to administer large quantities of pain medication in an untimely manner. There are four methods for an attacker to cause the controller to send the pump commands that trigger an over-infusion event are:

Programming-Focused: In this case, the caregiver's input is incorrect. The caregiver is not in our TCB and there-

fore can provide incorrect input to the devices (for SC) or the coordinator (AC and BC) either simply due to human error or incompetence. The caregiver can press incorrect keys when entering values, calculate rates incorrectly, or simply program the pump accurately, but use an incorrect concentration of the medication. **Mitigation:** These cases can be remediated using local solutions at the pump itself such as drug libraries, flow sensors, and barcode scanners [22]. One can push the remediation to the coordinator as well, but that would significantly increase the complexity of the coordinator, which is undesirable.

Communication-Focused: The inputs to the pump, `pump_in` and `bolus_req`, for the AC, BC and FC configurations, is incorrect. This is possible because: (a) some or all the information going out of the coordinator to the pump over `pump_in` has been altered (delayed, modified, corrupted) by adversaries, (b) bolus information going from the bolus button to the infusion pump over `bolus_req` has been altered (delayed, modified, corrupted) by adversaries; (c) some or all the information going into the coordinator from the sensors (i.e., `ox_data`, and `cap_data`), EHR (i.e., `EHR_data_in`), and the pump (i.e., `pump_out`) has been altered (delayed, modified, corrupted) by adversaries; and (d) the programming instructions from the caregiver to the coordinator, `care_in` has been altered (delayed, modified, corrupted). **Mitigation:** These can be prevented by using cryptographic primitives to preserve the confidentiality, integrity and authenticity properties of the lines of communication. Such techniques are considered best practices for securing network communication.

Hybrid : The caregiver's programming of the coordinator, `care_in`, in the AC and BC and FC configurations, is incorrect. **Mitigation:** All the reasons listed for the two aforementioned cases may apply and the same prevention strategies can be used.

Entity-Focused: If the the pump or the sensors or their environment are tampered with by adversaries, it is possible for the coordinator to be unaware of the actual state of the patient leading to over-infusion. **Mitigation:** In such cases, attack prevention (as in the three aforementioned cases) becomes very difficult. The only option is to detect problems with the patient's health based on data from the sensors and raise an alarm. However, if the sensors are not reporting correct data, the system simply lacks sufficient data to raise an alarm. The only way to deal with this situation is through redundancy of medical devices, assuming at least some of them are not compromised.

In summary, these vectors characterize the varied types of misinformation that could reach the PCA pump, the coordinator, and the caregiver. Within each vector, the attacker can devise a variety of actual attacks. The context of the IMD deployment plays a big role in identifying them. Any mitigation solution for these attacks have to therefore consider all of these cases.

4.4 Cryptographic Solutions

Several of the mitigation strategies rely on the use of cryptography, especially as a way to avoid MITM attacks. However, the use of cryptography is not without its problems.

- Medical devices typically do not support cryptographic operations, which may limit the deployability of the device. Cost in terms of their correct implementation, computational complexity and supporting infrastructure (e.g., certification authorities) is not non-trivial.

- Cryptography often relies on effective key distribution to work. Secure key distribution in a dynamic environment such as a hospital where the same device can be associated with multiple patients over a short span of time, is notoriously difficult. Approaches that are based on physiological signals [33] [3] may be applicable here, but they require diversity of signals which is not always available.

- When a new device is added to the interoperability setup, another concern would be if the device uses a protocol that relies on a *leap-of-faith (LoF)* mechanism. LoF mechanisms are those protocols in which the very first interaction between two parties assumes complete trust and results in the exchange of cryptographic primitives. All subsequent interactions then use this exchanged primitive for security [29]. This concern noticeably increases when considering the dynamic nature of IMDs and care facility workflows. Devices used for monitoring patients are continuously being added, removed and exchanged between different patients. As a consequence of this fluidity, devices will need to re-associate with network and re-establish connections leaving a space for potential vulnerabilities.

5. LESSONS LEARNED

The attack vectors in Figures 3, 4, and 5 highlight several important points:

- **Individual medical device safety does not equate to interoperability safety.** A device can be formally defined as "safe" if and only if none of its execution paths invoke a particular set of negative actions [22]. However, the safety of a particular medical device and the coordinator are insufficient to ensure that it remains safe in an interoperable setting. In our system model, adversary induced misinformation or bad input can cause an infusion pump to over-infuse medication, endangering patient safety. This condition can occur even if the infusion pump is guaranteed to meet its own safety requirements.

- **Secure communication within the IMD setup is paramount** As we transition from SC all the way to FC we can see that over-infusion will happen if the coordinator receives bad data or has faulty software or application. While the latter can be addressed with proper design and software verification techniques, the former condition is a simple transformation from today's caregiver scenario: rather than a human receiving inaccurate data, the coordinator receives it. The action taken is largely the same. Hence, it is not sufficient to develop safe coordinator unless it also has secure communication.

- **All security attacks are manifest as a confused deputy attack.** We assume that the pump software itself is designed to meet certain safety goals. Thus, the pump can only violate patient safety goals if it receives invalid input from a caregiver or coordinator. Likewise, when the coordinator and the caregiver are both considered trusted, patients can only be harmed if the pump is mis-programmed based on inaccurate/delayed/partial inputs from the sensors and EHR.

- **Best safety practices may thwart some attacks.** The techniques used to prevent data entry errors for caregivers, such as drug libraries, barcode scanners, and flow sensors, also play a role in preventing security failures. However, these techniques may not be exhaustive nor sufficient to thwart all security attacks. In particular, each of these devices and their interconnects must be trustworthy; otherwise, an attacker can simply tamper with the information they provide to the coordinator and pump.

- **Only pervasive misinformation attacks can silence the interoperability coordinator.** The sensor inputs ox_data and cap_data, plus the pump output pump_out and possibly the EHR, must simultaneously be manipulated; otherwise, an alarm may be raised. Such an attack would require manipulation between the coordinator and pump, along with incorrect sensor data, to be effective.

- **Attacks from compromised entities in the interoperability are difficult to prevent.** If any of the three main types of entities in the interoperability setup, namely the sensors, the caregiver, and pump can be compromised, then the traditional information security solutions described for securing the inputs are rendered moot. One can use redundancy to attempt to detect events of compromise, but this requires at least one uncompromised IMD.

- **Security may be the proper subset of safety for IMDs.** When privacy is not considered (as is the case in our analysis), security may be a subset of safety. If we do consider privacy, then loss of privacy may not always lead to immediate safety problems for the patient. We do note that reconnaissance and eavesdropping are often precursors to more active attacks and that privacy may itself be an important security and safety goal.

6. RELATED WORK

Though some work has been done in developing frameworks for enabling interoperability between medical devices, little work has been done in exploring security issues for interoperable medical devices. King *et al.* [25] present an open-source Medical Device Coordination Framework (MDCF) for exploring solutions related to designing, implementing, verifying, and certifying systems of integrated medical devices. The framework supports a publish-subscribe architecture and uses a model-based programming environment for rapid development of IMD systems. The scope of this project has largely been on enabling interoperability and doing it safely in a certifiable manner [19]. A complimentary system called Network-Aware Supervisory System (NASS) has been proposed in [23] [36], which provides a development environment for safe medical device supervisory control in the presence of network failures. In [24], the authors have extended NASS to consider wireless networks. Both MDCF and NASS frameworks focus primarily on safe interoperation. Security has not been explored in either of the two frameworks.

In our previous work [34], the security of ICE architecture was examined assuming the devices were using a wireless channel to communicate. The analysis was a very high level and was not specific to any interoperability setting. In later work [32, 35], we developed high-level models for classifying the security attacks and their consequences on interoperable medical devices. These models again did not deal in the specifics of a particular interoperability setup and consequently cannot be used to aid in designing security-conscious interoperability architectures. That being said, models developed from these efforts are certainly complimentary to this effort and can be incorporated to extend this work.

7. CONCLUSIONS AND FUTURE WORK

Medical device interoperability is an increasingly prevalent example of how computing and information technology will revolutionize and streamline medical care. However, one aspect that has not been considered thus far is ensuring IMDs do not harm patients in the presence of malicious adversaries. This work outlines our effort in understanding the threats faced by IMDs. It is an important first step in eventually designing secure interoperability architectures. In this regard, we presented a detailed attack-graph-based analysis of threats on PCA interoperability under various levels of interoperability. Assuming a trusted coordinator, most of the attacks were discovered to be various forms of the confused deputy attack. We then described mitigation approaches possible for each of the possible attack classes. Many of the communication channel-oriented attacks can be mitigated using existing best-practices and available cryptographic solutions. However, entity-focused attacks based on physical compromise of the devices themselves are very difficult to protect against technologically. Our analysis shows that individual medical device safety does not equate to IMD safety despite having a trusted coordinator.

In the future, we plan to extend the analysis by removing the coordinator from the trusted computing base and analyze the potential for attacks on constituents of the coordinator, namely the supervisor and network controller, the logs and the alarm system. We also plan to expand on this effort to design an interoperability architecture and coordinator that can handle many of the security problems that the coordinator in the ICE architecture cannot handle. Overall, we want to understand the relationship between safety and security in IMDs and other such medical cyber-physical systems (MCPS), which, as of now, is not entirely clear.

8. REFERENCES

[1] D. Arney, S. Fischmeister, J. Goldman, I. Lee, and R. Trausmuth. Plug-and-Play for Medical Devices: Experiences from a Case Study. *Biomedical Instrument & Technology*, 43(4):313–317, July 2009.

[2] ASTM F29.21. Medical devices and medical systems — essential safety requirements for equipment comprising the patient-centric integrated clinical environment (ICE) — part 1: General requirements and conceptual model.

[3] A. Banerjee, S. K. S. Gupta, and K. K. Venkatasubramanian. Pees: Physiology-based end-to-end security for mhealth. In *In Proc. 4th Annual Wireless Health Conference*, Nov 2013.

[4] K. Banitsas, S. Tachakra, and R. S. H. Istepanian. Operational parameters of a medical wireless lan: security, range and interference issues. In *Engineering in Medicine and Biology, 2002. 24th Annual Conference and the Annual Fall Meeting of the Biomedical Engineering Society EMBS/BMES Conference, 2002. Proceedings of the Second Joint*, volume 3, pages 1889–1890 vol.3, 2002.

[5] T. Choen. Medical and information technologies converg. *IEEE Eng. Med. Biol. Mag*, 23(3):59–65, May–June 2004.

[6] M. Clarke, D. Bogia, K. Hassing, L. Steubesand, T. Chan, and D. Ayyagari. Developing a standard for personal health devices based on 11073. In *EMBS*, 2007.

[7] T. Denning, K. Fu, and T. Kohno. Absence makes the heart grow fonder: New directions for implantable medical device security. In *HotSec*, 2008.

[8] T. Denning, Y. Matsuoka, and T. Kohno. Neurosecurity: security and privacy for neural devices. *Neurosurgical Focus*, 27(1), 2009.

[9] D. Dolev and A. C. Yao. On the security of public key protocols. *IEEE Transactions on Information Theory*, 29(2):198–208, 1983.

[10] FDA. Infusion pump improvement initiative. `http://www.fda.gov/downloads/MedicalDevices/ ProductsandMedicalProcedures/ GeneralHospitalDevicesandSupplies/ InfusionPumps/UCM206189.pdf`, April.

[11] D. Foo Kune, K. Venkatasubramanian, E. Vasserman, I. Lee, and Y. Kim. Toward a safe integrated clinical environment: a communication security perspective. In *Proceedings of the 2012 ACM workshop on Medical communication systems*, MedCOMM '12, pages 7–12, 2012.

[12] K. Grifantini. Plug and Play Hospitals. `http: //www.technologyreview.com/biomedicine/21052/`, July 2008.

[13] S. L. Grimes. Security: A new clinical engineering paradigm. *IEEE Eng. Med. Biol. Mag*, 23(4):80–82, July–August 2004.

[14] P. P. Gunn, A. M. Fremont, M. Bottrell, L. R. Shugarman, J. Galegher, and T. Bikson. The health

insurance portability and accountability act privacy rule: A practical guide for researchers. *Med. Care*, 42(4):321–327, April 2004.

[15] D. Halperin, T. Heydt-Benjamin, B. Ransford, S. Clark, B. Defend, W. Morgan, K. Fu, T. Kohno, and W. Maisel. Pacemakers and implantable cardiac defibrillators: Software radio attacks and zero-power defenses. In *IEEE Security and Privacy*, 2008.

[16] S. Hammouda and Z. Trabelsi. An enhanced secure arp protocol and lan switch for preveting arp based attacks. In *Proceedings of the 2009 International Conference on Wireless Communications and Mobile Computing: Connecting the World Wirelessly*, IWCMC '09, pages 942–946, 2009.

[17] S. Hanna, R. Rolles, A. Molina-Markham, P. Poosankam, K. Fu, and D. Song. Take two software updates and see me in the morning: The case for software security evaluations of medical devices. In *USENIX conference on Health security and privacy*, 2011.

[18] N. Hardy. The confused deputy: (or why capabilities might have been invented). *ACM SIGOPS Operating Systems Review*, 22(4):36–38, 1988.

[19] J. Hatcliff, A. King, I. Lee, A. Macdonald, A. Fernando, M. Robkin, E. Vasserman, S. Weininger, and J. Goldman. Rationale and architecture principles for medical application platforms. In *IEEE/ACM Third International Conference on Cyber-Physical Systems (ICCPS)*, pages 3–12, 2012.

[20] Health level seven international. http://www.hl7.org/.

[21] Integrating the healthcare enterprise. http://www.ihe.net/.

[22] B. G. Kim, A. Ayoub, O. Sokolsky, I. Lee, P. Jones, Y. Zhang, and R. Jetley. Safety-assured development of the gpca infusion pump software. In *Embedded Software (EMSOFT), 2011 Proceedings of the International Conference on*, pages 155–164, 2011.

[23] C. Kim, M. Sun, S. Mohan, H. Yun, L. Sha, and T. F. Abdelzaher. A framework for the safe interoperability of medical devices in the presence of network failures. In *Proceedings of the 1st ACM/IEEE International Conference on Cyber-Physical Systems*, ICCPS '10, pages 149–158, 2010.

[24] C. Kim, M. Sun, H. Yun, and L. Sha. A medical device safety supervision over wireless. In *Proceedings of the Reliable and Autonomous Computational Science*, RACS '10, pages 22–40, 2010.

[25] A. King, S. Procter, D. Andresen, J. Hatcliff, S. Warren, W. Spees, R. Jetley, P. Jones, and S. Weininger. An open test bed for medical device integration and coordination. In *Software Engineering - Companion Volume, 2009. ICSE-Companion 2009. 31st International Conference on*, pages 141–151, 2009.

[26] I. Lee, O. Sokolsky, S. Chen, J. Hatcliff, E. Jee, B. Kim, A. King, M. Mullen-Fortino, S. Park, A. Roederer, and K. Venkatasubramanian. Challenges and research directions in medical cyber physical systems. *Proceedings of the IEEE*, 100(1):75–90, 2012.

[27] Michael Wong. Physician-patient alliance for health and safety improving health and safety through innovation and awareness how often do errors with patient-controlled analgesia (PCA) occur? http://ppahs.org/2011/10/31/how-often-do-errors-with-pca-occur/.

[28] E. Morris, L. Levine, C. Meyers, D. Plakosh, and P. Place. Systems of systems interoperability. Technical report, Carnegie-Mellon University, April 2004.

[29] V. Pham and T. Aura. Security analysis of leap-of-faith protocols. In M. Rajarajan, F. Piper, H. Wang, and G. Kesidis, editors, *Security and Privacy in Communication Networks*, volume 96 of *Lecture Notes of the Institute for Computer Sciences, Social Informatics and Telecommunications Engineering*, pages 337–355. Springer Berlin Heidelberg, 2012.

[30] N. L. Snee and K. A. McCormick. The case for integrating public health informatics networks. *IEEE Eng. Med. Biol. Mag*, 23(1):81–88, January–February 2004.

[31] A. Tolk, S. Diallo, and C. Turnitsa. Applying the levels of conceptual interoperability model in support of integratability, interoperability, and composability for system-of-systems engineering. *Journal of Systemics, Cybernetics and Informatics*, 5(5):65–74, 2007.

[32] E. Vasserman, K. Venkatasubramanian, O. Sokolsky, and I. Lee. Security and interoperable-medical-device systems, part 2: Failures, consequences, and classification. *IEEE Security & Privacy*, 10(6):70–73, 2012.

[33] K. Venkatasubramanian, A. Banerjee, and S. K. S. Gupta. Pska: Usable and secure key agreement scheme for body area networks. *Information Technology in Biomedicine, IEEE Transactions on*, 14(1):60–68, Jan 2010.

[34] K. Venkatasubramanian, S. Gupta, R. Jetley, and P. Jones. Interoperable medical devices. *Pulse, IEEE*, 1(2):16–27, September–October 2010.

[35] K. Venkatasubramanian, E. Vasserman, O. Sokolsky, and I. Lee. Security and interoperable-medical-device systems, part 1. *IEEE Security & Privacy*, 10(5):61–63, 2012.

[36] P.-L. Wu, W. Kang, A. Al-Nayeem, L. Sha, R. B. Berlin, Jr., and J. M. Goldman. A low complexity coordination architecture for networked supervisory medical systems. In *Proceedings of the ACM/IEEE 4th International Conference on Cyber-Physical Systems*, ICCPS '13, pages 89–98, 2013.

Resilient Distributed Consensus for Tree Topology

Mark Yampolskiy[*]
University of South Alabama
Mobile, AL

Yevgeniy Vorobeychik
Vanderbilt University
Institute for Software
Integrated Systems
Nashville, TN

Xenofon D. Koutsoukos
Vanderbilt University
Institute for Software
Integrated Systems
Nashville, TN

Peter Horvath[*]
Budapest University of
Technology and Economics
Budapest, Hungary

Heath J. LeBlanc
Ohio Northern University
Ada, OH

Janos Sztipanovits
Vanderbilt University
Institute for Software
Integrated Systems
Nashville, TN

ABSTRACT

Distributed consensus protocols are an important class of distributed algorithms. Recently, an Adversarial Resilient Consensus Protocol (ARC-P) has been proposed which is capable to achieve consensus despite false information provided by a limited number of malicious nodes. In order to withstand false information, this algorithm requires a mesh-like topology, so that multiple alternative information flow paths exist. However, these assumptions are not always valid. For instance, in Smart Grid, an emerging distributed CPS, the node connectivity is expected to resemble the scale free network topology. Especially closer to the end customer, in home and building area networks, the connectivity graph resembles a tree structure.

In this paper, we propose a Range-based Adversary Resilient Consensus Protocol (R.ARC-P). Three aspects distinguish R.ARC-P from its predecessor: This protocol operates on the tree topology, it distinguishes between trustworthiness of nodes in the immediate neighborhood, and it uses a valid value range in order to reduce the number of nodes considered as outliers. R.ARC-P is capable of reaching global consensus among all genuine nodes in the tree if assumptions about maximal number of malicious nodes in the neighborhood hold. In the case that this assumption is wrong, it is still possible to reach Strong Partial Consensus, i.e., consensus between leafs of at least two different parents.

---

[*]The work was performed while the author was employed at Vanderbilt University, Institute for Software Integrated Systems.

Permission to make digital or hard copies of all or part of this work for personal or classroom use is granted without fee provided that copies are not made or distributed for profit or commercial advantage and that copies bear this notice and the full citation on the first page. Copyrights for components of this work owned by others than ACM must be honored. Abstracting with credit is permitted. To copy otherwise, or republish, to post on servers or to redistribute to lists, requires prior specific permission and/or a fee. Request permissions from permissions@acm.org.
HiCoNS'14, April 15–17, 2014, Berlin, Germany.
Copyright 2014 ACM 978-1-4503-2652-0/14/04 ...$15.00.
http://dx.doi.org/10.1145/2566468.2566485 .

Categories and Subject Descriptors

[**Security and privacy**]: Systems security—*Distributed systems security*; [**Security and privacy**]: Systems security—*Information flow control*; G.2.2 [**Mathematics of Computing**]: Graph Theory—*Trees*; G.1.0 [**Mathematics of Computing**]: General—*Parallel algorithms*

General Terms

Security, Algorithms

Keywords

Resilience, distributed consensus, tree topology, smart grids

1. INTRODUCTION

Several emerging classes of applications, such as Smart Grid, Vehicular Networks, or Distributed Person Tracking with multiple surveillance cameras, require coordinated behavior of all involved CPS systems. Smart Grid should be able to coordinate behavior of Smart Appliances to distribute load requirements over time and thus avoid energy spikes. Vehicular Networks should be able to distribute hazard information, thus preventing collisions and congestions on the roads. Multiple cameras can be used for coordinated distributed surveillance allowing tracking of persons in the field with the necessary grade of detail.

These are but a few of many emerging distributed CPS applications. What is common between all these applications is the need to coordinate actions of all involved CPS in a timely manner. Furthermore, often even coordination and/or optimization of local (i.e., in the neighborhood) parameters is sufficient to ensure global properties. Due to the vast amount of nodes in such scenarios as well as to the required robustness against node failures, distributed solutions should be applied.

Apart from coordinated tasks, the fundamental difference between those scenarios is that the coordination should be performed in various topologies, both network and overlay, which also have various grades of dynamicity. Smart Grids are expected to resemble scale-free networks with mesh-like core and tree-like topologies closer to the end customers, e.g., in the Home and Building Area Networks. With exception of the Smart Appliances, which can join and leave the network comparatively often, Smart Grid network topology evolves very slowly in time; therefore, it can be considered as static. In Vehicular Networks, a highly dynamic mesh topology should be taken into account. The Distributed Person Tracking, as it has been considered in [16], operates on a static mesh. Therefore, all of these scenarios might require different solutions optimized for the particular topology and the topological dynamics.

In this paper, we focus on the consensus problem in Building Area Networks (BAN) in Smart Grid, whose network and overlay topologies are trees. As Smart Appliances, which are leaf nodes in these trees, are owned by the end customers as well as exposed to the unrestricted physical access, it is reasonable to assume that they can be rigged. Therefore, a consensus protocol resilient to the false information provided by leaf nodes is needed.

We propose a Range-based Adversary Resilient Consensus Protocol (R.ARC-P). Compared to the ARC-P protocol introduced in [7, 9], it has three main differences. First, whereas ARC-P requires mesh topology in order to reach consensus, R.ARC-P operates on the tree topology. Second, ARC-P is an indiscriminate protocol, treating all nodes in the neighborhood equally; R.ARC-P is a discriminating protocol introducing different trust relationships based on the child-parent relation in the tree topology. Third, in ARC-P, the only value always trusted is the node's own value; in R.ARC-P, the range of values between its own value and the value of the parent node is considered as trustworthy.

The remainder of the paper is structured as follows. After discussing related work in Section 2, we describe the problem formulation in Section 3. In Section 4 we present the R.ARC-P protocol. The simulation results are presented in Section 5. We discuss the reasons behind consensus with R.ARC-P as well as outline concepts of the R.ARC-P based detection and localization of malicious nodes in Section 6.2. We conclude this paper with a short review and discussion of planned future work.

2. RELATED WORK

Two areas are relevant for this paper, Smart Grid and Consensus Protocols. As our proposal is based on the ARC-P protocol, we present it in more details.

The Smart Grid is an emerging distributed CPS, which should revolutionize the way in which energy is produced, distributed, stored, and used. It should provide benefits to all stakeholders. Customers should be able to benefit from the lower energy prices as well as from the capability of Smart Appliances (SA) to adjust dynamically to daily price fluctuations. Providers can benefit because they can buy and resell electricity produced at the customer site; moreover, providers have the additional option to store energy at the customer site. Coordinated energy usage by multiple SA can reduce the energy spikes in the electric power grid, thus reducing requirements and related costs of the power distribution systems. All this should support sustainable growth of the industry and reduce impact on the ecology.

In order to accomplish these tasks, beyond the physical grid infrastructure, an extensive logical connection and coordination between all involved Smart Grid components is needed, e.g., between multiple Smart Appliances (SA) in-

stalled at the customer site and Smart Metering Infrastructure (SMI) owned by the electrical service provider.

Recent surveys of communication/networking and of routing protocols in Smart Grid are given in [3] and [15], respectively. An overview of Smart Grid technologies and standards can be found in [4] and [1]. Cyber security and privacy issues in Smart Grid are discussed in [10] and [13]. Stealthy attacks on SCADA systems in Power Networks are studied in [14] and [2].

Distributed consensus protocols are an important class of distributed algorithms. The goal is to find an agreement between all nodes without having any centralized unit. In distributed consensus protocols, consensus is found based on the values exchanged between immediate neighbors. Consensus problems and conditions for reachability of consensus have been intensively studied in [12] and [11].

Resilient Distributed Consensus is a special case of distributed consensus. It is assumed that a limited number of malicious nodes are present that try to disrupt consensus by providing false status information to their neighbors. In [7, 9] a fully distributed Adversary Resilient Consensus Protocol (ARC-P) has been introduced. The topological properties necessary for reaching consensus with ARC-P have been studied in [8]. As we extend this protocol, we present it in more details.

ARC-P operates on mesh networks. The basic assumption is that the number of malicious nodes is bounded: there are at most $FTotal$ malicious nodes in the whole network and at most $FLocal$ malicious nodes in the neighborhood of every genuine (i.e., non-malicious) node. Based on this assumption, the ARC-P algorithm proceeds as follows. First, it sorts the status values from all neighboring nodes. Then it removes up to FLocal largest as well as up to FLocal smallest values, which are strictly smaller or respectively larger than the node's own value. After that, it computes the average of the remaining values (including its own value) and assigns this as the new value of the node.

Please note that ARC-P makes no assumptions about trustworthiness of any neighboring nodes. Due to the necessity for multiple information flow paths, ARC-P can only reach consensus in a mesh network topology.

3. PROBLEM FORMULATION

In this section, we first describe the Building Area Network (BAN) scenario and then present the considered threat model. Throughout this section we present arguments justifying our assumptions.

3.1 Scenario: Building Area Network (BAN) in Smart Grid

The Home Area Network (HAN) and Building Area Network (BAN) are important concepts in Smart Grid. They provide an envelope for the interconnection between Smart Appliances (SA) (e.g., washer, air conditioner, etc.) and Smart Metering Infrastructure (SMI). Theoretically, it is possible to provide redundant network connections between SA and SMI. However, economic considerations, such as costs of infrastructure, development, installation, and maintenance, are likely to prevent such solutions in HAN and BAN areas. Consequently, the physical network topology will be sparse, but sufficient for the purpose network infrastructure, and will resemble a tree topology (see Figure 1).

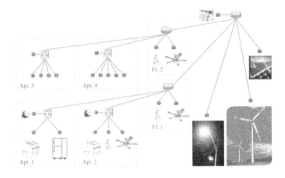

Figure 1: Building Area Network (BAN) Network Topology

Assuming the state of the art "plug and play" scenarios with auto-discovery capabilities, the logical topology of interconnection between nodes will resemble the physical topology with all communicating nodes arranged in a tree (see Figure 2). The numbers within nodes in both figures are voluntarily assigned IDs of all SA/AMI nodes. Numbers near nodes in Figure 2 are arbitrarily selected initial values, which will be discussed in more detail in Section 5.

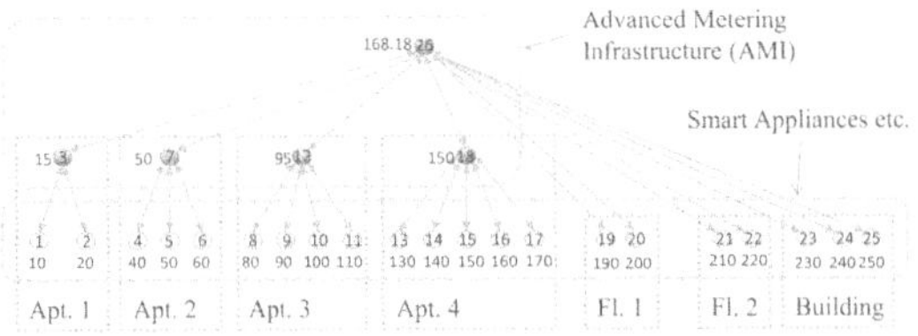

Figure 2: Building Area Network (BAN) Overlay Topology

Coordination between different SA is seen as one of the advantages of the Smart Grid, which, for instance, can reduce energy spikes caused by simultaneously turning appliances on or off. Such coordination between SA can be realized in a distributed manner, in which various SA exchange information among themselves either directly or indirectly via SMI. We assume that there will be no direct communication between SA for the following reasons. Technically, coordination between different classes of SA eventually produced by different manufacturers is a much harder problem than coordination via AMI with the standardized interface. Furthermore, within a single household such a solution remains very scalable as the number of SA is limited. Last, but not least, communication between SA from different households is not likely to be allowed because of privacy and security concerns.

3.2 Threat Model

In an environment like Smart Grid, or its constituent part BAN, there is a clear distinction between the exposure of its various components to attacks. For instance, physical access to AMI is usually restricted to authorized personnel. Usually, there are also mechanisms in place to detect physical or cyber manipulations on AMI.

On the other hand, various SA are owned by the residents who also have unrestricted physical access to it. This makes SA exposed to various manipulations. Moreover, as

the number or the type of SA is neither restricted nor controlled by the electricity provider, plugging in manipulated devices as well as computers impersonating SA can be seen as a plausible and cost-effective attack vector.

Consequently, we consider the following threat model. Only leaf nodes (which represent various SA) in the connectivity tree can be malicious. All non-leaf nodes (which represent AMI) are considered to be genuine and behave according to the consensus algorithm. The only attack we consider in this work is injection of the false information by the malicious nodes.

We are well aware that it is possible to perform at least two further classes of attacks. First, infection of AMI, e.g., via exploiting a buffer overflow attack. A second attack is DoS or DDoS attack either on the AMI or on SA. We explicitly omit consideration of these two classes of attacks for the following reasons. A buffer overflow attack requires significantly greater effort than injection of false information by compromised SA. Furthermore, AMI can be hardened to detect and to collect evidence of an attempted buffer overflow attack, thus opening the possibility of legal prosecution. Unlike the code injection attacks, DoS and DDoS attacks can be detected easily.

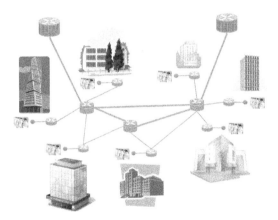

Figure 3: Neighborhood Area Network (NAN) Network Topology

In the present work, we also omit consideration of attacks on network components, e.g., on routers. Even though such attacks are possible, their complexity as well as resources required are way beyond those required for attacks on SA. This is especially true for the network infrastructure to which BAN is connected, e.g., the Neighborhood Area Network (NAN). At this level, it is common to have a core network with redundant physical topology (a schematic example is depicted in Figure 3), which is robust against both infrastructure failure and attacks on it.

3.3 Terms and Definitions

For the definition of various forms of consensus we use in this paper, we have to introduce the following terms for the tree $G = \{V, E\}$:

$$V = V^{SA} \cup V^{SMI} : V^{SA} \cap V^{SMI} = \emptyset$$
$$V^{SA} = V^g \cup V^m : V^g \cap V^m = \emptyset$$

Here, V^{SA} are all leaf nodes representing SA, V^{SMI} all non-leaf nodes representing SMI, V^g all genuine leaf nodes, and V^m all malicious leaf nodes. We also introduce the function $\pi(v_i)$, which returns the parent node of any non-root node v_i and which returns v_i if it is the root.

For this work, we are only interested in siblings among leaf nodes. We define leaf siblings as

$$\widetilde{V_k} = \{v_i : \forall v_i \in V^{SA} \wedge \pi\{v_i\} = v_k\}$$

In the considered scenario, Smart Grid leaf nodes, i.e., all kinds of SA, are the only active nodes. All non-leaf nodes, which represent Smart Metering Infrastructure, act rather as mitigating and filtering nodes.

We distinguish between following cases of consensus:

Global Consensus: We define *Global Consensus* as a consensus among all genuine leaf nodes. In mathematical terms,

$$\forall v_k(0) \; \exists t : v_i^g(t) = v_j^g(t) \; \forall v_i^g, v_j^g \in V^g,$$

where $v_k(0)$ represents initial value of any node, including non-leaf and malicious ones, and $v_i^g(t)$ and $v_j^g(t)$ are values of any two genuine leaf nodes after t rounds of a consensus algorithm. Please note that this definition emphasizes that there are no restrictions imposed on the initial values of any node, including non-leaf ones.

Weak Partial Consensus: We define *Weak Partial Consensus* as a consensus between all genuine nodes in at least one sibling neighborhood, i.e., sharing the same parent node:

$$\exists \widetilde{V_k}, t : \forall v_i, v_j \in \widetilde{V_k} \cap V^g : v_i^g(t) = v_j^g(t)$$

Strong Partial Consensus: We define *Strong Partial Consensus* as a consensus between all genuine nodes within at least two leaf neighborhoods:

$$\exists \widetilde{V_k}, \widetilde{V_q}, t : \forall v_i, v_j \in (\widetilde{V_k} \cup \widetilde{V_k}) \cap V^g : v_i^g(t) = v_j^g(t)$$

No Consensus: We say that *No Consensus* can be reached if no Weak Partial Consensus can be reached. We also speak about absence of consensus in the case where malicious node(s) can determine the consensus values of all genuine nodes.

We further distinguish between $FTotal$ and $FLocal$ values. Whereas FTotal is the overall number of malicious leaf nodes in the tree, FLocal is a reasonable assumption on how many nodes in the neighborhood can provide malicious information (because they are malicious or because they were outvoted by malicious nodes). FLocal acts as a parameter for the original ARC-P algorithm as well as for the R.ARC-P algorithm we will present in Section 4. We further assume that FLocal assumption can be wrong. Therefore, by the parents of leaf nodes, the maximal number of malicious nodes can reach in extreme case FTotal value.

4. RANGE-BASED ARC-P

Based on our assumption that only leaf nodes can be malicious, we can assume with the high confidence that parent nodes generally provide (more) genuine information and only child nodes can provide incorrect information. This allows us to extend the ARC-P by always trusting the value of a parent node, i.e., never exclude this value alongside with a node's own value. In our proposal, Range-based ARC-P (R.ARC-P), we go one step further. For every node, we declare that the range of values between the node's own value and its parent's value is valid. Selection of the valid values in R.ARC-P is graphically depicted in Figure 4.

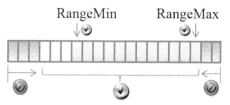

RangeMin = min (ownVal, parentVal)
RangeMax = max (ownVal, parentVal)

Figure 4: Selection of valid values in R.ARC-P

A C-like pseudo code of R.ARC-P executed by every node in the tree is depicted in Figure 5. The R.ARC-P algorithm works as follows. First, the minimum and maximum values of the – for this particular node in this particular round – always valid value range ($RangeMin$ and $RangeMax$) are defined as the minimum and maximum of its own and parent values, respectively. After sorting values from all peers (including its own and parent values), up to $FLocal$ smallest nodes are removed, as long as they are strictly smaller than $RangeMin$, and up to $FLocal$ largest values are removed, as long as they are strictly larger than $RangeMax$. In the pseudo code, we use indices to the smallest ($iRangeMin$) and biggest ($iRangeMax$) valid value as the means of "removal." After that, an average of all valid values is computed. Please note that $arrPeerVals$ should contain all values from all neighbors (including parent node) and its own value.

```
RARCP (arrPeerVals, ownVal, parentVal, FLocal)
{
  RangeMin = min (ownVal, parentVal);
  RangeMax = max (ownVal, parentVal);

  sort (arrPeerVals);

  iRangeMin = 0;
  for (i=0; i<FLocal; iRangeMin++, i++)
    if ((arrPeerVals[iRangeMin] >= RangeMin)
      break;

  iRangeMax = sizeof(arrPeerVals)-1;
  for (i=0; i<FLocal; iRangeMax--, i++)
    if ((arrPeerVals[iRangeMax] <= RangeMax)
      break;

  newVal = 0;
  for (i=iRangeMin; i<iRangeMax; i++)
    newVal += arrPeerVals[i];

  newVal /= (iRangeMax-iRangeMin+1);

  return newVal;
}
```

Figure 5: R.ARC-P Algorithm

5. EVALUATION

In this section, we first describe the settings for the experiments and later present some of test results.

Malicious Nodes		Reachability of Consensus		
FLocal	FTotal	ARC-P	ARC-P^d	R.ARC-P
0	0	√	√	√
0	1	–	–	–
1	0	–	(–)	√
1	1	–	(–)	√
1	2	–	(–)	(√)
2	0	–	(√)	√
2	1	–	(√)	√
2	2	–	(√)	√
2	3	–	(–)	(√)
2	5	–	(–)	(√)
		√	Global Consensus	
		(√)	Strong Partial Consensus	
		(–)	Weak Partial Consensus	
		–	No Consensus	

Table 1: Evaluation summary

5.1 Evaluation Setup

We have compared capabilities of ARC-P and R.ARC-P to reach consensus on different tree topologies with different initial values of all nodes. Furthermore, in order to overcome the obvious restriction of ARC-P in the case of leaf nodes (i.e., if FLocal is set to a value greater than zero no information will flow towards the leaf), we have evaluated how ARC-P with different FLocal values for leaf and non-leaf nodes will perform. We call this variant ARCP^d ("d" for **d**ifferentiated settings). In ARCP^d all non-leaf nodes perform like original ARC-P with the specified FLocal, for leafs FLocal is always set to 0.

For the sake of simplicity, all experiments presented in this paper are run on the topology depicted in Figure 2. In this figure, numbers within nodes indicate the arbitrarily selected IDs of the nodes. Before the consensus algorithm starts, we have initialized all leaf nodes with the value $10 * NodeID$. All non-leaf nodes are initialized with average values of their children nodes. In Figure 2, all initial values are depicted near nodes. Simulation experiments have been performed with MATLAB.

In our experiments, we have varied the total number of malicious nodes from zero to five, in all possible combinations of their placement in leaf nodes. Independently of the number of nodes, we have also varied the number of expected malicious nodes from zero to three. During simulation, all genuine nodes update their own value according to the selected protocol, all malicious values do not deviate from the initial value over time. This behavior simplifies visual distinction on the graphics between values of genuine and malicious nodes (values of malicious nodes are depicted as straight horizontal lines). Not presented in this section, we have also performed experiments with the values of malicious nodes changing periodically. Results regarding reaching consensus of different algorithms and their variations are not influenced by these fluctuations.

Please note that in this work we assume that all neighboring nodes exchange actual values, i.e., we don't consider the case when malicious nodes can provide different status values to different neighbors.

5.2 Simulation Results

The summary of various experiments is summarized in Table 1. The leftmost two columns specify FLocal and FTotal numbers of adversaries during the experiment, i.e., the expected (by the algorithm) maximal number of malicious nodes in the neighborhood and the real number of malicious nodes in the tree. The results of experiments are depicted in the remaining three columns for ARC-P, ARC-P^d, and R.ARC-P protocols respectively. The results reflect the worst case scenario, i.e., location of malicious nodes under which the particular protocol performs the worst. Please note that we assume that FLocal expectation can be wrong. Therefore, the worst case scenario can reflect the situation when up to FTotal malicious nodes are in the neighborhood of a single node. We distinguish between the following four cases of protocol performance: Global Consensus, Strong Partial Consensus, Weak Partial Consensus, and No Consensus (see Section 3.3 for the definition of these terms).

In the case when there are no malicious nodes in the system and none are expected, all ARC-P, ARC-P^d, and R.ARC-P perform similarly and produce identical convergence behavior (see Figure 6).

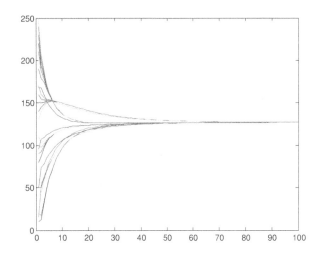

Figure 6: ARC-P, ARC-P^d, and R.ARC-P with FLocal=0, FTotal=0

In the case when there is one malicious node and none is expected, ARC-P, ARC-P^d, and R.ARC-P algorithms converge as well, but this time to the value of the malicious node (see Figure 7). Please note that in this figure, unlike all other presented in this paper, 500 rounds are depicted.

In the case when nodes expect that one of their neighbors is malicious, ARC-P cannot reach consensus even if there are no malicious nodes in the tree (see Figure 8). The reason is simple. As leaf nodes are only connected to their parents, there is no other information source which can be removed from the considerations nor are there any further information flow paths which would "feed" information to the node.

The ARC-P^d configuration of ARC-P performs slightly better (see Figure 9) - it is capable to reach Weak Partial Consensus for all sub-trees representing apartments of BAN as well as for the remaining SA of the building.

Under the same conditions, the proposed R.ARC-P algorithm is able to reach consensus among all nodes in the tree

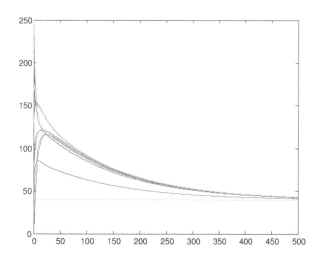

Figure 7: ARC-P, ARC-P^d, and R.ARC-P with FLocal=0, FTotal=1 (node 4)

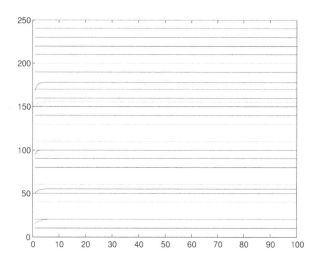

Figure 8: ARC-P with FLocal=1, FTotal=0

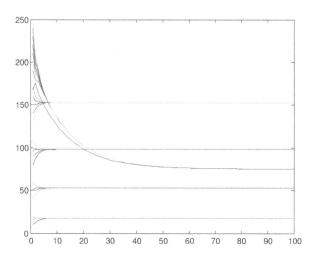

Figure 9: ARC-P^d with FLocal=1, FTotal=0

(see Figure 10). The reason is that all leaf nodes are trusting parents and – if they are genuine - their own value will always asymptotically converge to the value of their parent nodes.

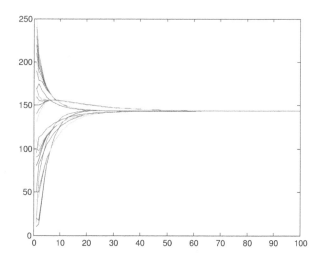

Figure 10: R.ARC-P with FLocal=1, FTotal=0

As even expectation of a single malicious node in the neighborhood prevents ARC-P protocol from converging, we will not present further examples with higher real and higher FLocal and FTotal.

Throughout our experiments, we have seen that R.ARC-P converges in all cases if the number of expected malicious nodes is correct, i.e., identical or greater than the real number of malicious nodes in the neighborhood. For instance, in Figure 11 an example is present with up to 3 malicious nodes in neighborhood, even though totally 5 malicious nodes are present in the system. R.ARC-P shows very fast convergence of all genuine nodes to the same value.

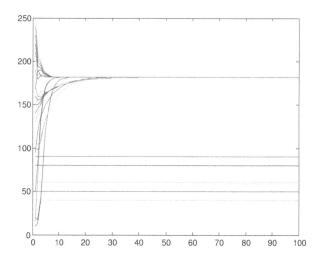

Figure 11: R.ARC-P with FLocal=3, FTotal=5 (malicious nodes: 4, 5, 6, 8, and 9)

Please note that, even under the same graph topology and initial values of nodes, the ultimate convergence value can vary influenced by the number of expected malicious nodes. This convergence error is introduced by removing outlier values from the computation of a new state value. The result is identical with the behavior of ARC-P protocol and is a "price" paid for the resilience against false information injection.

6. DISCUSSION

In this section, we first provide a brief discussion about underlying graph theoretical reasons for the different performance of the evaluated distributed consensus protocols. Then we outline ideas how the presence of false information can be detected and how malicious nodes can be localized if R.ARC-P protocol is used.

6.1 Reasoning about R.ARC-P Performance

Considering a generic graph in which ARC-P, ARC-P^d, and R.ARC-P tries to find a consensus can be seen as an information flow problem in a dynamic digraph, i.e., directed graph (for the related discussion see, e.g., [6, 5]). Exclusion of values of some neighbors is equivalent to the removing in edges comming from these nodes. Therefore, if ARC-P is applied in the tree with $FLocal \geq 1$, no information can flow towards leafs because edges from their parents are removed.

In the ARC-P^d, setting $FLocal = 0$ for all leafs fixes this problem only to some extent. This ensures that information is always flowing from the leaf parents to their leafs, thus creating preconditions for the Weak Partial Consensus around values of the leaf parents. However, indiscriminate treatment of all neighbors by non-leaf nodes enables removal of edges which makes graph disconnected, making global consensus impossible.

R.ARC-P fixes this problem by introducing hierarchical trust relationships between nodes. This alone ensures that there always exists a spanning tree in a digraph, starting at the root of the tree in which consensus should be reached. This, in turn, ensures that even in the worst case scenario all genuine nodes converge to the value of the root node. The introduction of the valid range (between own and parent node values) decreases the number of edges to be removed, thus fostering the "upstream" information flow from leafs to the root. Furthermore, the presence of the values in the range between own and parent node values, their number, and their values influence the convergence speed of a node's own value towards the value of the parent node. Therefore, R.ARC-P always reaches Global Consensus if FLocal is estimated correctly and tends to reach Strong Partial Consensus if the FLocal estimation was wrong.

6.2 Localization of Malicious Nodes

As we have thought during simulations, the R.ARC-P will not converge to a single consensus value if the number of malicious nodes in the neighborhood is underestimated. However, we would like to emphasize an interesting convergence behavior in this case. Figure 12 depicts the state development with nodes 5 and 6 malicious (i.e., FTotal=2) and expected number of malicious nodes FLocal=1.

According to the experimental setup, malicious nodes keep their own values unchanged. The genuine node 4 will converge to the value of its parent node 7. The node 7, however, will "stabilize" at the value between node 6 (an malicious nodes which considered genuine because of the wrong estimation) and node 26 (a parent node). This observation allows us to perform detection and – to some extent – lo-

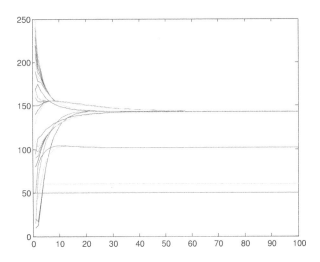

Figure 12: R.ARC-P with 1 malicious nodes expected and 2 present (nodes 5 and 6)

calization of the malicious node(s). We distinguish between the following cases:

- A parent node can monitor the behavior of the children leaf nodes. If they refuse to converge towards the value of the parent node, these nodes can be identified as malicious.

- In the case if child node, which is not a leaf node, does not converge, the assumption can be made that this child node was outvoted by an exceeding number of malicious children nodes.

- In the case of self-observation of a non-leaf node, its inability to converge with the parent node indicates that the number of malicious children is higher than expected.

These observations have two consequences. First of all, it is possible to identify misbehavior and – to some extent – localization of malicious node(s). Second, it opens the possibility for a dynamic adaptation of the number of expected malicious nodes in the neighborhood. We plan to evaluate both of these possibilities in more details in our future work.

7. CONCLUSIONS AND FUTURE WORK

In this paper, we have presented a novel resilient distributed consensus protocol, Range-based Adversary Resilient Consensus Protocol (R.ARC-P). Compared to the ARC-P protocol it extends, R.ARC-P has three main differences from ARC-P. First, whereas ARC-P requires mesh topology in order to reach consensus, R.ARC-P operates on the tree topology. Second, ARC-P is an indiscriminate protocol, treating all nodes in the neighborhood equally; R.ARC-P is a discriminating protocol introducing different trust relationships based on the child-parent relation in the tree topology. Third, in ARC-P, the only value that is always trusted is a node's own value; in R.ARC-P, the range of values between a node's own value and the value of the parent node is considered as trustworthy. With the simulation results we have shown that R.ARC-P can always reach Global Consensus if FLocal assumption is correct and can reach Strong Partial

Consensus if it is not. We have discussed the graph theoretical reasons behind this behavior. Furthermore, we have outlined a procedure allowing localization of malicious nodes if R.ARC-P algorithm is used.

In our future work, we plan to investigate the consensus problem in scale-free networks, which can be seen as a combination of mesh and tree sub-networks. An immediate assumption is that the original ARC-P should be applied for in the mesh part of such networks whereas the R.ARC-P protocol proposed in this paper in the tree sub-networks. We plan to evaluate the interplay of these two protocol variations.

Last but not least, even though in this work we have omitted discussing infection and DoS attacks, we are planning to investigate the influence of such attacks on the distributed consensus algorithm. Most interestingly, we are planning to analyze the question whether a combination of application and network level attacks can give an adversary a significant advantage, and, if it is the case, under what conditions.

Acknowledgments

This work is supported in part by the National Science Foundation (CNS-1238959, CNS-1035655) and NIST (70NANB13H169).

8. REFERENCES

[1] F. Cleveland. Iec tc57 security standards for the power system's information infrastructure-beyond simple encryption. In *Transmission and Distribution Conference and Exhibition, 2005/2006 IEEE PES*, pages 1079–1087. IEEE, 2006.

[2] G. Dán and H. Sandberg. Stealth attacks and protection schemes for state estimators in power systems. In *Smart Grid Communications (SmartGridComm), 2010 First IEEE International Conference on*, pages 214–219. IEEE, 2010.

[3] J. Gao, Y. Xiao, J. Liu, W. Liang, and C. Chen. A survey of communication/networking in smart grids. *Future Generation Computer Systems*, 28(2):391–404, 2012.

[4] V. C. Gungor, D. Sahin, T. Kocak, S. Ergut, C. Buccella, C. Cecati, and G. P. Hancke. Smart grid technologies: communication technologies and standards. *Industrial informatics, IEEE transactions on*, 7(4):529–539, 2011.

[5] P. Holme. Network reachability of real-world contact sequences. *Physical Review E*, 71(4):046119, 2005.

[6] P. Holme and J. Saramäki. Temporal networks. *Physics reports*, 519(3):97–125, 2012.

[7] H. J. LeBlanc and X. D. Koutsoukos. Consensus in networked multi-agent systems with adversaries. In *Proceedings of the 14th international conference on Hybrid systems: computation and control*, pages 281–290. ACM, 2011.

[8] H. J. LeBlanc, H. Zhang, X. Koutsoukos, and S. Sundaram. Resilient asymptotic consensus in robust networks. *Selected Areas in Communications, IEEE Journal on*, 31(4):766–781, 2013.

[9] H. J. LeBlanc, H. Zhang, S. Sundaram, and X. Koutsoukos. Consensus of multi-agent networks in the presence of adversaries using only local information. In *Proceedings of the 1st international conference on High Confidence Networked Systems*, pages 1–10. ACM, 2012.

[10] J. Liu, Y. Xiao, S. Li, W. Liang, and C. Chen. Cyber security and privacy issues in smart grids. 2012.

[11] R. Olfati-Saber, J. A. Fax, and R. M. Murray. Consensus and cooperation in networked multi-agent systems. *Proceedings of the IEEE*, 95(1):215–233, 2007.

[12] R. Olfati-Saber and R. M. Murray. Consensus problems in networks of agents with switching topology and time-delays. *Automatic Control, IEEE Transactions on*, 49(9):1520–1533, 2004.

[13] E. Quinn. Privacy and the new energy infrastructure. *Available at SSRN 1370731*, 2009.

[14] H. Sandberg, A. Teixeira, and K. H. Johansson. On security indices for state estimators in power networks. In *Preprints of the First Workshop on Secure Control Systems, CPSWEEK 2010, Stockholm, Sweden*, 2010.

[15] N. Saputro, K. Akkaya, and S. Uludag. A survey of routing protocols for smart grid communications. *Computer Networks*, 56(11):2742–2771, 2012.

[16] C. Soto, B. Song, and A. K. Roy-Chowdhury. Distributed multi-target tracking in a self-configuring camera network. In *Computer Vision and Pattern Recognition, 2009. CVPR 2009. IEEE Conference on*, pages 1486–1493. IEEE, 2009.

A Module for Anomaly Detection in ICS Networks

Matti Mantere
VTT Technical Research
Centre of Finland
Kaitovayla 1
90570 Oulu, Finland
matti.mantere@vtt.fi

Mirko Sailio
VTT Technical Research
Centre of Finland
Kaitovayla 1
90570 Oulu, Finland
mirko.sailio@vtt.fi

Sami Noponen
VTT Technical Research
Centre of Finland
Kaitovayla 1
90570 Oulu, Finland
sami.noponen@vtt.fi

ABSTRACT

Network security monitoring using machine learning algorithms is a topic that has been well researched and found to be difficult to use. We propose to use a specific approach in restricted IP network environments and leverage the network state information and information from individual connections for increased level of sensitivity. The approach is meant for use in restricted IP networks which exhibit a level of determinism that enables the use of machine learning approach. In this work we use algorithm called Self-Organizing Maps. We introduce an implementation of self-organizing maps engine built on top of the Bro network security monitor. An implemented selection of initial features for the Self-Organizing Maps is provided and a sample sub-set is used when training a SOM lattice for network data from an industrial control system environment. The anomaly detection prototype described in this paper is meant as a complementary mechanism, not a standalone solution for network security monitoring.

Categories and Subject Descriptors

H.0 [**Information Systems**]: General

Keywords

anomaly detection; cyber security; machine learning; network security monitoring

1. INTRODUCTION

In this paper we introduce a concept of using specific attributes of network state combined with individual connection information to provide meaningful features for network anomaly detection. The usage of network state attributes derived from a network security monitoring system as features for machine learning algorithm allows detection of changes in overall network environment, especially when combined with connection specific information.

Permission to make digital or hard copies of all or part of this work for personal or classroom use is granted without fee provided that copies are not made or distributed for profit or commercial advantage and that copies bear this notice and the full citation on the first page. Copyrights for components of this work owned by others than the author(s) must be honored. Abstracting with credit is permitted. To copy otherwise, or republish, to post on servers or to redistribute to lists, requires prior specific permission and/or a fee. Request permissions from permissions@acm.org.
HiCoNS'14, April 15–17, 2014, Berlin, Germany.
Copyright is held by the owner/author(s). Publication rights licensed to ACM.
ACM 978-1-4503-2652-0/14/04 ...$15.00.
http://dx.doi.org/10.1145/2566468.2566478.

Anomaly detection in industrial control system (ICS) networks is an important issue given the increased connectivity of these environments and their high susceptibility to damage once their perimeter has been breached. They also present a tempting target for various attackers with motives ranging from mischief to industrial espionage and sabotage. Our contribution to this aims to improve the overall state of network security monitoring in industrial environments.

A deployable machine learning based anomaly detection system with passive monitoring would strengthen the existing security measures for a industrial control system network. It would require very limited manual customization before and during deployment. After deployment changes would only be needed when there are changes made to the network environment. Similar activities are ongoing by other parties, as evident in the Section 2, but our systems aims to leverage the existing rich network analysis framework to provide increased capabilities.

In addition to the introduction of usage of specific network state information we introduce an initial module implementation using Bro network security monitor (Bro, Bro NSM) [25]. Bro is used as a base system and source of the information for forming the normalized features of the machine learning algorithm part. Bro NSM is an open source network security monitoring and traffic analysis framework originally written by Vern Paxson and available for download freely [4].

This paper is limited to the description of these techniques, the implementation and early testing with clean data from the test network. The machine learning algorithm used in this approach is a modified version of the basic self-organizing maps (SOM). The SOM implementation is carried out using Bro's inbuilt scripting language. SOM uses unsupervised learning and is used to map multi-dimensional data into the two-dimensional map. The resulting mapping preserves the topological relation of the inputs and is also easily understood and visualized. [18]

Network state attributes can be used as a part of the feature vector of the SOM setup but are optional. The system depicted can also be used without these features or easily extended to accommodate new features as long as they are available for the Bro NSM system at the time of individual connection terminations.

The envisioned operational context for a system leveraging this approach is a restricted network such as ICS network or a similar environment. The applicability of machine learning based anomaly detection for these restricted environments is dependent on the individual network and the protocols found therein.

For the initial testing we used near ideal instance of such an restricted network environment. Specifically the packet capture files from the PrintoCent state-of-the-art printed intelligence pilot factory located at VTT Oulu premises, and more accurately the control network of a printing machine called MAXI [1]. This environment offers relatively deterministic data flows in daily cycles. The term *deterministic* is used in this paper in the similar manner as in the work presented in the paper [16].

Network environments with relatively deterministic or predictable properties also alleviate the problem with false positives, a common issue with anomaly detection systems [9]. The used target network and its relatively deterministic properties are explained in Section 3.5.

Based on our review of related work in Section 2 and the studies on systems available to public our system differs from most. The main difference is that compared to the more generic anomaly and intrusion detection solutions currently commonly available it has a very specific intended context of use that is coupled with automated modeling of the network traffic through machine learning algorithm and allows user to easily select the various parameters or even extend the functionality. It is not meant to be usable in more open network environments, which means that many of the issues faced by systems in those environments are avoided. The selection of features and functionalities are geared towards this specific purpose. It is also the first artificial neural network (ANN) module for Bro NSM that has been published, and benefits from the wide array of functionality and extendability inherent in the underlying system. The rich stateful nature of Bro also allows the use of network features otherwise difficult to obtain. We have not yet fully exploited the state information in our system.

This paper follows the standard structure. In Section 2 the most relevant related work is presented. In Section 3 the material and methods are described, including the early implementation of a test set of features, the general implementation of the system and a short description of the network from which the packet captures are received from. This is followed by the Section 4 on results and Section 5 for a discussion and eventually the Section 6 for the conclusion.

2. RELATED WORK

This section discussing the related work contains much of the same information as found in the papers published earlier on by the authors, lastly in the paper [23].

Significant work has been done on using machine learning algorithms for network security monitoring and anomaly detection. Self-organizing maps algorithm has been also been investigated for this particular purposes, such as in the work presented in [26]. Research presented in [27] investigates a multilevel hierarchical approach and comparison to a single level approach, which is what we use here. The work presented in paper [19] investigates the training of neural network anomaly detectors for intrusion detection purposes and also brings up the challenge of the variability present in most networks. Work in [17] investigates the usage of fuzzy SOM's in comparison the the classical implementation.

In the paper [28] Sommer *et al.* discuss the applicability of machine learning for network intrusion detection and difficulties arising from bringing the system out of the laboratory and into the open. This work has been instrumental for our work in mapping the difficulties of using machine

learning for intrusion or anomaly detection. Concerning the aplicability of machine learning approaches to the monitoring and anomaly detection of industrial control system networks and other restricted networks we found several papers to describe work very important to ours. In work [16] Hadeli *et al.* investigate leveraging determinism in ICS network for anomaly detection, this stands in contrast to the challenge of diversity and variability for more open networks as stated in [19]. Linda *et al.* in paper [21] describe a neural network based method for detection intrusions in critical infrastructure settings with good test results. The authors of also investigate the issue in the light of leveraging machine learning for anomaly detection in ICS network context this work papers [24], [22] [23]. The paper by Yang *et al.* [32] also investigates the intrusion detection through anomaly -based approach presenting interesting work. The work presented by Lin *et al.* in [20] describes a new protocol parser for Bro specifically meant for a protocol used in supervisory control and data acquisition (SCADA) systems, namely DNP3. The advancement of the Bro in the field of SCADA systems is very important for the continuation of the work presented in this paper and therefore of great interest. The ability to parse most SCADA protocols would enable a machine learning approach to use protocol specific information as a basis of additional features. Important work on the Bro and work concerning leveraging the tool also includes work such as presented by the researchers in the following papers: [30][31][12][15]. Bro related information and downloads are available on the projects web site at [4].

The work presented in the paper [13] by Dreger *et al.* presents the idea of using host based context information for improving the accuracy of network intrusion detection systems (NIDS), and this might be something to be used as a source of features for the SOM implementation at a later stage.

Important previous work that we are building upon also includes other more generic seminal work done on intrusion and anomaly detection such as presented in the papers [10], [29]. A good treatise on more generic network security monitoring can be found in the book [8].

3. MATERIALS AND METHODS

The main software tool used in the work was the Network Security Monitor called Bro [25]. It is a very flexible and powerful system offering good extendability with its scripting language. A version 2.1 was used for the implementation of the SOM extension. The new module includes the SOM algorithm, needed functions for normalization and all the other functionality addressed to the handling of SOM and integration with Bro. The implementation is highly specific to Bro, due to the scripting language used which is intrinsic to Bro.

The scripting language was used to implement a instance of the SOM algorithm [18] with a number of features to select from at the end-users discretion. The feature set includes a number of connection specific features, as well as a number of features derived from the current state as reported by Bro internal functions. The highly stateful nature of the Bro allows us to use the network state information it has stored as additional features. As of this writing the implementation of the feature set is still work-in-progress, with only a limited number of features available. This will be further discussed in Section 3.1.

The system is taught to learn the normal connections and state of the network, and reports input which differs from traffic previously seen as an anomaly. The value which triggers this alert is user configurable variable which represent the minimum Euclidean distance between input and feature vectors that triggers an anomaly warning.

There are important Bro specific bits of information to be kept in mind. Such as that in addition to TCP traffic it also handles UDP and ICMP message flows as connections based on internal logic [25].This Bro behavior is reflected in this paper. When discussing ICMP or UDP connections, this Bro representation of the flows for these transport protocols is meant.

It is also important to note that the SOM implementation for anomaly detection is meant to be complementary to the usage of the network security monitoring and the Bro tool standard functionality, and not provide the capability to perform meaningfully effective intrusion detection by itself.

Other tools used for supporting the work include the applications used for packet capturing and analysis. Such as Tcpdump [7] and Wireshark[3].

The network traffic used for the proof-of-concept implementation was derived from the MAXI[1] and represents a novel setup with relatively pristine, deterministic and cyclic network environment. The network environment, it's specific design and the possibilities for network security monitoring therein are not in the scope of this paper and are only briefly described in Section 3.5.

3.1 Implementation

The current proof-of-concept level implementation as depicted in Figure 1 follows the standard SOM structure [18] with some tunable components. The implementation allows the envisioned end-user to tune the system to his or her needs by setting various attributes and variables defined in the configuration file.

The implementation is contained in two Bro script files, namely SOM.bro and SOM_config.bro with additional hook for calling the correct function in the connection handling script when a connection is terminated and to be logged. The built-in introspection function of Bro that produces information on the number of live connections is called right after the a connection terminates. The information from the introspection functionality is then combined with the information from the terminated connection to form the input vector.

Due to the limitations of the Bro scripting language the size of the SOM and the number of neurons that can be initialized is limited if done within Bro. Currently attempting to initialize overtly large lattices through recursive function calls results in a segmentation fault. In the future this initialization is to be done externally of the Bro by shell scripts or similar means.

The implementation as depicted in the Figure 1 consists of the core Bro functionality which has remained unchanged. The SOM functionality calls upon many of the Bro's internal functions for retrieving the network state at the time of the logging of a terminating connection. The terminating connection is processed both in the normal fashion of the standard system, as well as supplied to the SOM module for additional processing. The features selected for the use by the end user are then extracted. The features related to the terminating connection are processed and normalized,

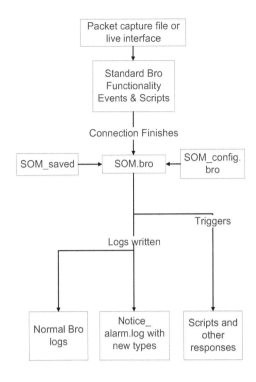

Figure 1: SOM extension for Bro NSM

and the same is done on the selected network and Bro state features, which are obtained from the internal state of Bro by the provided functions. The initial features implemented are discussed in more detail in the Section 3.2. For the normalization, the largest single value seen since the creation of the specific SOM lattice is used. The seen value is divided by the largest value seen so far, which leads to all the values in input function receiving normalized values in the range of $[0, 1]$. This leads to initial instability as the initial normalization values tend to be far lower than the level at which they stabilize. This phenomenon fades out as the training is carried out in a restricted and deterministic network environment where the normalization values reach their approximate highest values after a single period or interval. However, it must be noted that currently there is no handling for possible outliers during the learning period, and this is something that will need to be looked at as it might cause sub-optimal normalization behavior.

The completion of a single connection acts as a trigger to call the SOM functions provided in the additional scripts. A hook for this activity is added to the main script of the conn module of Bro.

The features used can be selected by the user in the configuration file, currently SOM_config, which contains the feature vector that can be modified. The variables and structures that are meant to be modified by the user are also marked open to redefinition in the Bro language. Therefore the user can also redefine the same variables again in other scripts as well, and not need to touch the original configuration file directly.

A detailed introduction of the SOM algorithm can be found in [18] and is only discussed in this paper to the ex-

Table 1: Currently implemented features for SOM extension

The number of live TCP connections at the moment of connection termination
The number of live UDP connections at the moment of connection termination
The number of live ICMP connections at the moment of connection termination
Duration of connection that terminated
Overall network fragments pending reassembly by Bro
The amount of data (bytes) sent by connection responder
The amount of data (bytes) sent by connection originator
Number of packets sent by the connection responder
Number of packets sent by the connection originator

tent that is required by the depiction of the approach and the implementation.

3.2 Features

The features extracted and combination of them used controls to a large extent the efficacy of a machine learning based anomaly detection system [21]. The decision on features is therefore one of the most interesting research topics. In the SOM module introduced in Figure 1 we propose to use Bro NSM internal state, interpreted network state as well as connection information as components of the feature vector used in the SOM implementation. The SOM_saved in the figure marking the saved SOM lattice.

Currently there is an initial implementation for the the features depicted in Table 1. The first three features the live tcp and udp connections and fragments pending reassembly during the termination of a connection triggering the SOM functions are based on the state information of the Bro NSM. The first four are network state features representing the Bro NSM's handling of UDP and ICMP flows as pseudo-connections [25]. The fragments that are pending reassembly reflects the Bro's internal state concerning the state of fragments it has seen.

The connection specific features implemented include the duration of an terminating connection, whether TCP, UDP or ICMP using Bro's definition of UDP and ICMP pseudo-connections as connections [25].

Features of data statistics of a connection, including packets and data sent to and fro between the connections originator and responder are also implemented. While the number of packets sent, the amount of data and durations each represent a single feature as depicted in Table 1 they are still normalized using the maximum corresponding value seen for the particular transport protocol in use for that connection. In the test network this resulted in significantly improved contrast between particularly UDP and TCP connections. In an earlier implementation the large maximum values for these features derived as seen in the TCP connections resulted in all UDP connections being normalized very close to zero and the contrast between different UDP connections for these features nearly vanished.

3.3 Learning phase

Prior to the use of the system for detecting anomalies a learning phase is required. Two modes are currently possible; manual and automatic. Saving of the modified SOM

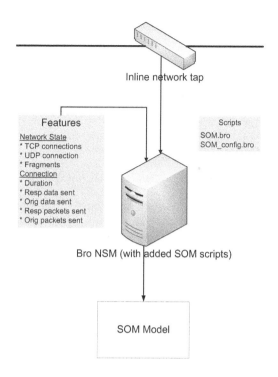

Figure 2: Depiction of SOM learning mode

lattice after learning phase is controlled by a flag, but running the system without saving the resulting SOM is mainly usable for debugging purposes.

In the automatic mode the system is set to switch to detection mode after a preset number of connections have been seen. The determination of the number of connections that is needed has to be decided by the user, and might result in a SOM lattice producing serious amount of false positives in the detection phase if not enough of connections are seen.

In the manual mode we repeatedly load the same saved SOM model and point to the packet capture file or network interface to be used for learning. Before each such learning run, the normal SOM variables can be tweaked, such as learning factor, the corresponding variables controlling the speed of the learning factor decrease, and the nature of the SOM neighbourhood function. As of this writing only one type of neighbourhood function is implemented, namely a 2-dimensional Moore neighbourhood of customizable size. The neighbourhood size is controlled by a variable that can be used to set the maximum Chebyshev distance for two dimensional plane with points having Cartesian coordinates: $D = \max(|x_2 - x_1|, |y_2 - y_1|)$ at which the neurons are still included in the neighbourhood. The 2-dimensional Moore neighbourhood used is also explained in the [18] for the basic SOM-implementation.

Figure 2 depics the learning phase of the system with some of the features already implemented. The inline network tap supplies connectivity to the network from which the traffic is to be learned by the SOM. In actual training situation, offline usage of a network traffic capture file would be more prudent.

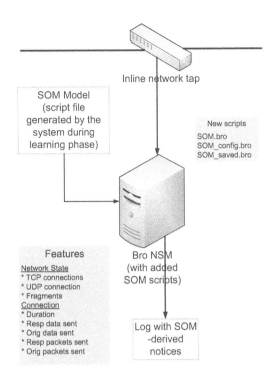

Figure 3: Depiction of SOM detection mode

Table 2: Notice report format for the SOM module

Possible_Anomaly_Seen Distance from nearest neuron[27,2]:[0.134853]

3.4 Detection phase

Figure 3 depicts the operational detection phase of the system. The detection mode requires that the learning mode has been run beforehand and the SOM model saved as a separate file, or the system is in automatic mode and the SOM map is in memory already. The SOM file also contains the features that were selected at the time of its initialization, and the SOM module retrieves this information from the file as well. For the detection several variables can be set to control the systems operation. The delta that marks the euclidean distance from the nearest SOM neuron that will trigger an alert should be set as low as possible to provide the desired balance of false negatives and false positives.

For the Bro logging framework additional alarm type has been defined for possible anomalies seen as deducted by the SOM algorithm. The new alarm type is accompanied by the additional information on which was the closest neuron in the SOM lattice for which the euclidean distance was still greater than `delta`. The exact euclidean distance from the nearest neuron is also logged in a format described Table 2.

The distance and the nearest neuron are logged for possible use to classify the connection, or deduce what type of traffic present in the network it most resembles. The code is to be instrumented in a way that will allow the user to flag certain clusters in the SOM as a type of traffic they represent. In the detection phase no changes are implemented in to the SOM model, this renders the system more resistant to slow attacks targeted towards the machine learning algo-

rithm. During a slow attack the system is gradually taught to accept subtle changes as normal, but since the system is no longer learning anything new, this approach will not work.

When reacting to an attack or an anomaly raised by the SOM module, normal Bro NSM functionality is available, which provides a rich set of possible responses such as logging the incident or arbitrary triggering scripts.

3.5 Test network

Printocent is one of the world's first pilot factory environments for Intelligent Printing which is also capable of mass production. The latest printing line, called MAXI [1], was installed during 2012 and it can be used for prototype, ramp-up and small scale industrial production. Simplified network structure and the location of our monitoring tap is depicted in Figure 4. Simatics and Rexroth are controllers that read, and set new drive parameters to different units in the printing line. The parameters affect the quality of the end result of the printing process. Human-machine interfaces (HMI) are used to monitor and manually adjust parameters on the line.

Copper Tap -device from Black Box provides a complete copy of data from a full-duplex link to the network analyzer. The tap replicates the full-duplex signal from the network and sends one signal back to the network and the other signal to a monitoring laptop equipped with two distinct network interfaces. The Tap causes a 200-250 nanoseconds latency to the traffic passing through, but is otherwise completely transparent to the environment. There is no physical connection between the receive port on the analyzer side of the Tap and the Tap's internal processor.

Tcpdump [7] was used to record the traffic captures to libpcap packet capture format. Local traffic from the laptop is filtered out with tcpdump capture options and the capture interface is set to promiscuous mode. Two captures are automatically merged into daily capture files with scripts and mergecap which is a part of Wireshark [3].

The overall available network data consists of several months worth of traffic. The target network environment has several noteworthy attributes. The attributes are listed in Table 3. The start and shutdown are hardware controlled, specifically via one master switch controlling power. The network environment is relatively pristine, not having evolved much over time or since its inception. Due to the start in the morning and shutdown in the evening the system had a cycle length of around one short business day, from 6-8 hours on average.

Not all of the attributes listed in 3 are required for deployment of the system. The daily reboot cycle of start in the morning and shutdown in the evening is merely convenient, but by no means necessary. While it provides a clear daily cycle, the cycle could be of an arbitrary length, as long as the required traning data would contain the necessary amount of cycles for the target network. Having a relatively pristine environment is also more of a convenience for the development of our module, and not a requirement for deployment. However, having noise in the network can have an effect on the predictability of the network traffic.

The traces also consisted in large part of a proprietary Siemens protocols, namely S7 communication, for which there is no analyzer for in the Bro system. However, an open source plugin for Wireshark[3] is available at [5].

Table 3: Network attributes

Start in the morning, shudown in the evening
Environment is pristine
Low number of different protocols present in the network
Very stable and cyclic
Very deterministic or predictable throughout its daily cycles

Table 4: Used feature vector

global features = vector("tcp_connections", "udp_connections", "duration", "orig_data_sent", "resp_data_sent") &redef;

These presence of these attributes make for a very controllable environment to test and developed network monitoring systems aimed at ICS networks and restricted network environments using internet protocl (IP) based communication schemes. Especially the deterministic nature is important [16].

The important downside of this is, that there are not that many pristine environments around, as most tend to be built over time and gone through multiple rounds of network evolution, as the systems have been replaced and added to. This typically leaves obsolete systems and protocols to use, which are required for compatibility, but have no other contribution for the overall system. This also contributes to the number of vulnerabilities found in these types of systems [11].

This issue creates a risk that the anomaly detection system developed for this type of an environment might require customization to be applicable to the more cluttered legacy systems. This might also add to the customization burden or even make the approach not feasible to use at all.

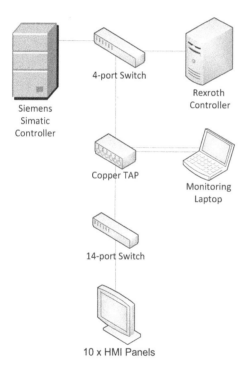

Figure 4: Simplified diagram of Printocent MAXI's network

For the initial testing of the algorithm we used several days worth of data, namely the packet captures ranging from 10. December 2012 to 31. January 2013 and some additional one day captures done during the time after this. Then we

proceeded to test the system using the packet captures that had not been used during the training. The feature vector used in the initial testing is depicted in Table 4.

The rate of false positives was mostly between 0-3 false alarms a day. These features did behave in a very deterministic manner, and the low number of false positives was not a surprise. However, whether these features can identify attacks and anomalies remains to be tested. That is to be the next phase of our work, and finding out what new features are needed and in what combination to catch as many of target anomalies and attacks as possible. The initial testing was also done with just a few test traces, as verification through testing was not in the focus of this paper.

The network packet rate that was seen in our monitoring location as depicted in the Figure 4 was an average of 68-73 packets per second during its uptime of generally 6-8 hours daily. The number of connections and pseudo-connections seen fluctuated, but typically around two to three thousand of them were seen during a typical day, including unnecessary traffic.

The reason behind this testing was merely to test that the system is implemented correctly, is capable of constructing the SOM lattice properly and provides anomalies when the euclidean distance threshold is violated. Elaborated results on testing the system with data including embedded attacks or attack-like activity are upcoming.

The further results with 6 clean and 5 dirty traces resulted in all the dirty traces yielding significantly increased number of alarms compared to the normal false positive rate. For example, an Nmap [6] operating systems detection traffic embedded in the test trace resulted in over 1000 new alarms being produced. This stands in stark contrast to the typical number of false positives reported in the initial tests. The promising test results are submitted for publication in a detailed form.

4. RESULTS

After the SOM was properly trained through several training runs with the capture data from the target network 4 several clusters formed as expected. The training took some manual tweaking of the various SOM learning factors, such as manipulation of neighborhood function size and the learning factor alpha, which controls the degree by which a winning weight vector in the SOM is moved towards the values of the input vector subject to learning. The learning mode worked as expected. A script wrapper to automatize the iterative process of teaching the SOM solves some of the issues, but the systems is susceptible to converge to a suboptimal stable state as is a possibility in SOM algorithm [14]. This behavior is difficult to predict, and requires at times the initialization of new lattices in a trial-and-error manner.

In the detection mode the system was configurable to yield a low amount of false positives, typically in the range from zero to three false positives a day when testing with a few later packet captures from the test network not used for training. The false positives typically were a result of one type of the long TCP connections terminating at the end of the day, for which only few occurrences were found in each days traffic. However, as this was just testing of the basic functionality, the actual operational false positive rate might be different.

In the learning mode the system was able to process a day-long capture from the MAXI network in roughly 30 seconds on a system with i5 Intel CPU, 8GB of memory and a SSD disk using a lattice of size $[x = 30, y = 20]$ and the same feature vector as depicted in Table 4. The Bro NSM currently utilizes only one core per running instance. Despite subtly differing computational tasks the detection mode took the roughly same amount of time when run on the same packet capture file.

5. DISCUSSION

Our previous work on anomaly and intrusion detection and machine learning in ICS context was carried out with different data. The data was received from a large factory installation which had gone through several changes during its time of existence. The nature of that traffic was very different to what we found when analyzing the MAXI data, and will be a target of further investigation if more traffic captures can be arranged to be procured from the site. The difference between a pristine network environment and one that has a considerable presence of obsolete components, systems and noise that has been built over time requires further study. This will be critical if the approach is to be of value to a greater number of end users.

It is also possible, that legacy networks exhibit characteristics that make it unfeasible to use this type of approach for them. The deterministic attributes are needed.

Also, it could be said that we are not actually using the network state attributes as features, but more the network state as interpreted by the Bro system. However, we feel that for simplicity's sake it is a close enough approximation, as Bro attempts to report the state as it sees it as accurately as possible.

The handling of outliers during the learning phase that might have an undesired effect on the normalization of input vectors must also be investigated further. Some heuristic to control the change of the normalization values will also need to be implemented. Further features for which a protocol analyzer is available in Bro are also to be investigated. Usage of the protocol parser investigated and presented in [20] is also to be undertaken.

It might also be prudent to divide the single SOM lattice into several lattices, each representing a single protocol or a set of protocol for which the features extracted are sufficiently similar for improved distribution after normalization. Currently the durations of the connections in the test network explained in Section 4 are normalized with a value that leads to a very uneven distribution, with a bulk of the values very near to value 0, and the day-long TCP connections near value 1. This decreases the sensitivity of the system to slight changes in durations, since after the normalization the change is also very near to zero.

Inclusion of additional lattice to provide functionality for periodically checking the network state independent of terminating connections would improve the detection possibilities for on-going attacks.

6. CONCLUSIONS

We have implemented a proof-of-concept SOM engine using Bro NSM script and have tested the engine to work as expected. The performance evaluation needs to be commenced and more features implemented to improve the versatility of the system. The large feature set is meant for the user to select from to customize the system for his specific network. One set of features will not work for all types of networks.

The system is not designed to catch all attacks, but to complement existing solutions and the capabilities of network security monitoring solutions like the Bro NSM framework which it is built upon. The standard functionality of the Bro NSM system is available simultaneously with the SOM module, and the SOM modules information can be further processed by other scripts.

The SOM engine is currently operational, and efforts are ongoing to implement more features for accurate detection and the start of test runs for the MAXI[1] environment depicted in Figure 4. The exact sub-set of features to be selected from the total pool for the specific MAXI use case is also under investigations.

After further work and additional protocol specific features the system is expected to provide additional anomaly detection capability for existing ICS environments with minimal manual customization.

Acknowledgments

The research presented in this paper was mainly done as a collaborative effort in two research projects at VTT. Namely the DIAMONDS project [2], which is an EUREKA ITEA2 European Research Program project funded by TEKES, and INCYSE or Industrial Cyber Security Endeavour, which is a VTT internal research project.

7. REFERENCES

[1] PrintoCent, (accessed 1/6/2013).
    http://www.printocent.net.
[2] DIAMONDS ITEA2 Project, (accessed 17/3/2013).
    www.itea2-diamonds.org/.
[3] Wireshark, (accessed 2/5/2013).
    http://http://www.wireshark.org/.
[4] Bro Network Security Monitor, (accessed 2/6/2013).
    http://www.bro-ids.org/.
[5] S7comm wireshark dissector plugin, (accessed 6/6/2013).
[6] Nmap Network Security Scanner, (accessed 7/2/2013).
    http://www.nmap.org/.
[7] Tcpdump, (accessed 7/6/2013).
    http://www.tcpdump.org/.
[8] R. Bejtlich. *The Tao Of Network Security Monitoring: Beyond Intrusion Detection*. Addison-Wesley Professional, 2004.
[9] E. Cole. *Network Security Bible*. Bible (eBooks). Wiley, 2009.

[10] D. Denning. An intrusion-detection model. *Software Engineering, IEEE Transactions on*, SE-13(2):222 – 232, feb. 1987.

[11] DHS CSSP National Cyber Security Division. Common Cybersecurity Vulnerabilities in Industrial Control Systems, 2011.

[12] H. Dreger, A. Feldmann, V. Paxson, and R. Sommer. Predicting the resource consumption of network intrusion detection systems. In R. Lippmann, E. Kirda, and A. Trachtenberg, editors, *Recent Advances in Intrusion Detection*, volume 5230 of *Lecture Notes in Computer Science*, pages 135–154. Springer Berlin / Heidelberg.

[13] H. Dreger, C. Kreibich, V. Paxson, and R. Sommer. Enhancing the accuracy of network-based intrusion detection with host-based context. In K. Julisch and C. Kruegel, editors, *Detection of Intrusions and Malware, and Vulnerability Assessment*, volume 3548 of *Lecture Notes in Computer Science*, pages 584–600. Springer Berlin / Heidelberg.

[14] E. Erwin, K. Obermayer, and K. Schulten. Self-organizing maps: Ordering, convergence properties and energy functions. *Biological Cybernetics*, 67:47–55, 1992.

[15] J. Gonzalez and V. Paxson. Enhancing network intrusion detection with integrated sampling and filtering. In D. Zamboni and C. Kruegel, editors, *Recent Advances in Intrusion Detection*, volume 4219 of *Lecture Notes in Computer Science*, pages 272–289. Springer Berlin / Heidelberg.

[16] H. Hadeli, R. Schierholz, M. Braendle, and C. Tuduce. Leveraging determinism in industrial control systems for advanced anomaly detection and reliable security configuration. In *Emerging Technologies Factory Automation, 2009. ETFA 2009. IEEE Conference on*, pages 1–8, 2009.

[17] W. Hu, D. Xie, T. Tan, and S. Maybank. Learning activity patterns using fuzzy self-organizing neural network. *Systems, Man, and Cybernetics, Part B: Cybernetics, IEEE Transactions on*, 34(3):1618–1626, 2004.

[18] T. Kohonen, M. R. Schroeder, and T. S. Huang, editors. *Self-Organizing Maps*. Springer-Verlag New York, Inc., Secaucus, NJ, USA, 3rd edition, 2001.

[19] S. Lee and D. Heinbuch. Training a neural-network based intrusion detector to recognize novel attacks. *Systems, Man and Cybernetics, Part A: Systems and Humans, IEEE Transactions on*, 31(4):294–299, 2001.

[20] H. Lin, A. Slagell, C. Di Martino, Z. Kalbarczyk, and R. K. Iyer. Adapting bro into scada: building a specification-based intrusion detection system for the dnp3 protocol. In *Proceedings of the Eighth Annual Cyber Security and Information Intelligence Research Workshop*, CSIIRW '13, pages 5:1–5:4, New York, NY, USA, 2013. ACM.

[21] O. Linda, T. Vollmer, and M. Manic. Neural network based intrusion detection system for critical infrastructures. In *Proceedings of the 2009 international joint conference on Neural Networks*, IJCNN'09, pages 102–109, Piscataway, NJ, USA, 2009. IEEE Press.

[22] M. Mantere, M. Sailio, and S. Noponen. Feature selection for machine learning based anomaly detection in industrial control system networks. In *Green Computing and Communications (GreenCom), 2012 IEEE International Conference on*, pages 771–774, 2012.

[23] M. Mantere, M. Sailio, and S. Noponen. Network traffic features for anomaly detection in specific industrial control system network. *Future Internet*, 5(4):460–473, 2013.

[24] M. Mantere, I. Uusitalo, M. Sailio, and S. Noponen. Challenges of machine learning based monitoring for industrial control system networks. In *2012 26th International Conference on Advanced Information Networking and Applications Workshops*, march 2012.

[25] V. Paxson. Bro: a system for detecting network intruders in real-time. *Computer Networks*, 31(23-24):2435 – 2463, 1999.

[26] M. Ramadas, S. Ostermann, and B. Tjaden. Detecting anomalous network traffic with self-organizing maps. In *In Proceedings of the Sixth International Symposium on Recent Advances in Intrusion Detection, LNCS*, pages 36–54. Springer Verlag, 2003.

[27] S. Sarasamma, Q. Zhu, and J. Huff. Hierarchical kohonen net for anomaly detection in network security. *Systems, Man, and Cybernetics, Part B: Cybernetics, IEEE Transactions on*, 35(2):302–312, 2005.

[28] R. Sommer and V. Paxson. Outside the closed world: On using machine learning for network intrusion detection. In *Security and Privacy (SP), 2010 IEEE Symposium on*, pages 305 –316, may 2010.

[29] M. Thottan and C. Ji. Anomaly detection in ip networks. *Signal Processing, IEEE Transactions on*, 51(8):2191–2204, 2003.

[30] M. Vallentin, R. Sommer, J. Lee, C. Leres, V. Paxson, and B. Tierney. The nids cluster: Scalable, stateful network intrusion detection on commodity hardware. In C. Kruegel, R. Lippmann, and A. Clark, editors, *Recent Advances in Intrusion Detection*, volume 4637 of *Lecture Notes in Computer Science*, pages 107–126. Springer Berlin / Heidelberg.

[31] N. Weaver, V. Paxson, and R. Sommer. Work in progress: Bro-lan pervasive network inspection and control for lan traffic. In *Securecomm and Workshops, 2006*, pages 1 –2, 28 2006-sept. 1 2006.

[32] D. Yang, A. Usynin, and J. Hines. Anomaly-based intrusion detection for scada systems. In *Proceedings of the 5th Intl. Topical Meeting on Nuclear Plant Instrumentation, Control and Human Machine Interface Technologies*, NPIC&HMIT 05, 2006.

Energy Efficiency via Incentive Design and Utility Learning[*]

Lillian Ratliff, Roy Dong, Henrik Ohlsson, S. Shankar Sastry

Department of Electrical Engineering and Computer Sciences
University of California, Berkeley
Berkeley, CA 94720-1776
ratliffl@eecs.berkeley.edu, roydong@eecs.berkeley.edu
ohlsson@eecs.berkeley.edu, sastry@eecs.berkeley.edu

ABSTRACT

Utility companies have many motivations for modifying energy consumption patterns of consumers such as revenue decoupling and demand response programs. We model the utility company–consumer interaction as a principal–agent problem and present an iterative algorithm for designing incentives while estimating the consumer's utility function.

General Terms

Theory

Keywords

game theory; incentive design; utility learning; energy disaggregation

1. INTRODUCTION

Utility companies have many motivations for changing energy consumption patterns of users. Many regions are beginning to implement revenue decoupling policies, whereby utility companies are economically motivated to decrease energy consumption [3]. Additionally, the cost of producing energy depends on many variables, and being able to control demand via demand response programs can help alleviate the costs of inaccurate load forecasting [7].

In brief, the problem of behavior modification in energy consumption can be understood as follows. Utility companies provide incentives to energy consumers, who seek to

[*]The work presented is supported by the NSF Graduate Research Fellowship under grant DGE 1106400, NSF CPS:Large:ActionWebs award number 0931843, TRUST (Team for Research in Ubiquitous Secure Technology) which receives support from NSF (award number CCF-0424422), and FORCES (Foundations Of Resilient CybEr-physical Systems), the European Research Council under the advanced grant LEARN, contract 267381.

Permission to make digital or hard copies of part or all of this work for personal or classroom use is granted without fee provided that copies are not made or distributed for profit or commercial advantage, and that copies bear this notice and the full citation on the first page. Copyrights for third-party components of this work must be honored. For all other uses, contact the owner/author(s). Copyright is held by the author/owner(s).

HiCoNS April 15-17, 2014, Berlin, Germany
ACM 978-1-4503-2652-0/14.04.
http://dx.doi.org/10.1145/2566468.2576849.

maximize their own utility by selecting energy consumption patterns. Figure 1 depicts the abstract view of the behavior modification problem. The design of incentives can be

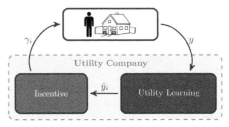

Figure 1: Behavior modification via incentives abstractly is a *control* and *estimation* problem.

thought of as a control problem for utility companies. Further, consumers do not report any measure of their satisfaction directly to the utility companies. Thus, it must be estimated. In this abstract, we formulate the problem of designing incentives for behavior modification given utility companies do not know consumers' utility functions and must learn them iteratively by issuing incentives in order to gather information about how consumers respond. We propose an algorithm for iteratively solving the incentive design and utility learning problem.

2. INCENTIVE DESIGN PROBLEM

A principal-agent problem occurs when the principal interacts with the agent to perform a task, but the agent is not incentivized to act in the principal's best interests [5]. This conflict is often the result of asymmetric information between the principal and the agent or a disconnect between their goals and objectives. We cast the utility–consumer interaction model in the framework of a principal–agent model in which the utility company is the principal and the consumer is the agent [9]. Both the principal and the agent wish to maximize their pay–off determined by the functions $J_p(v,y)$ and $J_a(v,y)$ respectively. The principal's decision is denoted v; the agent's decision, y; and the incentive, $\gamma : y \mapsto v$ where $\gamma \in \Gamma$ and Γ is the set of admissible controls from Y to $\mathbb{R}$. Let v and y take values in $V \subset \mathbb{R}^{n_p}$ and $Y \subset \mathbb{R}^{n_a}$, respectively; $J_p : \mathbb{R}^{n_p} \times \mathbb{R}^{n_a} \to \mathbb{R}$; $J_a : \mathbb{R}^{n_p} \times \mathbb{R}^{n_a} \to \mathbb{R}$. The incentive problem can be stated as follows. Determine the desired actions

$$(v^d, y^d) = \arg \max_{v \in \mathcal{I}_v, y \in \mathcal{I}_y} J_p(v,y) \qquad (1)$$

where $\mathcal{I}_v$ and $\mathcal{I}_y$ are constraints on v and y respectively. Then, solve the following problem:

PROBLEM 1. *Find* $\gamma : Y \to V$, $\gamma \in \Gamma$ *such that*

$$\arg \max_{y \in \mathcal{I}_y} J_a(\gamma(y), y) = y^d \qquad (2)$$

$$\gamma(y^d) = v^d \qquad (3)$$

where Γ is the set of admissible incentive mechanisms.

3. ALGORITHM

The principal's true utility is assumed to be given by

$$J_p(v, y) = g(y) - v \qquad (4)$$

where v is the value of the incentive paid to the agent and $g(\cdot)$ is a function of the consumer's energy usage y over a billing period and may represent an objective derived from *revenue decoupling* or *demand response* programs [3, 7].

The agent's true utility is assumed to be

$$J_a(\gamma(y), y) = -py + \gamma(y) + f(y) \qquad (5)$$

where p is the fixed price of energy known to both the agent and the principal and $\gamma : Y \to \mathbb{R}$ is the incentive mechanism. The principal does not know the agent's satisfaction function $f(\cdot)$, and hence, must estimate it as he solves the incentive design problem. We will use the notation $\hat{f}$ for the estimate of the satisfaction and $\hat{J}_p$ and $\hat{J}_a$ for the player's cost functions using the estimate of f.

We propose an algorithm for solving the incentive design problem iteratively. We assume that the agent's satisfaction function is parameterized using the following finite–dimensional, affine parameterization

$$f = \sum_{i=1}^{N} \alpha_i f_i \qquad (6)$$

where f_i are basis functions, $\alpha = (\alpha_1, \cdots, \alpha_N) \in \mathcal{A}$. We can interpret $\mathcal{A}$ as the prior information we have about the agent's satisfaction function f.

The proposed algorithm is as follows. Find (v^d, y^d) by solving the problem formulated in (4). Suppose we are given $\gamma^{(0)}$. Then, at iteration k, we execute the following steps:

1. Estimate $\hat{f}^{(k)}$ using $\{y^{(\ell)}, \gamma^{(\ell)}\}_{\ell=0}^{k}$.

2. Determine $\gamma^{(k+1)}$ by solving Problem 1 replacing J_a with $\hat{J}_a^{(k)} = -py + \gamma^{(k+1)}(y) + \hat{f}^{(k)}(y)$.

3. Issue $\gamma^{(k+1)}$ and observe the agent's response $y^{(k+1)}$. If $y^{(k+1)} = y^d$, stop. Otherwise, $k \leftarrow k + 1$ and return to step 1.

4. DISCUSSION

Preliminary results on discussed algorithm are presented in [9]. We are able to show that if the satisfaction function is the sum of polynomial basis functions up to a finite order and under some mild assumptions on the linear dependence of the incentives, then after a finite number of iterations we know the satisfaction function exactly and at the next iteration we can design an incentive to induce the desired behavior.

We are currently working on using tools from non–linear programming such as constraint qualification and second–order optimality conditions including Kharush-Kuhn-Tucker

conditions to solve the estimation problem when we allow for the agent to play an *approximately optimal* strategy at each iteration [4]. In addition, we are developing an experimental platform in which we deploy sensors to 12 homes and design incentives to induce energy efficient behavior.

Another interesting direction for future work is device–level feedback. Studies have shown that providing device–level feedback on power consumption patterns to consumers can modify behavior and improve energy efficiency [6, 8]. However, the current infrastructure only has sensors to measure the aggregated power consumption signal for a household. Additionally, deploying plug–level sensors would require entering households to install these devices. A low cost alternative to the deployment of a large number of sensors is *non–intrusive load monitoring* (or *energy disaggregation*) which refers to recovering the power consumption signals of individual devices from the aggregate power consumption signal [1]. Returning to Figure 1, we remark that the estimation problem is extended to include energy disaggregation so that utility companies may design device–level incentives. Again, preliminary results are reported in [9]. With an ε–error bound disaggregation algorithm in place [1], we are able to design incentives to induce a consumption pattern that is approximately the desired behavior. We are currently using fundamental limits on energy disaggregation algorithms [2] to derive rigorous bounds on the behavior modification and utility learning problem.

References

[1] R. Dong, L. Ratliff, H. Ohlsson, and S. S. Sastry. Energy disaggregation via adaptive filtering. In *Proceedings of the 50th Allerton Conference on Communication, Control, and Computing*, 2013.

[2] R. Dong, L. Ratliff, H. Ohlsson, and S. S. Sastry. Fundamental limits of non–intrusive load monitoring. In *In Proceedings of 3rd Conference on High Confidence Networked Systems*, 2014 (arXiv:1310.7850v1 preprint).

[3] J. Eom. Shareholder incentives for utility-delivered energy efficiency programs in California. In *Proceedings of the 28th USAEE/IAEE North American Conference*, 2008.

[4] A. Keshavarz, Y. Wang, and S. Boyd. Imputing a convex objective function. In *2011 IEEE International Symposium on Intelligent Control (ISIC)*, pages 613–619. IEEE, 2011.

[5] J.-J. Laffont and D. Martimort. *The theory of incentives: the principal-agent model*. Princeton University Press, 2009.

[6] J. A. Laitner, K. Ehrhardt-Martinez, and V. McKinney. Examining the scale of the behaviour energy efficiency continuum. In *European Council for an Energy Efficient Economy*, 2009.

[7] J. L. Mathieu, T. Haring, and G. Andersson. Harnessing residential loads for demand response: Engineering and economic considerations. In *Interdisciplinary Workshop on Smart Grid Design and Implementation*, 2012.

[8] L. Perez-Lombard, J. Ortiz, and C. Pout. A review on buildings energy consumption information. *Energy and buildings*, 40:394–398, 2008.

[9] L. J. Ratliff, R. Dong, H. Ohlsson, and S. S. Sastry. Behavior modification and utility learning via energy disaggregation. *arXiv:1312.1394*, 2013.

Decisions for Autonomous Vehicles: Integrating Sensors, Communication, and Control

Katherine Driggs-Campbell
Universiy of California, Berkeley
krdc@eecs.berkeley.edu

Victor Shia
Universiy of California, Berkeley
vshia@eecs.berkeley.edu

Ruzena Bajcsy
Universiy of California, Berkeley
bajcsy@eecs.berkeley.edu

ABSTRACT

This paper details the work in progress to formalize methods and algorithms for autonomous decision making, focusing on the implementation of autonomous vehicles. Many different scenarios are to be considered while focusing on a heterogeneous environment of human driven, semi-autonomous, and fully autonomous vehicles. As this work is in its early stages of development, this paper summarizes the work that has been done in the areas of vehicle to vehicle communication with control applications and high-level decision making for autonomous vehicles. The proposed method to be implemented is also presented, which aims to guarantee feasibility, safety, and stability of autonomous systems.

Categories and Subject Descriptors

I.2.9 [**Robotics**]: Autonomous Vehicles

Keywords

intelligent transportation; autonomous vehicles

1. INTRODUCTION

Recently, multiple car companies have announced that autonomous vehicles will be available for consumers in the near future[1]. While there are many questions to be answered concerning legal issues and social acceptance, one of the major technical issues to be resolved is the high-level control decisions to determine how the autonomous vehicle will interact with the surrounding cars. How will the autonomous car handle this heterogeneous environment? What exactly needs to be known by the autonomous vehicle to make correct, informed decisions? This work proposes looking at the interaction between an autonomous vehicle and the surrounding vehicles to make the high-level decisions by considering work done in control theory, communication, artificial intelligence, and hybrid systems. A simple sketch of the proposed plan is shown in Figure 1.

[1]http://www.pcmag.com/article2/0,2817,2428697,00.asp

Permission to make digital or hard copies of part or all of this work for personal or classroom use is granted without fee provided that copies are not made or distributed for profit or commercial advantage, and that copies bear this notice and the full citation on the first page. Copyrights for third-party components of this work must be honored. For all other uses, contact the owner/author(s). Copyright is held by the author/owner(s).

HiCoNS'14, April 15–17, 2014, Berlin, Germany.
ACM 978-1-4503-2652-0/14/04.
http://dx.doi.org/10.1145/2566468.2576851.

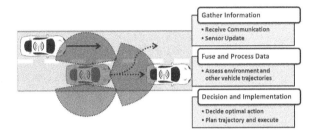

Figure 1: (Left) Illustrates potential actions (dotted arrow) for gray autonomous car, while receiving sensor data emitting from car and communicated data from surrounding cars, like intended trajectories. (Right) A flow diagram of proposed project.

As this work is in its preliminary stages, the following section will summarize the work that has been done in the area of vehicle to vehicle (V2V) communication with control applications and of high-level control and decision making for autonomous vehicles. Then, the proposed solution and the current work will be summarized, including the simulator that has been set up for data collection.

2. RELATED WORK

As previously mentioned, a great deal of work has been done in research concerning autonomous vehicles. The open problems that remain primarily focus on incorporating control with environmental constraints (using vision, radar, or other sensors), through methods such as model predictive control, as the low-level control theory for vehicles has been achieved [4, 8]. Therefore, we focus on the previous work in V2V communication and high-level decision making.

When considering V2V communication, most research has considered threat assessment, privacy and security, and infrastructure concerns [6]. In the 90s to the early 2000s, many V2V systems considered platooning or vehicle formations, both with and without packet loss. This is important as it not only shows that centralized control for autonomous vehicles is possible, but also that the integration of control and communication is achievable [3, 7, 9]. Many engineering studies have demonstrated applications that address the critical crash scenarios including warning systems for forward collisions and vehicle control loss. They also can assist drivers execute safe lane changes and intersection movement to avoid accidents. Occasionally, the driver monitoring is mentioned, by stating that the mental state of the driver might affect the desired safety impact of a V2V system[2]. As shown, it appears that there is little to no work currently being done in autonomous-driver interactive situations in V2V literature.

In academia, there has not been much consideration for high-level decision making for autonomous vehicles since the DARPA Grand Challenge and the DARPA Urban Grand Challenge[3]. These demonstrations showed promising results using heuristic approaches for autonomous vehicles [5]. The most complete experiment testing the feasibility of autonomous vehicles was by Forbes in the artificial intelligence community in the mid-90s. In his study, a simulator was built to test the control of autonomous vehicles using dynamic probabilistic network learning and reinforcement learning, among other techniques [2]. More recently, Abbeel mimicked simplified driving behaviors using apprenticeship learning with inverse reinforcement learning [1]. As shown, there is little to no current work being done on the high-level decision making for autonomous vehicles that utilizes current technology, V2V communication, and the complete dynamics of the vehicle and the environment.

3. METHODS

This section presents the components that will contribute to the proposed plan, combining sensor data, driver monitoring, and information from other vehicles. Here, when we refer to the environment, we refer to both the environment in terms of the road, obstacles, weather, etc., as well as the surrounding vehicles. When considering these other cars, we must consider driver intent as behavior is highly dependent upon this. Since we are considering autonomous vehicle decision making, we do not have to deal with driver intent from the ego vehicle. However, intent will be of concern for the surrounding vehicles, especially when making future predictions of how the vehicle (and therefore potential threat) will move forward with time. We have already obtained results in driver modeling, in which we create precise and accurate predictions of an individual's driving behavior. This model essentially creates a useful reachable set, depending on the driver mode. Derivation of this model can be found in [4, 8]. We must consider how to incorporate this model into the system, decide if additional information must be communicated to the ego vehicle, and determine if high-level information should be communicated or inferred (e.g. does the driver intend to stay in her lane or change lanes?). In order to safely introduce the autonomous vehicle onto the road, the system must be equipped with sensors to assess the states of the environment (e.g. radar, vision, etc.). The data needed for accurate, safe decision making must be explored.

We propose that the system integrates said data and outputs a high-level decision for an autonomous vehicle. The system proposed is a hybrid system that switches modes when a new high-level command is given, which would be defined by the guards. Therefore, experiments need to be carried out to learn how human drivers make decisions and switch mode of behavior, using techniques like inverse reinforcement learning, to motivate our system.

To implement this, a car simulator with a motion platform has been setup for experiments to collect driver data in a realistic manner[4]. This platform provides a testing environment that allows the investigator to have complete control over the experiment, without sacrificing realism. The setup uses PreScan[5], which simulates various V2V mechanisms. This includes methods for dedicated short range communication receivers and transmitters using a selected protocol, as well as more general receiver/transmitter options.

4. CONCLUSION

In summation, this paper briefly outlines the work to be done in developing an autonomous vehicle system that fuses information from multiple sources. This can be used to make intelligent decisions, in a manner that has not been done before. While this work is still in its preliminary stages, the algorithms are in progress and the experimental setup has been completed.

5. ACKNOWLEDGMENTS

This material is based upon work supported by the National Science Foundation under Award ECCS-1239323 and by the MURI Award ONR-N000141310341.

6. REFERENCES

[1] P. Abbeel and A. Y. Ng. Apprenticeship learning via inverse reinforcement learning. *In Proceedings of ICML*, 2004.

[2] R. P. Jeffrey Forbes, Nikunj Oza and S. Russell. Feasibility study of fully automated vehicles using decision-theoretic control. *California PATH Research Report UCB-ITS-PRR-97-6*, January 1997.

[3] S. Sheikholeslam and C. Desoer. Longitudinal control of a platoon of vehicles with no communication of lead vehicle information: a system level study. *IEEE Transactions on Vehicular Technology*, 42(4):546–554, 1993.

[4] V. Shia, Y. Gao, R. Vasudevan, K. Driggs-Campbell, T. Lin, F. Borrelli, and R. Bajcsy. Driver modeling for real-time semi-autonomous vehicular control. *IEEE Transactions on Intelligent Transportation Systems*, accepted, pending revision.

[5] S. Thrun and et al. Stanley: The robot that won the darpa grand challenge. *Journal of Field Robotics, 2006*, 23(9):661–692, 2006.

[6] S. Tsugawa. Inter-vehicle communications and their applications to intelligent vehicles: an overview. In *IEEE Intelligent Vehicle Symposium.*, volume 2, pages 564–569 vol.2, 2002.

[7] P. Varaiya. Smart cars on smart roads: problems of control. *IEEE Transactions on Automatic Control*, 38(2):195–207, 1993.

[8] R. Vasudevan, V. Shia, Y. Gao, R. Cervera-Navarro, R. Bajcsy, and F. Borrelli. Safe semi-autonomous control with enhanced driver modeling. In *American Control Conference*, pages 2896–2903, 2012.

[9] Q. Xu, K. Hedrick, R. Sengupta, and J. VanderWerf. Effects of vehicle-vehicle/roadside-vehicle communication on adaptive cruise controlled highway systems. In *IEEE Vehicular Technology Conference.*, volume 2, pages 1249–1253 vol.2, 2002.

---

[2]http://www.its.dot.gov/research/v2v.htm
[3]http://archive.darpa.mil/grandchallenge/overview.asp

[4]http://arxiv.org/abs/1401.5039
[5]https://www.tassinternational.com/prescan

Forecasting the Resilience of Networked Dynamical Systems Under Environmental Perturbation

[Extended Abstract]

Tua A. Tamba
Department of Electrical Engineering
University of Notre Dame, USA
ttamba@nd.edu

M. D. Lemmon
Department of Electrical Engineering
University of Notre Dame, USA
lemmon@nd.edu

Categories and Subject Descriptors

G.4 [**Mathematics of Computing**]: Mathematical Software; I.1 [**Symbolic & Algebraic Manipulation**].

Keywords

Resilience, distance-to-bifurcation, sum-of-square relaxation.

1. INTRODUCTION

Many real life systems can be viewed as networked systems that are composed of interconnected compartments exchanging mass or energy between each other and with their environment through fluxes. Such interactions with the environment make these systems sensitive to external perturbations that cause system parameters to vary away from their nominal values. For nonlinear networked systems, such parameter variations can change the qualitative behavior of the system (i.e. phase portrait or stability) through a bifurcation [6]. These changes may result in a *regime shifts* [8] in which the system "flips" from a nominal operating state to an alternative state. Regime-shifts can be catastrophic for users who have grown accustomed to the quality of services provided by the system prior to the shift. Examples of this can be found in the eutrophication of shallow lakes as a result of human-induced nutrient enrichment or the decline of fisheries due to overfishing practices [8]. Another prime example occurs when voltage collapses cascade through the electric power grid [4]. Each of these shifts has the potential to disrupt the services that these systems provide to the society. Forecasting the resilience of these networked systems to parameter variations is therefore crucial for managing their security and sustainability [1, 5].

Consider networked systems $\dot{x} = f(x, \mu)$ whose equilibrium x^* depend on parameter μ. The resilience of a system under parameter variation can be measured by the distance $\gamma = |\mu^* - \mu^0|$ between the nominal parameter μ^0 and the closest critical paramater μ^* at which a bifurcation occur. The quantity γ, often called *distance to closest bifurcation,*

is an indicator of how close the system is to a collapse. The computation of γ is generally difficult since the *bifurcation set* containing μ^* is usually unknown. Prior works [2, 4] have used numerical optimization techniques to search for the minimum γ subject to the necessary constraints that are satisfied when a bifurcation occurs at μ^*. These methods, however, are computationally demanding since the search for minimum γ requires the computation of the equilibrium x^* at every iteration.

This paper uses sum-of-square (SOS) relaxations [7] to obtain a lower bound on the global minimum of the "distance-to-bifurcation", γ, in networked dynamical system. Our approach uses algebraic geometric methods [3] to reduce the size of the constraints and to avoid the computation of equilibrium x^* at every iteration of the optimization. We have recently applied this method to a class of non-negative systems that has a kinetic realization [9]. This paper extends the method in [9] to systems that may not be non-negative. The method is illustrated on an example predicting voltage collapse in electrical power networks [2].

2. BIFURCATION CONDITIONS

Consider an n-dimensional *polynomial system* whose state trajectories $x(t; x_0)$ satisfy

$$\dot{x}(t) = f(x(t), \mu), \quad x(0) = x_0, \quad (1)$$

for all $t \geq 0$ in which $f(x, \mu) \in \mathbb{R}^n(\mu)[x]$ is polynomial in the unknown $x \in \mathbb{R}^n$ with coefficient $\mu \in \mathbb{R}^p$. The system's *equilibria* are vectors in the field, $\mathbb{Q}^n(\mu)$, of rational functions that are zeros of the right hand side of (1). In other words, $x^*(\mu)$ is an equilibrium if

$$x^*(\mu) \in \{x \in \mathbb{Q}^n(\mu) : f(x, \mu) = 0\}. \quad (2)$$

Computing the algebraic expression for $x^*(\mu)$ in high dimensional systems usually requires the use of symbolic methods. These methods are based on the fact that a set of polynomials generate an *ideal* in the polynomial ring and that the zeros of the system of polynomials are equivalent to the zeros of any Gröbner basis of that ideal [3].

Let $J = \frac{\partial f(x, \mu)}{\partial x}|_{x^*}$ be the Jacobian matrix of (1) with characteristic polynomial $p(s) = a_0 s^n + a_1 s^{n-1} + \cdots + a_{n-1}s + a_n$, where the coefficients $a_i(\mu)$ are function of the parameter, μ. For $z = 1, \ldots, n$, let $\triangle_z$ denotes the zth Hurwitz determinant of $p(s)$. A local bifurcation can be characterized in term of the *eigenvalue condition* of J with some additional *transversality conditions* [6]. Let Ω^{SN} and Ω^H be the set of parameters for which a saddle node (also pitchfork

Permission to make digital or hard copies of part or all of this work for personal or classroom use is granted without fee provided that copies are not made or distributed for profit or commercial advantage, and that copies bear this notice and the full citation on the first page. Copyrights for third-party components of this work must be honored. For all other uses, contact the owner/author(s). Copyright is held by the author/owner(s).

HiCoNS'14, April 15–17, 2014, Berlin, Germany.
ACM 978-1-4503-2652-0/14/04.
http://dx.doi.org/10.1145/2566468.2576848.

and transcritical) and Hopf bifurcations occur. As shown in [9], these sets are semi-algebraic sets characterized by $a_i(\mu)$ and $\triangle_z$. One may then denote the parameter set for which at least one type of bifurcation occurs as $\Omega = \Omega^{SN} \cup \Omega^H$. Thus, system (1) will not have a bifurcation if Ω is empty.

When system (1) is *non-negative* and has a *kinetic realization*, the bifurcation set can be expressed only in terms of the parameters, rather than the parameters and the equilibria. As a result, this parameterization simplifies the computation of the distance-to-bifurcation [9].

3. DISTANCE-TO-BIFURCATION

The previous section suggests that the non-existence of a particular bifurcation is equivalent to the emptiness of the corresponding bifurcation set. In general, checking the emptiness of Ω^{SN} can be difficult. In recent years, however, it has proven fruitful to consider convex relaxations of the problem [7] in which one checks for the emptiness of the set $\tilde{\Omega}(\beta) \cap \Omega^{SN}$, where $\tilde{\Omega}(\beta)$ is a semi-algebraic set defined by a positive semi-definite *certificate* function $V(\mu)$. In particular, let β be a real constant and let $\alpha(|\mu - \mu^0|)$ be a class $\mathcal{K}$ function in which μ is the parameter set and μ^0 is a known initial parameter. The *certificate* set is defined as

$$\tilde{\Omega}(\beta) = \left\{ \mu \in \mathbb{R}^p \, : \, \alpha(|\mu - \mu^0|) \le \beta \right\}. \quad (3)$$

Given a specific $\beta > 0$, if the intersection $\tilde{\Omega}(\beta) \cap \Omega^{SN} = \emptyset$, then the distance to a saddle node bifurcation cannot be less than $\alpha^{-1}(\beta)$. The key point is that verifying whether the set $\tilde{\Omega}(\beta) \cap \Omega^{SN}$ is empty or not can be done using the SOS program. By defining the certificate function as $V(\mu) = \alpha(|\mu - \mu^0|)$, a bound $\bar{\beta}$ for the minimum distance to a saddle node bifurcation can be obtained by the following SOS program [9].

maximize $\quad \bar{\beta}$
such that $\quad a_{n-1}^2(\mu)(V(\mu) - \bar{\beta}) + r(\mu)a_n(\mu)$ is SOS.

A similar result would also hold for the Hopf bifurcation.

4. THE VOLTAGE COLLAPSE PROBLEM

Consider a simple power network [2] in figure 1 whose underlying differential equations are given by

$$\dot{\omega} = \frac{1}{M}[P_m - P_{e1}(\delta, V) - D_G \omega],$$

$$\dot{\delta} = \omega - \frac{1}{D_L}[P_{e2}(\delta, V) - P_d], \quad (4)$$

$$\dot{V} = \frac{1}{\tau}[Q_e(\delta, V) - Q_d],$$

where $\delta = \delta_1 - \delta_2$, $P_{e1} = G - V(G \cos \delta - B \sin \delta)$, $P_{e2} = -V^2 G + V(G \cos \delta + B \sin \delta)$, $Q_e = -V^2(B - B_c) - V(G \sin \delta - B \cos \delta)$, $G = R/[R^2 + (X_L - X_x)^2]$, $B = (X_L - X_x)/[R^2 + (X_L - X_x)^2]$. We will use the methods in previous section to

determine the distance to saddle node bifurcation (i.e. voltage collapse). We pose the problem in term of parameters $\mu = (P_d, Q_d)$ (the load powers) and compute the minimum $\beta = |\mu^* - \mu^0|$ such that the equilibrium and the bifurcation conditions are satisfied. Assuming $\omega = 0$, $X_c = B_c = 0$, $R = 0.1$, $X_L = 0.5$ and letting $x = \sin \delta$ and $y = \cos \delta$, one can verify that these conditions satisfy the following equations.

$$0 = -V^2 G + V G y + V B x - P_d,$$
$$0 = -V^2 B - V G x + V B y - Q_d,$$
$$0 = B^2 + G^2 - 2B^2 V y - 2G^2 V y$$
$$0 = x^2 + y^2 - 1.$$

For simplicity, let's assume a constant power factor of $Q_d = 0.25 P_d$. Computing a Gröbner basis, $\mathbb{G}$, for the ideal generated by the above polynomials yield a single polynomial

$$\mathbb{G} = B^4 - B^3 P_d + 2B^2 G^2 - 4B^2 G P_d - 4B^2 P_d^2 - BG^2 P_d$$
$$+ 2BGP_d^2 + G^4 - 4G^3 P_d - 0.25G^2 P_d^2,$$

and the minimum distance to bifurcation can be recasted as

maximize: $\quad \beta$
such that: $\quad (P_d^* - P_d^0)^2 + (Q_d^* - Q_d^0)^2 - \beta + r(\mu)\mathbb{G}$ is SOS.

The SOSTOOLS [7] were used to solve the above SOS program and found a minimum $\beta = 0.443$ which corresponds to $\mu^* = (0.6661, 0.1665)$. These are the same results obtained in [2], but the underlying optimization problem is much simpler than that used in [2] as it only uses a single constraint.

5. ACKNOWLEDGMENTS

The authors gratefully acknowledge the partial financial support of Notre Dame's Environmental Change Initiative and the National Science Foundation (CNS-1239222).

6. REFERENCES

[1] F. Alvarado et al. Engineering foundations for the determination of security costs. *Power Systems, IEEE Transactions on*, 6(3):1175–1182, 1991.

[2] C. A. Canizares. Calculating optimal system parameters to maximize the distance to saddle-node bifurcations. *Circuits and Systems I, IEEE Transactions on*, 45(3):225–237, 1998.

[3] D. A. Cox, J. B. Little, and D. O'Shea. *Using algebraic geometry*. Springer New York, 1998.

[4] I. Dobson. Computing a closest bifurcation instability in multidimensional parameter space. *Journal of nonlinear science*, 3(1):307–327, 1993.

[5] C. Holling. Engineering resilience versus ecological resilience. *Foundations of Ecological Resilience*, pages 51–66, 1996.

[6] Y. A. Kuznetsov. *Elements of applied bifurcation theory*. Springer-Verlag New York, Inc., 1998.

[7] P. A. Parrilo. Semidefinite programming relaxations for semialgebraic problems. *Mathematical programming*, 96(2):293–320, 2003.

[8] M. Scheffer et al. Catastrophic shifts in ecosystems. *Nature*, 413(6856):591–596, 2001.

[9] T. A. Tamba and M. D. Lemmon. The distance-to-bifurcation problem in non-negative dynamical systems with kinetic realizations. *Submitted to ICCA*, 2014. Available at http://nd.edu/~ttamba.

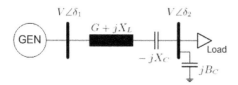

Figure 1: A simple power network [2].

User Interface Design and Verification for Semi-Autonomous Driving

Dorsa Sadigh
UC Berkeley
dsadigh@eecs.berkeley.edu

Katherine
Driggs-Campbell
UC Berkeley
krdc@eecs.berkeley.edu

Ruzena Bajcsy
UC Berkeley
bajcsy@berkeley.edu

S. Shankar Sastry
UC Berkeley
sastry@coe.berkeley.edu

Sanjit A. Seshia
UC Berkeley
sseshia@eecs.berkeley.edu

ABSTRACT

This paper presents a project in its early stages of development, in which we propose a solution to the problem of human interaction with autonomous vehicles. We have devised a method for design of a user interface that displays sufficient and crucial information to the driver. Our contribution in this work is (i) identifying different modes of driving behavior, (ii) building an expectation model of a driver, and (iii) implementing an interface system.

1. INTRODUCTION

Recently, there has been a great deal of research and media attention focused on the future of the car industry, primarily concerning autonomous vehicles. Since Google announced commercialization of the Google Car [1] by 2018, nearly all major car manufacturers have invested in research promising fully autonomous vehicles in the next five to ten years [1].

Many function specific automations are available in cars today. For example, Volvo's city braking system intervenes if a collision is unavoidable [1], and BMW's self-parallel-parking feature handles only steering maneuvers when engaged [2]. The major difficulty in these semi-autonomous systems is the interaction with the human driver, as there is often disparity between how the system functions and how the human *expects* the system to perform. When the system does not perform expected, drivers tend to either abuse the functionality or reject the system entirely [3].

---

[1] http://en.wikipedia.org/wiki/Google-driverless-car
[2] http://www.bmw.com/com/en/newvehicles/7series/sedan/2012/showroom/convenience/park-assistant.html
[3] http://online.wsj.com/news/articles/SB10001424052748703734504575125883649914708

Permission to make digital or hard copies of part or all of this work for personal or classroom use is granted without fee provided that copies are not made or distributed for profit or commercial advantage, and that copies bear this notice and the full citation on the first page. Copyrights for third-party components of this work must be honored. For all other uses, contact the owner/author(s). Copyright is held by the author/owner(s).
HiCoNS'14, April 15–17, 2014, Berlin, Germany.
ACM 978-1-4503-2652-0/14/04.
http://dx.doi.org/10.1145/2566468.2576851 .

In order for these autonomous systems to be well-received and be completely integrated into our everyday lives, many important questions need to be answered. Here, we focus on one imperative question: How do we guarantee a safe interaction between the human driver and the autonomous car to improve driver experience and comfort?

This work in progress suggests an innovative, practical solution to assist the intercommunication between human and autonomous systems. By modeling these human-in-the-loop systems and using formal methods to develop provably correct user interfaces (UIs), we can relay crucial information that will improve driver performance and experience in this autonomous environment.

2. METHODS

We propose developing a system that incorporates driver, vehicle, and environment data with user interfaces to act as a communication medium between the driver and autonomous systems. The following subsections describe our approach.

2.1 Data Integration.

The data that needs to be presented to the driver through the UI in the vehicle includes information about the driver, the surrounding environment, and the vehicle. This information can be collected using different methods. We gather our data from three sources:

Vehicle-to-Vehicle (V2V) Communication: Nearby vehicles can communicate states and status to the ego vehicle (i.e. the vehicle in which the driver of interest resides).

Sensory Information: Data is collected from front and side radar, LiDAR, and CAN bus readings. The collected data gives us information about the surrounding environment and the state of the vehicle.

Driver Monitoring: Eye trackers[4], cameras, the MS Kinect[5], optical tracking setup[6], and steering wheel touch sensors are used to monitor driver behavior.

From the collected data, we can estimate the driver state to provide appropriate information, by learning an individual's behavior using past driving data, estimated mental and

---

[4] http://www.eyetracking-glasses.com/
[5] http://www.xbox.com/en-US/KINECT
[6] http://www.naturalpoint.com/

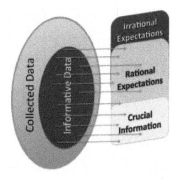

Figure 1: One-to-one mapping from the informative part of the full data collection to the rational expected and the crucial set.

perception state, and the outside environment. As described in [4, 6], driver modes can be identified to predict driver behavior using the described dataset. In our previous work, we have estimated the driver behavior using the k-means clustering algorithm, where each cluster corresponds to a specific driving behavior.

2.2 Meeting Expectations of the Driver.

The UI must satisfy the following criteria: (i) meet the expectations of the driver; (ii) avoid mode confusion by displaying the correct data for a given driver state; (iii) display concise and informative data; and (iv) present information in a user-friendly manner. In addition, an expectation model that identifies what information the driver desires must be generated from surveying drivers.

Acknowledging that not all expectations can be met and that the driver might not be aware of crucial information she needs while driving, the data presented through the UI will be a portion of the expected data in addition to crucial information in a given mode. Figure 1 shows the mapping from the collected data to what needs to be displayed to the driver. Additionally, not all the data collected is useful and informative to the driver. Therefore, we create this one-to-one mapping from the informative part of the collected dataset to the data that must be presented to the driver.

3. EXPERIMENTAL SETUP

To carry out experiments and collect data, we setup a force feedback car simulator [7], equipped with software to simulate all the sensory data and V2V communication. This setup provides a realistic driving platform that guarantees safety of the user, while allowing complete control over the experimental conditions [2]. Additionally, we have a set of eye tracker glasses that provide accurate gaze detection [8]. With these tools and setups, we gather all necessary data described in Section 2.1 for monitoring and modeling the human behavior as well as evaluating our UI.

4. IMPLEMENTATION AND VALIDATION

To implement the models and UI, a variety of mediums that can be used in a car are to be tested, including mobile applications that can be mounted in a vehicle; mobile applications that can use audio and haptic feedback; simulated windshield displays; and new wearable computers like Google Glass [9]. Once the systems are developed and methodically tested for usability, the methods can be systematically compared to evaluate the performance. We define logical properties that represent the brevity and clarity of the UI model and the one-to-one mapping previously described. We use formal methods and verification techniques to validate the correctness of our model as motivated by Sturton et al. in evaluating UIs for electronic voting machines [5]. Then, to ensure effectiveness of the UI, driver performance is quantified by applying probabilistic model checking techniques and verifying logical properties on performance models before and after using the UI, as demonstrated in our previous work [3].

5. CONCLUSION

In conclusion, the autonomous vehicle race has begun and will eventually affect our everyday lives. While in transition, we present a high impact project to assist drivers as well as increase the public's acceptance of autonomous vehicles. In developing this unique, verifiable, and accurate interface, we provide the drivers insight to the autonomous system's intent without overloading them with unnecessary information. With the proposed UI from integrated data, we believe that we can improve driver performance and address many of the important questions that are raised by the autonomous movement.

6. ACKNOWLEDGMENT

This work is supported by the NSF grants CCF-1116993 and CCF-1139138.

7. REFERENCES

[1] E. Coelingh et al. Collision Warning with Auto Brake: a Real-Life Safety Perspective. In *Innovations for Safety: Opportunities and Challenges*, 2007.

[2] K. Driggs-Campbell et al. Experimental design for human-in-the-loop driving simulations. *Available on arXiv*, January 2014.

[3] D. Sadigh et al. Data-driven probabilistic modeling and verification of human driver behavior. In *Formal Verification and Modeling in Human-Machine Systems (AAAI Spring Symposium)*, 2014.

[4] V. Shia et al. Driver modeling for semi-autonomous vehicular control. *IEEE Transactions on Intelligent Transportation Systems*, in review.

[5] C. Sturton et al. On voting machine design for verification and testability. In *Proceedings of the 16th ACM conference on Computer and communications security*, CCS '09, pages 463–476, New York, NY, USA, 2009. ACM.

[6] R. Vasudevan et al. Safe Semi-Autonomous Control with Enhanced Driver Modeling. In *American Control Conference (ACC), 2012*, pages 2896–2903. IEEE, 2012.

---

[7]http://www.force-dynamics.com/
[8]http://www.eyetracking-glasses.com/

---

[9]http://www.google.com/glass/start/

Is This a Good Time?
Deciding When to Launch Attacks on Process Control Systems

Marina Krotofil
Hamburg University of Technology
21079 Hamburg, Germany

Álvaro A. Cárdenas
University of Texas at Dallas
Richardson, TX75080, USA

ABSTRACT

We introduce a new problem formulation for understanding the threats and vulnerabilities of process control systems. In particular, we consider an adversary that has compromised sensor or actuator signals of a control system and needs to identify the best time to launch an attack. We have previously shown that attackers might not be able to reach if the timing of their Denial-of-Service (DoS) attacks is not chosen strategically: Therefore, if the timing of a DoS attack is not chosen correctly, the attack can have limited impact; however, if the timing of the attack is chosen carefully, the attack has higher chances of succeeding. We formulate the problem of selecting a good time to launch DoS attacks as an optimal stopping problem that the adversary has to solve in real-time. In particular, we use the theory for the Best-Choice Problem to identify an optimal stopping criteria and then use a low pass filter to identify when the time series of a process variable has reached its peak. We identify some of the complexities associated with solving the problem and outline directions for future work.

1. INTRODUCTION

One of the growing research areas for securing cyber-physical systems is the work on threat models that considers an adversary which can manipulate sensor or actuator signals in order to drive the physical process under control to an undesired state. While most of the work in this area explores the implications of manipulating signals, there has been little work on understanding the complexity of launching successful attacks, and in particular, on finding a "good time" to launch an attack. In our study we consider an attacker that can read sensor signals for a given process variable, and then has to select a time to launch a DoS attack on the communication channel, which in turn will freeze the process value in the controller's memory [3]; and therefore the controller will select control commands based on a value that is not being updated.

We formulate the problem as an optimal stopping time problem for the attacker. In particular, we formulate the problem as a Best-Choice Problem (also known as the "Secretary Problem"), in which the adversary is presented with a time series of system states (obtained by sensors) and has

Permission to make digital or hard copies of part or all of this work for personal or classroom use is granted without fee provided that copies are not made or distributed for profit or commercial advantage, and that copies bear this notice and the full citation on the first page. Copyrights for third-party components of this work must be honored. For all other uses, contact the owner/author(s). Copyright is held by the author/owner(s).

HiCoNS'14, April 15–17, 2014, Berlin, Germany.
ACM 978-1-4503-2652-0/14/04.

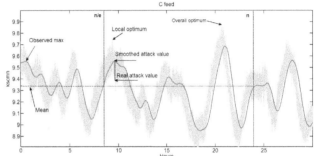

Figure 1: The learning phase $\frac{n}{e}$ of the Best-Choice problem identifies a peak that is used as a reference point to find a better peak between $\frac{n}{e}$ and n. Because the signal is noisy it is difficult to identify a peak in real-time–a downward trend might be a noisy artifact masking a general upward trend– therefore we use a low-pass filter so we can identify a peak as soon as the signal has a downward trend. If we do not find a peak higher than the learning period before reaching n we call this a "non-selection."

to select the optimal time to attack based on these measurements.

Optimal stopping problems are studied in statistics and they are generally concerned with the problem of choosing a time to take a particular action in order to maximize an expected reward. Recall that the attacker faces the following problem: given a time-series of N sensor signal samples that will exhibit a sequence of peaks, how should the attacker select one of peaks to launch her attack? This particular formulation in the context of the Secretary Problem was solved by Freeman [2], which showed that one can select the best signal sample with maximum probability $(1/e)$ by using the following rule: do not select any sample among the first (N/e) candidates (the learning period), and after that, select the first sample whose value exceeds the value of all candidates seen so far, or the last sample in the series.

There are multiple variations or formulations to the secretary problem. In this paper we consider the classical solution, and a recent result that assumes the order in which the candidates arrive is not completely random, but has a probability distribution satisfying a hazard rate condition [4]. This assumption is commonly used in standard engineering applications. Gaussian, uniform, and exponential distributions satisfy this property. Under this assumption it can be shown that the learning period can be cut down to $N/log(N)$; which is significantly smaller than N/e.

Because the Best-Choice Problem formulation assumes non-correlated time measurements, the attacker has to add an additional stopping criteria to identify when the sensor signal has reached its peak; this is a non-trivial task in many

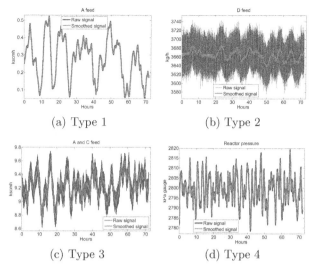

Figure 2: Different types of sensor signals with their correspondent smoothed signals, $m=250$

practical situations as sensor measurements tend to be noisy and have sudden fluctuations. To this end we explore two methods: signal smoothing with low pass filters (completed work to appear in the 2014 International Conference on Critical Infrastructure Protection) and quickest change detection theory (future work). A summary of our approach can be seen in Fig. 1.

2. EXPERIMENTAL RESULTS

For our experimental analysis we use the C and Matlab model of the full Tennessee Eastman (TE) challenge process developed by Ricker [5]. The TE process is a modified model of a real plant-wide industrial process [1] which was created to equip the process control community with a realistic and accurate model for testing process control technologies. We have extended this line of work to test and evaluate the performance of the system under adversarial attacks [3].

Although the TE model provides a solid platform for process and control engineering experimentation, we had to extend the system to incorporate two new requirements. First, we modified the original process code to introduce randomness into the sensor and actuator signals noise, without disturbing the underlying dynamic behavior of the process. This enabled statistical evaluation of the experiments. Second, due to low sampling frequency of the final simulated data available in Matlab (100 samples per hour), we implemented in C a way to export the exact process simulation data into the Matlab workspace, which are a sampled at a rate 2000 samples per hour and thus are much closer to real-world scenarios.

As mentioned before, in addition to using the Best-Choice theory to identify a peak, we use a low pass filter to remove short-term fluctuations or "noise" and highlight long-term trends of the data. The simplest form of smoothing is the "moving average" which is the mean of the previous m samples. In TE process, sensor signals can be roughly divided into 4 groups (Fig. 2). Type 1 is characterized by few distinct peaks and low noise level. Type 2 is distinguished by the slow signal amplitude change with high frequency noise. Type 3 can be described as a very noisy variation of Type 1 signal. Type 4 signal distinguishes itself with the multiple noisy signal peaks. Our experimental results show that to succeed, the attacker has to take into account type of the signal she is dealing with.

We evaluate the performance of our approach based on three metrics: (1) fractional error in identifying the peak, in %; (2) fractional error in selecting the highest possible peak in the series, in %; and (3) number of non-selections (when no peak is higher than the one observed in the learning phase, and last sample in the series is taken). Our results confirm that the learning period can be indeed cut down to $N/log(N)$ while achieving results comparable to the the N/e strategy; in particular, because if the learning phase is short, the number of non-selections reduces substantially (almost to zero). For the same reason the fractional error in selecting the highest possible peak increases as the attacker has less time to achieve sufficient aspiration level. Since for the classic solution the number of non-selections reaches on average 25%, it can be a decisive factor to favor $N/log(N)$ strategy.

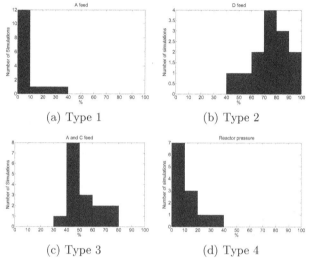

Figure 3: Distribution of the fractional error in selecting the highest possible value, $m = 250$

Because of space considerations, we illustrate the performance of our approach in a form of the histogram of the distribution of the fractional error in selecting the highest possible value in the time series (Fig. 3). As can be seen, the best results can be achieved for sensor signals of Type 1 and 4. In contrast the methodology proposed in this paper is not well suited for conducting attacks on the sensor signals of Type 2 and 3 because of their noise. While applying a low-pass filter delivers good results for the attacks on the low-noise signals, an alternative solution is required for dealing with the noisy process variables.

3. REFERENCES

[1] J. J. Downs and E. F. Vogel. A plant-wide industrial process control problem. *Computers & Chemical Engineering*, 17(3):245–255, 1993.

[2] P. Freeman. The secretary problem and its extensions: A review. *International Statistical Review/Revue Internationale de Statistique*, pages 189–206, 1983.

[3] M. Krotofil and A. A. Cárdenas. Resilience of Process Control Systems to Ccyber-Pysical Attacks. In *NordSec'14, Secure IT-Systems*, volume 8208 of *LNCS*, pages 166–182, 2013.

[4] M. Mahdian, R. P. McAfee, and D. Pennock. The secretary problem with a hazard rate condition. In *Internet and Network Economics*, pages 708–715. 2008.

[5] N. L. Ricker. Tennessee Eastman Challenge Archive. http://depts.washington.edu/control/LARRY/TE/download.html. retrieved: May, 2013.

A Formal Verification Approach To Revealing Stealth Attacks on Networked Control Systems

Nikola Trčka, Mark Moulin, Shaunak Bopardikar, Alberto Speranzon
United Technologies Research Center
411 Silver Ln
East Hartford, CT

ABSTRACT

We develop methods to determine if networked control systems can be compromised by stealth attacks, and derive design strategies to secure these systems. A stealth attack is a form of a cyber-physical attack where the adversary compromises the information between the plant and the controller, with the intention to drive the system into a bad state and at the same time stay undetected. We define the discovery problem as a formal verification problem, where generated counterexamples (if any) correspond to actual attack vectors. The analysis is entirely performed in Simulink, using Simulink Design Verifier as the verification engine. A small case study is presented to illustrate the results, and a branch-and-bound algorithm is proposed to perform optimal system securing.

1. INTRODUCTION

A Cyber-Physical System (CPS) is a system consisting of computational (i.e. cyber) components that interact with physical entities. In this paper we focus on networked control systems, a special class of CPSs, where the main components are sensors, actuators, and controllers, all interconnected through, for example, ethernet or WiFi, and operating in a closed loop to maintain desired behavior of a physical plant.

Today, networked control systems support many critical infrastructures, like e.g. water and gas distribution and transportation systems, to name a few. To ensure safe and reliable behavior of these systems, their security must be of primary importance. Security analysis, or sometimes called risk assessment, is a process that identifies and evaluates system vulnerabilities, typically based on a system model and a predefined set of attack models. In this paper we propose a novel model-based security analysis technique for networked control systems, focusing on stealth attacks, a special class of cyber-physical attacks, where a possible adversary tries to compromise the system while staying undetected at the same time.

Permission to make digital or hard copies of part or all of this work for personal or classroom use is granted without fee provided that copies are not made or distributed for profit or commercial advantage, and that copies bear this notice and the full citation on the first page. Copyrights for third-party components of this work must be honored. For all other uses, contact the owner/author(s). Copyright is held by the author/owner(s).
HiCoNS'14, April 15–17, 2014, Berlin, Germany.
ACM 978-1-4503-2652-0/14/04.
http://dx.doi.org/10.1145/2566468.2566484.

The mechanism of a stealth attack on a networked control system is depicted in Figure 1. We assume that the control and measurement signals are communicated over a network that is either physically or only logically composed of several secure and non-secure links. The attacker has the ability to intercept packets that flow over the non-secure links and replace them with arbitrary packets (or achieve the same effect by directly compromising sensors/actuators), and is not able to compromise any of the block components of the system. The intention of the attacker is to guide the system into a bad state, while at the same time making sure that the controller does not see any irregularities in the measurements (cf. Figure 1). For this paper we do not consider any specific diagnostic procedure, but rather a general (albeit strict) method where the measure of detectability is simply based on the difference between the attacked and the nominal measurements. Our techniques, however, can be easily applied to other monitoring and diagnostics procedures as well. In addition to the main detection mechanism operating in the control block, we also assume that a range check on the actuator signal is performed at the plant.

Stealth attacks came into prominence owing to the several recent orchestrations of attacks on CPSs such as the Stuxnet [7], a power grid by the infamous "Dr. Chaos" [6], and a company's internal heating ventilation and cooling system [5]. In control systems literature, Smith, in [10], first introduced and demonstrated a *stealth/covert attack* on a closed-loop control system. In this scenario, the attacker can compromise, with a judicious choice, both the input (actuators) and the output (measurements) of a closed loop control system so that the it is not possible to detect the attack from the output. Teixeira et al. [12, 11] study the problem in the linear, yet similar, setting and provide methods to change the system model so that a class of stealthy attacks on the actuators gets revealed. Dan and Sandberg in [4] consider stealth attacks on static linear systems and provide algorithms to secure measurements that require a maximum amount of attacker resources. Pasqualetti et al. [9] provide a more general framework to analyze several types of attacks on power systems and networks. In particular, general conditions for attack detection and identifiability for descriptor linear time-invariant systems are considered. More recently, in [3], we extended the analysis for linear systems to account for attacks on several points of a closed loop linear control system, along with techniques to prevent stealth attacks.

Not restrictive to having a *physical* element, stealth attacks can also be envisioned to occur on software systems in which threads between two interacting pieces of code can be compromised. Therefore, our goal is to design tools that can analyze not only systems modeled as differential algebraic equations but can in principle also handle complex, possibly non-linear or discrete-event systems.

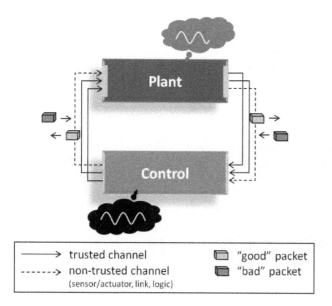

Figure 1: Depiction of a stealth attack on a networked control system

Formal verification [1, 2, 8] (in the context of checking safety) is an automated technique that given an open (and thus non-deterministic) model of a system and a desired safety property for this system, checks whether the property is always satisfied on the system or not. If the property is proven false, a counterexample is usually provided, in the form of an (external) input signal that drives the system from its initial state to the first violation point. For scalability reasons, the search space covering all possible behaviors is rarely constructed in full, and typically exists in an implicit form only. In addition, the analysis is most often bounded in depth, i.e. performed only from time 0 to some predefined model time T. Formal verification is very flexible, and can in principle handle a large class of systems, requiring only a model for which an executable semantics is provided.

This paper proposes to use formal verification to prove that a system is secure against stealth attacks of the form from Figure 1. The source of non-determinism in this context comes from the degrees of freedom the attacker has, namely the network links he has access to and the packet content he can inject, while the property to verify characterizes the attack itself, namely its stealth dynamics and its intended outcome (or goal). If the system is proven safe by formal verification, we are sure that no stealth attacks can exist on this system, meaning that every attack will be detectable from the measurements. If it is proven insecure, the generated counterexample directly maps to a stealth attack, i.e. to a sequence of inputs that guarantees stealth behavior and guides the system into a "bad" state that corresponds to the intended attack outcome. This attack can then be analyzed and, based on the gained insight, additional components of the system are secured and the verification process

is repeated. Conceptually, the approach can be visualized as in Figure 2.

For broader applicability, our approach is entirely implemented in the Matlab/Simulink environment, the commercial framework commonly used for modeling control systems. We provide a generic Simulink template to cover a large class of networked control systems, only requiring from users to instantiate the system dynamics and the control logic, and to set desired verification parameters. The actual formal verification analysis is performed using Simulink Design Verifier [8], the verification engine of Matlab/Simulink, using its property proving capability in particular.

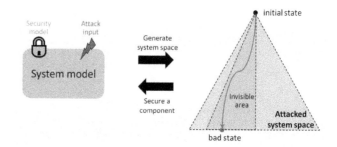

Figure 2: Formal verification approach to revealing stealth attacks

The remainder of the paper is organized as follows. In the next section we give some preliminaries. Section 3 introduces the notions of stealth attack and system security. In Section 4, we study three special cases of stealth attacks in more detail. The formal verification approach to system security is explained in Section 5. Section 6 shows a small case study to illustrate the formal verification approach. In Section 7 we cover the system design problem by presenting an algorithm for optimal system securing. Finally, in Section 8 we give conclusions and directions for future work.

2. PRELIMINARIES

$\mathbb{N}$ denotes the set of natural numbers, including zero, and $\mathbb{N}^+ = \mathbb{N} \setminus \{0\}$. $\mathbb{R}$ is the set of real numbers, and $\mathbb{R}^{\geq 0}$ is the set of non-negative reals. $\mathbb{R}^{m \times n}$, for $m, n \in \mathbb{N}^+$, is the set of all real matrices of dimension $m \times n$. We define $\mathbb{R}^n = \mathbb{R}^{n \times 1}$. $\wp(A)$ denotes the power set of a set A. Given a function f, we write $dom(f)$ and $range(f)$ for the domain and the range of f respectively.

3. SYSTEM UNDER STEALTH ATTACK

We consider a closed-loop discrete time dynamical system (P, Q, C) described by the equations in Figure 3, where for every *time instant* $k \in \mathbb{N}$, the vector $x_k \in \mathbb{R}^n$ denotes the *state* of the system, $y_k \in \mathbb{R}^m$ is the *measurement* vector, $u_k \in \mathbb{R}^p$ is the *control input* vector, $P : \mathbb{R}^n \times \mathbb{R}^p \to \mathbb{R}^n$ is the *plant dynamics* function, $Q : \mathbb{R}^n \to \mathbb{R}^m$ is the *measurement function*, and $C : \mathbb{R}^m \to \mathbb{R}^p$ is the *control (law)* function. We call (P, Q) the *plant*, and (P, Q, C, x_0) is the *initialized system* from some *initial state* $x_0 \in \mathbb{R}^n$.

Given an initialized system (P, Q, C, x_0), we define the set of all *reachable states* of (P, Q, C, x_0) by $reach(P, Q, C, x_0) = \{x_0, x_1, x_2, \ldots\}$. This notion is generalized to an arbitrary initial set $X_0 \subseteq \mathbb{R}^n$ by defining $reach(P, Q, C, X_0) = \bigcup_{x_0 \in X_0} reach(P, Q, C, x_0)$.

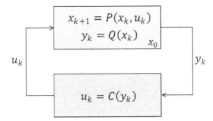

Figure 3: Discrete-time dynamical system

a)

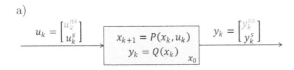

b)

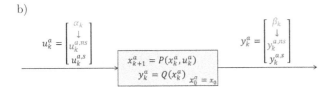

Figure 4: a) Nominal system with signal decomposition, and b) the same system under a stealth attack

3.1 Signal partitioning and attacked system

To formalize the notion of stealth attack, we first divide the measurement and the control vector into their non-secure and secure parts. In other words, we assume that u_k has a block vector form $(u_k^{ns} \ u_k^s)^T$, where $u_k^{ns} \in \mathbb{R}^{p_{ns}}$, $u_k^s \in \mathbb{R}^{p_s}$ and $p_{ns} + p_s = p$ for some $p_{ns}, p_s \in \mathbb{N}^+$, and similarly that $y_k = (y_k^{ns} \ y_k^s)^T$ with $y_k^{ns} \in \mathbb{R}^{m_{ns}}$, $y_k^s \in \mathbb{R}^{m_s}$ and $m_{ns} + m_s = m$ for some $m_{ns}, m_s \in \mathbb{N}^+$. Given a set of measurement and control vectors V, we write V^{ns} for the set of vectors containing only the non-secure parts of the vectors in V, and similarly for the secure case. Given a matrix $M \in \mathbb{R}^{m \times p}$, the matrix $M^{ns,s} \in \mathbb{R}^{m_{ns} \times p_s}$ denotes the block of M that corresponds to the non-secure part of y_k and the secure part of u_k. Similarly, we define $M^{ns,ns} \in \mathbb{R}^{m_{ns} \times p_{ns}}$, $M^{s,ns} \in \mathbb{R}^{m_s \times p_{ns}}$ and $M^{s,s} \in \mathbb{R}^{m_s \times p_s}$.

Figure 4a shows the nominal system from Figure 3 with the measurement and the control vectors decomposed into their secure and non-secure parts. Figure 4b shows the dynamics of this system when it is under attack. At every time instant k, the non-secure part of the input is replaced by some vector $\alpha_k \in \mathbb{R}^{p_{ns}}$, called the attack-intention vector, that is used to directly control the system towards the intended bad state, while at the same time the non-secure part of the measurements is replaced by a masking vector $\beta_k \in \mathbb{R}^{m_{ns}}$ to hide the effect of intention vectors from previous steps and possibly manipulate the controller into producing an incorrect command. Given this, we define the notion of stealth attack as follows.

DEFINITION 1 (STEALTH ATTACK). *Let* $\varepsilon \in \mathbb{R}^{\geq 0}$ *and* $\Pi \subseteq \mathbb{R}^n \times \mathbb{N}$. *A pair of sequences* $\alpha_0, \ldots, \alpha_K \in \mathbb{R}^{p_{ns}}$ *and* $\beta_0, \ldots, \beta_K \in \mathbb{R}^{m_{ns}}$, *for* $K \in \mathbb{N}$, *is called a* (Π, ε)-*(stealth)*

attack *on an initialized system* $(P, Q, \mathcal{C}, x_0)$ *if the following holds:*

1. $\alpha_k \in range(\mathcal{C})^{ns}$ *and* $\beta_k \in range(Q)^{ns}$ *for every* $k \in [0, K]$ - *every injected signal is in the acceptable (i.e. nominal) range,*

2. $(x_K^a, K) \in \Pi$ - *the last state of the attack is according to the given relation* Π,

3. $\| y_k - y_k^a \| \leq \varepsilon$ *for every* $k \in [0, K]$ - *attack is undetectable (up to the given* ε *and the norm function) on the measurements, and*

4. $\alpha_k \neq u_k^{ns}$ *for at least one* $k \in [0, K]$ - *attack is not trivial (this condition is of importance only if* Π *does not involve system state; see next section).*

We call K *the* length *of the attack,* Π *the* attack intention property *(representing the "bad state" condition in terms of state value and time stamp) and* ε *the* detectability threshold *(representing the sensitivity of the potential monitoring facility in the controller).*

We now define what it means for a dynamical system and its plant to be considered secure, modulo some detectability threshold and an attack intention property. Intuitively, a system is secure from some initial state if it cannot be attacked from that state. This definition further extends to a class of initial states by requiring security property for each element of the class. Finally, a plant is considered secure if no matter what control algorithm is attached to it, the corresponding system is secure.

DEFINITION 2 (SECURE SYSTEM). *Given* $\varepsilon \in \mathbb{R}^{\geq 0}$ *and* $\Pi \subseteq \mathbb{R}^n \times \mathbb{N}$, *an initialized system* $(P, Q, \mathcal{C}, x_0)$ *is* (Π, ε)-secure *if there exists no* (Π, ε) *attack on* $(P, Q, \mathcal{C}, x_0)$. *Given a non-empty set* $X_0 \subseteq \mathbb{R}^n$, *the system* $(P, Q, \mathcal{C})$ *is* (Π, ε, X_0)-secure *if* $(P, Q, \mathcal{C}, x_0)$ *is* (Π, ε)-secure *for every* $x_0 \in X_0$. *The plant structure* (P, Q) *is* (Π, ε, X_0)-secure *if the corresponding system structure* $(P, Q, \mathcal{C})$ *is* (Π, ε, X_0)-secure *for every control law function* $\mathcal{C}$.

4. SPECIAL CASES

In this section we identify certain special classes of stealth attacks. These special cases are interesting as they often arise in practice, and can accelerate the formal verification approach by reducing complexity or even enable efficient analytic/closed-form solutions.

4.1 Case 1: Equality of measurement signals

The first case is the singular case where $\varepsilon = 0$ and the norm function is the entry-wise absolute value. In this case the attacker can only form the masking signal by taking $\beta_k = y_k^{ns}$ for every $k \in [0, K]$, which simplifies the undetectability requirement in Definition 1 to:

- $y_k^s = y_k^{a,s}$ for every $k \in [0, K]$ - attack is undetectable on the secure part of the measurements (and thus completely).

Given this and the fact that the attacked control signal would now always be equal to the nominal signal, the attack can be depicted as in Figure 5. The benefit of this simplification is that it eliminates one degree of freedom the

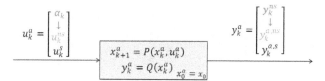

$$u_k^a = \begin{bmatrix} \alpha_k \\ \downarrow \\ u_k^{ns} \\ u_k^s \end{bmatrix} \qquad x_{k+1}^a = P(x_k^a, u_k^a) \qquad y_k^a = \begin{bmatrix} y_k^{ns} \\ \downarrow \\ y_k^{a,ns} \\ y_k^{a,s} \end{bmatrix}$$

$$y_k^a = Q(x_k^a) \quad x_0^a = x_0$$

Figure 5: System under a stealth attack for the special case of $\varepsilon = 0$

attacker has, drastically reducing the search space that formal verification needs to explore. It is important to note, however, that in this case the corresponding security analysis would not capture attacks that e.g. take advantage of system noise to achieve the stealth property.

4.2 Case 2: State-independent attack intention property

Another special case to consider is when $\Pi \overset{\text{def}}{=} \Pi_K = \mathbb{R}^n \times \{K\}$ for some $K \in \mathbb{N}$, i.e. when the attack intention property is trivial on the attack state condition, but holds only at time K. This case is relevant when we want to secure our system for all possible stealth attacks of length K, irrespective of their intentions that regard system state. In this case the following result naturally follows:

THEOREM 1. *Let $X_0 \subseteq \mathbb{R}^n$ be such that $reach(P, Q, \mathcal{C}, X_0) \subseteq X_0$, i.e. a set of system states closed under reachability. If there exists a one-step attack (Π_1, ε) from every $x_0 \in X_0$, then there is also a K-step attack (Π_K, ε) (for any $K \in \mathbb{N}$) from every such x_0. More importantly, if the system $(P, Q, \mathcal{C})$ is proven $(\Pi_1, \varepsilon, X_0)$-secure, then there is no state from which it can be attacked (for any attack length).*

4.3 Case 3: Linear system case

We now consider the important case when the system under consideration has linear dynamics. The purpose of this is to clarify the definitions of the previous section; for a more thorough treatment of the stealth attack prevention problem in the linear setting, please see [3].

Central to this section is the following theorem that gives a convenient matrix rank condition for system security when the system is linear and in addition satisfies the requirements of Case 1 and Case 2.

THEOREM 2. *Let $(P, Q, \mathcal{C})$ be a system where $P(x_k, u_k) \equiv Ax_k + Bu_k$ and $Q(x_k) \equiv Cx_k$ for some matrices $A \in \mathbb{R}^{n \times n}$, $B \in \mathbb{R}^{n \times p}$ and $C \in \mathbb{R}^{m \times n}$. Then, for every $K \in \mathbb{N}^+$ and every $x_0 \in \mathbb{R}^n$, the initialized system $(P, Q, \mathcal{C}, x_0)$ is $(\Pi_K, 0)$-secure, for $\Pi_K = \mathbb{R}^n \times \{K\}$, iff $rank([CA^iB]^{s,ns}) = p_{ns}$, where $i \in \mathbb{N}$ is the smallest index for which $CA^iB \neq 0$.*

PROOF. The proof is based on the unfolding of the third condition in Definition 1. First, for $k = 0$, we have $[Cx_0]^s = [Cx_0^a]^s$ which always holds because $x_0^a = x_0$. For $k = 1$, we have

$$[Cx_1]^s = [Cx_1^a]^s$$
$$\text{iff } \left[C\left(Ax_0 + B\begin{pmatrix} u_0^{ns} \\ u_0^s \end{pmatrix}\right)\right]^s = \left[C\left(Ax_0 + B\begin{pmatrix} \alpha_0 \\ u_0^s \end{pmatrix}\right)\right]^s$$
$$\text{iff } [CAx_0]^s + [CB]^{s,ns}u_0^{ns} + [CB]^{s,s}u_0^s$$
$$\qquad = [CAx_0]^s + [CB]^{s,ns}\alpha_0 + [CB]^{s,s}u_0^s$$
$$\text{iff } [CB]^{s,ns}(u_0^{ns} - \alpha_0) = 0.$$

Further, for $k = 2$, we derive

$$[Cx_2]^s = [Cx_2^a]^s$$
$$\text{iff } \left[C\left(Ax_1 + B\begin{pmatrix} u_1^{ns} \\ u_1^s \end{pmatrix}\right)\right]^s = \left[C\left(Ax_1 + B\begin{pmatrix} \alpha_1 \\ u_1^s \end{pmatrix}\right)\right]^s$$
$$\text{iff } [CAx_1]^s + [CB]^{s,ns}u_1^{ns} = [CAx_1]^s + [CB]^{s,ns}\alpha_1$$
$$\text{iff } \left[CA\left(Ax_0 + B\begin{pmatrix} u_0^{ns} \\ u_0^s \end{pmatrix}\right)\right]^s + [CB]^{s,ns}u_1^{ns}$$
$$\qquad = \left[CA\left(Ax_0 + B\begin{pmatrix} \alpha_0 \\ u_0^s \end{pmatrix}\right)\right]^s + [CB]^{s,ns}\alpha_1$$
$$\text{iff } [CAB]^{s,ns}u_0^{ns} + [CB]^{s,ns}u_1^{ns} = [CAB]^{s,ns}\alpha_0[CB]^{s,ns}\alpha_1$$
$$\text{iff } [CAB]^{s,ns}(u_0^{ns} - \alpha_0) + [CB]^{s,ns}(u_1^{ns} - \alpha_1) = 0.$$

Taking index i into account and extending the derivation to $k = K + i + 1$, the result can be written in matrix form as follows:

$$M = \begin{pmatrix} [CA^iB]^{s,ns} & 0 & \dots & 0 \\ [CA^{i+1}B]^{s,ns} & [CA^iB]^{s,ns} & \dots & 0 \\ \vdots & \vdots & \ddots & 0 \\ [CA^{i+K}B]^{s,ns} & [CA^{i+K-1}B]^{s,ns} & \dots & [CA^iB]^{s,ns} \end{pmatrix}$$

$$M \cdot \begin{pmatrix} u_0^{ns} - \alpha_0 \\ u_1^{ns} - \alpha_1 \\ \vdots \\ u_K^{ns} - \alpha_K \end{pmatrix} = 0$$

From this it follows that a non-trivial attack of length K does not exist iff the above matrix M has full column rank. This is, however, only possible when $[CA^iB]^{s,ns}$ is full column rank, i.e. when its rank is p_{ns}. Note that the first condition of Definition 1 can always be taken care of by scaling. $\square$

Note that the condition in Theorem 2 does not depend on the control law function. Therefore, in the linear case, with Π only looking at the attack length and $\varepsilon = 0$, all the notions of Definition 2 coincide.

Although this very special case allows for an analytical solution and does not require the formal verification approach, it is unfortunately not often seen in practice. Its solution efficiency, however, may potentially be exploited to guide the verification procedure (not studied in this paper).

5. SECURITY AS A FORMAL VERIFICATION PROBLEM

In this section we show how to apply formal verification to analyze system security. As explained in the introduction, the basic idea is to encode the negation of the attack conditions from Definition 1 as a verification property, so that when a counterexample is generated it directly maps to a stealth attack of the shortest length. More importantly, if no counterexample is generated, we can conclude that no stealth attack is possible, i.e. that the system is secure. We use Simulink to model the control system and Simulink Design Verifier [8] as the formal verification engine. The overall approach is illustrated in 6.

Figure 7 shows the generic Simulink template we use to prove system security. Blocks Plant and Controller represent nominal behavior, while their counterparts on the bottom represent the attacked system with exactly the same internal

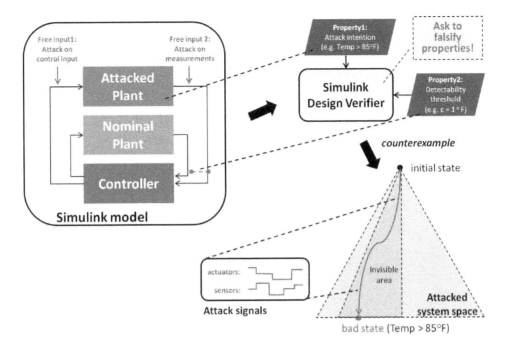

Figure 6: Using Simulink Design Verifier to discover stealth attacks (or prove their absence)

dynamics but different input signals. Initial state is modeled as a free input block, with an assumption block that captures the desired range of initial conditions. Signals α and β form the attack we are searching for, so they are also modeled as free inputs and have associated assumption blocks to restrict their ranges in accordance with the first condition of Definition 1. We use Demux blocks to split control and output signals into their secure and non-secure parts, and Mux blocks to merge these parts back together.

The remaining three conditions of Definition 1 are captured inside the Attack_Condition block. This block takes the following signals as input: i) the difference between the nominal and the attacked output (for the attack undetectability property), ii) the attacked state (for the attack intention property), and iii) the difference between the injected α signal and the original non-secure part of the control signal (to ensure that the attack is not trivial). For every $k \in [0, K]$ the block outputs the joint validity of the three corresponding conditions from Definition 1 and sends it to the property block of Simulink Design Verifier for falsification. It is implemented as a conjunction of the Π signal, which includes a time counter and only operates on the last value of the state signal, and two more signals that correspond to the other two attack conditions that must be evaluated over the complete trajectory. The first signal ensures that we have the undetectability property holding along the whole trajectory, while the second one ensures that at least one α_k along this trajectory is different from the part of the nominal control output it replaces. The values of the trajectory properties for these signals are stored in their corresponding delay blocks, with initial values 0 and 1 respectively.

Figure 8 shows how the setup simplifies drastically when we assume the special case of a single fixed initial state and with $\varepsilon = 0$. The free input blocks for the initial state and the β signal are removed, and there is no need to replicate the control block anymore because the controller now receives

the same input both in the nominal and the attacked case. The only degree of freedom that now needs to be considered in security analysis is the injection signal α on the controller output.

We note that the models in Figures 7 and 8 are both for the case where a specific controller is taken into consideration; proving security for all possible controllers simply means replacing the controller block in these figures by a free input block (restricted to the same range).

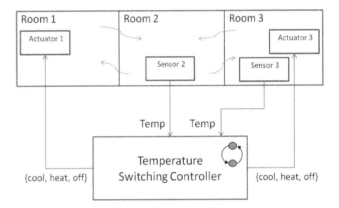

Figure 9: Three-room temperature control system

6. CASE STUDY

We illustrate our approach on a small case study, a simple temperature control system depicted in Figure 9. The plant in the system comprises of three adjoint rooms, where the first and the third room have a cooling/heating device in them (which can be actuated by the controller), and the second and the third room have temperature sensors (which can be read by the controller). The controller implements

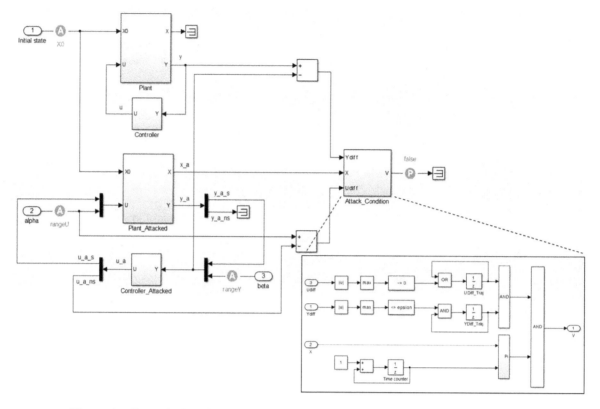

Figure 7: Generic Simulink model template for generation of stealth attacks

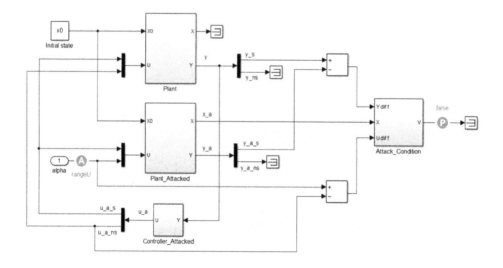

Figure 8: Simulink model template for the special case 1 ($\varepsilon = 0$) and unique initial state

$$\begin{pmatrix} T_{1,k+1} \\ T_{2,k+1} \\ T_{3,k+1} \end{pmatrix} = \begin{pmatrix} 1-c_{12} & c_{12} & 0 \\ c_{21} & 1-c_{21}-c_{23} & c_{23} \\ 0 & c_{32} & 1-c_{32} \end{pmatrix} \cdot \begin{pmatrix} T_{1,k} \\ T_{2,k} \\ T_{3,k} \end{pmatrix}$$

$$+ \begin{pmatrix} 1 & 0 \\ 0 & 0 \\ 0 & 1 \end{pmatrix} \cdot \begin{pmatrix} u_{1,k} \\ u_{2,k} \end{pmatrix}$$

$$y_k = \begin{pmatrix} y_{1,k} \\ y_{2,k} \end{pmatrix} = \begin{pmatrix} 0 & 1 & 0 \\ 0 & 0 & 1 \end{pmatrix} \cdot \begin{pmatrix} T_{1,k} \\ T_{2,k} \\ T_{3,k} \end{pmatrix}$$

$$u_{i,k} = \begin{cases} -0.25, & y_{i,k} \geq T_{\max} \\ 0, & T_{\min} < y_{i,k} < T_{\max} \\ 0.25, & y_{i,k} \leq T_{\min}, \text{ for } i \in \{1,2\}. \end{cases}$$

Table 1: Dynamics of the three-room temperature control system from Figure 9

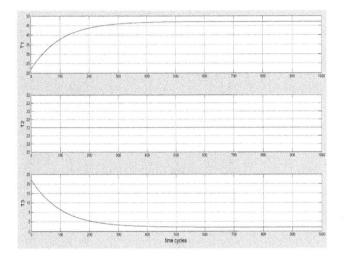

Figure 10: Nominal open-loop behavior of the three-room temperature control system

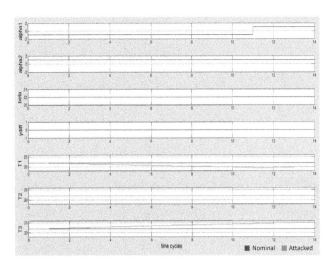

Figure 11: Analysis of the three-room temperature control system. Experiment 1: Only the link from the sensor in room 2 is secure and $\varepsilon = 0$.

an on/off control, i.e. it chooses to cool or heat the rooms, or do nothing, based on two predefined set points $T_{\min}$ and $T_{\max}$. The choice to heat/cool room 1 is based on the measured temperature of room 2. The change of temperature between the rooms is assumed to follow the discretized basic first-order heat balance model, given in Table 1, where positive constants c_{12}, c_{21}, c_{23}, c_{32} represent the heat transfer coefficients between the rooms. For this paper, we assume a symmetric scenario and set $c_{12} = c_{21} = c_{23} = c_{32} = 0.01$.

Figure 10 shows the nominal system behavior from state $T_1 = T_2 = T_3 = 22$ when it operates in open-loop. Constant symmetric heating of room 1 and cooling of room 2 does not change the temperature in room 2. Moreover the heat transfer between rooms 1 and 3 through room 2 stabilizes the temperatures in these rooms at the unacceptable levels of $T_1 = 47$ and $T_3 = -3$. The goal of attacker is to drive this stable system into some unacceptable state. In order to analyze feasible scenarios of such stealth attacks, we made several experiments changing system secure and non-secure links, and changing the level of detectability ε.

In our first experiment, the system is initialized with values $T_1 = 22$, $T_2 = 22$ and $T_3 = 22$, and we set $T_{\min} = 21$ and $T_{\max} = 23$. We assume that the links from the controllers to the actuators in room 1 and room 3, and the link from

the sensor in room 3 to the controller, are not-secure, and that the link from the sensor in room 2 to the controller is secure. Further, we take $\varepsilon = 0$ and define $\Pi = \{(x,k) \mid x \in \mathbb{R}^n, \max_{i \in [1,n]}\{x(i)\} > 25, k \in [0,20] \subseteq \mathbb{N}\}$. The intention of the attacker in this case is to be completely stealth for the maximum of 20 time units and, if physically possible, make sure that in this interval at least one room has temperature above 25 degrees. Applying our method to this setup we receive the results presented in Figure 11. The plot of signal T_2 is showing stealth behavior of the attack, while the signals for T_1 and T_3 are showing that there is a clear difference between the nominal $T_1^{\text{nom}} = T_3^{\text{nom}} = 22$ and the attacked system state. The length of the generated attack is 14, meaning that the system entered a bad state (where at least one state element exceeded the given bound of 25 - in this case T_3) before the bound 20 was reached. The α and β signals indicate that the attack was executed by simultaneous cooling of room 1 (signal α_1), heating of room 3 up to a point after which this room does not influence the system (signal α_2), and sending a fake measurement signal (equal to nominal) to the controller.

Our second experiment is similar to the first one except that we set $\varepsilon = 1$, and we assume that the link from the controller to the actuator in room 3 is now secure. Figure 12 shows that an attack of length 14 still exists, where the system hits a bad state in room 1 (where T_1 is above 25). In this case the attack is still based on simultaneous heating of rooms 1 and 3. However, the cooling is not anymore enforced directly through an actuator (which is now secure) but through the β signal sending the fake measurement value of $T_{\max} = 23$. Note that this attack is only possible for detectability thresholds that are bigger or equal $23 - 22 = 1$.

For the third experiment, we secure all components but the actuator in room 1, and we reduce the detectability threshold ε to 0.3. Figure 13 shows that in this case room 1 can be directly attacked through an actuator to reach level 25, while the temperature in room 2 is only deviated by 0.2 from the nominal case. According to this experiment, the initial phase of attack can target only the room 1, while the change of temperature in room 2 is small due to low heat

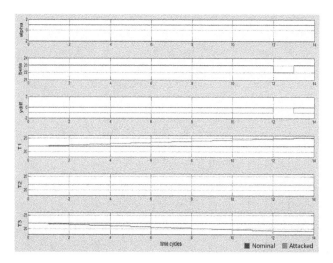

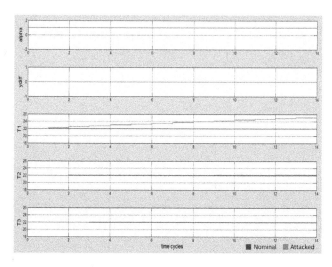

Figure 12: Analysis of the three-room temperature control system. Experiment 2: The link from the sensor in room 2 and the link to the actuator in room 3 are secure, and $\varepsilon = 1$.

transfer constants and undetected due to the low sensitivity of the detector (high ε).

For our final experiment, we set the detectablity threshold back to zero and weaken Π to Π_K for some arbitrary $K \in \mathbb{N}$. As our plant is linear, we can now apply the matrix rank condition from Theorem 2. We consider two cases: i) when only the sensor in room 2 is secure (as in Experiment 1 above), and ii) when both the sensor in room 2 and the actuator in room 3 are (as in Experiment 2). The calculation results in i) $[CB]^{s,ns} = (0\ 0)$, $[CAB]^{s,ns} = (0.01\ 0.01)$ and ii) $[CB]^{s,ns} = (0)$, $[CAB]^{s,ns} = (0.01)$. In the first case $[CAB]^{s,ns}$ is not full column rank, meaning that the attacker can inject non-trivial stealth behavior into the system (with or without a real intention) for an arbitrary period of time. In the second case $[CAB]^{s,ns}$ is full column rank and so this behavior is not possible (under the given strict detectability threshold).

7. OPTIMAL SECURE SYSTEM DESIGN

In this section we present a branch-and-bound algorithm that traverses the space of possible secure/non-secure system decompositions and returns a secure configuration of the minimal cost. For the search we assume that all security elements have a certain predefined cost. Algorithm 1 shows the pseudo code of the algorithm, while Figure 14 depicts the algorithm in operation.

The algorithm takes the user defined cost function as input, as well as all the parameters needed for formal verification analysis. It maintains a priority queue (lowest cost first) of candidate *configurations*, where a configuration is defined as a set of secure components (components 1 to p correspond to actuators, while components $p+1$ to $p+m$ correspond to sensors). Initially, the queue contains the empty configuration only, i.e., we first assume that all components are not secure. When the configuration from the top of the queue is taken, it is immediately discarded if its cost is not lower than the cost of the current optimum final configuration $conf_{\min}$ (line 7); otherwise, it is passed to the formal verification engine. If the verification analysis results in no

Figure 13: Analysis of the three-room temperature control system. Experiment 3: Only the actuator in room 1 is non-secure, and $\varepsilon = 0.3$.

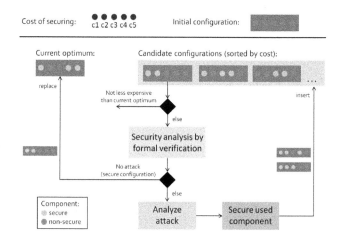

Figure 14: Algorithm for optimal system securing - Snapshot of operation

attack (line 15), the configuration is considered final and the current optimum is updated. If the analysis generated an attack (line 9), for each component used at some place in the attack a new configuration is created containing this component and all the components of the original configuration. The new configurations are then added to the queue based on their costs (line 13), unless they are already in the queue. The algorithm stops when the configuration queue becomes empty, in which case the current optimal configuration represents the global optimum and the solution to the problem.

8. CONCLUSIONS

We presented a formal verification based methodology for discovering stealth attacks on networked control systems. The formal analysis is entirely performed in Simulink, using Simulink Design Verifier, and generates explicit attacks vectors in case the system is found to be non secure. The technique was demonstrated on a simple temperature control system, for different input parameters. To facilitate

Algorithm 1: Branch-and-Bound Algorithm For Optimal System Securing

---

Input: $\mathcal{M}$ - Simulink model template from Figure 7
$K \in \mathbb{N}$ - time bound for verification
$\mathbb{R}^{\geq 0} \ni \varepsilon$ - observability threshold
$\Pi \subseteq \mathbb{R}^n \times \mathbb{N}$ - attack intention property
$cost : [0, p + m] \to \mathbb{N}$ - costs for actuator/sensor
(link) securing

---

1   $Conf = \wp([0, p + m])$ - configuration space
2   $Conf \ni conf_{\min} = \bot$ - current minimum-cost
    configuration (undefined initially)
3   $\mathbf{Queue}\langle Conf\rangle \ni queue = [\emptyset]$ - queue of candidate
    configurations (containing empty configuration initially)

    `// explore queue until empty`
4   **while** $queue \neq []$ **do**
     `// take first configuration and remove it from`
     `queue`
5     $conf = \mathbf{head}(queue)$
6     $queue = \mathbf{tail}(queue)$
     `// proceed with configuration only if its cost is`
     `smaller than current minimum`
7   **if** $conf_{min} = \bot \vee cost(conf) < cost(conf_{min})$ **then**
      `// apply formal verification`
8       $(\alpha, \beta) = \mathbf{FormalVerification}(\mathcal{M}, K, \varepsilon, \Pi, conf)$
      `// check if an attack was discovered or not`
9   **if** $(\alpha, \beta) \neq \bot$ **then**
       `// system not secure; analyze attack`
       `signals to see what components are used`
10   **for** $i \in [0, p + m] \setminus conf$ **do**
        `// if actuator/sensor i is used at some`
        `place in attack, secure it and make a`
        `new candidate configuration`
11   **for** $k \in [0, K]$ **do**
12   **if** $i \leq p \wedge \alpha_k(i) \neq u_k^{ns}(i) \vee i >$
        $p \wedge \beta_k(i - p) \neq y_k^{ns}(i - p)$ **then**
         `// insert based on cost (lowest`
         `cost first)`
13          $\mathbf{insert}(queue, conf \cup \{i\})$
14   **break**
15   **else**
      `// new secure configuration found; update`
      `current minimum`
16       $conf_{\min} = conf$

---

system securing, an algorithm that generates optimal secure configurations based on a user-defined cost function was proposed.

For our future work we plan to address the following challenges: i) scalability - find the right level of overapproximation for our model that would simplify the analysis and make it more scalable, while at the same time not introduce many spurious attacks; ii) metrics - come up with a set of metrics to quantify the negative impact of the attack, and subsequently use them in cost/security tradeoff analysis; and iii) extend analysis to other types of attacks.

9. REFERENCES

[1] A. Armin, A. Cimatti, E. Clarke, M. Fujita, and Y. Zhu. Symbolic model checking using SAT procedures instead of BDDs. In *Proceedings of the 36th annual ACM/IEEE Design Automation Conference*, pages 317–320. ACM, 1999.

[2] C. Baier and J.-P. Katoen. *Principles of model checking*, volume 26202649. MIT press Cambridge, 2008.

[3] S. Bopardikar and A. Speranzon. On analysis and design of stealth-resilient control systems. In *6th IEEE International Symposium on Resilient Control Systems*, 2013.

[4] G. Dan and H. Sandberg. Stealth attacks and protection schemes for state estimators in power systems. In *IEEE Int. Conf. on Smart Grid Communications*, 2010.

[5] D. Goodin. Intruders hack industrial heating system using backdoor posted online, 2012. Available online at: `http://arstechnica.com/security/2012/12/intruders-hack-industrial-control-system-using-backdoor-exploit/`.

[6] F. W. Jr. 'Dr. Chaos' gets seven more years in jail, 2005. Available online at: `http://www.scmagazine.com/dr-chaos-gets-seven-more-years-in-jail/article/32757/`.

[7] J. Leyden. Stuxnet 'a game changer for malware defence', 2010. Available online at: `http://www.theregister.co.uk/2010/10/09/stuxnet\_enisa\_response/`.

[8] MathWorks. Simulink Design Verifier. `http://www.mathworks.com/products/sldesignverifier/`.

[9] F. Pasqualetti, F. Dorfler, and F. Bullo. Attack detection and identification in cyber-physical systems. *IEEE Transaction on Automatic and Control*, 2012. Conditionally accepted.

[10] R. Smith. A decoupled feedback structure for covertly appropriating networked control systems. In *18th International Federation of Automatic Control World Congress*, 2011.

[11] A. Teixeira, D. Pérez, H. Sandberg, and K. Johansson. Attack Models and Scenarios for Networked Control Systems. In *Proceedings of the 1st International Conference on High Confidence Networked Systems*, HiCoNS '12, pages 55–64. ACM, 2012.

[12] A. Teixeira, I. Shames, H. Sandberg, and K. H. Johansson. Revealing Stealthy Attacks in Control Systems. In *50th Annual Allerton Conf. on Communication, Control and Comp.*, 2012.

Graph-Based Verification and Misbehavior Detection in Multi-Agent Networks

Phillip Lee[§], Omar Saleh[†], Basel Alomair[†], Linda Bushnell[§], Radha Poovendran[§]
[§]Department of Electrical Engineering, University of Washington, Seattle, WA 98195
[†] King Abdulaziz City for Science and Technology, Riyadh, Saudi Arabia
Email: leep3@uw.edu, {osaleh, alomair}@kacst.edu.sa, {lb2, rp3}@uw.edu [*]

ABSTRACT

Multi-agent networks consist of autonomous nodes, where each node maintains and updates its state based on exchanged information with its neighboring nodes. Due to the collaborative nature of state updates, if one or more nodes were to misbehave by deviating from the pre-specified update rule, they can bias the states of other nodes and thus drive the network to an undesirable state. In this paper, we present a query-based mechanism for a third-party verifier to detect misbehaving nodes. The proposed mechanism consists of two components. The first component determines whether the state of the queried node is consistent with its ideal value. The second component identifies the set of misbehaving nodes that induced the inconsistency. We prove that our approach detects the set of misbehaving nodes, as well as the times of their misbehaviors, by establishing the equivalence of our approach to a tree-generation algorithm. We evaluate our approach through simulation study which corroborates the theoretical guarantees, and analyzes the performance of our scheme as a function of the number of queried nodes.

Categories and Subject Descriptors

C.2.0 [**General**]: Security and protection

General Terms

Security

Keywords

security; misbehavior; multi-agent network; graph-based verification

1. INTRODUCTION

Formation flight [15], environmental monitoring [1] and wide-area surveillance [18] are applications where networked nodes collaborate in order to perform maneuvering, sensing and computation. This collaboration is typically achieved by having each node

maintain an internal state, which is updated according to a pre-specified rule, based on information exchanged with the node's neighbors [14]. The objective of the system can be quantified as a desired set of node states to be achieved. Under this approach, the update and broadcast of individual node state forms part of the network control signals that are required for coordination of network missions.

Since the state update relies on inputs provided by neighboring nodes, a set of misbehaving nodes can bias the state updates of their neighbors by broadcasting incorrect state values. A node could be misbehaving because it is faulty or malicious [17]. These errors in the node states introduced by misbehaving nodes will propagate through the network via the local update. Detecting such misbehaving nodes has received significant attention from the control and fault tolerant computing literatures [9, 10, 17, 20].

Existing methods consider detection of misbehaving nodes at a local level [17, 20] by the nodes themselves. However, in applications such as formation flight of unmanned vehicles [11] and network consensus [7, 19] , there exists an external entity with knowledge of the deployed network (initial states, state dynamics, and network topology) that can communicate with a subset of nodes at any given time and hence can participate in the detection process. An example is leader-follower systems [11] where the set of leader nodes receive control inputs from the external entity, and act as actuators that drive the system to a desired operating point.

In this paper, we study the problem of detecting misbehaving nodes in a multi-agent network in the presence of a third-party verifier. Under our approach, each node cryptographically signs its state update messages, which are stored by the neighboring nodes. We propose a detection mechanism in which a third party verifier queries the subset of network nodes and receives the signed messages stored by the queried nodes. In developing this detection mechanism, we make the following specific contributions:

- We develop a query-based mechanism for a third-party verifier to detect misbehaving nodes. The proposed mechanism consists of two components. In the first component, the verifier determines whether the nodes are updating their states correctly by comparing the queried states to the ideal states. Upon detection of inconsistent states, the second component identifies the set of misbehaving nodes that are inducing the inconsistency.

- We classify three types of disjoint events that could lead to an inconsistent state of a node: the event where the node computes its state according to the correct update rule, but receives inconsistent inputs; the event where the node computes the update rule incorrectly; and the case where both of these events occur. We present an algorithm that identifies which type of event caused an inconsistent state.

[*]This work was supported by a grant from the King Abdulaziz City for Science and Technology (KACST).

Permission to make digital or hard copies of all or part of this work for personal or classroom use is granted without fee provided that copies are not made or distributed for profit or commercial advantage and that copies bear this notice and the full citation on the first page. Copyrights for components of this work owned by others than ACM must be honored. Abstracting with credit is permitted. To copy otherwise, or republish, to post on servers or to redistribute to lists, requires prior specific permission and/or a fee. Request permissions from permissions@acm.org.
HiCoNS'14, April 15–17, 2014, Berlin, Germany.
Copyright 2014 ACM 978-1-4503-2652-0/14/04 ...$15.00.
http://dx.doi.org/10.1145/2566468.2566477.

- We develop a decision-tree growing algorithm that identifies misbehaving nodes and times of their misbehaviors by systematically searching for sources of inconsistency based on the identified type of event. Under the assumption that misbehaving nodes do not share cryptographic information (non-colluding), we show the proposed tree growing algorithm detects and identifies misbehaving nodes that are inducing inconsistent states of nodes.

The rest of the paper is organized as follows. In Section 2, we review relevant related work on detection of misbehaving nodes in multi-agent networks. In Section 3, we state the definitions and assumptions used in this paper. In Section 4, we formulate the problem of detecting and identifying misbehaving nodes in multi-agent networks and propose a query-based detection mechanism. The effectiveness of the proposed detection mechanism is then proved. In Section 5, we present a simulation to illustrate the effectiveness of our approach. Section 6 presents our conclusions and future work.

2. RELATED WORK

Ensuring reliable performance of a distributed system in the presence of faulty and malicious components has been studied in the context of Byzantine failures in distributed computing [13], fault-tolerant control of dynamic systems [4], and secure routing in networking [2]. The Byzantine failure model in distributed computing assumes a set of nodes (processors) can fail in arbitrary ways while executing an algorithm in a distributed manner. A successful termination of an algorithm requires a bound on the number of failed nodes [13]. Specifically, if f nodes can fail simultaneously, at least $(2f + 1)$ nodes must be deployed in the network.

An analogous result was proved in the context of distributed consensus in multi-agent networks [20] where each node updates its state using linear iteration to obtain correct initial states of other nodes. In these works, the state dynamics is represented as a linear dynamical system, and incorrect state values of malicious nodes as unknown inputs. It was proved that if f nodes are malicious in the network, a graph connectivity of at least $(2f + 1)$ is required for every node to agree on the initial states of other nodes. This work is based on the theory of unknown input observer (UIO) [5, 6, 8]. Moreover, it was also shown that once a node has obtained correct initial states of other nodes, it can detect and identify malicious nodes in the network given the full network topology and state update dynamics of all other nodes. However, this approach requires that each node has the knowledge of the entire network topology and state dynamics, and is computationally hard for each node due to combinatorial search.

To overcome this difficulty, a detection scheme based on decentralized UIO was introduced in [17] where a set of nodes cooperatively detect misbehaving nodes. Similar approach was also taken in [16] where the authors designed a distributed intrusion detection system based on UIO. Malicious nodes in wireless control networks was studied in [21], where the authors proved that if the connectivity of the wireless network is sufficiently high, it suffices to observe only a set of nodes in the network to jointly diagnose faults in the plant and detect malicious nodes.

A related body of work that focuses on providing resilience of multi-agent networks against misbehaving nodes has been explored in [12,22]. These approaches are based on local filtering techniques where a node chooses from the set of received inputs to update its state. In [12], a low complexity algorithm based on local filtering was introduced where a node removes f largest and smallest inputs. A sufficient condition for consensus was given as a function of the in-and out degree distributions. A consensus protocol based

on similar local filtering technique was studied in [22]. The authors introduce the notion of r-robustness, and characterize conditions in terms of r-robustness to guarantee consensus when there are at most r malicious nodes in the neighborhood of any node. However, these works do not consider proactive detection and identification of misbehaving nodes.

Existing works utilize mathematical structures of network dynamics and topology of the network to provide detection and mitigation strategies at a local level. These methods, however, do not incorporate the available cryptographic primitives to facilitate detection, and do not leverage the presence of external entities that have knowledge of the network dynamics.

In our view, our work is complementary to the existing methods in that we employ cryptographic mechanisms to detect and identify misbehaving nodes by an external entity. Therefore, our proposed methods may be used in conjunction with the existing methods.

3. PRELIMINARIES

In this section, we present models of the network, state update dynamics, misbehaving nodes and third party verifier. Table 1 lists the notations used in this paper.

3.1 Network Model

We consider a homogeneous network with N nodes where each node communicates with a set of neighboring nodes $\mathcal{N}(n_i)$, which is assumed to be time-invariant for all nodes n_i. We assume a broadcasting communication model where each node transmits its message to all its neighbors simultaneously. A suitable media access control (MAC) protocol [3] is assumed to be implemented so that whenever a node broadcasts its message, it will be received by all its neighboring nodes. We assume the deployed network is connected, i.e., there exists at least one path between any two nodes in the network.

Each node n_i is assigned a unique public and private key pair $(K_{n_i}, K_{n_i}^{-1})$. Every node stores its own private key and public keys of its neighboring nodes. Each node is also required to store all messages received from its neighbors in the previous M time slots.

Table 1: A summary of notations used

Symbol	Definition
n_i	Identity of node i
$\mathcal{V}$	Third party verifier
$\mathcal{N}(n_i)$	Set of neighboring nodes of node i
M	Time slot of inspection
Q	Set of queried nodes
$x_{n_i}(m)$	State of node i at time m
$X(m)$	$\{x_{n_i}(m) \mid \forall n_i\}$
$X_{\mathcal{N}(n_i)}(m)$	$\{x_{n_j}(m) \mid n_j \in \mathcal{N}(n_i)\}$
$\hat{x}_{n_i}(m)$	Ideal state of node i at time m
$f_i(\cdot)$	Node n_i's state update function.
$IN_{n_i}(m)$	Set of input values for node n_i's state update at time m
$\widehat{IN}_{n_i}(m)$	Set of ideal input values for node n_i's state update at time m
$\widetilde{IN}_{n_i}(m)$	Elements in $IN_{n_i}(m)$ that are inconsistent
$ID(x)$	ID of the node that transmitted message x
K_{n_i}	Public key assigned to node n_i
$K_{n_i}^{-1}$	Private key assigned to node n_i
$sig_{K_{n_i}^{-1}}(x)$	Message x signed with private key $K_{n_i}^{-1}$

3.2 State Update Dynamics

We consider a discrete-time multi-agent network where time is slotted into intervals of equal duration. It is assumed that each node is aware of the beginning and end of each time slot.

During mth time slot, each node n_i is responsible for updating its state $x_{n_i}(m)$ to $x_{n_i}(m+1)$ before the beginning of $(m+1)$th time slot in a specified manner. To update its state during mth time slot, each node n_i first constructs a message by concatenating its ID, current time slot, and its current state. Node n_i then digitally signs the constructed message with its private key, attaches the signature to the constructed message, and broadcasts the message to its neighboring nodes. In addition, after receiving signed messages from its neighbors, node n_i verifies validity of received messages by verifying signatures using stored public keys of neighbors.

If the verification test is successful, then node n_i accepts the message as valid. If not, node n_i discards the message. If node n_i does not receive a valid message from node n_j during the mth time slot, node n_i sets $x_{n_j}(m) = $ Null. It is assumed that Null is a valid input parameter for the function $f_i(\cdot)$, but not a valid output. Each node is responsible for broadcasting its state to its neighbors for all time slots.

After verification, node n_i extracts the current states of neighbors, $X_{\mathcal{N}(i)}(m) = \{x_{n_j}(m)|n_j \in \mathcal{N}(n_i)\}$, and updates its state with its current state and current states of neighbors. The update process of node n_i during mth time slot is described as below.

1. n_i constructs the message described as above and broadcasts the message to its neighbors.

$$n_i \to \mathcal{N}(n_i) : \left(n_i||m||x_{n_i}(m)||sig_{K_{n_i}^{-1}}(n_i||m||x_{n_i}(m))\right)$$

2. n_i verifies validity of the message received from node n_j. If valid, accept the message. If not, discard. If node n_i does not receive a valid message from node n_j, record n_j's state as Null.

3. n_i extracts $X_{\mathcal{N}(i)}(m) = \{x_{n_j}(m)|n_j \in \mathcal{N}(n_i)\}$, current state of neighbors that are valid from received messages.

4. Update its state using the specified update function $f_i(\cdot)$

$$x_{n_i}(m+1) = f_i(X_{\mathcal{N}(n_i)}(m), x_{n_i}(m), Nulls)$$

The set of input values node n_i uses to update its state during time slot m is denoted as $IN_{n_i}(m) = \{X_{\mathcal{N}(n_i)}(m-1)\}, x_{n_i}(m-1)\}$.

3.3 Adversary Model

We say that a node n_i is misbehaving if it broadcasted its initial state falsely during time slot $m = 0$ or if it computed its updated function $f_i(\cdot)$ incorrectly for at least one time slot $m \geq 0$. Mathematically, node n_i is misbehaving if

$$x_{n_i}(m+1) \neq f_i(X_{\mathcal{N}(n_i)}(m), x_{n_i}(m))$$

for at least one time slot $m \geq 0$. The set of misbehaving nodes is classified into two categories: faulty and malicious. We assume that malicious nodes are capable of following behaviors. First, when asked by a third party verifier to give its current or previous states, a malicious node is capable of returning false states. Second, while a faulty node always broadcasts its current state truthfully to its neighbors, a malicious node is capable of broadcasting its state untruthfully. We assume, however, that malicious nodes are not colluding with each other. Specifically, each malicious node is unaware of the identity or private key of any other malicious node.

We also assume that there exists at least one node that is not malicious in $\mathcal{N}(n_i)$ for every node n_i that is capable of returning correct message to the third party verifier at the time of query.

3.4 Third Party Verification Model

A third party verifier who is aware of the initial states of nodes, and the set of specified update functions can generate ideal states of nodes at any given time slot. The table of ideal states of every node till the current time slot is referred to as the truth table. In what follows, the third party verifier will be referred to as the verifier and is denoted as $\mathcal{V}$.

The verifier can be the network owner if he is within a communication range of at least one node in the network. If not, the network owner relegates the responsibility of the verifier to a trusted third party that is within the communication range of at least one node. In order to relegate, the network owner sends the third party its truth table, set of update functions for every node, and public keys associated with each node.

Given the ideal state of node n_i at time m, $\hat{x}_{n_i}(m)$, the verifier is capable of checking whether the actual state is within an acceptable bound. The state of node n_i at time m is defined to be inconsistent if

$$|\hat{x}_{n_i}(m) - x_{n_i}(m)| \geq \epsilon(n_i, m)$$

where $\epsilon(n_i, m) > 0$ is a predefined threshold. $\epsilon(n_i, m)$ is chosen based on how much deviation the verifier is willing to tolerate for node n_i at time m. In this paper, a Null state is classified as an inconsistent state. For example, consider a distributed averaging update dynamics given as

$$X(m+1) = WX(m).$$

In such scenario, the network may stop further linear iteration when every node reaches a value that is within some ϵ range of the true average to save further communication and computation overhead. Furthermore, it is known [14] that the linear update dynamics for distributed averaging is marginally stable, i.e., matrix W has one eigenvalue equal to 1 and all other eigenvalues have magnitude less than 1. Moreover, the eigenvector that is associated with the eigenvalue 1 has same values in all entries. This implies that, as long as $|\hat{x}_{n_i}(m) - x_{n_i}(m)| < \epsilon$, for all n_i, the deviation on the $m + 1$th time slot is bounded as $|\hat{x}_{n_i}(m+1) - x_{n_i}(m+1)| < \epsilon$. Such deviations can be tolerated since the state of every node will converge to a value that lies within ϵ of the average of the initial states.

This notion of tolerable deviation from the ideal behavior can be generalized in the following way. The verifier can choose $\epsilon(n_i, m)$ such that if all inputs were consistent at time m, and $f_i(\cdot)$ was computed correctly, then $x_{n_i}(m+1)$ would also be consistent. A sufficient condition for the existence of such ϵ values is given in the following lemma.

LEMMA 3.1. *If the update function $f_i(\cdot)$ for each node n_i is continuous around the ideal input states for all time slots $m \leq M$, then $\epsilon(n_i, m) > 0$ values can be constructed such that if $|\hat{x}_{n_j}(m-1) - x_{n_j}(m-1)| < \epsilon(n_j, m-1)$ for all $n_j \in \mathcal{N}(n_i)$, and $|\hat{x}_{n_i}(m-1) - x_{n_i}(m-1)| < \epsilon(n_i, m-1)$, then $|\hat{x}_{n_i}(m) - x_{n_i}(m)| < \epsilon(n_i, m)$ for all time $m \leq M$.*

PROOF. Choose $\epsilon(n_i, M) > 0$. From the definition of continuity, there exists $\epsilon(n_j, M-1)$ for $n_j \in \mathcal{N}(n_i)$ and $\epsilon(n_i, M-1)$ such that if $|\hat{x}_{n_j}(M-1) - x_{n_j}(M-1)| < \epsilon(n_j, M-1)$ and $|\hat{x}_{n_i}(M-1) - x_{n_i}(M-1)| < \epsilon(n_i, M-1)$, then $|\hat{x}_{n_i}(M) - x_{n_i}(M)| < \epsilon(n_i, M)$. The same argument can be made for time slot $M - 1$. Therefore, $\epsilon(n_i, m)$ values can be constructed recursively starting from any time slot $M > 0$. $\square$

4. QUERY-BASED DETECTION

Under our approach, the external verifier periodically checks whether the network states are consistent. Further inspections are made as needed to determine the source of any inconsistencies.

We propose a detection mechanism where the verifier queries the stored state information in nodes to detect inconsistent states and identify misbehaving nodes. The detection process starts at the beginning of time slot M. The verifier selects a set of nodes, Q to be queried. Each node in Q is queried to return the messages it received from its neighbors during the previous time slot. If no inconsistent states are found, then the detection process ends. For each inconsistent state found during time slot $M - 1$, further inspections are required to identify the set of misbehaving nodes that induced the inconsistent state at time $M - 1$. The following two subsections describe the query-based algorithms that are building blocks of the detection mechanism.

4.1 Determining Cause of Inconsistency

In Section 3.4, we defined the notion of consistent state such that if all input states were consistent, and update function was computed correctly, then the resulting updated state is also consistent. Hence, if $x_{n_i}(m)$ was inconsistent for some time slot $m \geq 1$, it would be due to the occurrence of one of the following events. We label these different types of events as E_1, E_2, E_3.

- E_1: Node n_i computed $f_i(\cdot)$ correctly but one or more elements of the set $IN_{n_i}(m - 1)$ were inconsistent.

- E_2: Node n_i computed $f_i(\cdot)$ incorrectly during the $(m-1)$th time slot but every element of $IN_i(m - 1)$ was consistent.

- E_3: Node n_i computed $f_i(\cdot)$ incorrectly during the $(m-1)$th time slot and one or more elements of $IN_{n_i}(m - 1)$ were inconsistent.

During the initial time slot $m = 0$, if the broadcasted state $x_{n_i}(0)$ was inconsistent, we label this event as type E_2. A illustration of the three types of events is shown in Figure 1.

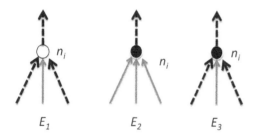

Figure 1: Illustration of the three types of events that could result in inconsistent state of node n_i. Dashed lines indicate inconsistent states. Filled circles indicate incorrect computation of the update function. (a) E_1: Node n_i computes the function $f_i(\cdot)$ correctly but resulting state is inconsistent due to inconsistent inputs. (b) E_2: All inputs are consistent but node n_i computes $f_i(\cdot)$ incorrectly. (c) E_3: Node n_i computes $f_i(\cdot)$ incorrectly and one or more inputs are inconsistent.

Determining which type of event induced inconsistency of a given state is the first step of the detection process. We propose an algorithm that determines which type of event led to a given inconsistent state.

Given an inconsistent state $x_{n_i}(m)$, the verifier must first reconstruct the input values node n_i has used during time slot $m - 1$ to

update its state. To do so, The verifier sends a request to node n_j for the messages received from node n_i during time slot $(m - 1)$. The verifier also requests to node n_i for the messages n_i received from its neighbors during time slot $(m - 1)$. Since we assume that malicious nodes are capable of responding to queries with incorrect state values, no node is queried to return its own state.

Both n_i and n_j sign the requested messages with their respective private keys and send the requested messages back to the verifier. After having received requested messages, the verifier authenticates the received messages via the attached digital signatures and extracts $X_{n_i}(m - 1)$ and $X_{\mathcal{N}(n_i)}(m - 1)$ from the messages. A pseudocode description of the algorithm to construct $IN_{n_i}(m - 1)$ is given as algorithm **ConstructIN**.

Algorithm ConstructIN	
Input: $x_{n_i}(m)$	
Output: $IN_{n_i}(m - 1)$	
Query $n_j \in \mathcal{N}(n_i)$	1
$n_j \to \mathcal{V}$: signed message n_i sent to n_j or Null	2
Query n_i	3
$n_i \to \mathcal{V}$: signed message n_i received from $\mathcal{N}(n_i)$ or Nulls	4
Return $IN_{n_i}(m - 1) = \{X_{\mathcal{N}(n_i)}(m - 1), x_{n_i}(m - 1)\}$	5

Figure 2: Algorithm for reconstructing input values node n_i has used to update its state during time slot $(m - 1)$

After constructing the input values $IN_{n_i}(m - 1)$ using the algorithm ConstructIN, the next step for the verifier is to determine which type of event led to the inconsistent state $x_{n_i}(m)$. There are two separate cases to be considered.

Case 1. $IN_{n_i}(m - 1)$ did not contain a Null message: In the case when $IN_{n_i}(m - 1)$ did not contain a Null message, the verifier computes $\bar{x}_{n_i}(m) = f_i(IN_{n_i}(m - 1))$ using the returned output values from ConstructIN, $IN_{n_i}(m - 1)$. If $\bar{x}_{n_i}(m) = x_{n_i}(m)$, then the verifier concludes that event type E_1 has occurred since the function was computed correctly at time slot $(m-1)$. If $\bar{x}_{n_i}(m) \neq x_{n_i}(m)$, then the verifier needs to distinguish between E_2 and E_3.

The verifier collects inconsistent elements from the set $IN_{n_i}(m-1)$ by comparing the values with the truth table and constructs a subset $\widetilde{IN}_{n_i}(m - 1)$. If $\widetilde{IN}_{n_i}(m - 1) = \emptyset$, (there was no inconsistent element in $IN_{n_i}(m - 1)$) then E_2 must have occurred. If there is an inconsistent element $\widetilde{IN}_{n_i}(m - 1) \neq \emptyset$, then E_3 has occurred.

Case 2. $IN_{n_i}(m - 1)$ contained at least one Null message: Unlike a valid signed state which cannot be forged, any node can falsely claim that it did not receive any message from its neighbors at a given time slot, since Null message does not have any signature attached to it by nature. If n_i claims that it did not receive any message from its neighbor n_j at time slot $(m-1)$, the verifier takes the following steps to determine whether node n_i is falsely reporting or not. First, the verifier requests to every node in $\mathcal{N}(n_j)$ for the message it received from node n_j at time slot $(m - 1)$.

If at least one node in $\mathcal{N}(n_j)$ returns a valid signed message from node n_j during time slot $(m - 1)$, then the verifier concludes that node n_i is falsely claiming that it did not receive any input state from n_j. Consequently, n_i is identified as a misbehaving node for ignoring a received input. The verifier now needs to distinguish between event types E_2 and E_3. To do so, the verifier reconstructs the message $IN_{n_i}(m - 1)$ by replacing a falsely claimed Null with the signed message of n_j and check whether newly constructed $IN_{n_i}(m - 1)$ has contained any inconsistent element. If $\widetilde{IN}_{n_i}(m - 1) = \emptyset$, then E_2 has occurred, if not E_3 has occurred.

On the other hand, if all nodes in $\mathcal{N}(n_j)$ claim that no message was transmitted from n_j at time slot $(m-1)$, or if n_i is the only neighboring node of n_j, then it is concluded that n_j did not transmit any message during time slot $m-1$. Since Null state is classified as an inconsistent state by convention, the verifier now needs to distinguish between event types E_1 and E_3. The verifier computes $\bar{x}_{n_i}(m) = f_i(IN_{n_i}(m-1))$. If $\bar{x}_{n_i}(m) = x_{n_i}(m)$, then verifier concludes E_1 has occurred. If $\bar{x}_{n_i}(m) \neq x_{n_i}(m)$, then E_3 has occurred. A pseudocode description of the algorithm is given as algorithm **DecideType**.

Algorithm DecideType

Input: Inconsistent state $x_{n_i}(m)$

Output: Type of Event

Initialization:

$IN_{n_i}(m-1) \leftarrow \text{ConstructIN}(x_{n_i}(m))$	1
if Null $\notin IN_{n_i}(m-1)$	2
$\quad \bar{x}_{n_i}(m) \leftarrow f_i(IN_{n_i}(m-1))$	3
$\quad$ **if** $\bar{x}_{n_i}(m) = x_{n_i}(m)$	4
$\quad\quad$ **return** E_1; **exit**	5
$\quad$ **else**	6
$\quad\quad$ Construct $\widetilde{IN}_{n_i}(m-1)$	
$\quad\quad$ **if** $\widetilde{IN}_{n_i}(m-1) = \emptyset$	7
$\quad\quad\quad$ **return** E_2; **exit**	8
$\quad\quad$ **else**	9
$\quad\quad\quad$ **return** E_3; **exit**	10
$\quad$ **end**	11
else Null $\in IN_{n_i}(m-1)$	12
For all n_j such that $x_{n_j}(m-1) = \text{Null}$	13
Request to all $n_k \in \mathcal{N}(n_j)$ for $x_{n_j}(m-1)$	14
if exists at least one n_k such that	15
$n_k \rightarrow \mathcal{V}$: signed message n_j sent to n_k during time $(m-1)$	16
Replace Null with $x_{n_j}(m-1)$ in $IN_{n_i}(m-1)$	17
Construct $\widetilde{IN}_{n_i}(m-1)$	18
$\quad$ **if** $\widetilde{IN}_{n_i}(m-1) = \emptyset$	19
$\quad\quad$ **return** E_2; **exit**	20
$\quad$ **else**	21
$\quad\quad$ **return** E_3; **exit**	22
else	23
$\quad \bar{x}_{n_i}(m) \leftarrow f_i(IN_{n_i}(m-1))$	24
$\quad$ **if** $\bar{x}_{n_i}(m) = x_{n_i}(m)$	25
$\quad\quad$ **return** E_1; **exit**	26
$\quad$ **else**	27
$\quad\quad$ **return** E_3; **exit**	28

Figure 3: Algorithm for determining which event led to inconsistent state $x_{n_i}(m)$

The algorithm DecideType cannot be executed for an inconsistent state $x_{n_i}(m)$ at time slot m if the necessary data required to construct $IN_{n_i}(m-1)$ is not stored in any nodes. Since each node is required to store all messages it received from its neighbors in the previous M time slots, DecideType can be executed for any inconsistent state during time slots $m \in \{1...M-1\}$. Using the algorithm DecideType as the building block, we now proceed to describe the main algorithm which detects all misbehaving nodes that induced an inconsistent state at time slot $M-1$.

4.2 Identifying Misbehaving Nodes

The intuition behind the proposed algorithm is the following: Given an inconsistent node state, the cause for the inconsistency is either E_2 or other types of events (E_1 or E_3). If the event type is E_2, then the node's misbehavior during the previous time slot was

the sole cause of inconsistency. If the type is not E_2, then there existed at least one inconsistent state used by the node to update its state during the previous time slot, and the same argument can be made for each inconsistent state during the previous time slot.

This detection process is represented as a tree-generation algorithm. The output of the algorithm is a tree $\mathcal{T}$ with root vertex $x_{n_i}(M-1)$ and maximum depth of M. Vertices at depth d (denoted as V_d) represent the set of inconsistent states at time slot $(M-d)$ that contributed to the inconsistency of $x_{n_i}(M-1)$. Every vertex is labeled with the event type ($E_1, E_2, or E_3$) of the inconsistency of the vertex.

The algorithm starts by setting an inconsistent state $x_{n_i}(M-1)$ as a root vertex. The root vertex is at depth $d = 1$. Root vertex is labeled with the output of DecideType($x_{n_i}(M-1)$). If the output is E_2, then the algorithm terminates. If not, then $\widetilde{IN}_{n_i}(M-2)$ are added as children vertices to the root vertex. The same process is repeated for every vertex v at depth d. Vertex v is labeled with DecideType(v), and $\widetilde{IN}_{ID(v)}(M-(d+1))$ are added as children vertices to v. The algorithm is terminated if all vertices in V_d are labeled with E_2 or the depth of the tree is equal to M. A pseudocode description of the algorithm is given as algorithm **GrowTree**.

Algorithm GrowTree

Input: Inconsistent state $x_{n_i}(M-1)$

Output: Tree $\mathcal{T}$ with root vertex $x_{n_i}(M-1)$, depth $d \leq M$

Initialization:

Set $x_{n_i}(M-1)$ as root vertex of tree $\mathcal{T}$,

$d \leftarrow 1$;

$\quad$ **While** $d < M$	1
$\quad\quad$ **For** $v \in V_d$	2
$\quad\quad$ Label v with DecideType(v);	3
$\quad\quad$ **if** DecideType($x_{n_i}(m)$) $\neq E_2$	4
$\quad\quad\quad$ Add children vertices $\widetilde{IN}_{ID(v)}(M-(d+1))$ to v;	5
$\quad\quad$ **end**	6
$\quad\quad$ **If** $|V_{d+1}| == 0$	7
$\quad\quad\quad$ **Return** $\mathcal{T}$ **exit**;	8
$\quad\quad$ **else**	9
$\quad\quad\quad$ $d \leftarrow d + 1$	10
$\quad\quad$ **end**	11
$\quad$ **Return** $\mathcal{T}$	

Figure 4: Algorithm of tree generation to detect misbehaving nodes that contributed to the inconsistent state of node n_i at time $M-1$

After having obtained the output tree $\mathcal{T}$, the verifier can identify misbehaving nodes in the following way. If a vertex that resides in depth d, v_d is labeled with E_2 or E_3, this implies the node that broadcasted v_d misbehaved during $M-(d+1)$.

In order for the proposed algorithm to be executed successfully at time slot M, each node needs to store all signed states from its neighbors in the previous M slots. Assuming each node is equipped with the same amount of memory, the least amount of memory required is $M \cdot \max_{n_i} |\mathcal{N}(n_i)|$ messages. We now proceed to prove properties of the proposed algorithm.

DEFINITION 4.1. *We define the set of misbehaving nodes $B(x_{n_i}(M-1))$ as* inconsistency-inducing nodes *of an inconsistent state $x_{n_i}(M-1)$ if the following two conditions are true:*

- *Node $n_j \in B(x_{n_i}(M-1))$ misbehaved at least once during time slots $\{0...M-2\}$.*

- *If $x_{n_j}(m+1) = f_j(IN_{n_j}(m))$ for all time slots $m \in \{0...M-2\}$, then $x_{n_i}(M-1)$ would be a consistent state.*

Definition 4.1 states that if every node in $B(x_{n_i}(M-1))$ behaved correctly from time 0 to time $M-2$, then $x_{n_i}(M-1)$ would be a consistent state.

DEFINITION 4.2. *A full information tree $\mathcal{T}_F$ with root vertex $x_{n_i}(M-1)$ is a tree with depth M where each vertex represents a state of a node and children vertices are input states used to compute the parent vertex.*

An example of a full information tree with $M=4$ is shown in Figure 5.

THEOREM 4.3. *$GrowTree(x_{n_i}(M-1))$ detects all inconsistency-inducing nodes of $x_{n_i}(M-1)$, $B(x_{n_i}(M-1))$.*

PROOF. Consider a full information tree $\mathcal{T}_F$ with root vertex $x_{n_i}(M-1)$. The tree $\mathcal{T}$ generated by the algorithm **GrowTree** is a subtree of $\mathcal{T}_F$ with the same root vertex. Note that every leaf vertex v_{leaf} of $\mathcal{T}$ is labeled with E_2, and all vertices on the path from a leaf vertex to the root vertex is labeled with either E_1 or E_3. If all misbehaving nodes that induced events E_2, E_3 behaved correctly, then the tree will only be left with vertices with label E_1, but all information flow through vertices labeled E_1 will be consistent since children vertices of v_{leaf} in $\mathcal{T}_F$ are all consistent states. Since **GrowTree** can detect all nodes that are responsible for vertices labeled E_2, E_3 in the tree, **GrowTree** detects all nodes in $B(x_{n_i}(M-1))$. $\square$

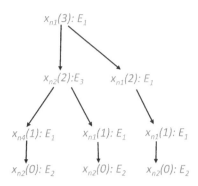

Figure 6: Illustration of the tree-generation algorithm executed on the example 5 (Figure 5). DecideType($x_{n_1}(3)$) returns event 1, inconsistent inputs used by node n_1 at time slot 2 is added as children vertices to the root vertex. Each vertex at depth 2 are labeled with outputs of DecideType($x_{n_2}(2)$), DecideType($x_{n_1}(2)$) and children vertices are added accordingly. Same process is run at depth 3. The verifier concludes that node n_2 broadcasted inconsistent initial state during time slot 0 and updated its state incorrectly during time slot 1.

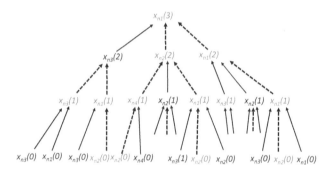

Figure 5: Example of inconsistent states from previous time slots affecting the state of node n_i at time slot 3. Dashed lines indicate inconsistent states transmitted to neighboring nodes.

The verifier runs the algorithm **GrowTree**($x_{n_i}(M-1)$) for each inconsistent state $x_{n_i}(M-1)$ to identify the set of misbehaving nodes that induced the inconsistency of $x_{n_i}(M-1)$.

5. SIMULATION STUDY

In this section, we conduct a numerical study using MATLAB. The goal of this study is to evaluate relationships between the inspection time slot M, average number of nodes being queried $|Q|$, and the probability of detecting misbehaving nodes in the network.

A wireless network consisting of 300 nodes is simulated. Nodes are distributed uniformly on a square with side length of 2000 units. Transmission range of each node is 200 units.

Each node's state dynamics is given as

$$X(m+1) = (I - \alpha \cdot L)X(m) \qquad (1)$$

where L is the Laplacian matrix [14] of the deployed network, and $\alpha = 0.01$ to guarantee convergence. Under the dynamics 1, each node's state converges to the average value of the initial states of the nodes, provided the network is connected. Each node is given an initial state drawn uniformly from the interval $(0, 100)$. Five percent of nodes are chosen at random as misbehaving nodes. At each time slot, a misbehaving node adds a Gaussian random variable of zero mean and variance 4 to its updated state. Each node is independently chosen as a queried node with probability q. An example of the simulated network topology is shown in Figure 7.

The detection probability is estimated via Monte-Carlo methods. We performed 30 trials for each $M = 3, 5, 7$. Probability of detection is given as number of detected nodes divided by the number of misbehaving nodes in the network. We simulated two scenarios. In the first scenario, a state of node n_i is considered to be inconsistent at time slot m if $|\hat{x}_{n_i}(m) - x_{n_i}(m)| > 0$ for all m. In the second scenario, the verifier is willing to tolerate a small deviation from the ideal state, and a node's state is considered to be inconsistent if $|\hat{x}_{n_i}(m) - x_{n_i}(m)| > 0.3$. The acceptable range of 0.3 is chosen to be small compared to the average of the initial states of nodes. The simulation results of the first and second scenarios are shown in Figures 8 and 9, respectively.

For the networks simulated in our study, misbehaving nodes were detected with high probability (Figure 8). The probability of detection increases monotonically in q and M. As q increases from 0.01 to 1, the probability of detection increases in a logarithmic rate for all simulated values of M. This implies that there exists a threshold value of q such that once q exceeds the threshold value, detection probability does not increase as q increases. The fraction of nodes that needs to be queried to detect all misbehaving nodes is approximately 0.4 for $M = 3$, 0.2 for $M = 5$, and 0.1 for $M = 7$. In this case, any misbehaving node always induces inconsistency and any misbehaving node that is within M hops away from the queried node will be detected with probability one.

Figure 9 illustrates the detection probability of misbehaving nodes when small deviations from the ideal state are accepted. In this case, only the misbehaving nodes that induced deviations greater than the acceptable range are detected. It is observed that probability of detection increases in a similar logarithmic rate in q as in

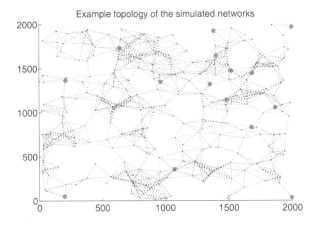

Figure 7: **Example topology of the simulated network. 300 Nodes were uniformly deployed in a squre with length 2000 units. Each node has a communication range 200 units. 5 % of the nodes were chosen as misbehaving nodes. Filled red circles indicate locations of misbehaving nodes.**

Figure 8. On the other hand, it is observed that increase in M does not increase the probability of detection as much as it did in the first scenario. Since each misbehaving node injects a zero mean Gaussian noise independently from each other at each state update iteration, positive and negative errors from different nodes may cancel out, resulting in a consistent state update within the acceptable range by the non-misbehaving nodes. Therefore, the overall induced inconsistency does not propagate throughout the network as fast as in the first scenario.

6. CONCLUSION AND FUTURE WORK

In this paper, the problem of detecting and identifying misbehaving nodes in multi-agent networks was studied. We considered a class of multi-agent networks where a third-party verifier has a knowledge of the deployed network topology and node dynamics. We proposed a detection mechanism where the verifier queries a partial set of nodes periodically, obtains the node state values from the query responses, and detects inconsistent states by comparing the state values from the queries with the ideal state values. We proposed an algorithm that systematically searches for misbehaving nodes that could have caused the detected inconsistent state. We proved that the proposed approach is equivalent to as a rooted tree-generation algorithm where the verifier can identify detected misbehaving nodes and their types of misbehaviors by examining the output tree. The effectiveness of the proposed detection mechanism was analyzed. Specifically, it was proved that starting from a node with an inconsistent state, the tree-generation algorithm detects all misbehaving nodes such that if these nodes have not misbehaved, the identified inconsistent state would instead be a consistent state.

In future work, we will investigate detection mechanisms against colluding misbehaving nodes where the misbehaving nodes are operated by one adversarial entity in a coordinated manner. We will also study how to deterministically choose the set of queried nodes Q given the network topology. Also, in this paper, we considered a broadcast communication model where if a node transmits a message, it will be received by all its neighbors. In future work, we will consider a more general case where communication links fail prob-

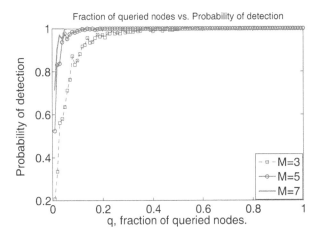

Figure 8: **Simulation results comparing probability of detection with inspection period M. The fraction of nodes being queried ranges from $q = 0.01$ to $q = 1$. Three different values of $M = 3, 5, 7$ were simulated via Monte-Carlo methods with 30 trials each. Misbehaving nodes update its state incorrectly at each time slot by adding an zero mean Gaussian noise with variance of 4, causing each state to deviate from its ideal state with probability one. The fraction of nodes that needs to be queried to detect all misbehaving nodes is approximately 0.4 for $M = 3$, 0.2 for $M = 5$, and 0.1 for $M = 7$.**

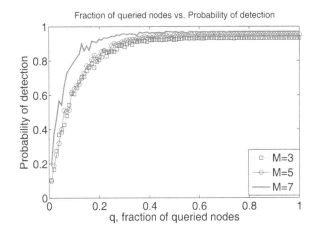

Figure 9: **Simulation results comparing probability of detection with inspection period M. The fraction of nodes being queried ranges from $q = 0.01$ to $q = 1$. Three different values of $M = 3, 5, 7$ were simulated via Monte-Carlo methods with 30 trials each. Misbehaving nodes update its state incorrectly at each time slot by adding an zero mean Gaussian noise with variance of 4. A state of node n_i was considered inconsistent at any given time slot m if $|\hat{x}_{n_i}(m) - x_{n_i}(m)| > 0.3$. In this case, only the misbehaving nodes that induced deviations greater than the acceptable range are detected.**

abilistically, and the quality of the communication channel differs for each sender/receiver pair.

7. REFERENCES

[1] I. N. Athanasiadis and P. A. Mitkas, "An agent-based intelligent environmental monitoring system," *Management of Environmental Quality: An International Journal*, vol. 15, no. 3, pp. 238–249, 2004.

[2] B. Awerbuch, D. Holmer, C. Nita-Rotaru, and H. Rubens, "An on-demand secure routing protocol resilient to Byzantine failures," *Proceedings of the 1st ACM Workshop on Wireless Security*, pp. 21–30, 2002.

[3] D. Bertsekas and R. Gallager, *Data Networks*. Prentice-Hall International, 1992, vol. 2.

[4] M. Blanke, *Diagnosis and Fault-Tolerant Control*. Springer, 2003.

[5] J. Chen, R. J. Patton, and H.-Y. Zhang, "Design of unknown input observers and robust fault detection filters," *International Journal of Control*, vol. 63, no. 1, pp. 85–105, 1996.

[6] W. Chen and M. Saif, "Fault detection and isolation based on novel unknown input observer design," *American Control Conference*, pp. 5129–5134, 2006.

[7] A. Clark and R. Poovendran, "A submodular optimization framework for leader selection in linear multi-agent systems," *IEEE Conference on Decision and Control and European Control Conference*, pp. 3614–3621, 2011.

[8] Y. Guan and M. Saif, "A novel approach to the design of unknown input observers," *IEEE Transactions on Automatic Control*, vol. 36, no. 5, pp. 632–635, 1991.

[9] A. Haeberlen, P. Kouznetsov, and P. Druschel, "The case for Byzantine fault detection," in *Proc. of the 2nd Workshop on Hot Topics in System Dependability*, 2006.

[10] ——, "Peerreview: Practical accountability for distributed systems," *ACM SIGOPS Operating Systems Review*, vol. 41, no. 6, pp. 175–188, 2007.

[11] M. Ji, A. Muhammad, and M. Egerstedt, "Leader-based multi-agent coordination: Controllability and optimal control," *American Control Conference*, pp. 1358–1363, 2006.

[12] H. J. LeBlanc and X. D. Koutsoukos, "Low complexity resilient consensus in networked multi-agent systems with adversaries," *Proceedings of the 15th ACM International Conference on Hybrid Systems: Computation and Control*, pp. 5–14, 2012.

[13] N. A. Lynch, *Distributed Algorithms*. Morgan Kaufmann, 1996.

[14] M. Mesbahi and M. Egerstedt, *Graph Theoretic Methods in Multiagent Networks*. Princeton University Press, 2010.

[15] R. Olfati-Saber, "Flocking for multi-agent dynamic systems: Algorithms and theory," *IEEE Transactions on Automatic Control*, vol. 51, no. 3, pp. 401–420, 2006.

[16] F. Pasqualetti, A. Bicchi, and F. Bullo, "Distributed intrusion detection for secure consensus computations," *IEEE Conference on Decision and Control*, pp. 5594–5599, 2007.

[17] F. Pasqualetti, R. Carli, A. Bicchi, and F. Bullo, "Identifying cyber attacks via local model information," *IEEE Conference on Decision and Control*, pp. 5961–5966, 2010.

[18] J. Pavón, J. Gómez-Sanz, A. Fernández-Caballero, and J. J. Valencia-Jiménez, "Development of intelligent multisensor surveillance systems with agents," *Robotics and Autonomous Systems*, vol. 55, no. 12, pp. 892–903, 2007.

[19] W. Ren, R. W. Beard, and T. W. McLain, "Coordination variables and consensus building in multiple vehicle systems," in *Cooperative Control*. Springer, 2005, pp. 171–188.

[20] S. Sundaram and C. N. Hadjicostis, "Distributed function calculation via linear iterative strategies in the presence of malicious agents," *IEEE Transactions on Automatic Control*, vol. 56, no. 7, pp. 1495–1508, 2011.

[21] S. Sundaram, M. Pajic, C. N. Hadjicostis, R. Mangharam, and G. J. Pappas, "The wireless control network: monitoring for malicious behavior," *IEEE Conference on Decision and Control*, pp. 5979–5984, 2010.

[22] H. Zhang and S. Sundaram, "Robustness of information diffusion algorithms to locally bounded adversaries," *American Control Conference*, pp. 5855–5861, 2012.

Safety Envelope for Security[*]

Ashish Tiwari
Bruno Dutertre
SRI International

Dejan Jovanović
Thomas de Candia
SRI International

Pat Lincoln
John Rushby
SRI International

Dorsa Sadigh
Sanjit Seshia
U California Berkeley

ABSTRACT

We present an approach for detecting sensor spoofing attacks on a cyber-physical system. Our approach consists of two steps. In the first step, we construct a *safety envelope* of the system. Under nominal conditions (that is, when there are no attacks), the system always stays inside its safety envelope. In the second step, we build an *attack detector* monitor that executes synchronously with the system and raises an alarm whenever the system state falls outside the safety envelope. We synthesize safety envelopes using a modifed machine learning procedure applied on data collected from the system when it is not under attack. We present experimental results that show effectiveness of our approach, and also validate the several novel features that we introduced in our learning procedure.

Categories and Subject Descriptors

G.3 [**Probability and Statistics**]: Correlation and regression analysis; I.2.6 [**Artificial Intelligence**]: Learning; D.2.5 [**Software Engineering**]: Testing and Debugging—monitors

Keywords

Hybrid Systems; Invariants; Safety Envelopes; Security

1. INTRODUCTION

On 4 December 2011, an American Lockheed Martin RQ-170 Sentinel unmanned aerial vehicle (UAV) was captured by Iranian forces. It was speculated that a GPS spoofing attack was partly responsible for that incident, wherein the UAV was fed false GPS data to make it land in Iran at what the drone thought was its home base in Afghanistan [1].

[*]Supported in part by DARPA under contract FA8750-12-C-0284 and NSF grant SHF:CSR-1017483. Any opinions, findings, and conclusions or recommendations expressed in this material are those of the authors and do not necessarily reflect the views of the funding agencies.

Permission to make digital or hard copies of all or part of this work for personal or classroom use is granted without fee provided that copies are not made or distributed for profit or commercial advantage and that copies bear this notice and the full citation on the first page. Copyrights for components of this work owned by others than ACM must be honored. Abstracting with credit is permitted. To copy otherwise, or republish, to post on servers or to redistribute to lists, requires prior specific permission and/or a fee. Request permissions from permissions@acm.org.
HiCoNS'14, April 15–17, 2014, Berlin, Germany.
Copyright 2014 ACM 978-1-4503-2652-0/14/04 ...$15.00.
http://dx.doi.org/10.1145/2566468.2566483.

Separately, modern automobiles were shown to have several attack surfaces that an attacker can use to compromise computers/networks within a car and inject sensor spoofing attacks [4,9]. These incidents underline the need to enhance security of complex networked cyber-physical systems.

One way to improve security of any system would be to eliminate the attack vectors. However, the attack surface is growing swiftly as we increase complexity of these systems and introduce new features and capabilities into these complex systems. Inevitably, there will always be some channels available for an attacker to exploit.

An alternate approach for improving security would be to build systems that are resilient to attacks. A system that is resilient to attacks can be built by having a module that *detects attacks*. If all attacks can be successfully detected, the system can respond appropriately whenever attacked. For example, a controller can simply ignore inputs from a sensor that are marked as spoofed by an *attack detector*.

The goal of this paper is to build an *attack detector*. An *attack detector* is a "runtime monitor": it runs continuously, monitors the state of the system, and raises an alarm whenever it believes there is an attack; moreover, it also predicts which component of the system is misbehaving. Our focus here is on detecting sensor spoofing attacks: an attack where the adversary behaves as a sensor of the system, and sends/publishes spurious values for that sensor.

A good attack detector should have very low false positives (where the detector says there is an attack when there is none) and very low false negatives (where the detector says there is no attack when there is one). False negatives are clearly bad. False positives are bad too: they unnecessarily deteriorate the performance of the system.

What are the challenges in building a good attack detector? First, we may not have a *model* of a complex cyber-physical system that is simultaneously good and amenable to analysis. So, we have no information on the normal behavior of the system *a priori*. We do have access to the system, and hence, we have the ability to operate the system under normal conditions. Second, we have no knowledge of the noise characteristics of the sensors. We assume that we know informally the meaning of the value produced by a sensor, but we do not have any formal models of the sensor. Since sensors are noisy, a key challenge in building a detector is separating an attack from normal sensor noise: when a sensor output is unusually high/low, is that just the result of the system behavior and sensor noise behavior under normal conditions, or is that due to a spoofing attack?

Note that an attack detector is just a *classifier*: it distinguishes system states reached when the system is operating under normal conditions from the states reached when the system is under attack. So, we use an *invariant* – an over-approximation of the reachable states – of the system *under normal conditions* as the classifier. We call this set the *safety envelope*. The safety envelope is represented as constraints. When the system is attacked, its state will most likely fall outside the safety envelope, and hence, we will detect it. The intuition is as follows: a system typically has several sensors, and under normal conditions, there are relationships that exist between different sensor values. For example, if a system has two velocity sensors, then under normal conditions, these two sensor values must be "equal". So, if one of the sensor is spoofed, the invariant that "the two sensor values must be equal" is violated and this violation indicates an attack. This is the basic idea, but in reality, it gets complicated because of sensor noise and different characteristics/behaviors of different sensors.

We present a new algorithm for synthesizing a safety envelope of a system using data gathered from normal operation of the system. Our algorithm is inspired by ideas from the field of machine learning. It is important to note that machine learning is broadly interested in learning patterns/generalizations from concrete data: a key aspect being that the procedure should *not* learn the noise, but only the underlying pattern after somehow ignoring noise. In our case, the situation is different. We are here *interested in learning the noise characteristics* of the sensors so that we can use the learnt normal noise characteristics to *differentiate normal behavior from a sensor spoofing attack*.

Our main contributions are: (a) a new algorithm for synthesizing safety envelopes from data, (b) several extensions and variants of the algorithm that incorporate key insights about invariant generation into the algorithm, and (c) experimental validation of the algorithm on a real robot.

Our approach has one drawback: if learning is performed in one environment (e.g., on road), but the system is then deployed in a completely different one (e.g., on sand, or with a heavy payload), then the attack detector, despite the generalization during learning, will likely give many false positives. This drawback can be potentially overcome by noting that the learning procedure is fast and automatic and we can learn (new mode) invariants on-the-fly (assuming we can be sure that the system is not under attack when learning).

2. PROBLEM FORMULATION

In this section, we formulate the *sensor spoofing detection problem*.

We have a networked cyber-physical system that interacts with its environment through a set of sensors and actuators. The sensor data can potentially be spoofed by an adversary. The goal is to detect such sensor attacks.

Formally, let X denote the state variables of the system whose dynamics are given by

$$\begin{aligned} \dot{X} &= f(X, c(Y), D) \\ Y &= g(X) \end{aligned}$$

where $c(Y)$ are values computed by the controllers, D are the external disturbances and Y are the variables denoting the measurements produced by the sensors on the system. For simplicity, assume that Y also includes outputs of *virtual*

sensors; that is, values that can be computed, or inferred, from the real sensor readings.

We assume that we do *not* have access to the dynamical model f of the system and the sensor-values generating function g.

The data Y generated by the sensors can be spoofed by an adversary. For example, the adversary can add a constant offset to a variable $y_i \in Y$. Since the system dynamics are influence by Y, the adversary can potentially change the set of reachable states of the system.

The *sensor spoofing detection problem* seeks to identify such attacks, and if there is an attack (at any given time or time interval), then detect which sensor variable $y_i \in Y$ was attacked.

3. SAFETY ENVELOPES

In this section, we describe our high-level approach for solving the sensor spoofing detection problem.

Safety envelopes form the central concept in our approach. A safety envelope is simply *any over-approximation of the states of the system that are reachable under nominal conditions*. The safety envelope contains all system states that the system can reach when there are no sensor attacks. Thus, a safety envelope is just an *invariant* set for the system under normal operating conditions.

We use safety envelopes to detect sensor attacks at runtime. We continuously monitor the system, and if the system state falls outside the safety envelope, then we raise a "sensor attack detected" alarm.

In Section 4, we present a technique for computing a safety envelope for a cyber-physical system, which can be used to not only detect attacks, but also find the sensors that are being spoofed.

3.1 Why Safety Envelopes?

We learn safety envelopes from data collected during normal runs of the system. Since it uses an *over-approximation*, the safety envelope approach may appear inferior to an approach that computes the *best possible predictive model* from the data (using, say, Kalman filters). But, there is good reason why they are, in fact, *better* suited for attack detection: the actual system is often complex and linear templates are insufficient for describing the actual model. So, if we use fixed linear templates to learn the model, we will likely learn relations that are not physically meaningful, but are sufficient to "describe the data". Overfitting will occur. There will be lack of generalization. Consequently, either we will need a large amount of data to learn, or, if we use limited data to learn, we will get plenty of "false positives" since any behavior that is slightly different from the training set will be classified as an "attack". As a simple example, if we have distance and speed data for a robot moving at *almost constant* speed v, the best learnt model might predict that the speed of the robot remains set at v, whereas an "over-approximating" safety envelope might just learn the relationship between distance covered and speed, and generalize away from the actual speed. Furthermore, we do not really need a model, but just a good over-approximation to achieve our goal of detecting sensor attacks.

Safety envelopes are also models, but they are highly non-deterministic and abstract models of the system. When learning safety envelopes, we do not want to over-approximate (abstract) too much: the more we abstract, the more false negatives are generated.

4. LEARNING SAFETY ENVELOPES

In this section, we describe a technique based on machine learning for synthesizing safety envelopes.

Recall that we are assuming that we do not have access to the model of the dynamics (f) of the system. However, we have access to *sensor data generated during some normal runs* of the system. We will use the data as a surrogate for the dynamical model.

Let t denote a sampling period and let

$$Y(0), Y(t), Y(2t), Y(3t), \ldots, Y((m-1)t)$$

denote the sequence of m samples of sensor data generated under nominal conditions. Let $Y(it)$ be a column vector with n entries. Consider the $(m \times n)$-matrix

$$\mathbf{Y} = \begin{bmatrix} Y(0)^T \\ Y(t)^T \\ \vdots \\ Y((m-1)t)^T \end{bmatrix}$$

Here $Y(it)^T$ denotes the transpose of $Y(it)$, and hence each $Y(it)^T$ is a row vector. Our algorithm for learning invariants is inspired by principal component analysis (PCA), but differs in one key aspect: we retain components corresponding to the small eigenvalues, and throw away components corresponding to large eigenvalues.

More formally, we present the pseudocode for our procedure `learnInvariant` that learns invariants from data in Figure 1. The input to the procedure is the $\mathbf{Y}$ data matrix defined above and the row vector Y of the n variable names. The procedure outputs a constraint (formula) that denotes the invariant set. The procedure computes the eigenvalues and eigenvectors of the $(n \times n)$-matrix $\mathbf{Y}^T\mathbf{Y}$. The matrix $\mathbf{Y}^T\mathbf{Y}$ is positive semi-definite, so all eigenvalues are non-negative reals. Each eigenvector $\vec{v}$ corresponding to a *small* eigenvalue defines a linear invariant $l \leq \vec{v}^T Y \leq u$, where (l, u) are the minimum and maximum of the values in the vector $\mathbf{Y}\vec{v}$. The eigenvectors corresponding to *large* eigenvalues are discarded. The procedure returns the conjunction of linear invariant corresponding to all the small eigenvalues.

The correctness of the procedure is obvious: the choice (l, u) of the lower- and upper-bounds guarantees that all the data points used to learn the invariant set clearly belong to the invariant set.

Why use small eigenvalues to define the invariant? This is because, in an ideal system (devoid of any sensor noise or errors), linear equational invariants will be defined by eigenvectors corresponding to 0 eigenvalues. For example, if we have two sensors – one giving the velocity v of a vehicle and the other giving the acceleration a of that vehicle, then we expect a linear relationship

$$v((i+1)t) = v(it) + \frac{(a(it) + a((i+1)t))}{2}t \quad (1)$$

to exist between the velocity and acceleration readings of two successive time steps. Consider the $(m \times 2)$-matrix $\mathbf{Y}$ constructed using data for the two *virtual sensor* variables $v((i+1)t) - v(it)$ and $(a((i+1)t) + a(it))t/2$. *If* the vehicle was indeed moving with constant $\frac{da}{dt}$, and *if* the sensors for measuring v and a were accurate, then the (2×2)-matrix $\mathbf{Y}^T\mathbf{Y}$

```
1: procedure LEARNINVARIANT(Y, Y)
2:     Input: (m × n)-matrix Y of sampled sensor data
3:     Input: (n × 1)-column vector Y of variable names
4:     Output: Formula φ denoting the invariant
5:     compute the (n × n)-matrix Yᵀ Y
6:     compute the eigenvalues λ and corresponding eigen-
           vectors v⃗ of this matrix
7:     initialize invariant φ to True
8:     initialize templates to the emptyset ∅
9:     initialize λ_th to a small positive constant, say 0.2
10:    for each eigenvalue, eigenvector pair λ, v do:
11:        if λ > λ_th then continue
12:        else
13:            add v⃗ to (the set of) templates
14:        end if
15:    end for
16:    for (each template v⃗ in templates) do:
17:        set φ to (φ and min(Yv⃗) ≤ v⃗ᵀY ≤ max(Yv⃗))
18:    end for
19:    return invariant φ
20: end procedure
```

Figure 1: Modified PCA for synthesizing invariants from data

would have an eigenvector (namely, $[1; -1]$) corresponding to eigenvalue 0 in the data matrix because:

$$\begin{aligned} \text{By assumption Equation 1} \qquad \mathbf{Y}[1; -1] &= \vec{0} \\ \text{therefore,} \qquad \mathbf{Y^T Y}[1; -1] &= \vec{0} \\ \text{therefore,} \qquad (\mathbf{Y^T Y})[1; -1] &= 0[1; -1] \end{aligned}$$

However, in reality, *since* the vehicle may not be moving with constant $\frac{da}{dt}$, and *since* the sensors for measuring v and a will necessarily be noisy, $\mathbf{Y}[1; -1]$ will not be identically equal to $\vec{0}$ (but it will be close to 0), and hence, the matrix $\mathbf{Y}^T\mathbf{Y}$ is unlikely to have 0 as an eigenvalue (but it will have an eigenvalue close to 0). So, *how to find the invariant in reality?* Rather than finding $\vec{v}$ such that $\mathbf{Y}\vec{v}$ is identically $\vec{0}$, we can find a $\vec{v}$ that minimizes the 2-norm of $\mathbf{Y}\vec{v} - \vec{0}$. Let us compute the 2-norm of $\mathbf{Y}\vec{v} - \vec{0}$.

$$\begin{aligned} ||\mathbf{Y}\vec{v} - \vec{0}||_2 = ||\mathbf{Y}\vec{v}||_2 &= (\mathbf{Y}\vec{v})^T(\mathbf{Y}\vec{v}) \\ &= (\vec{v}^T\mathbf{Y}^T)(\mathbf{Y}\vec{v}) \\ &= \vec{v}^T(\mathbf{Y}^T\mathbf{Y})\vec{v} \end{aligned}$$

If $\vec{v}$ is an *unit* eigenvector of $\mathbf{Y}^T\mathbf{Y}$ with eigenvalue λ, then the above expression evaluates to λ. Thus, among all eigenvectors, the eigenvector $\vec{v}^*$ corresponding to the smallest eigenvalue λ^* is the best candidate for defining equational invariant; see also illustration in Figure 2. We should remark here that the eigenvector $\vec{v}^*$ may *not* globally minimize $\vec{v}^T\mathbf{Y}^T\mathbf{Y}\vec{v}$, but it can be shown that *the vector which achieves global minimum approaches* $\vec{v}^*$ *as the ratio of any other eigenvalue to* λ^* *approaches* ∞. This is the justification for using small eigenvalues to construct the safety envelope in Procedure `learnInvariant` in Figure 1.

The next natural question to ask is *why throw away large eigenvalues?* The reason is *generalization*. From a few runs of the system, we wish to generate a safety envelope that is valid for *all* runs. Hence, we need to avoid finding invariants that "overfit" to the particular data being used to learn the invariants. Throwing away the eigenvectors corresponding to large eigenvalues is an effective way for generalizing.

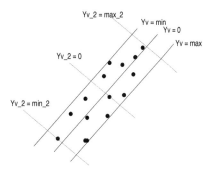

Figure 2: Illustrating modified PCA: The dark lines define the invariant $\min \leq Y\vec{v} \leq \max$ generated using the eigenvector $\vec{v}$ corresponding to a small eigenvalue; the dotted lines show the possible invariant $\min_2 \leq Y\vec{v_2} \leq \max_2$ that would be generated using the larger eigenvalue. We throw away the dotted invariant.

We illustrate the intuition with the same example as above. Recall that in the above example, the (2×2)-matrix $\mathbf{Y}^T\mathbf{Y}$ will have an eigenvector $[1; -1]$ corresponding to a small eigenvalue. Now, since $\mathbf{Y}^T\mathbf{Y}$ is symmetric, it has to be approximately equal to $[a, a; a, a]$. The other eigenvalue for this matrix will be approximately equal to $2a$ with $[1; 1]$ as the corresponding eigenvector. This eigenvector gives us the following expression over Y:

$$(v((i+1)t) - v(it)) + \frac{(a(it) + a((i+1)t))}{2}t$$

Any (lower or upper) bound for this expression is essentially equivalent to a bound for the acceleration. Thus, *if* we include a bound for this expression in the invariant, then our invariant will have a bound for the acceleration of the vehicle *based on the values of acceleration that were seen in the runs of the systems used to generate the data*. There may be other runs of the system where these bounds are violated. These runs will violate our invariant, and get wrongly classified as *attacks*. This is the reason for not using the large eigenvalues to define the safety envelope; see also illustration in Figure 2.

Our intuitive reasoning given above was confirmed in our experiments. Using the large eigenvalues in the invariant resulted in an increase in the number of *false positives* – that is, the system detected an "attack" when there was no real attack.

Procedure `learnInvariant` in Figure 1 is our high-level procedure for synthesizing a safety envelope for a system starting from data collected from runs of the system under nominal conditions. We enhance the basic procedure using some key new ideas that improve the quality of the computed safety envelopes. These improvements can be summarized as follows:

- **Learning for Hybrid Systems.** Rather than learning *one* invariant set, one can get better quality invariants if we learn the invariant set as a *disjunction* of smaller invariant sets. This is especially useful if the underlying system is multi-modal or hybrid – in which case, intuitively, we would like to have one invariant set for each mode of the hybrid system. Section 4.1 de-

scribes how to extend the basic `learnInvariant` procedure to *identify modes* and then learn the safety envelope as a disjunction of invariant sets for each mode.

- **Learning Relational Invariants at Multiple Time Scales.** Traditional invariants are subsets of the state space of the system, but often we are interested in *relational invariants*; that is, invariants between two successive states of the system. Relational invariants are a subset of the *square of the state space* of the system. An important parameter for defining relational invariants is the time duration between the successive states and increasing the time duration has implications on the quality of the invariants. Section 4.2.1 describes this aspect in detail.

- **Learning Using Virtual Sensors and Multiple Feature Vectors.** Using the raw data generated by the sensors for learning may not be beneficial, and one can improve quality of safety envelope using synthetic sensors – values that can be computed using the raw sensor values, usually using nonlinear transformers. Section 4.2.2 describes the benefits of using such virtual sensors and many different feature vectors for learning invariants.

We describe these three enhancements in the subsequent sections.

4.1 Learning Modes and Mode Invariants

In this section, we extend our basic learning procedure to also identify modes and invariants for these modes.

The learning procedure `learnInvariant` only learns polytopes as invariants; that is, conjunctions of linear inequality constraints. It identifies just one mode and one polytope invariant for that mode.

If a system operates in multiple modes (such as a hybrid system), then finding one polytope that includes reachable states of all modes can lead to severe over-approximation. Figure 3 provides an illustration of this phenomena. The figure depicts the reachable states for a 3-mode hybrid system. The reachable states in each of the three modes are shown by solid blob. An over-approximating polytope of the union of the three blobs is depicted using a dotted line, whereas polytope over-approximations of each of the three blobs is shown using dashed lines. The union of the dashed polytopes is a better over-approximation of the union of the blobs, compared to the dotted polytope. Procedure `learnInvariant` would find one dotted polytope. We wish to modify/extend it to find the three dashed polytopes.

The basic idea for inferring modes and mode invariants is as follows: instead of processing all data points (all rows in $\mathbf{Y}$) in one step (as is done in Procedure `learnInvariant`), we process rows of $\mathbf{Y}$ one at a time. If we ever find a row that does not belong to any of the mode invariants learnt so far, we use Procedure `learnInvariant` on the *next k rows of $\mathbf{Y}$* to learn a new mode invariant. We then continue processing the rows in matrix $\mathbf{Y}$. Note here that we are implicitly assuming that the rows of $\mathbf{Y}$ are ordered by time and that the system possibly remains in the same mode during the time duration spanning the next k data points.

More formally, we present the pseudocode for the recursive procedure `learnModeInvariants` in Figure 4. The procedure has the same inputs as Procedure `learnInvariants`, and also one additional argument Φ, which is a set of mode

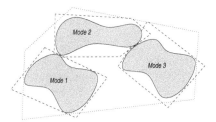

Figure 3: Learning safety envelope as a disjunction of smaller safety envelopes for each mode (dashed lines), versus as a single safety envelope for all modes (dotted line). The sum of the areas inside dashed lines is smaller than the area inside the dotted line, indicating the former is a better invariant.

```
1: procedure LEARNMODEINVARIANTS(Y, Y, Φ)
2:     Input: (m × n)-matrix Y of sensor data
3:     Input: (n × 1)-column vector Y of sensor variables
4:     Input: Set Φ of mode invariants learnt so far
5:     Output: Set Φ of (final) mode invariants
6:     Fix parameter k to a positive number
7:     if Y has zero rows then
8:         return Φ
9:     end if
10:    Let Y[0] denote the first row vector of Y
11:    if Y[0] belongs to some formula φ ∈ Φ then
12:        update φ in Φ by including Y[0]
13:        update Y by removing first row
14:        return learnModeInvariants(Y, Y, Φ)
15:    else
16:        slice Y as [ Y1 ] s.t. Y1 contains the first k
                       [ Y2 ]
       rows of Y
17:        φ = learnInvariant(Y1, Y)
18:        Φ = Φ ∪ {φ}
19:        return learnModeInvariants(Y2, Y, Φ)
20:    end if
21: end procedure
```

Figure 4: Identifying Modes and Learning Mode Invariants

invariants (found so far). In the first call, this argument is the empty set ∅. Procedure `learnModeInvariants` is a wrapper over Procedure `learnInvariant`. It picks the next unprocessed data point, namely the first row Y[0] of the matrix Y (line 10), and then checks if the data point belongs to one of the existing mode invariants in Φ (line 11). If it does, then the first row of Y is removed (line 13) and Φ is updated (line 12, discussed more below), and the procedure recursively calls itself (line 14). If not, then the next k rows of Y are used to learn a new mode invariant using Procedure `learnInvariant` (line 16,17), and the procedure recursively calls itself on the updated Φ and unprocessed data Y2 (line 19).

There are a few important undefined parameters and undefined functions in Procedure `learnModeInvariants`. The parameter k used in line 16 determines how many rows to use to construct a new mode invariant. We usually pick k to be at least twice the length of vector Y (length of the feature vector). Procedure `learnModeInvariants` also uses

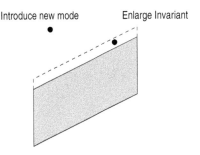

Figure 5: Introducing new mode versus enlarging an existing mode invariant depending on distance of new data point from the existing invariant.

a notion of *when a row* Y[0] *of data belongs to a multi-mode invariant* (line 11). We use a notion of distance of a point from a set for this purpose. Ideally, if this distance is zero, then the point belongs to the invariant set. But this interpretation is too strict and does not allow generalization of the learnt mode invariants – we need to generalize since we are now using *partial* data set to learn the initial mode invariants. Hence, even when the distance of a data point from an mode invariant set φ is nonzero, the data point may be considered as *belonging to the mode invariant set φ if the distance is less than some fixed small constant*. In such a case, we update φ by enlarging it to include the data point (line 12); see Figure 5 for graphical illustration of this process.

4.2 Picking the Feature Vector

One key aspect in designing a good learning procedure is identifying the feature vector. In our case, this is the vector Y that defines the columns of the data matrix Y. In this section and the next, we present two ideas for defining columns of the data matrix Y that will yield useful invariants.

An "invariant" usually is a subset of the *state space* of the system. The state space of a system is defined as the set of all possible valuations for all state variables. For learning an invariant, the ideal choice for defining the feature vector (the vector Y) would be the state variables of the system. In our context, this would be the variables representing the outputs of all sensors in the system. However, this is a not a good choice for our learning-based invariant generation procedures. This is because the learning procedures find only *linear* expressions over the feature vector Y as invariants. And there may not exist linear relationships between the outputs of the sensors.

The first idea here is to use the learning procedure to find "relational invariants" rather than "invariants". This is helpful to find relationships between the *derivative* of a sensor output and other sensor outputs (Section 4.2.1). The second idea is to use "virtual sensors" in place of the raw sensors to define the feature set Y (Section 4.2.2).

4.2.1 Learning Relational Invariants at Multiple Time Scales

Let us assume we have n sensors, say $s_1, \ldots, s_n$. Let $s_j(it)$ denotes the output of the sensor s_j at time it for some natural number i and sampling period t. The natural choice of feature vector Y for learning invariants would be $s_1, \ldots, s_n$. For learning "relational invariants", we use a feature vector of twice the length; namely

$$Y = [s_1; \ldots; s_n; s_1'; \ldots; s_n']$$

where the prime variables denote the sensor value in the *next* sample. Thus, the matrix $\mathbf{Y}$ is given as follows:

$$\mathbf{Y} = \begin{bmatrix} s_1(0), & \ldots, & s_n(0), & s_1(t), & \ldots, & s_n(t) \\ s_1(t), & \ldots, & s_n(t), & s_1(2t), & \ldots, & s_n(2t) \\ s_1(2t), & \ldots, & s_n(2t), & s_1(3t), & \ldots, & s_n(3t) \\ & & \vdots & & \vdots & \end{bmatrix}$$

We note that using the feature vector Y defined above, we can learn (relational) invariants that relate the *change* in a sensor output (derivative of the signal) with other sensor outputs. For example, relational invariants can capture relationship between velocity and acceleration, and similarly between angular velocity and orientation. These relationships will be missed if we only use current velocity and current acceleration in the feature vector, since there will likely be no relationship between them.

In our experimental setup, different sensors published (time stamped) data at different rates – in a completely asynchronous manner. In this case, the value $s_1(it)$ is computed by averaging all the values published by sensor s_1 in the time interval $[it - t/2, it + t/2]$. The sampling period t becomes an important parameter that could determine what attacks are detected.

Noisy Sensor. If a sensor is really noisy, then the relational invariants computed using small values of t will be of poor quality, but those computed using large values of t will be more useful. Specifically, assume s_1 is noisy. If t is small and about the same as the publishing rate of s_1, then s_1 is likely to publish just one value in the interval $[it - t/2, it + t/2]$. So, averaging has minimal/no effect. As a result, due to the high noise, the range $[min(\mathbf{Y}\vec{v}), max(\mathbf{Y}\vec{v})]$ (line 17 of Figure 1) for any expression containing s_1 will be large. If s_1 is spoofed, it will be impossible to say if it is just noise or an attack. However, if we use a larger sampling period t, say 10 times larger, then s_1 is likely to publish about 10 values in the interval $[it - t/2, it + t/2]$. So, averaging will partially eliminate the effect of noise and the range $[min(\mathbf{Y}\vec{v}), max(\mathbf{Y}\vec{v})]$ will be small – indicating a better quality invariant that will be better in discriminating attacks (unless the attack looks just like noise).

Fast Dynamics Sensor. If a sensor is measuring a fast-changing attribute of the system, then the relational invariants computed using small values of t will be of high quality, but those computed using large values of t will likely be of poor quality. This is because averaging over the larger time period would give a value that is less likely to be the true value.

Slowly Drifting Attacks. Consider the scenario where an adversary spoofs a sensor in a way that the spoofed value remains inside the "noise envelope" at every time instance, but with a bias so that over a longer time horizon, the spoofed value has a considerable deviation from the real value. Relational invariants computed over longer time horizons can help detect such attacks, whereas relational invariants over small sampling period t will fail to detect such attacks.

4.2.2 Using Virtual Sensors and Multiple Feature Vectors for Learning

It is often the case that we have some knowledge of the physical interpretation of the value returned by all the sensors in a system. Moreover, we also know the relationships that should exist between all the physical quantities being measured by the various sensors. It is wasteful to not use that information for learning invariants.

We use 'virtual sensors' in the feature vector. These virtual sensors perform some computation on the raw data produced by the sensors and publish the result. The intuition is that there is more likely to be linear invariants that hold between the virtual sensors. Moreover, if we expect no linear invariants to hold for some raw sensor data, we drop it from the feature vector.

We provide a concrete example scenario now. Consider a system that has a GPS providing location information and an inertial measurement unit (IMU) providing the velocity data. We expect that the location and velocity should be related in some way. But this relationship is not linear. In this case, clearly the raw data provided by the GPS is not very useful as a feature in our feature vector. The distance travelled in the last t time units is more useful as a feature – since we expect it to be linearly related to the velocity. Therefore, we add to our feature vector a 'virtual sensor' that publishes the distance traveled in the last t time units. It computes this distance using the data published by the GPS in the last t time units. The function that computes this distance from the GPS coordinates is nonlinear and complex. But once we have the distance, we expect to find a *linear* relationship between distance and velocity. Furthermore, since the raw GPS longitude and GPS lattitude data is not useful, we remove both from the feature vector.

The final idea we use to define the feature vector is *creating multiple small feature vectors* rather than one large feature vector. This allows us to learn targetted invariants. Consider the system described above that has a virtual sensor providing "distance traveled" (`distance`) information and an inertial measurement unit (IMU) providing linear velocity (`vel`), angular velocity (ω), and orientation (θ) data. We expect a linear relationship to exist between the distance traveled and linear velocity, and a separate linear relationship to exist between the angular velocity and (change $\theta' - \theta$ in) orientation. To find these invariants, our feature vector Y would be

$$Y = [\texttt{distance}, \texttt{vel}, \omega, \theta, \theta']$$

However, since we expect invariants involving only a few of the variables (and not all), we can instead use *two different feature vectors* Y_1 and Y_2.

$$Y_1 = [\texttt{distance}, \texttt{vel}], \quad Y_2 = [\omega, \theta, \theta']$$

We then find invariant ϕ_1 using Y_1 and invariant ϕ_2 using Y_2. Finally, we return the *conjunction* ϕ_1 and ϕ_2 of the two learnt invariants.

4.3 Attack Detector

Once we have learnt the safety envelope (for all identified modes), we use it to detect attacks in the natural way. In fact, the pseudocode for monitoring the system is similar to that of Procedure `learnModeInvariants`: we construct the row vector defined by the virtual sensors, and check if the row vector belongs to some formula $\phi \in \Phi$, where Φ is the learnt (multi-mode) safety envelope. If it does not, then the monitor raises an alarm.

How to detect which sensor is spoofed? Due to the use of virtual sensors and multiple feature vectors, as suggested in Section 4.2.2, we know exactly which invariants are violated by the new data. For each invariant, we know exactly which sensors were used to compute the virtual sensors used in that invariant. Thus, each violated invariant gives a set of candidate spoofed sensors. By just intersecting all such sets, we get a list of one or more sensors that are being most likely spoofed.

We can not only generate the candidate list of spoofed sensors, but also a confidence number on our prediction. Specifically, depending on the distance of the new data point from the invariant set, we can compute a confidence measure: if the new data point is really far away from the learnt invariant set, then we are sure that the system is under attack *with high confidence*, and if the new data point is outside, but relatively close to the learnt invariant set, then we predict that the system is under attack *with lower confidence*.

5. EXPERIMENTS

Our motivating case study was a customized LandShark. The LandShark is a fully electric unmanned ground vehicle (UGV) developed by Black I Robotics [2]. We focused on the following sensors and commands in our customized Land-Shark for purposes of learning a safety envelope and detecting spoofing attacks: (a) global positioning system (GPS), (b) wheel odometers, (c) inertial measurement unit (IMU), and (d) user input consisting of commanded speed and rotation. The software stack on the customized LandShark is based on robot operating system (ROS) (www.ros.org), which is a publish-subscribe middleware. All sensors publish *time-stamped* data at some specific frequency. Different sensors publish data at different rates.

The GPS sensor publishes the longitude, latitude and altitude. The wheel odometers publish the linear velocity, angular velocity, position, and orientation data: all in either 3-d cartesian coordinates, or as quaternions. The IMU publishes data for linear acceleration, angular velocity, and orientation. We use these sensor values to define a few virtual sensors; for example, a sensor that publishes values for the distance covered in the last sampling period; and also sensors that publish speed (not velocity) computed using different sources.

We use six feature vectors for learning invariants:
(1) $Y_1 = \{$ linear speed gv calculated using GPS, linear speed ov calculated using odometry $\}$,
(2) $Y_2 = \{$ linear acceleration oa calculated using odometry, linear acceleration ia calculated using IMU $\}$,
(3) $Y_3 = \{$ angular speed about z-axis owz calculated using odometry, commanded angular speed $cw\}$
(4) $Y_4 = \{ ov$, commanded linear speed $cv \}$
(5) $Y_5 = \{ owz$, change in orientation oo about z-axis, calculated using odometry $\}$
(6) $Y_6 = \{$ angular speed about z-axis iwz calculated using IMU, $owz \}$
Note that several features are "virtual sensors" whose values are calculated from the "actual sensors". Invariant generated using feature vector Y_i will be called *Type-i invariant* below.

We should remark here that we do not need to be completely confident that the values computed for the virtual sensors actually correspond to the names used for them

above. For example, we observed that variables that appear to be measuring the same entity (such as, imu-angular-speed-about-z-axis and odometer-angular-speed-about-z-axis) turned out to be almost never equal in the data!

The landshark was run and data collected (in five different rosbags). We used three rosbags (about 800 seconds of real time) to learn the safety envelope. We then injected multiple attacks into each of the other two rosbags (about 200 seconds of real time each). We then tried to see if our attack detector based on the safety envelope (learnt from three bags) could detect attacks correctly in the other two bags.

5.1 Understanding the Results

We now present experimental evaluation of our learing-based attack detection procedure. Our algorithm has several parameters. In our default setting:
(a) we use a sampling period of 100ms,
(b) we use 20 samples to learn invariants of a new mode,
(c) we introduce a new mode whenever the distance of the next 3 data points from an existing invariant is more than 10% the length of the interval defining that invariant, and
(d) we ignore eigenvalues greater-than 0.2 when generating invariants.
In our experiments, we found that the performance of the attack detector was, surprisingly, mostly robust to minor changes in the values of these parameters. Hence, we will describe results using the default setting here.

In the default setting, our learning algorithm finds 5 modes. The first mode corresponds to the scenario where the land-shark is stationary. The Type-1 invariant in this mode is

$$\text{Mode-1, Type-1}: \quad 1.00 * ov \in [0.00, 0.00] \quad \text{eigenvalue } 0.0$$

Providing physical intuition for the other modes is not as easy. The Type-1 (T-1) and Type-2 (T-2) invariants for the second mode (M-2) are:

$$\text{M-2, T-1}: \qquad 1.00 * ov \in [0.00, 0.02] \qquad 0.0$$
$$\text{M-2, T-2}: \quad -0.76 * oa + 0.65 * ia \in [-0.11, 0.06] \qquad 0.04$$

The rightmost constant is the corresponding eigenvalue. Note that the eigenvalues are close to 0. The second mode corresponds, roughly, to scenario where the landshark is moving very slowly (the Type-1 invariant), the sensors (such as, the odometer acceleration and the IMU acceleration) are in close agreement (the Type-2 invariant), and there is little or no rotation (the Type-5 invariant, not shown above). Mode-2 was learnt by our procedure from data generated by an *accelerating* landshark (when the run of the landshark started). The last mode (Mode-5) is similar to Mode-2, but it was learnt from data generated by a *slowing down* landshark.

The two other modes identified by our learning algorithm cover the case when the landshark is in motion. A sample of their invariants is provided below:

$$\text{M-3, T-1}: \quad -0.56 * gv + 0.83 * ov \in [-1.47, 0.11] \quad 0.10$$
$$\text{M-3, T-2}: \quad -0.87 * oa + 0.49 * ia \in [-0.19, 0.39] \quad 0.06$$
$$\text{M-4, T-1}: \quad -0.53 * gv + 0.85 * ov \in [-0.05, 0.04] \quad 0.01$$
$$\text{M-4, T-2}: \quad -0.98 * oa + 0.20 * ia \in [-0.10, 0.09] \quad 0.03$$

In Mode-3, linear acceleration ia calculated using IMU is less-than twice the linear acceleration oa calculated using wheel odometry, whereas in Mode-4, ia is almost *five* times oa.

Note that one would expect that oa and ia are equal, and that gv and ov are also equal – because they represent the same physical quantity. But they are not equal in the data and the invariant captures the 'actual relationship' between them. The actual relationship is different from the expected relationship because
(a) sensors are noisy, and the noise need not be pure white noise, but it can have a certain characteristic (e.g. bias),
(b) sensors, in particular the IMU, is mounted on the landshark in a certain way, and this influences its reading,
(c) the values for the virtual sensors are computed making certain assumptions about the system (for e.g., the landshark is on a flat surface, or the landshark is moving with constant (linear or angular) acceleration), which can be wrong,
(d) the terrain and landshark's maneuvers influence the sensor behavior: for example, when the landshark is moving in straight-line without making any turns, the odometer is very accurate, but when the landshark rotates, the odometer data is less reliable. Similarly, the noise characteristics of the IMU data vary with the operating condition of the landshark.
It is difficult to model the parts (a)–(d) described above. But we need to have some model of them to be able to distinguish normal behavior from attacks. The learning algorithm can be seen as a way to learn the effect of these difficult-to-model aspects of a complex cyber-physical system.

5.2 Evaluating the Attack Detector

How good are the learnt invariants? We now evaluate the attack detector built using the above 5-mode invariant set that describes all the good states that the system can reach (when not under attack).

We take a new set of data (collected using another real run of the landshark), *which was not used for learning the invariant set*, and inject GPS, Odometer, and IMU spoofing attacks into the data. We insert attacks by just modifying the data published by the respective sensors. If a sensor publishes value $v(t)$ at time t, then we modify it to publish the value $v(t) + \texttt{offset}$ for a fixed offset, for all t in some predefined time interval $[t_0, t_1]$ (*translation attack*)[1].

We used the 5-mode invariant to detect GPS, odometer, and IMU spoofing attacks. The results are summarized in Table 1. The first column lists the attack: an attack name consists of the sensor being spoofed (e.g., gps, and the offset by which its value was translated). The table indicates if the attack was detected (Column 2); and if so, which invariants were violated (Column 3). Based on which invariants are violated, it is easy to predict the faulty/spoofed sensor (Column 4), and provide a confidence measure (Column 5) on the prediction.

As Table 1 shows, we easily detect GPS spoofing attacks where either the longitude or the latitude was translated by 0.001 (roughly $80m$). Similarly, translations to odometry velocity (by 2 m/s) and odometry angular velocity (by 3 rad/s) were also detected. Attacks on IMU linear acceleration were harder to detect – when the acceleration was translated by 10 m/s^2, we detected the attack but with low confidence. We were unable to detect spoofing on IMU angular velocity.

---

[1]We also tried some *drifting attack*, where the sensor publishes $v(t_0) + (\texttt{offset}/(t_1 - t_0) * (t - t_0))$ for all $t \in [t_0, t_1]$, but the results were the same as for translation with $\texttt{offset}$ – most likely because we were not clever in designing the drifting attacks.

attack +offset	detected?	invariants violated	predicted sensor	confidence
gps +0.001	yes	1	GPS	1.0
Odo.v +2	yes	1,2	Odo	0.99
Odo.ω +5	yes	3,5	Odo	0.83
IMU.a +10	yes	2	IMU	0.58
IMU.ω +5	no			

Table 1: **Detecting sensor spoofing using the learnt safety envelope: Col. 1 is the attack, Col. 2 says if it was detected, Col. 3 lists the invariants that are violated by the attack data, Col. 4 is the sensor predicted as under attack and Col. 5 lists the confidence number output by our tool.**

Sensor	Offset	Detected?	Confidence
GPS	0.0001	yes	0.97
GPS	0.00001	no	
Odo.v	1	yes	0.87
Odo.v	0.1	no	
Odo.ω	3	yes	0.67
Odo.ω	1	no	
IMU.ω	100	no	
IMU.a	10	yes	0.58
IMU.a	5	no	

Table 2: **Limits for detecting translation attacks: For each attack, we list the offset that was detected and the offset that was not detected.**

5.3 Exploring the Limits

The results in Table 1 will change as we change the offset. So, we experimented and tried to find limits of what attacks can be detected.

The results are summarized in Table 2. For GPS, translations of either the longitude or the latitude by 0.00001 degrees (roughly $0.8m$) were not detected. Similarly, changing the odometry velocity by 0.1 m/s was not detected, and changing odometry angular velocity by 1 rad/s was also not detected. The limits for IMU acceleration were poor: we could not detect translations by 5 m/s^2. The attack detector performed worst for IMU angular velocity attacks. Even when it was translated by 100 rad/s, the attack detector failed to detect. *Why?* The reason is that the IMU on the landshark is a very very noisy sensor. The data generated by the IMU has plenty of high-frequency large spikes, which causes the invariants to become too liberal. In fact, in many cases, the eigenvalues of the $\mathbf{Y}^T\mathbf{Y}$ matrix when considering IMU angular velocity (i.e., when using feature vector Y_6) were larger than our threshold! So, our learning algorithm ignored the invariants involving IMU angular velocity (that is, there were no Type-6 invariants in many modes). As a result, attacks on IMU.ω were not detected.

What if we change the threshold that is used to decide if an eigenvalue is small enough? The result is that we start getting plenty of false positives. Several normal IMU spikes get classified as attacks.

Apart from the missing Type-6 invariants, Type-4 invariants are also missing in the list of *violated invariants* in Table 1. The reason is not entirely clear, but it appears that the commanded velocity is not directly related to the landsharks current velocity in a significant way, and hence the discrimating power of the generated invariants is weak. In fact, just like Type-6 invariants, Type-4 invariants are missing from certain modes because the corresponding eigenvalues were all bigger than the threshold.

5.4 Single-mode versus multi-mode detectors

How does the procedure perform if we do not introduce modes and instead have just one large safety envelope? The procedure performs poorly compared to our baseline procedure in two ways:

(a) It produces more false negatives. The "one-mode" attack detector is unable to detect any GPS spoofing attacks. This is because the "one-mode" learning procedure looks at all the data to learn global invariants. It observes too much variance in the data involving the GPS, and it fails to find a small eigenvalue in the matrix involving the GPS.

(b) New false positives are observed: Our baseline procedure did not produce any false positives, but the "one-mode" procedure reports attacks when there were no attacks. This was a little surprising. On further investigation, we found that the false positives were caused by invariants whose eigenvalues happened to be just below the threshold of 0.2.

Nevertheless, we should mention that the one-mode attack detector performed as well as the baseline detector on odometry and IMU spoofing data. There are a few reasons for this: (1) Our test data, although separate from the training data, is similar to it because the landshark was performing similar maneuvers in both cases. The one-mode attack detector will likely give much more false negatives if it was evaluated on the actual landshark performing different maneuvers. (2) The landshark does not really have different operating modes. Modes are being used here just to improve precision. If the system really had modes (for e.g., if the training and test data had landshark moving on hard surface and on sand), then the difference in performance of one-mode and multi-mode detectors would be more pronounced.

5.5 Single versus Multiple Feature Vectors

How does the procedure perform if we do not introduce multiple feature vectors and instead have just one feature vector comprising of all real and virtual sensors?

When using just one feature vector, the learning algorithm produced a safety envelope consisting of 10 modes, with around 7 invariants in each mode. It is difficult to interpret the modes or the invariants in any way: all the invariants had nonzero coefficients for most of the Y variables. The performance of the attack detector based on the learnt safety envelope is shown in (left half of) Table 3. On GPS attacks, the performance matches the performance of the baseline attack detector: attacks that offset GPS longitude or latitude by 0.0001 (degrees) are detected, whereas attacks that offset GPS values by 0.00001 (degrees) are undetected. The performance of the new detector matches the performance of the baseline detector also on odometry linear velocity attacks: offset 1 is detected, but offset 0.1 is not. However, performance of the new detector is much worse on the odometry angular velocity attacks (offset 3 not detected) and on the IMU linear acceleration attacks (offset 10 not detected). The new detector performs better than the baseline detector on IMU angular velocity attacks: it detects offset 10 attacks, and fails to detect offset 5 attacks. Recall that the baseline detected had failed to detect all IMU angular veloc-

Sensor	One Feature Vector Offset		$T = 500ms$ Offset	
	Detected	Undetected	Detected	Undetected
GPS	0.0001	0.00001	0.0001	0.00001
Odo.v	1	0.1	1	0.1
Odo.ω	-	3	3	1
IMU.ω	10	5	5	-
IMU.a	-	10	10	5^-
false positives	observed		not observed	

Table 3: Performance of attack detector when (a) using one feature vector consisting of all (virtual) sensor values (Columns One Feature Vector) and (b) using invariants that relate states 500ms apart. A - indicates we did not find a suitable value (due to limited experimentation).

ity attacks, since the invariant involving IMU.ω was deemed to be of poor quality (and hence discarded) in the baseline detector. We believe this is reflected in the *false positives*: the new detector reported (about 3) false positives on (data from) a 200 second landshark run. Recall that the baseline detector had reported zero false positives on the same run.

5.6 Changing time scale for relational invariants

How does performance change if we use larger time scales for generating and monitoring invariants? We show the results in (right half of) Table 3. Recall from Section 5.1 that the baseline procedure used intervals that related states that were 100ms apart. We now use 500ms as the time interval, and 10 samples to learn invariants of a new mode. The other parameters were the same as for the baseline experiment. We also removed feature vector Y_4 from the list of feature vectors used to construct the invariants, since it was consistently observed to yield poor quality invariants (that were not discriminating and caused false positives in many different experiments – an indication that Y_4 is not a good feature vector.)

We had hypothesized that invariants over large time intervals will be effective in detecting clever *drifting attacks*, where the sensor value remains inside the "noise" term in every time step, but it has a "constant bias" so that over a longer time horizon, the spoofed value is significantly different from the true value. Since we did not generate such attacks, we are unable to experimentally confirm the above hypothesis. We had also hypothesized that invariants over large time intervals will be more effective in generating useful invariants for very noisy sensors. The baseline detector was unable to detect IMU angular velocity attacks for this reason. Using the larger time scale, the learning procedure found useful Type-6 invariants (involving IMU.ω). For example, in one of the modes (out of 5 that were learnt), the following Type-6 invariant was generated:

$$\text{M-5,T-6}: \quad -0.83 * iwz - 0.56 * owz \in [-0.05, 0.01] \quad 0.00$$

The resulting attack detector performed better than the baseline overall as Table 3 shows: it was able to detect translation attacks (by 5) on IMU.ω, and translation attacks (by 10 and by 5 too, but the latter with very low confidence) on IMU.a.

Finally, we note that, in all experiments, we used the same training data (generated from about 800 seconds of land-shark run) and the same testing data (about 200 seconds of landshark run, which was disjoint from the training data).

6. RELATED WORK

In this paper, we detect sensor spoofing by constructing a safety envelope using learning techniques and then monitoring the system to detect if it stays inside the safety envelope. Broadly, our work is an instance of *anomaly detection* [3]. Our problem formulation and high-level approach are close to the work in [7], but our work falls in between those that assume availability of detailed models and those that use no information about the system.

The construction of safety envelopes is related to the field of system identification. In the area of hybrid systems identification, Paoeltti et al. [11] study multiple approaches for identifying switched affine and piecewise affine (PWA) models based on input, output observations. The system is typically represented in the form of the well-known *Switched AutoRegressive eXogenous (SARX)* model [8, 13], wherein the current output is represented as a linear combination of an extended regression vector and an error term, where the regression vector includes the observed inputs and outputs. The identification problem is solved by finding the parameters of the extended regression vector for each mode [11]. Our work also starts with the observed data. However, our goal is not to find models, but *relations or constraints* that are mode invariants. Note that our invariants can also depend on the current output observations. Unlike many system identification approaches, we do not disregard the noise term; on the contrary, we are interested in finding invariants that capture the usual noise characteristics. Our algorithm is not restricted to learning linear invariants: we can generate linear and non-linear invariants by appropriately choosing the feature vectors. Unlike work in identification, our work uses a novel method for learning mode invariants of a hybrid system that does not assume any *a priori* bound on the number of modes [11].

Liu et al. [10] study the problem of robust hybrid systems identification with unknown continuous fault inputs. They model every faulty mode as a discrete state in the estimation model. Although they consider faults (attacks) in their input data, and take the approach of decoupling the faults from the error dynamics, they make the strong assumption that dynamical models of the system (system matrices) are provided. Our work does not make any assumptions on the model that generates the input and output traces.

Fawzi et al. [6] study the problem of secure estimation and control for cyber-physical systems under attacks. The authors provide theoretical guarantees on the maximum number of errors that can be detected by a decoder function. In their approach, they assume the knowledge of system matrices, and the guarantees are based on the existence of extended observability matrix. In addition, the noise and attack models are not decoupled. In our work, we separate the learning phase from the detection phase; therefore, our invariants represent a realistic bound on the noise level, and we differentiate between noise and attack.

Our algorithm is inspired by the famous PCA method; however, we are interested in finding invariants instead of the "principal components". It is the dual of PCA in some sense. An attractive way to describe about our procedure

– especially the invariant generalization aspect of Figure 5 – is to see it as performing abstract interpretation [5] on data, rather than on programs. We also note that the multi-mode invariant (that we are learning) is just a disjunctive invariant [12].

7. CONCLUSION

We presented a learning-based procedure for detecting sensor attacks in a cyber-physical system. We plan to improve the attack detector by using information learnt about transitions through modes and by experimenting with better attacks and other data sets.

8. REFERENCES

[1] Wikipedia, the free encyclopedia. `en.wikipedia.org/wiki/Iran-U.S._RQ-170_incident`.

[2] Black I Robotics. Basic operations manual, 2010. Revision 1.2, 12/1/10.

[3] V. Chandola, A. Banerjee, and V. Kumar. Anomaly detection: A survey. *ACM Comput. Surv.*, 41(3), 2009.

[4] S. Checkoway, D. McCoy, B. Kantor, D. Anderson, H. Shacham, S. Savage, K. Koscher, A. C. an, F. Roesner, and T. Kohno. Comprehensive experimental analyses of automotive attack surfaces. In *USENIX Security*, 2011.

[5] P. Cousot and R. Cousot. Abstract interpretation: A unified lattice model for static analysis of programs by construction or approximation of fixpoints. In *4th ACM Symp. on Principles of Programming Languages, POPL 1977*, pages 238–252, 1977.

[6] H. Fawzi, P. Tabuada, and S. Diggavi. Secure estimation and control for cyber-physical systems under adversarial attacks. *ArXiv e-prints*, May 2012.

[7] R. Fujimako, T. Yairi, and K. Machida. An approach to spacecraft anomaly detection problem using kernel feature space. In *Proc. 11th ACM SIGKDD Intl. Conf. on Know. Disc. in Data Mining*, 2005.

[8] F. Gustafsson. *Adaptive Filtering and Change Detection*. Wiley, Oct. 2000.

[9] K. Koscher, A. Czeskis, F. Roesner, S. Patel, T. Kohno, S. Checkoway, D. McCoy, B. Kantor, D. Anderson, H. Shacham, , and S. Savage. Experimental security analysis of a modern automobile. In *Proceedings of the IEEE Symposium and Security and Privacy*, Oakland, CA, 2010.

[10] W. Liu and I. Hwang. Robust estimation algorithm for a class of hybrid systems with unknown continuous fault inputs. In *American Control Conference (ACC), 2010*, pages 136–141, 2010.

[11] S. Paoletti, A. L. Juloski, G. Ferrari-Trecate, and R. Vidal. Identification of hybrid systems a tutorial. *European Journal of Control*, 13(2-3):242–260, 2007.

[12] J. Rushby. Verification diagrams revisited: Disjunctive invariants for easy verification. In *Computer-Aided Verification, CAV '2000*, volume LNCS 1855, pages 508–520, 2000.

[13] R. Vidal. Recursive identification of switched ARX systems. *Automatica*, 44(9):2274–2287, 2008.

Distributed Switching Control to Achieve Resilience to Deep Fades in Leader-Follower Nonholonomic Systems

Bin Hu
Department of Electrical Engineering
University of Notre Dame
Notre Dame, Indiana
bhu2@nd.edu

Michael D. Lemmon
Department of Electrical Engineering
University of Notre Dame
Notre Dame, Indiana
lemmon@nd.edu

ABSTRACT

Leader-follower formation control is a widely used distributed control strategy that often needs systems to exchange information over a wireless radio communication network to coordinate their formations. These wireless networks are subject to *deep fades*, where a severe drop in the quality of the communication link occurs. Such deep fades may significantly impact the formation's performance and stability, and cause unexpected safety problems. In many applications, however, the variation in channel state is a function of the system's kinematic states. This suggests that channel state information can be used as a feedback signal to recover the performance loss caused by a deep fade. Assuming an exponentially bursty channel model, this paper proposes a distributed switching scheme under which a string of leader-follower nonholonomic system is almost surely practical stable in the presence of deep fades. Sufficient conditions are derived for each vehicle in the leader follower chain to decide which controller is placed in the feedback loop to assure almost sure practical stability. Simulation results are used to illustrate the main findings in the paper.

Categories and Subject Descriptors

B.1.0 [**Control Structures and Microprogramming**]: General; H.1.1 [**Models and Principles**]: Systems and Information Theory—*General Systems Theory*

Keywords

Distributed switching control, Deep fading, Resilience, Channel state information, Almost sure practical stability

1. INTRODUCTION

In the past decade, *formation control* has found extensive applications in industry and academia [2, 11, 8, 10, 5]. In formation control, the agents coordinate with each other to form and maintain a specified formation. The coordination is often conducted distributedly over a wireless radio communication network. It is well known that such communication networks are subject to deep

Permission to make digital or hard copies of all or part of this work for personal or classroom use is granted without fee provided that copies are not made or distributed for profit or commercial advantage and that copies bear this notice and the full citation on the first page. Copyrights for components of this work owned by others than ACM must be honored. Abstracting with credit is permitted. To copy otherwise, or republish, to post on servers or to redistribute to lists, requires prior specific permission and/or a fee. Request permissions from permissions@acm.org.

HiCoNS'14, April 15–17, 2014, Berlin, Germany.
Copyright 2014 ACM 978-1-4503-2652-0/14/04 ...$15.00.
http://dx.doi.org/10.1145/2566468.2566473.

fading, which causes a severe drop in the network's quality-of-service (QoS). These deep fades negatively impact the formation's performance and stability by interfering with the coordination between agents. The loss of coordination may cause serious safety issues in applications like smart transportation system [16], unmanned aerial vehicles system[13] and underwater autonomous vehicles[12]. These issues can be addressed by developing a resilient control system that detect such deep fades and adaptively reconfigures its controller to maintain a minimum performance level.

Channel fading is often characterized in terms of channel gain [15]. Channel gain represents the signal strength ratio of receiving signal over transmission signal. It is usually modeled as an *independent and identical distributed (i.i.d)* random process with Rayleigh or Rician distribution. This model may be reasonable in most stationary wireless network, it is however inadequate for vehicular communication in two aspects. First, the fading process exhibits memory and is better modeled as a two state Markov random process[17]. Second, the i.i.d. channel model fails to characterizing the impact that the formation's kinematic states have on the channel, which is crucial in safety-critical applications like Vehicle-to-Vehicle (V2V)[4] system where the velocity and relative distance of the vehicles significantly change the channel state. Moreover, for those wireless communication systems using directional antennae [20, 1], changes in the vehicles' orientations could also lead to a deep fade.

The presence of deep fades inevitably injects a great deal of uncertainty into the physical system which negatively limits the performance that can be achieved by the control system. Prior work [18, 14, 6] characterize the minimum stabilizing data rate for linear time-invariant system but assuming constant channel gain. As noted above, the assumption on constant channel gain is overly simplistic for fading channels. Recent work of [9] studies the impact of the time-varying channel gains on mean square stability. This work, however, assumes the channel gain is functionally independent from the physical system's dynamics. In [7], the authors examine a more realistic fading channel model in which the channel is exponentially bursty and is dependent on the norm of the physical system's states. This paper extends the prior work in [7] to a two-dimensional leader-follower formation control problem.

Another unique aspect of this paper is the use of almost-sure practical stability to characterize system safety. By "safety", we mean that the probability of a system's deviation from a bounded set asymptotically goes to zero as time gets large. The asymptotic nature of such probability bounds is captured in almost-sure stability concepts. Much of the prior work has instead focused on mean-square stability (MSS) which does not provide strong safety guarantees in the sense mentioned above. The focus on almost-sure characterizations of safety is therefore another unique feature of this paper.

Leader-follower formations are useful for their simplicity and scalability. This paper studies a chain of leader-follower control scheme for nonholonomic systems using directional antennae to access the wireless communication network. The leader follower chain formation consists of a collection of leader follower pairs that are required to attain and maintain a desired separation and relative bearing. Each leader follower pair transmits its leading vehicle's bearing angle to its follower, and requires the follower to adjust its speed and angular velocity to achieve the formation. Assuming an exponentially bursty channel model, this paper proposes a distributed switching control scheme under which the separation and bearing angle of each leader follower pair are guaranteed to reach and remain in a "safe" set almost surely. Sufficient conditions are derived for each vehicle to decide which controller is selected to assure almost sure practical stability. Simulation results are provided to demonstrate the merits of the proposed method.

2. MATHEMATICAL PRELIMINARIES

Let $\mathbb{Z}$ and $\mathbb{R}$ denote the set of integers and real numbers, respectively. Let $\mathbb{Z}_+$ and $\mathbb{R}_+$ denote the set of non-negative integers and real numbers, respectively. Let $\mathbb{R}^n$ denote the n-dimensional Euclidean vector space. The ∞-norm on the vector $x \in \mathbb{R}^n$ is $|x| = \max |x_i| : 1 \leq i \leq n$, and the corresponding induced matrix norm is $\|A\| = \max_{1 \leq i \leq n} \sum_{j=1}^{n} |A_{ij}|$. Given a vector $x \in \mathbb{R}^n$, we let $x_i \in \mathbb{R}$ for $i = 1, 2, \ldots, n$ denote the ith element of vector x. We let $f(\cdot) : \mathbb{R} \to \mathbb{R}^n$ denote a function mapping the real line onto vectors in $\mathbb{R}^n$.

Let $f(t) \in \mathbb{R}^n$ denote the value that function f takes at time $t \in \mathbb{R}$. Let $\{\tau_k\}_{k=0}^{\infty}$ denote a strictly monotone increasing sequence with $\tau_k \in \mathbb{R}_+$ for all $k \in \mathbb{Z}_+$ and $\tau_k < \tau_{k+1}$. Then, $f(\tau_k)$ denotes the value of function f at time τ_k. For simplicity, we let $f(k)$ denote $f(\tau_k)$ if its meaning is clear in the context. The left-hand limit at $\tau_k \in \mathbb{R}$ of a function $f(\cdot) : \mathbb{R} \to \mathbb{R}^n$ is denoted by $f(k^-)$. Similarly, the right-hand limit of the function $f(k)$ is denoted by $f(k^+)$.

Consider a continuous-time random process $\{x(t) \in \mathbb{R}^n : t \in \mathbb{R}_+\}$ whose sample paths are right-continuous and satisfy the following differential equation,

$$\dot{x}(t) = f(x(t), u(t), w(t), d(t)) \tag{1}$$

where $f(0,0,0,0) = 0$, $u(\cdot) : \mathbb{R}_+ \to \mathbb{R}^m$ is a control input, $d(t)$ is an external $\mathscr{L}_\infty$ disturbance with $|d(t)|_{\mathscr{L}_\infty} = D$ and $w(t)$ is a jump process

$$w(t) = \sum_{\ell=1}^{\infty} w_\ell \delta(t - \tau_\ell) \tag{2}$$

in which $\{w_\ell, \ell \in \mathbb{Z}_+\}$ is a Markov process describing the ℓth jump's size at jump instants $\{\tau_\ell\}_{\ell=1}^{\infty}$. The expectation of this stochastic process at time t will be denoted as $\mathbb{E}(x(t))$.

Given a constant positive $\Delta^* \in \mathbb{R}_+$, let $\Omega(\Delta^*)$ be a bounded set defined as $\Omega(\Delta^*) = \{x \in \mathbb{R}^n \,||x| \leq \Delta^*\}$. The system in equations (1-2) is said to be *almost-surely practical stable* with respect to $\Omega(\Delta^*)$, if there exists $\Delta > 0$ with $\Delta^* > \Delta$ such that if $|x(0)| \leq \Delta$, then

$$\lim_{t \to \infty} \Pr \left\{ \sup_t |x(t)| \in \Omega(\Delta^*) \right\} = 1$$

The system is almost-surely *safe* if it is almost-surely practically stable with respect to the set of safe states, $\Omega(\Delta^*)$.

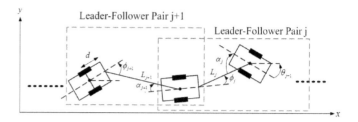

Figure 1: A cascaded formation of nonholonomic vehicular system

3. SYSTEM DESCRIPTION

3.1 System Model

Figure 1 shows a string formation of N mobile robots. For each mobile robot, we consider the following kinematic model,

$$\dot{x}_i = v_i \cos(\theta_i), \; \dot{y}_i = v_i \sin(\theta_i), \; \dot{\theta}_i = \omega_i, \, i = 0, 1, \ldots, N-1 \tag{3}$$

where $(x_i(t), y_i(t))$ denotes the vehicle i's position at time $t \in \mathbb{R}_+$, $\theta_i(t)$ is the orientation of the vehicle relative to the x axis at time t. v_i and ω_i are the vehicle's speed and angular velocity that represent the control input.

As shown in Figure 1, the cascaded formation with N mobile robots consists of $N-1$ leader-follower pairs. In each leader-follower pair j, we assume that the leader can directly measure its relative bearing angle α_j to the follower. Similarly, the follower can measure its bearing angle ϕ_j to the leader. Both of the vehicles are able to measure the relative distance L_j. What is not directly known to the follower is the relative bearing angle α_j. In this paper, we consider the case when information about leader's bearing angle α_j is transmitted over a wireless channel. The channel is accessed through a directional antenna whose radiation pattern is shown in Figure 2. The control objective of the cascaded formation is to have the follower in each leader-follower pair to regulate its speed and angular velocity to achieve and maintain a desired distance and bearing angle. Let L_{d_j} and α_{d_j} denote the desired inter-vehicle distance and relative bearing angle, respectively, in the jth leader-follower pair. It will therefore be convenient to characterize the time rate of change of the relative distance L_j and leader's relative bearing angle α_j as follows [5]

$$\begin{aligned} \dot{L}_j &= v_{j-1} \cos \alpha_j - v_j \cos \phi_j - d\omega_j \sin \phi_j \\ \dot{\alpha}_j &= \frac{1}{L_j} \left(-v_{j-1} \sin \alpha_j - v_j \sin \phi_j + d\omega_j \cos \phi_j \right) + \omega_{j-1} \end{aligned} \tag{4}$$

where d is the distance from the vehicle's center to its front.

3.2 Information Structure

As discussed in the previous section, the leader's bearing angle α_j in each leader-follower pair must be transmitted to the follower over a wireless channel. In this regard, the information about α_j that is available to the follower is limited by the following two constraints,

- The state measurement $\alpha_j(t)$ is only taken at a sequence of time instants $\{\tau_k\}_{k=0}^{\infty}$ that satisfies $\tau_k < \tau_{k+1}, k = 1, 2, \ldots, \infty$.

- The sampled data $\alpha_j(\tau_k)$ is quantized with a finite number of bits $\bar{R}_j$, and is transmitted over an unreliable wireless channel with only first $R_j(k)$ bits ($R_j(k) \leq \bar{R}_j$) received at the follower.

At kth sampling time instant, the triple $\{\hat{\alpha}_j(k^-), U_j(k), c_j(k)\}$ characterizes the information structure of the leader's bearing angle

$\alpha_j(\tau_k)$ at the leader side. Assume that the measurement $\alpha_j(\tau_k)$ lies in an interval $[-U_j(k)+\hat{\alpha}_j(k^-), U_j(k)+\hat{\alpha}_j(k^-)]$ with $\hat{\alpha}_j(k^-)$ representing the "center" of the interval and $U_j(k)$ representing the length of the interval. The codeword $c_j(k) = \{b_{jl}(k)\}_{l=1}^{\bar{R}_j}$ consists of bits $b_{jl}(k) \in \{-1,1\}$, and is constructed by truncating the first $\bar{R}_j$ bits of the following infinity bit sequence

$$\{\{b_{jl}(k)\}_{l=1}^{\infty} \in \{-1,1\}^{\infty} | \alpha_j(\tau_k) = \hat{\alpha}_j(k^-) + U_j(k)\sum_{l=1}^{\infty}\frac{1}{2^j}b_{jl}(k)\}$$

This corresponds to a uniform quantization of the sampled state within the interval $[-U_j(k)+\hat{\alpha}_j(k^-), U_j(k)+\hat{\alpha}_j(k^-)]$ with $\bar{R}_j$ number of bits.

We assume that the follower only successfully receives the first $R_j(k)$ bits in the codeword $c_j(k)$. The information structure at the follower side is another triple $\{\hat{\alpha}_j(k), U_j(k), \hat{c}_j(k)\}$ with $\hat{c}_j(k) = \{b_{jl}\}_{l=1}^{R_j(k)}$ and $\hat{\alpha}_j(k)$ being constructed as follows

$$\hat{\alpha}_j(k) = \hat{\alpha}_j(k^-) + U_j(k)\sum_{l=1}^{R_j(k)}\frac{1}{2^j}b_{jl}(k). \tag{5}$$

$\hat{\alpha}_j(k)$ is an estimate of the leader's bearing angle $\alpha_j(k)$ at time instant τ_k.

In order to reconstruct the estimate $\hat{\alpha}_j(k)$, it is necessary to synchronize the leader and follower in the sense that they have the same information structure. We assume a noiseless feedback channel, with each successfully received bit being acknowledged to the leader. This allows one to ensure that the information structures are synchronized between the leader and follower.

The follower then uses the estimated bearing angle $\hat{\alpha}_j(k)$, and the measured inter-vehicle distance L_j, to select its speed, v_j, and angular velocity ω_j to achieve the control objective.

3.3 Wireless Channel

As shown in Figure 2, the leading vehicle in each pair uses a directional antenna to access the wireless channel. We assume the channels are free of interference from other leader-follower pairs, but the channel does exhibit deep fading. Deep fades occur when the channel gain drops below a threshold and stays below that threshold level for a random interval of time. Such fades are often modeled using two-state Markov chains[17].

We adopt an exponentially bounded burstiness (EBB) characterization of the fading channel. In particular, let $h(\cdot,\cdot)$ and $\gamma(\cdot,\cdot)$ denote continuous, positive and monotone decreasing functions from $\mathbb{R}_+ \times \mathbb{R}_+$ to $\mathbb{R}_+$. Assume the probability of successfully decoding $R_j(k)$ bits at each sampling time τ_k satisfies

$$\text{Pr}\{R_j(k) \leq h(|\alpha_j(\tau_k)|,|L_j(\tau_k)|) - \sigma\} \leq e^{-\gamma(|\alpha_j(\tau_k)|,|L_j(\tau_k)|)\sigma} \tag{6}$$

for $|\alpha_j(\tau_k)| \leq \pi/2$ and $\sigma \in [0, h(|\alpha_j(\tau_k)|,|L_j(\tau_k)|)]$ with

$$\text{Pr}\{R_j(k) = 0\} = 1 \tag{7}$$

for $|\alpha_j(\tau_k)| > \pi/2, \forall k \in \mathbb{Z}_+$. We say such channels exhibit exponentially bounded burstiness (EBB). EBB characterizations can be used to describe a wide range of Markov channel models that include traditional i.i.d models as well as two-state Markov chain models [19]. The analysis methods in this paper apply to a wide range of realistic channel conditions.

The equations (6) and (7) characterize the fact that if the follower vehicle is out of the antenna's radiation scope, i.e. $|\alpha_j(\tau_k)| > \pi/2$, then the communication link between the vehicles is broken. If the vehicle is within the scope, i.e. $|\alpha_j(\tau_k)| \leq \pi/2$, the probability of having a low bit rate is exponentially bounded.

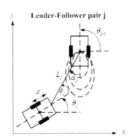 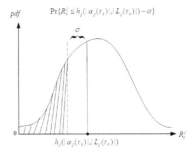

Figure 2: Exponential Bounded Burstiness (EBB) Model for directional wireless channel

As shown in Figure 2, the function $h(|\alpha_j|,|L_j|)$ in EBB model may be seen as a threshold characterizing the low bit rate region as a function of current formation's state. The exponent associated with exponential decrease is represented by a similar function $\gamma(|\alpha_j|,|L_j|)$. The two functions play different roles in the EBB model. Function $h(|\alpha_j|,|L_j|)$ characterizes the fact that as the absolute value of the formation's state L and α increase, the low bit rate threshold shrinks and moves toward the origin. Such activity can be induced due to path loss that is widely considered in the wireless communication community. On the other hand, the function $\gamma(|\alpha_j|,|L_j|)$ in the exponential bound models the fact that the likelihood of exhibiting a low bit rate increases as the formation state is away from the origin.

What should be apparent from the EBB model is that we are explicitly accounting for the relationship between channel state $(R_j(k))$ and formation configuration. A major goal of this paper is to exploit that relationship in deciding how to switch between different controllers to assure almost sure performance.

3.4 Distributed Switching Control

In this paper, the control objective is to steer the cascaded vehicular system shown in Figure 1 to a sequence of desired distances $\{L_{d_j}\}_{j=1}^{N-1}$ and bearing angles $\{\alpha_{d_j}\}_{j=1}^{N-1}$ in a distributed fashion, and then maintain around those set-points.

At each time instant $\{\tau_k\}_{k=0}^{\infty}$, the follower of each leader-follower pair switches among a group of controller gains to regulate its velocity and angular velocity to achieve the control objective. Let $K(k) := \{K_{\alpha_j}(k), K_{L_j}(k)\}$ denote the controller gain pair used for leader-follower pair j at time instant τ_k. These controller gains are selected from one pair of a collection of values $\mathcal{K}_j = \{K_{j_1}, K_{j_2}, \ldots, K_{j_M}\}$. Recall that the dynamics of formation configuration is equation (4), we use standard input to state feedback linearization to generate the control input

$$\begin{bmatrix} v_j \\ \omega_j \end{bmatrix} = \begin{bmatrix} -\cos\phi_j & -L_j\sin\phi_j \\ -\frac{\sin\phi_j}{d} & \frac{L_j}{d}\cos\phi_j \end{bmatrix} \begin{bmatrix} K_{L_j}(k)(L_{d_j}-L_j) \\ K_{\alpha_j}(k)(\alpha_{d_j}-\hat{\alpha}_j) \end{bmatrix} \tag{8}$$

over the time interval $[\tau_k, \tau_{k+1}]$. The variable $\hat{\alpha}_j(t)$ is a continuous function over $[\tau_k, \tau_{k+1})$, and satisfies the following initial value problem,

$$\dot{\hat{\alpha}}_j = K_{\alpha_j}(k)(\alpha_{d_j}-\hat{\alpha}_j), \hat{\alpha}_j(\tau_k) = \hat{\alpha}_j(k) \tag{9}$$

where the estimate $\hat{\alpha}_j(k)$ is obtained from equation (5). With this control, the inter-vehicle distance L_j and bearing angle α_j satisfy the following differential equations over $[\tau_k, \tau_{k+1}]$ for $k \in \mathbb{Z}_+$,

$$\begin{bmatrix} \dot{L}_j \\ \dot{\alpha}_j \end{bmatrix} = \begin{bmatrix} \cos\alpha_j & 0 \\ \frac{-\sin\alpha_j}{L_j} & 1 \end{bmatrix} \begin{bmatrix} v_{j-1} \\ \omega_{j-1} \end{bmatrix} + \begin{bmatrix} K_{L_j}(k)(L_{d_j}-L_j) \\ K_{\alpha_j}(k)(\alpha_{d_j}-\hat{\alpha}_j) \end{bmatrix} \tag{10}$$

The equations (9-10) represent the closed-loop system for the leader-follower pair j and can be viewed as an example of a jump nonlinear system given in equations (1-2). The $\mathcal{L}_\infty$ disturbance in the jth leader-follower system is $[v_{j-1}, \omega_{j-1}]$. The estimate of the bearing angle $\hat{\alpha}_j$ forms a jump process with jumps occurring at discrete time instants $\{\tau_k\}_{k=1}^\infty$. As shown in equation (5), the magnitude of the jump at each time instant is stochastically governed by the length of the uncertainty interval $U_j(k)$ and the number of received bits $R_j(k)$. Such jump process significantly impacts the formation performance of the cascaded system by pushing the formation state away from the equilibrium, which in turn leads to deep fades with a high probability. In the next section, we will show how to reconfigure the local controller gain in response to the changes of $U_j(k)$ and $R_j(k)$ such that almost sure performance is assured.

It is apparent from Figure 1 that vehicle j for $j = 1, 2, \ldots, N - 2$ plays a leader in leader-follower pair $j + 1$ as well as a follower in leader-follower pair j. In this regard, vehicle j could observe the full state α_{j+1} of the leader-follower subsystem $j + 1$ because it serves the leadership in that system. By observing the behavior of the following vehicle, vehicle j for $j = 1, 2, \ldots, N - 1$ can adjust its controller gain to overcome large overshoots in the following system. Such cooperative control strategy lessens the amplification on the disturbance from the upper leader-follower systems to the lower systems.

4. MAIN RESULTS

This paper's main results consist of two parts regarding to the behavior of inter-vehicle distance L_j and bearing angle α_j for each leader-follower pair. The first part of the results provide a sufficient condition under which the inter-vehicle distance L_j for $j = 1, 2, \ldots, N - 1$ is convergent to a compact invariant set. The second part of the results derive sufficient conditions for the almost sure practical stability for the bearing angle $\alpha_j, j = 1, 2, \ldots, N - 1$.

In the main results, we use the fact that the leader's action in each leader-follower pair can be constrained as a function of the following system's state to assure the stability for the whole leader-follower system. Proposition 4.1 provides an explicit characterization of the bound on the leader's action, as well as a distributed way to achieve that bound. Using the results from Proposition 4.1, one can easily prove the first main result in this paper (Lemma 4.4), i.e. the convergence of inter-vehicle distance since the distance is measurable to both leader and follower. The more challenging and interesting part of the results is to guarantee the almost sure practical stability for the bearing angle α_j, which is presented in section 4.2.

The following Proposition is provided to assure the control input from upper leader-follower subsystem is bounded as a function of state estimates of the bottom system. The proof is provided in Appendix.

PROPOSITION 4.1. *Consider the closed-loop system in equations (9-10), let $d \geq 1$, if there exists a sequence of controller gains $\{K_j(k)\}_{k=0}^\infty$, $K_j(k) = \{K_{L_j}(k), K_{\alpha_j}(k)\} \in \mathcal{K}_j$ such that for given bounded increasing positive functions $W_j(\cdot) : \mathbb{R}_+ \to \mathbb{R}_{>0}$ with $\sup_s W_j(s) = W_j^*, j = 1, 2, \ldots, N - 1$, the following inequality holds for all $k \in \mathbb{Z}_+$*

$$\max\left\{K_{L_j}(k)(M_{L_j}(k) + L_{d_j}), K_{\alpha_j}(k)|\tilde{\alpha}_j(k)|\right\} \leq \frac{W_j(|\tilde{\alpha}_{j+1}(k)|)}{(1 + M_{L_j}(k))} \tag{11}$$

Where

$$M_{L_j}(k) = \max\left\{\overline{L}_j(\tau_k), \overline{L}_j(\tau_{k+1})\right\}$$

$$\overline{L}_j(t) = \left(L_{d_j} + \frac{W_{j-1}(|\alpha_j(k)|)}{K_{L_j}(k)}\right)\left(1 - e^{-K_{L_j}(k)(t - \tau_k)}\right)$$
$$+ L_j(k)e^{-K_{L_j}(k)(t - \tau_k)}$$

$$\tilde{\alpha}_j(k) = \alpha_{d_j} - \hat{\alpha}_j(k)$$

then

$$\sup_t \left|\left[\begin{array}{c} v_j(t) \\ \omega_j(t) \end{array}\right]\right| \leq W_j(|\tilde{\alpha}_{j+1}(k)|), t \in [\tau_k, \tau_{k+1}] \tag{12}$$

Because of inequality (12), each leader-follower subsystem j in equation (10) can bound the external disturbance $[v_{j-1}, \omega_{j-1}]$ by observing its local state estimate $\tilde{\alpha}_j$ at each time instant τ_k. Meanwhile, the subsystem $j - 1$ can select its controller gain so that the control input $[v_{j-1}, \omega_{j-1}]$ satisfies the bound in inequality (12) because the estimate of bearing angle $\tilde{\alpha}_j$ is always available to subsystem $j - 1$. Such property provides a basis to design a distributed and cooperative switching law to assure the stability for the whole formation system.

REMARK 4.2. *Functions $W_j(\cdot)$ are upper bounds on the control inputs of upper leader-follower system and the values of $W_j(\cdot)$ at each time instant τ_k can also be seen as feedback signals from the bottom system. Such feedback signals directly constrain the magnitude of control input from upper system, so that the disturbances are not amplified from upper system to bottom system.*

REMARK 4.3. *The inequality (11) could be viewed as a switching rule for the leader-follower pair j to react to the changes on system $j + 1$'s bearing angle. The switching rule applied over each time interval $[\tau_k, \tau_{k+1}]$ is feasible because it is only based on the information that is available at time τ_k. Since the function W_j is bounded and positive, we can always find sufficiently small controller gains such that the inequality (11) holds.*

4.1 Convergence of Inter-vehicle Distance L_j

In this section, we present the first main result of this paper involving the convergence of inter-vehicle distance. The following lemma provides a sufficient condition on the controller gain K_{L_j}, under which one can show $L_j(t)$ converges at an exponential rate to an invariant set $\Omega_{\text{inv,j}}$ centered at the desired inter-vehicle distance L_{d_j}, for $j = 1, 2, \ldots, N - 1$.

LEMMA 4.4. *Let the hypothesis of proposition 4.1 hold, consider the system (9-10) with the selected controller gain $\{K_{L_j}, K_{\alpha_j}\} \in \mathcal{K}_j$. If $K_{L_j} > \frac{W_j^*}{\delta(L_{d_j} - d)}$ and $L_j(0) > d$, then for any sample path, $L_j(t) \geq d$ for all $t \in \mathbb{R}_+$ and there exists a finite time $\overline{T} > 0$ such that $L_j(t)$ enters and remains in the set*

$$\Omega_{\text{inv,j}} \equiv \left\{L_j \in \mathbb{R}_+ \,|\, |L_j - L_{d_j}| \leq \frac{W_j^*}{\delta K_{L_j}}\right\}$$

for all $t \geq \overline{T}$ and any $\delta \in (0, 1]$.

PROOF. Consider the function $V(L_j) = \frac{1}{2}(L_j - L_{d_j})^2$ and closed-loop state equation (10). Taking the directional derivative of V, one obtains

$$\dot{V}(L_j) = -K_{L_j}(L_j - L_{d_j})^2 + (L_j - L_{d_j}) \cdot v_{j-1}\cos\alpha_j$$

$$\leq -K_{L_j}(1 - \delta)(L_j - L_{d_j})^2 - \delta \cdot K_{L_j}(L_j - L_{d_j})^2 + |L - L_d|W_j^*$$

for any $\delta \in (0,1]$. The last inequality holds because of proposition 4.1. When $|L_j - L_{d_j}| \geq \frac{W_j^*}{\delta K_{L_j}}$, the following dissipative inequality holds,

$$
\begin{aligned}
\dot{V}(L_j) &\leq -K_{L_j}(1-\delta)(L_j - L_{d_j})^2 \\
&= -2K_{L_j}(1-\delta)V(L_j) \qquad (13)
\end{aligned}
$$

This is sufficient to imply that $V(L_j(t))$ is an exponentially decreasing function of time that enters the set $\Omega_{\text{inv,j}}$ in finite time. $L_j(t) > d$ for all time since all L_j in $\Omega_{\text{inv,j}}$ satisfy

$$
L_j \geq -\frac{W_j^*}{\delta K_{L_j}} + L_{d_j} > d \qquad (14)
$$

$\square$

REMARK 4.5. *Note that d is the distance from the center of the vehicle to the front of the vehicle. As shown in Figure 1, $L_j(t) > d$ simply means that the two vehicles do not collide with each other.*

4.2 Almost Sure Practical Stability for Bearing Angle α_j

In this section, we provide the second main result of this paper that assures almost sure practical stability for the bearing angle α_j. Figure 3 is used to interpret the basic idea and results in this section. Two types of sets are depicted in Figure 3 with one enclosed by the blue curve, and the other one enclosed by the red curve. The blue curve enclosed set represents the partition generated by inequality $G(|\alpha_j|, |L_j|) \leq \eta_j$ with associated threshold $\eta_j \in (0,1)$, which is shown in Lemma 4.7. The red-curve enclosed area characterizes the target set where the system trajectory will converge to almost surely. The size of the target set is Δ_j^*.

The main result states that the bearing angle α_j will almost surely converge to the target set if the system trajectory enters and remains in the set enclosed by the blue curve. To assure the invariance of the blue curve enclosed set, we adopt a switching control strategy to reconfigure the control gain for each leader-follower pair. Figure 3 shows one possible evolution of the system trajectory α_j and L_j with the switching strategy. We use black dots to represent the estimates of the bearing angle $\hat{\alpha}_j(\tau_k)$ at each sampling time τ_k. A bar is used to characterize the uncertainty interval with the estimate $\hat{\alpha}_j(\tau_k)$ as its center. The length of bar can be viewed as an upper bound of the quantization error $|\alpha_j(\tau_k) - \hat{\alpha}_j(\tau_k)|$, and increases as the channel condition decreases. Therefore, the basic idea for switching is that when the system trajectory approaches the blue set's boundary with an increasing uncertainty length, an appropriate controller is re-selected to assure the stochastic variation on the uncertainty length satisfies a supermartingale like inequality, which guarantees the system states converge to the target set with probability one.

To be more specific about the main result, we first use a dynamic quantization method to show that the quantization error $|\alpha_j(\tau_k) - \hat{\alpha}_j(\tau_k)|$ can be bounded by a sequence that is recursively constructed (Lemma 4.6). Then, we present a sufficient condition on the selection of controller, under which the sequence satisfies a supermartingale like inequality (Lemma 4.7). Finally, the super-martingale inequality condition leads to the proof of almost sure practical stability for the bearing angle α_j (Theorem 4.9).

Recall that $\{\alpha_j(k^-), U_j(k)\}_{k=0}^{\infty}$ characterizes the quantizer's state at each time instance τ_k. The following lemma gives a recursive construction for this sequence such that the quantization error remains bounded by some function of $U_j(k)$ for all $k \geq 0$. Such predictable bound is used to switch controllers to assure almost sure

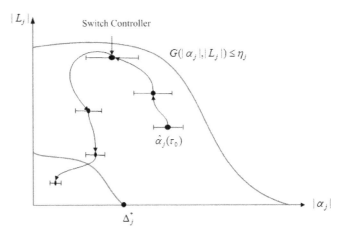

Figure 3: Partition of formation state space.

performance. Note that the technique used to prove the Lemma follows the pattern in traditional dynamical quantization [14, 3].

LEMMA 4.6. *Consider the closed-loop system (9-10), given the transmission time sequence $\{\tau_k\}_{k=0}^{\infty}$, and controller pairs $\{K_{L_j}(k), K_{\alpha_j}(k)\}_{k=0}^{\infty}$. Let $T_k = \tau_{k+1} - \tau_k$, let the hypothesis of proposition 4.1 and Lemma 4.4 hold, the initial ordered pair $\{\hat{\alpha}_j(0), U_j(0)\}$ is known to both leader and follower, and the initial state $\alpha_j(0) \in [-U_j(0), U_j(0)]$, $U_j(0) \leq \frac{\pi}{2}$. If the sequence $\{\alpha_j(k^-), U_j(k)\}_{k=0}^{\infty}$ is constructed by the following recursive equation,*

$$
U_j(k+1) = B_j(k)T_k + 2^{-R_j(k)}U_j(k) \qquad (15)
$$

$$
\hat{\alpha}_j(k+1^-) = (\hat{\alpha}_j(k^+) - \alpha_{d_j})e^{-K_{\alpha_j}(k)T_k} + \alpha_{d_j} \qquad (16)
$$

where

$$
B_j(k) = \max\left\{\frac{1}{\min\{L_{jmin}, L_j(k)\}}, 1\right\} W_{j-1}(|\tilde{\alpha}_j(k)|)
$$

$$
L_{jmin} = \left[-\tilde{L}_j(k) + \frac{W_{j-1}(|\tilde{\alpha}_j(k)|)}{K_{L_j}(k)}\right]e^{-K_{L_j}(k)T_k} + L_{d_j} - \frac{W_{j-1}(|\tilde{\alpha}_j(k)|)}{K_{L_j}(k)}
$$

$$
\tilde{L}_j(k) = L_{d_j} - L_j(k)
$$

then the bearing angle $\alpha_j(k)$ for all $j = 1, 2, \ldots, N-1$ generated by system equations (9-10) can be bounded as

$$
|\alpha_j(k) - \hat{\alpha}_j(k^+)| \leq \overline{U}_j(k) \qquad (17)
$$

where $\overline{U}_j(k) = 2^{-R_j(k)}U_j(k)$ and $R_j(k)$ is the number of bits received over the time interval $[\tau_k, \tau_{k+1}]$.

PROOF. Let $e_j(t) = \alpha_j(t) - \hat{\alpha}_j(t)$ denote the estimation error, and we consider the dynamic of $e_j(t)$ over time interval $[\tau_k, \tau_{k+1}]$,

$$
\dot{e}_j = \begin{bmatrix} -\frac{\sin\alpha_j}{L_j} & 1 \end{bmatrix} \begin{bmatrix} v_{j-1} \\ \omega_{j-1} \end{bmatrix}
$$

By inequality $\frac{d|e_j|}{dt} \leq \left|\frac{de_j}{dt}\right|$, we have

$$
\begin{aligned}
\frac{d|e_j|}{dt} &\leq \left|\begin{bmatrix} -\frac{\sin\alpha_j}{L_j} & 1 \end{bmatrix} \begin{bmatrix} v_{j-1} \\ \omega_{j-1} \end{bmatrix}\right| \qquad (18) \\
&\leq \left(\frac{1}{|L_j|} + 1\right)\left|\begin{bmatrix} v_{j-1} \\ \omega_{j-1} \end{bmatrix}\right| \\
&\leq \left(\frac{1}{|L_j|} + 1\right)W_{j-1}(|\tilde{\alpha}_j(k)|) \qquad (19)
\end{aligned}
$$

The last inequality holds because of Proposition 4.1. The explicit bound on $|L_j|$ over time interval $[\tau_k, \tau_{k+1})$ can be derived as follows,

$$\dot{L}_j \geq K_{L_j}(k)(L_{d_j} - L_j) - |v_{j-1}|$$
$$\geq K_{L_j}(k)(L_{d_j} - L_j) - W_{j-1}(|\tilde{\alpha}_j(k)|)$$

Using Gronwall-Bellman inequality over $[\tau_k, \tau_{k+1})$ yields,

$$L_j(t) \geq \left[L_j(\tau_k) - \left(L_{d_j} - \frac{W_{j-1}(|\tilde{\alpha}_j(k)|)}{K_{L_j}(k)}\right)\right]e^{-K_{L_j}(k)(t-\tau_k)}$$
$$+ \; L_{d_j} - \frac{W_{j-1}(|\tilde{\alpha}_j(k)|)}{K_{L_j}(k)})$$

Since $L_{d_j} \geq \frac{W_{j-1}(|\tilde{\alpha}_j(k)|)}{K_{L_j}(k)}$ and $L_j(t) > d$ from Lemma 4.4, we know $\inf_{\tau_k \leq t < \tau_{k+1}} L_j(t)$ is obtained at either $t = \tau_k$ or $t = \tau_{k+1}$,

$$L_j(t) \geq \inf_{\tau_k \leq t < \tau_{k+1}} L_j(t) = \min\{L_{jmin}, L_j(\tau_k)\} \quad (20)$$

$$L_{jmin} = \left[-\tilde{L}_j(k) + \frac{W_{j-1}(|\tilde{\alpha}_j(k)|)}{K_{L_j}(k)}\right]e^{-K_{L_j}(k)T_k}$$
$$+ \; (L_{d_j} - \frac{W_{j-1}(|\tilde{\alpha}_j(k)|)}{K_{L_j}(k)})$$

By inequality (20), (19) is rewritten as

$$\frac{d|e_j|}{dt} \leq \left(\frac{1}{\min\{L_{jmin}, L_j(\tau_k)\}} + 1\right)W_{j-1}(|\tilde{\alpha}_j(k)|)$$

Solving above differential inequality, we have

$$|e_j(t)| \leq \underbrace{\left(\frac{1}{\min\{L_{jmin}, L_j(\tau_k)\}} + 1\right)W_{j-1}(|\tilde{\alpha}_j(k)|)(t - \tau_k) + |e_j(\tau_k)|}_{B_j(k)}$$

For $t \to \tau_{k+1}$, one can get $|e(k+1^-)| \leq B_j(k)T_k + |e_j(k)|$. And assume that $|e_j(k)| \leq \overline{U}_j(k)$, then $|e(k+1^-)| \leq B_j(k)T_k + \overline{U}_j(k)$. We know that

$$|e(k+1^+)| \leq 2^{-R_j(k+1)}|e(k+1^-)| \leq 2^{-R_j(k+1)}\left(B_j(k)T_k + \overline{U}_j(k)\right)$$

From equation (15) and $\overline{U}_j(k+1) = 2^{-R_j(k+1)}U_j(k+1)$, we have $|e(k+1^+)| \leq \overline{U}_j(k+1)$. The equation (16) holds by simply considering the solution to the ODE $\dot{\tilde{\alpha}}_j = -K_{\alpha_j}\tilde{\alpha}_j$ with initial value $\tilde{\alpha}_j = \alpha_{d_j} - \hat{\alpha}_j(k^+)$. $\square$

With Lemma 4.6, the following lemma provides a sufficient condition on the selection of controller gains that leads to almost-surely practical stability for the bearing angle $\alpha_j, j = 1, 2, \ldots, N-1$.

LEMMA 4.7. *Consider the closed loop system in equations (9-10). Let*

$$G(|\alpha_j|, |L_j|) = e^{-h(|\alpha_j|, |L_j|)\gamma(|\alpha_j|, |L_j|)}(1 + h(|\alpha_j|, |L_j|)\gamma(|\alpha_j|, |L_j|))$$

be non-negative, monotone increasing function with respect to $|\alpha_j|$ and $|L_j|$ respectively. If there exists a sequence of controller gains $\{K_{L_j}(k), K_{\alpha_j}(k)\}_{k=0}^\infty$ with $K_j(k) = \{K_{L_j}(k), K_{\alpha_j}(k)\} \in \mathcal{H}_j$ for all $k \in \mathbb{Z}$ such that the Proposition 4.1 and following inequality hold for any $\eta_j \in (0, 1)$

$$G(\overline{\alpha}_j(k+1), \overline{L}_j(k+1)) \leq \eta_j \quad (21)$$

$$\overline{\alpha}_j(k+1) = |-\tilde{\alpha}_j(k)e^{-K_{\alpha_j}(k)T_k} + \alpha_{d_j}| + B_j(k)T_k + \overline{U}_j(k)$$
$$\overline{L}_j(k+1) = L_{d_j} + \frac{W_{j-1}(|\tilde{\alpha}_j(k)|)}{K_{L_j}(k)} - \left[\tilde{L}_j(k) + \frac{W_{j-1}(|\tilde{\alpha}_j(k)|)}{K_{L_j}(k)}\right]e^{-K_{L_j}(k)T_k}$$

then

$$\mathbb{E}\left[\overline{U}_j(k+1)|\overline{U}_j(k)\right] \leq \eta_j\overline{U}_j(k) + \eta_jB_j(k)T_k, \forall k \in \mathbb{Z}_+ \quad (22)$$

PROOF. Consider the sequence $\{\overline{U}_j(k)\}_{k=0}^\infty$ that satisfies equation (15) in Lemma 4.6, using the argument in [7], the conditional expectation $\mathbb{E}\left[\overline{U}_j(k+1)|\overline{U}_j(k)\right]$ can be bounded as

$$\mathbb{E}\left[\overline{U}_j(k+1)|\overline{U}_j(k)\right] \leq G(|\alpha_j(k+1)|, |L_j(k+1)|)\left(B_j(k)T_k + \overline{U}_j(k)\right)$$

Let $G(|\alpha_j(k+1)|, |L_j(k+1)|) \leq \eta_j$, we have final conclusion (22) hold. In order to select the controller gain $\{K_{L_j}(k), K_{\alpha_j}(k)\}$ for the time interval $[\tau_k, \tau_{k+1})$, the selection decision is made based only on the information at time instant τ_k. Thus, we further bound the state $|\alpha_j(k+1)|$ and $|L_j(k+1)|$ by considering

$$|e_j(k+1^-)| = |\alpha_j(k+1^-) - \hat{\alpha}_j(k+1^-)|$$
$$\leq U_j(k+1) = B_j(k)T_k + \overline{U}_j(k)$$

since $\alpha_j(k+1) = \alpha_j(k+1^-)$, we have

$$|\alpha_j(k+1)| \leq |\hat{\alpha}_j(k+1^-)| + B_j(k)T_k + \overline{U}_j(k)$$
$$\leq |\alpha_{d_j} - \left(\alpha_{d_j} - \hat{\alpha}_j(k)\right)e^{-K_{L_j}(k)T_k}| + B_j(k)T_j + \overline{U}_j(k)$$
$$\triangleq \overline{\alpha}_j(k+1)$$

Similarly, we can also bound $|L_j(k+1)|$ by $\overline{L}_j(k+1)$ that is shown in Proposition 4.1,

$$|L_j(k+1)| \leq \overline{L}_j(k+1) = \left(L_{d_j} + \frac{W_{j-1}(|\tilde{\alpha}_j(k)|)}{K_{L_j}(k)}\right)\left(1 - e^{-K_{L_j}(k)T_k}\right)$$
$$+ L_j(k)e^{-K_{L_j}(k)T_k}$$

Since the function $G(|\alpha_j(k+1)|, |L_j(k+1)|)$ is monotone increasing function w.r.t $|\alpha_j(k+1)|$ and $|L_j(k+1)|$, then if

$$G\left(\overline{\alpha}_j(k+1), \overline{L}_j(k+1)\right) \leq \eta_j$$

we have

$$G\left(|\alpha_j(k+1)|, |L_j(k+1)|\right) \leq \eta_j$$

then the final conclusion holds. $\square$

REMARK 4.8. *Function $G(\alpha_j, L_j)$ in condition (21) is directly related to the EBB model, and it generates a partition of the formation state space as shown in Figure 3. Each partition associates with a threshold η_j that characterizes the convergent rate for the uncertainty set. The aim of switching control strategy is to guarantee the condition (21) holds with a selected η_j.*

With Lemma 4.6, the following theorem proves that the bearing angle of each leader follower pair asymptotically converges to a "safe" set $\Omega_j := \{\alpha_j(t) | |\alpha_j(t) - \alpha_{d_j}| \leq \Delta_j^*\}$ with probability one as time goes infinity.

THEOREM 4.9. *Consider the closed loop system in equations (9-10). Let the hypothesis of Lemma 4.7 hold, for given positive value $\Delta_j^*, j = 1, 2, \ldots, N-1$, if there exists a controller pair $\{K_{L_j}(k), K_{\alpha_j}(k)\}$ with $\eta_j(k)$ for all $k \in \mathbb{Z}_+$ such that*

$$B_j(k) \leq \frac{1 - r_j(k)}{J_j(k)}\min\{\Delta_j^*, |\tilde{\alpha}_j(k)| + \overline{U}(k)\}, j = 1, 2, \ldots, N-1$$

$$(23)$$

with $r_j(k) < 1$ where

$$r_j(k) = \max\{\eta_j(k) + 1 - 2^{-\bar{R}_j}, e^{-K_{\alpha_j}^*T_k}\} \quad (24)$$
$$J_j(k) = (\eta_j(k) + 1 - 2^{-\bar{R}_j})T_k \quad (25)$$

then the bearing angle $\alpha_j(t)$ of leader follower pair j almost surely converges to a bounded set defined by $\Omega_j = \{\alpha_j(t)||\alpha_j(t) - \alpha_{d_j}| \leq \Delta_j^*\}$, i.e. $\lim_{t\to\infty} \Pr\{|\alpha_j(t) - \alpha_{d_j}| \leq \Delta_j^*\} \to 1$.

PROOF. Consider sampling time interval $[\tau_k, \tau_{k+1})$, by equation (9), we know that

$$\dot{\hat{\alpha}}_j = K_{\alpha_j}(k)\left(\alpha_{d_j} - \hat{\alpha}_j(t)\right)$$

with initial value $\hat{\alpha}_j(\tau_k)$. Therefore, let $\tilde{\alpha}_j(k) = \alpha_{d_j} - \hat{\alpha}_j(k)$, we have

$$\tilde{\alpha}_j(k+1^-) = e^{-K_{\alpha_j}(k)T_k}\tilde{\alpha}_j(k)$$

Let $E_j(k+1) = \tilde{\alpha}_j(k+1) - \tilde{\alpha}_j(k+1^-)$, then

$$\tilde{\alpha}_j(k+1) = e^{-K_{\alpha_j}(k)T_k}\tilde{\alpha}_j(k) + E_j(k+1)$$

Let $K_{\alpha_j}^* = \min\{K_{\alpha_j}|K_{\alpha_j} \in \mathcal{K}_j\}$, then

$$|\tilde{\alpha}_j(k+1)| \leq e^{-K_{\alpha_j}^*T_k}|\tilde{\alpha}_j(k)| + |E_j(k+1)| \qquad (26)$$

The term $|E_j(k+1)|$ can be bounded as

$$|E_j(k+1)| \leq \left(B_j(k)T_k + \overline{U}_j(k)\right)\left(1 - 2^{-R_j(k+1)}\right)$$

Taking the conditional expectation on both sides of inequality (26) with respect to the information $\mathscr{I}_k = \{\tilde{\alpha}_j(k), \overline{U}_j(k)\}$ available at time instant τ_k and using above bound on $|E(k+1)|$ yields

$$\mathbb{E}\left[|\tilde{\alpha}_j(k+1)||\mathscr{I}_k\right] \leq \left(B_j(k)T_k + \overline{U}_j(k)\right)\left(1 - 2^{-R_j(k+1)}\right)$$
$$+ e^{-K_{\alpha_j}^*T_k}|\tilde{\alpha}_j(k)|$$

Combining inequality (22) in Lemma 4.7, one has

$$\mathbb{E}\left[|\tilde{\alpha}_j(k+1)| + \overline{U}_j(k+1)|\mathscr{I}_k\right]$$
$$\leq \max\{\eta_j(k) + 1 - 2^{-\bar{R}_j}, e^{-K_{\alpha_j}^*T_k}\}\left(|\tilde{\alpha}_j(k)| + \overline{U}_j(k)\right)$$
$$+ (\eta_j(k) + 1 - 2^{-\bar{R}_j})T_k B_j(k) \qquad (27)$$

Let $V_j(k) = |\tilde{\alpha}_j(k)| + \overline{U}_j(k)$, and consider function $V_j(k)$ as a candidate Lyapunov function. It is clear that $V_j(k) \geq 0$ for any $k \in \mathbb{Z}_+$. Then, one can rewrite inequality (27) into

$$\mathbb{E}[V_j(k+1)|V_j(k)] \leq \mathbb{E}[V_j(k+1)|\mathscr{I}_j(k)]$$
$$\leq r_j(k)V_j(k) + J_j(k)B_j(k)$$

Furthermore, if the controller gains $\{K_{L_j}(k), K_{\alpha_j}(k)\}$ are selected to assure $r_j(k) < 1$ and condition (23) hold, then

$$\mathbb{E}[V_j(k+1)|V_j(k)] \leq V_j(k) - \left[(1 - r_j(k))V_j(k) - J_j(k)B_j(k)\right]$$
$$\leq V_j(k) + (1 - r_j(k))\min\{\Delta_j^* - V_j(k), 0\}$$
$$= V_j(k) - (1 - r_j(k))\max\{V_j(k) - \Delta_j^*, 0\} \qquad (28)$$

From inequality (28), one can prove the bounded set $\hat{\Omega}_j = \{V_j(k) : V_j(k) \leq \Delta_j^*\}$ is invariant with respect to system in equations (9) and (10) almost surely by considering

(1) : when $V_j(k) \leq \Delta_j^*$, inequality (28) is reduced to $\mathbb{E}[V_j(k+1)|V_j(k)] \leq V_j(k)$, which implies that sequence $\{V_j(k)\}$ is a super-martingale and remains in the set $\hat{\Omega}_j$ almost surely.

(2) : when $V_j(k) > \Delta_j^*$, $\exists \varepsilon > 0$ such that $\mathbb{E}[V_j(k+1)|V_j(k)] \leq V_j(k) - \varepsilon$. Clearly, the trajectory of $V_j(k)$ will asymptotically decrease until reaching the set $\hat{\Omega}_j$ almost surely.

This condition can be viewed as a stochastic version of the LaSalle Theorem in discrete time system. With condition (28), one can easily attain the following almost sure convergence property for $V_j(k)$ with respect to set $\hat{\Omega}_j$

$$\lim_{k\to+\infty}\Pr\left\{\sup_k V_j(k) \leq \Delta_j^*\right\} \to 1$$

Since $|\alpha_j(k) - \alpha_{d_j}| \leq |\tilde{\alpha}_j(k)| + \overline{U}_j(k) = V_j(k)$, the almost sure convergence property for $V_j(k)$ leads to almost sure convergence for $|\alpha_j(k) - \alpha_{d_j}|$ with respect to set Ω_j. Since the state trajectories remains bounded within each transmission time interval $[\tau_k, \tau_{k+1})$ for all $k \in \mathbb{Z}_+$. Therefore, we have

$$\lim_{t\to+\infty}\Pr\left\{\sup_t |\alpha_j(t) - \alpha_{d_j}| \leq \Delta_j^*\right\} \to 1$$

□

REMARK 4.10. *Inequality (23) characterizes an upper bound on the propagated disturbance $B_j(k)$ under which the leader follower pair j is almost sure practically stable. This upper bound is a increasing function of the size of target set Δ_j^* and the worst-case of bearing angle $|\tilde{\alpha}_j(k)| + \overline{U}(k)$, and a decreasing function of the ratio η_j.*

REMARK 4.11. *Inequality (23) can be viewed as a distributed rule to select $\eta_j(k)$ to assure almost sure practical stability for each leader follower pair. The selected $\eta_j(k)$ is used in Lemma 4.7 to switch controller.*

5. SIMULATION EXPERIMENTS

This section presents simulation experiments examining the resilience of our proposed switched controller to deep fades, and also demonstrates the benefits of using almost sure practical stability as a safety measurement over the traditional mean square stability.

5.1 Simulation Setup

In the simulation, we consider $N = 4$ vehicles that is cascaded in a string as shown in Figure 1. Each leader-follower pair uses a two-state Markov chain model to simulate the fading channel between the leader and follower. The two-state Markov chain has two states with one representing the good channel condition and the other one representing the bad channel condition. Here, the "good channel state" simply means the transmitted bit is successfully received, while the "bad channel state" means the failure of receiving the bit.

Following the characterization of Makov chain model in [17], one can find that the conditional probability for good channel state is a monotone decreasing function of $\frac{L_j(t)}{\cos\alpha_j(t)}$, while the conditional probability for bad channel state is a monotone decreasing function of $\frac{\cos\alpha_j(t)}{L_j(t)}$. The explicit function form depends on the distribution of the channel gain. In this simulation, we therefore use $p_{11} = e^{-3\times10^{-3}(\frac{L_j(t)}{\cos\alpha_j(t)})^2}$ to denote the conditional probability for the good channel state. Let $p_{22} = e^{-6\times10^2(\frac{\cos\alpha_j(t)}{L_j(t)})^2}$ represent the conditional probability for the bad channel condition. Hence, the corresponding transition probabilities between these states are $1 - p_{11}$ and $1 - p_{22}$. Then, we utilize the EBB model in equation (6) to characterize the low bit region generated by the two-state markov chain model. The corresponding functions in EBB model (6) are

$$h(\alpha_j, L_j) = \bar{R}_j e^{-3\times10^{-4}(\frac{L_j(t)}{\cos\alpha_j(t)})^2}, \gamma(\alpha_j, L_j) = e^{-4.5\times10^{-3}(\frac{L_j(t)}{\cos\alpha_j(t)})^2}$$

with $\bar{R}_j = 2$ representing two bits are transmitted at each sampling period.

The 100 ms sampling time that is widely used in mobile robot system, is selected for each leader-follower pair ($j = 1, 2, 3$), i,e, $T_k = 0.1$ sec for all $k \in \mathbb{Z}_+$. The functions $W_{j-1}(\cdot)$ in Proposition 4.1 are selected to be linear functions $W_{j-1}(|\tilde{\alpha}_j(t)|) = a_j |\tilde{\alpha}_j(t)| + b_j$ with parameters selected as follows

$$a_1 = 0.1, b_1 = 0.01; a_2 = 0.8, b_2 = 2; a_3 = 1, b_3 = 4$$

The value of the parameter sets are chosen to be increasing with respect to j to guarantee the feasibility of the controller selection for each leader-follower system.

In this simulation, we consider an interesting and realistic scenario that the fourth vehicle from far distance intends to merge into the other three closed-clustered vehicles. Hence, the initial states for three leader-follower pairs ($j = 1, 2, 3$) are set as

$$\alpha_1(\tau_0) = \frac{\pi}{3}, \alpha_2(\tau_0) = \frac{\pi}{4}, \alpha_3(\tau_0) = \frac{\pi}{6}.$$

with initial uncertainty length $U_j(\tau_0) = \frac{\pi}{6}$, and

$$L_1(\tau_0) = 7.1, L_2(\tau_0) = 7.1, L_3(\tau_0) = 99.$$

By switching controller pairs from the following pool

$$\mathcal{K}_j = \left\{ (K_{L_j}, K_{\alpha_j}) : 0 < K_{L_j} \leq 100, 0 < K_{\alpha_j} \leq 100 \right\}.$$

each leader-follower pair is required to achieve and maintain around desired setpoints $\alpha_{d_j} = 0, L_{d_j} = 2, j = 1, 2, 3$.

5.2 Simulation Results

A Monte Carlo method was used to verify that the system has almost surely practical stability when Proposition 4.1 and Lemma 4.7 hold. Each simulation example is run 100 times over a time interval from 0 to 10 seconds.

In the first simulation, we select the controllers for each leader-follower pair from $\mathcal{K}_j, j = 1, 2, 3$ so that Proposition 4.1 and Lemma 4.7 hold at each time instant τ_k. Figures 4-5 show the maximum and minimum values of the system states L_j and α_j, $j = 1, 2, 3$ evaluated over all the 100 runs. In both figures, the maximum value is marked by red lines and the minimum value is marked by blue lines. The two dashed lines in Figure 5 represent the upper and lower bound for the relative bearing α, i.e. $|\alpha_j| \leq \pi/2$, which characterizes the safety region. We can see from Figures 4-5 that the maximum and minimum values of the system states asymptotically converge to a bounded set containing the desired set-points $\alpha_{d_j} = 0$ and $L_{d_j} = 2$. This is precisely the behavior that one would expect if the system is almost sure practical stable. These results therefore, seem to confirm our statement in Theorem 4.9. Figures 6-7 show one sample of switching controller profile and channel state for each leader-follower pair. The top plot in Figure 6 shows the switching controller profile for the leader-follower pair 1 with red line marked as controller gain K_{α_1} and blue line as controller gain K_{L_1}. The bottom one is the switching controller profile for leader-follower pair 2 with the same marking rule. These plots show that the controller gains stay low at the first two seconds to avoid causing large disturbance to the bottom system, then switch from low to high when the systems approach the equilibrium and are confident that the channel state will always stay good. The top plot in Figure 7 is the switching controller profile for the leader-follower system 3 with same marking rule, and the bottom plot is the channel state $R_3(k)$ that characterizes the number of successfully received bits at each time interval. We can clearly see from the plots that the controller for system 3 starts with low gains to compensate the effect caused by a short string of zero bits at the beginning, and then

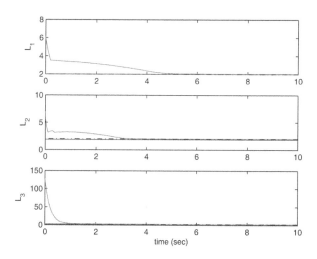

Figure 4: **The maximum and minimum value of inter-vehicle distance L_j for leader-follower pair, $j = 1, 2, 3$.**

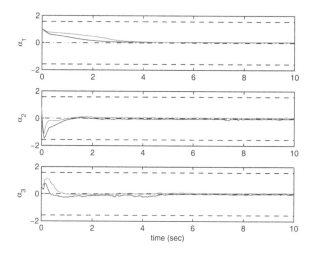

Figure 5: **The maximum and minimum value of bearing angle α_j for leader-follower pair, $j = 1, 2, 3$.**

switches from low gain to high gain when channel condition stays good. These results demonstrate that channel state indeed is used as a feedback signal to switch the controller. In the second simulation, we studied the benefits of almost sure practical stability as a safety measurement over the traditional mean square stability. Traditional mean square stability requires the second moment of the system state converges to a positive constant value, but it does not put any constraint on the sample path which might potentially cause safety issues. For a fair comparison, the same simulation setup and parameters are applied in this simulation with the only difference on the controllers. One type of controller used in this simulation is a mean square stabilizing controller, which is selected to guarantee mean square stability for each leader-follower pair. The other type of controller is the switching controller proposed in this paper to guarantee almost sure practical stability for each leader-follower pair. The switching control strategy uses the mean square stabilizing controller as its initial controller.

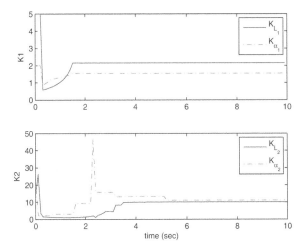

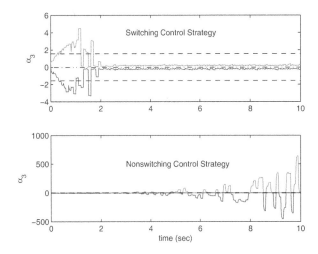

Figure 6: One sample of switching controller profile for leader-follower pair 1 and 2

Figure 8: The maximum and minimum system trajectory for leader-follower pair 3 with switching controller (Top) and non-switching controller pair(Bottom) $K_{L_3} = 2$ **and** $K_{\alpha_3} = 50$

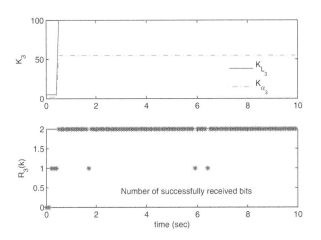

Figure 7: One sample of switching profile and channel state for leader-follower pair 3

Figure 8 shows a comparison of the maximum and minimum values of the bearing angle α_3 for leader-follower pair 3 with the switching controller case in the top plot and the mean square controller $K_1 = (5, 0.5); K_2 = (5, 0.5); K_3 = (2, 50)$ in the bottom plot. It is worth noting that (K_1, K_2, K_3) is just one of the many selections in our simulation. Because of the space limitation, we only use (K_1, K_2, K_3) as an example to demonstrate the results. It is clear from Figure 8 that the system's sample path goes unbounded as time increases by using a mean square stabilizing controller, but it converges asymptotically to a bounded set by using a switching controller. These results suggest that the composition of mean square stable systems does not guarantee mean square stability for the whole system, while the composition of almost sure stable systems may still guarantee almost sure stability for the whole system.

6. CONCLUSIONS

This paper studied the almost sure practical stability for leader-follower formation control of a class of nonholonomic system in the presence of deep fades exhibiting exponentially bounded burstiness. The main results are the sufficient conditions to select distributed switching controller to assure almost sure practical stability. The simulation results support our theoretical analysis and also illustrate the benefit of using almost surely practical stability as a safety measurement over traditional mean square stability.

Acknowledgments

The authors acknowledge the partial financial support of the National Science Foundation (NSF-CNS-1239222).

7. REFERENCES

[1] C. A. Balanis. *Antenna theory: analysis and design/Constantine A. Balanis.* J. Wiley, New York, 1982.

[2] T. Balch and R. C. Arkin. Behavior-based formation control for multirobot teams. *Robotics and Automation, IEEE Transactions on*, 14(6):926–939, 1998.

[3] R. W. Brockett and D. Liberzon. Quantized feedback stabilization of linear systems. *Automatic Control, IEEE Transactions on*, 45(7):1279–1289, 2000.

[4] L. Cheng, B. E. Henty, D. D. Stancil, F. Bai, and P. Mudalige. Mobile vehicle-to-vehicle narrow-band channel measurement and characterization of the 5.9 ghz dedicated short range communication (dsrc) frequency band. *IEEE Journal on Selected Areas in Communications*, 25(8):1501–1516, 2007.

[5] J. P. Desai, J. Ostrowski, and V. Kumar. Controlling formations of multiple mobile robots. In *Robotics and Automation, 1998. Proceedings. 1998 IEEE International Conference on*, volume 4, pages 2864–2869. IEEE, 1998.

[6] N. Elia and S. K. Mitter. Stabilization of linear systems with limited information. *Automatic Control, IEEE Transactions on*, 46(9):1384–1400, 2001.

[7] B. Hu and M. D. Lemmon. Using channel state feedback to achieve resilience to deep fades in wireless networked control systems. In *Proceedings of the 2nd international conference on High Confidence Networked Systems*, April 9-11 2013.

[8] M. Mesbahi and M. Egerstedt. *Graph theoretic methods in multiagent networks*. Princeton University Press, 2010.

[9] P. Minero, M. Franceschetti, S. Dey, and G. N. Nair. Data rate theorem for stabilization over time-varying feedback channels. *Automatic Control, IEEE Transactions on*, 54(2):243–255, 2009.

[10] N. Moshtagh and A. Jadbabaie. Distributed geodesic control laws for flocking of nonholonomic agents. *Automatic Control, IEEE Transactions on*, 52(4):681–686, 2007.

[11] R. Olfati-Saber, J. A. Fax, and R. M. Murray. Consensus and cooperation in networked multi-agent systems. *Proceedings of the IEEE*, 95(1):215–233, 2007.

[12] D. J. Stilwell and B. E. Bishop. Platoons of underwater vehicles. *Control Systems, IEEE*, 20(6):45–52, 2000.

[13] D. M. Stipanović, G. Inalhan, R. Teo, and C. J. Tomlin. Decentralized overlapping control of a formation of unmanned aerial vehicles. *Automatica*, 40(8):1285–1296, 2004.

[14] S. Tatikonda and S. Mitter. Control under communication constraints. *Automatic Control, IEEE Transactions on*, 49(7):1056–1068, 2004.

[15] D. Tse and P. Viswanath. *Fundamentals of wireless communication*. Cambridge university press, 2005.

[16] P. Varaiya. Smart cars on smart roads: problems of control. *Automatic Control, IEEE Transactions on*, 38(2):195–207, 1993.

[17] H. Wang and N. Moayeri. Finite-state markov channel - a useful model for radio communication channels. *IEEE Transactions on Vehicular Technology*, 44(1):163–171, 1995.

[18] W. S. Wong and R. W. Brockett. Systems with finite communication bandwidth constraints. ii. stabilization with limited information feedback. *Automatic Control, IEEE Transactions on*, 44(5):1049–1053, 1999.

[19] O. Yaron and M. Sidi. Performance and stability of communication networks via robust exponential bounds. *IEEE/ACM Transactions on Networking*, 1(3):372–385, 1993.

[20] S. Yi, Y. Pei, and S. Kalyanaraman. On the capacity improvement of ad hoc wireless networks using directional antennas. In *International Symposium on Mobile Ad Hoc Networking & Computing: Proceedings of the 4 th ACM international symposium on Mobile ad hoc networking & computing*, volume 1, pages 108–116. Citeseer, 2003.

8. APPENDIX

Proof of Proposition 4.1:

PROOF. Consider the infinite norm of the control input given in equation (8),

$$
\left\| \begin{bmatrix} v_j(t) \\ \omega_j(t) \end{bmatrix} \right\| = \left\| \begin{bmatrix} -\cos\phi_j & -L_j\sin\phi_j \\ -\frac{\sin\phi_j}{d} & \frac{L_j}{d}\cos\phi_j \end{bmatrix} \begin{bmatrix} K_{L_j}(k)(L_{d_j}-L_j) \\ K_{\alpha_j}(k)(\alpha_{d_j}-\hat{\alpha}_j) \end{bmatrix} \right\|
$$
$$
\leq \left\| \begin{bmatrix} -\cos\phi_j & -L_j\sin\phi_j \\ -\frac{\sin\phi_j}{d} & \frac{L_j}{d}\cos\phi_j \end{bmatrix} \right\| \left\| \begin{bmatrix} K_{L_j}(k)(L_{d_j}-L_j) \\ K_{\alpha_j}(k)(\alpha_{d_j}-\hat{\alpha}_j) \end{bmatrix} \right\|
$$
$$
\leq \left(1+|L_j(t)|\right)\max\{K_{L_j}(k)|\tilde{L}_j(t)|, K_{\alpha_j}(k)|\tilde{\alpha}_j(t)|\} \tag{29}
$$

with $\tilde{L}_j(t) = L_{d_j} - L_j(t)$. The supreme of $|L_j(t)|$ over time interval $[\tau_k, \tau_{k+1})$ can be obtained by considering

$$
\dot{L}_j(t) \leq K_{L_j}(k)(L_{d_j}-L_j)(t) + W_{j-1}(|\tilde{\alpha}_j(k)|)
$$

Using Gronwall Bellman theorem to solve above inequality and yield,

$$
L_j(t) \leq \left(L_{d_j} + \frac{W_{j-1}(|\alpha_j(k)|)}{K_{L_j}(k)}\right)\left(1 - e^{-K_{L_j}(k)(t-\tau_k)}\right)
$$
$$
+ L_j(k)e^{-K_{L_j}(k)(t-\tau_k)}
$$
$$
\triangleq \overline{L}_j(t)
$$

Assume $L_j(t) > 0$ (In Lemma 4.6, we prove that if controller gain $K_{L_j}(k)$ is selected sufficiently large, $L_j(t) > d > 0$ holds for all $t \geq 0$), and because

$$
\frac{d\overline{L}_j}{dt} = \left[K_{L_j}(k)L_{d_j} + W_{j-1}(|\tilde{\alpha}_j(k)|) - K_{L_j}(k)L_j(k)\right]e^{-K_{L_j}(k)(t-\tau_k)}
$$

$\frac{d\overline{L}_j}{dt} \geq 0$ or $\frac{d\overline{L}_j}{dt} < 0$ over interval $[\tau_k, \tau_{k+1})$. In other words, $\overline{L}_j(t)$ is a monotone function over $[\tau_k, \tau_{k+1})$. Thus $\sup_{\tau_k \leq t < \tau_{k+1}} L_j(t)$ is obtained when $t = \tau_k$ or $t \to \tau_{k+1}$, i.e.

$$
L_j(t) \leq \sup_{\tau_k \leq t < \tau_{k+1}} L_j(t)
$$
$$
= \max\left\{\overline{L}_j(\tau_k), \overline{L}_j(\tau_{k+1})\right\} \triangleq M_{L_j}(k) \tag{30}
$$

Note that $|\tilde{L}_j(t)| = |L_{d_j} - L_j(t)| \leq L_j(t) + L_{d_j}$, thus

$$
|\tilde{L}_j(t)| \leq L_{d_j} + M_{L_j}(k) \tag{31}
$$

By inequalities (30-31), (29) can be further bounded

$$
\sup_t \left\| \begin{bmatrix} v_j(t) \\ \omega_j(t) \end{bmatrix} \right\|
$$
$$
\leq (1+M_{L_j}(k))\max\left\{K_{L_j}(k)(L_{d_j}+M_{L_j}(k)), K_{\alpha_j}(k)|\tilde{\alpha}_j(t)|\right\} \tag{32}
$$

with $\tilde{\alpha}_j(t) = \alpha_{d_j} - \hat{\alpha}_j(t)$ satisfying

$$
\dot{\tilde{\alpha}}_j = -K_{\alpha_j}(k)\tilde{\alpha}_j, t \in [\tau_k, \tau_{k+1})
$$

with initial value $\tilde{\alpha}_j(\tau_k)$. From the solution of the above ODE, it is obvious that $|\tilde{\alpha}_j(t)| < |\tilde{\alpha}_j(\tau_k)|$, then it is straightforward to show that if the condition (11) is satisfied, the inequality (12) holds. □

On the Cost of Differential Privacy in Distributed Control Systems *

Zhenqi Huang
Coordinate Science
Laboratory
University of Illinois at
Urbana-Champaign
Urbana, IL 61801, USA
zhuang25@illinois.edu

Yu Wang
Coordinate Science
Laboratory
University of Illinois at
Urbana-Champaign
Urbana, IL 61801, USA
yuwang8@illinois.edu

Sayan Mitra
Coordinate Science
Laboratory
University of Illinois at
Urbana-Champaign
Urbana, IL 61801, USA
mitras@illinois.edu

Geir E. Dullerud
Coordinate Science
Laboratory
University of Illinois at
Urbana-Champaign
Urbana, IL 61801, USA
dullerud@illinois.edu

ABSTRACT

Individuals sharing information can improve the cost or performance of a distributed control system. But, sharing may also violate privacy. We develop a general framework for studying the cost of differential privacy in systems where a collection of agents, with coupled dynamics, communicate for sensing their shared environment while pursuing individual preferences. First, we propose a communication strategy that relies on adding carefully chosen random noise to agent states and show that it preserves differential privacy. Of course, the higher the standard deviation of the noise, the higher the cost of privacy. For linear distributed control systems with quadratic cost functions, the standard deviation becomes independent of the number agents and it decays with the maximum eigenvalue of the dynamics matrix. Furthermore, for stable dynamics, the noise to be added is independent of the number of agents as well as the time horizon up to which privacy is desired. Finally, we show that the cost of ϵ-differential privacy up to time T, for a linear stable system with N agents, is upper bounded by $O(\frac{T^3}{N\epsilon^2})$.

Keywords

Differential Privacy; Distributed Control; Cyber-physical Security

---

*This work is supported by NSA SoS grant (No. W911NSF-13-0086).

Permission to make digital or hard copies of all or part of this work for personal or classroom use is granted without fee provided that copies are not made or distributed for profit or commercial advantage and that copies bear this notice and the full citation on the first page. Copyrights for components of this work owned by others than ACM must be honored. Abstracting with credit is permitted. To copy otherwise, or republish, to post on servers or to redistribute to lists, requires prior specific permission and/or a fee. Request permissions from permissions@acm.org.
HiCoNS'14, April 15–17, 2014, Berlin, Germany.
Copyright 2014 ACM 978-1-4503-2652-0/14/04 ...$15.00.
http://dx.doi.org/10.1145/2566468.2566474.

1. INTRODUCTION

In distributed control systems there is a trade-off between privacy and cost. A vehicle with a smart navigation device may provide some information about its trajectory for crowd sourced traffic data collection [7]. Aggregates of this data can then be used by the navigation device for traffic-aware routing. Similarly, a consumer in a power-grid may share some information about her energy demands to then use the aggregate demands for deciding her own consumption plans and save energy costs. At one extreme is the completely private society in which agents neither share nor receive any information through communication. They only interact through their coupled dynamics. The other extreme is the completely non-private or broadcast society. Agents share complete information which at least in principle allows, all agents to make accurate predictions (e.g., traffic or electricity demands) and to make optimal decisions. Between these two extremes lie a multitude of other possible communication strategies. The privacy-cost trade-off can formalized as the *cost of privacy* measured by the difference between the cost achieved through a given communication strategy and the cost achieved by the completely non-private strategy.

In this paper, we present a general framework for studying cost of privacy for distributed control systems in which a collection of agents pursue individual goals and communicate for the purpose of sensing their shared environment. Each agent i has a *preference p_i*—an infinite sequences of points that it wants to visit in a Euclidean space. These preference capture, for example, a sequence of waypoints for a vehicle or the electric power demand of a household. The evolution of an agent depends on (a) its dynamics, (b) the control action it takes, and also (c) the environment or the aggregate state of the other agents. If the communication strategy shares more information about its preference, then all agents in the society can estimate the environment more accurately, and therefore, make better control decisions. On the other hand, such a communication strategy may leak information about agent preference. For a given communication strategy (r), the difference between the actual sequence of states visited by an agent following r and the preferred trajectory p_i defines the cost incurred by the agent i.

In our formulation, once the underlying dynamics of the system, the individual preferences, and the communication strategy are fixed the overall system is deterministic[1]. We show (Proposition 1) that knowing the preference for the agents and an observation of the system allows an adversary to uniquely infer the complete state trajectory of an agent over time. That is, there is a one-to-one correspondence between the observation sequences and the state trajectories. Therefore, protecting the privacy of the state trajectories is tantamount to protecting the preferences.

The notion of privacy we adopt in this paper is differential privacy [1, 2] as applied to continuous bit streams in [4]. We have to make two technical adjustments to the earlier definition. First, since preferences are infinite sequences, we define adjacency of preferences over a time horizon, say T. Secondly, we define a pair of agent preferences p and p' to be *adjacent up to time* T, if they differ about the preference of at most one agent, say agent i, and for any time before T, the L^1-norm of difference $p_i - p'_i$ at that time is bounded. The resulting notion of ϵ-differential privacy then ensures that an adversary with access to all the communication in the system—we call this an *observation sequence*—cannot gain information about the preference of any agent up to time T with any significant probability.

Contributions. (1) We present an ϵ-differential privacy preserving communication strategy for distributed control systems. For a given privacy parameter ϵ, and a given agent state x_i, the strategy adds noise to x_i from a Laplace distribution with zero mean and standard deviation proportional to the sensitivity of a particular function to changes in agent preferences. The function in question maps observations to sets of executions η^{-1} (see Section 4).

(2) We show that for a linear distributed system with quadratic cost functions, the sensitivity of η^{-1}, and therefore the required standard deviation of the noise, is independent of the number of participating agents (see Theorem 4). Roughly, the sensitivity of η^{-1} with respect to the changes in an individual agent's preference is influenced by the number of agents N in two opposing directions. As N increases, a larger number of agents are influenced by the changes in the preference of an individual. In contrast, with larger N, the influence of i on another individual agent through the environment weakens in an environment which aggregates the state of all the agents. In the linear case, these two effects roughly cancel out making the sensitivity independent of N.

(3) We show that the required standard deviation of noise decreases with the stability of the dynamics and with the weakening of the environment's influence on an individual. When the modulus of the maximum eigenvalue of the dynamics matrix is smaller, the effect of changes in an individual's preference on the system's trajectory decays faster over time. Furthermore, as the time horizon goes to infinity, the sensitivity converges to a constant for stable systems. Thus, the amount of noise to be added for differentially private

communication is independent of the number of participating agents as well as the time horizon up to which privacy is desired. For unstable dynamics, on the other hand, the sensitivity can grow exponentially with the time bound T.

(4) We establish that the cost of ϵ-differential privacy using our communication strategy up to time T for a system with N agents is at most $O(\frac{T^3}{N\epsilon^2})$ for stable systems and the cost can also grow exponentially with T for unstable systems. This suggests that the proposed strategy is more likely to be useful for stable systems with short-lived participants (e.g., drivers with short commutes), and further research is needed for strategies that scale better with time.

Organization. Section 2 discusses related research. Section 3 defines Markov chains with observation maps and their semantics. Section 4 develops the general framework. Section 5 presents the Laplace communication mechanism for general distributed control systems and Section 6 develops specialized results for linear systems. Several proofs are omitted because of limited space; details can be found in the online version of the paper [9].

2. RELATED WORK ON DIFFERENTIAL PRIVACY

While there are several notions of data privacy in the Computer Science literature, the quantitative and statistical nature of differential privacy makes it suitable for adoption in distributed control. The notion used in this paper follows the definition of differential privacy introduced originally in the context of statistical queries on databases [1] (see [2] for a survey). Differential privacy requires that the change of an individual agent's data can only result in *unsubstantial* changes in the statistics of any output. It follows that an adversary looking at the output of any analysis cannot reason with high confidence about the individual's data. Various mechanisms for achieving differential privacy have been studied in the literature [13, 12, 3]. The Laplace mechanism requires adding a Laplace noise to the query output and was proposed in [1]. In the recent paper [5], a staircase mechanism is shown to be the optimal noise-adding mechanism in terms of maximizing the accuracy of a query. In [4], the notion of differential privacy is expanded to include streaming and online computations in which the adversary can look at the entire sequence of outputs from the analysis algorithm.

Our work is concerned with protecting the privacy of the agent's states and preferences instead of its participation status. Consequently, like the definitions presented in [6, 15], we define differential privacy in terms of adjacent preferences that are identical for all agents excepting one agent whose preferences are close as measured by the L^1 norm. Our notion of ϵ-differential privacy ensures that an adversary with access to all the communication in the system cannot gain information about the preference of any agent up to time T with any significant probability.

In the paper [10], the authors develop a notion of differential privacy which ensures that an adversary cannot tell the exact input to a dynamical system by looking at its output stream. Laplace and Gaussian mechanisms are presented for converting an ordinary dynamical system to a differentially private one. Unlike our message-based and distributed implementation schemes, here the privacy-preserving implementation consists of a filter and an estimator which are de-

---

[1]If the communication strategy uses randomization, the the overall system is purely probabilistic.

signed to minimize the mean-squared error from the outputs of the ideal system. In the follow-up work [11], a Kalman filter is designed to estimate the states of differentially private systems with minimized error. The sufficient condition of the minimization problem is established in the form of linear matrix inequalities. The problem studied in this paper is different from the ones introduced in these two papers in several ways. First, in the class of systems studied here, an agent's dynamics is coupled with the environment which depends on the aggregate of all other agents' states. Secondly, these systems are "closed loop" and the noise added for privacy in one round affects all future states of the system.

The results in this paper generalize our previous work on differentially private iterative consensus [8] where the agent are required to converge to a common value while preserving the privacy of their initial values. Setting the coupling to zero, it is possible to recover the mechanism in [8] from the communication strategy proposed here.

3. PRELIMINARIES

For a set S, S^k and S^ω denote the k-arity and infinite Cartesian products of S. For a natural number $N \in \mathbb{N}$, we denote the set $\{1, \dots, N\}$ by $[N]$.

For a set S, $\mathcal{P}(S)$ is the set of probability distributions over S. For a random variable X taking values in S with distribution $\mu \in \mathcal{P}(S)$, we write $X \sim \mu$. The mechanisms presented in this paper rely on random real numbers drawn according to the Laplace distribution. $Lap(b)$ denotes the Laplace distribution with probability density function $p_L(x|b) = \frac{1}{2b} e^{-|x|/b}$. This distribution has mean 0 and variance $2b^2$.

For a vector v of length N, the ith component is denoted by v_i. For a vector v in $\mathbb{R}^n$, $|v|_p$ $(1 \leq p \leq \infty)$ stands for the standard L^p-norm for v. Without a subscript, $|\cdot|$ stands for L^1-norm by default. For a matrix $A \in \mathbb{R}^{m \times n}$, $|A|_p = \max_{|v|_p = 1} |Av|_p$ stands for the standard induced p-norm of matrix A. Without a subscript, $|A|$ stands for induced 1-norm of A.

A matrix $K \in \mathbb{R}^{n \times n}$ is said to be stable, if the modulus of all the eigenvalues of K are smaller than unity. The smaller the maximum modulus of eigenvalues of K, the more stable K is. If some of the eigenvalues are larger than 1, it is said to be unstable. A property of a stable matrix A is that for any x, $A^t x \to \mathbf{0}$ vector as $t \to 0$.

The behavior of the complete system in this paper is modeled as a Markov chain parametrized by a quantity p, and which produces some observations. This Markov chain $\mathcal{M}(p) = \langle Q, Y, q_0, \mu, \eta \rangle$, where each of the following components may depend on p: (i) Q is a measurable set of states, (ii) Y is a set of observations, (iii) $q_0 \in Q$ is the initial state, (iv) $\mu : Q \to \mathcal{P}(Q)$ is a *probabilistic state transition function*, and (v) $\eta : Q \to Y$ is the *observation function*. We will denote the components of $\mathcal{M}(p)$ by $Q_{\mathcal{M}(p)}, Y_{\mathcal{M}(p)}, \mu_{\mathcal{M}(p)}$, etc.

An *execution* of length k of $\mathcal{M}(p)$ is a sequence of states $\alpha = q_0, q_1, \dots, q_{k-1}$, such that for each $i \in [k]$, $\mu(q_{k-1}, q_k) > 0$. The probability measure over the space of executions $\mathbb{P}_{\mathcal{M}(p)}$ is defined in the standard way by first defining a σ-algebra of cones over the space of executions, and then by defining the probability of the cones by integrating over μ (see for example [14]).

For the execution α of length k, the corresponding *observation* is a sequence in Y^k obtained by point-wise ap-

plication the observation function to α, that is, $\eta_{\mathcal{M}(p)}(\alpha) \triangleq \eta_{\mathcal{M}(p)}(q_0), \dots, \eta_{\mathcal{M}(p)}(q_{k-1})$. For a given observation sequence $\beta \in Y^k$, the corresponding set of executions $\eta_{\mathcal{M}(p)}^{-1}(\beta)$ is defined as the set $\{\alpha \mid \eta_{\mathcal{M}(p)}(\alpha) = \beta\}$ and the functions $\eta_{\mathcal{M}(p)}$ and $\eta_{\mathcal{M}(p)}^{-1}$ are extended to sets of executions and observations in the usual way.

4. DISTRIBUTED CONTROL SYSTEMS

We begin by defining a distributed control system abstractly (see Figure 1) ; Section 6 provides more concrete instantiations of these definitions in terms of linear models. A control system consists of N agents operating in a shared environment. Agent i, $i \in [N]$, has a preference p_i. The agent's behavior consists of a physical part which evolves according to some deterministic dynamics and a controller which computes the control inputs for the physical dynamics. The agent uses a communication strategy r to broadcast some noisy version of its state to the other agents. The broadcasts are noisy to preserve privacy and are used to estimate the state of the environment. These estimates are used by the i's controller for computing the inputs (along side its own state).

Fixing the vector of preferences p for all agents, the evolution of the complete system becomes a stochastic process, specifically a Markov chain with observations $\mathcal{M}(p)$ with the stochasticity arising from the noise values used in the communication strategy of the individual agents.

The Markov chain modeling the distributed control system is specified by the following parameters: (a) Euclidean spaces $\mathcal{X}, \mathcal{U}$ and $\mathcal{Z}$ which define an individual agent's state space, its control input space, and the state space of the environment, respectively. (b) The preferences of each agent i ($p_i \in \mathcal{X}^\omega$) consisting of a sequence of points in the individual agent's state space $\mathcal{X}$ which defines a path agent i wants to follow. (c) A *dynamics function* $f : \mathcal{X} \times \mathcal{U} \times \mathcal{Z} \to \mathcal{X}$ which defines the next state of an agent as a function of its current state, control input and the environment's state. (d) An *aggregation function* $h : \mathcal{X}^N \to \mathcal{Z}$ which defines the state of the environment as a function of the agent states. (e) A *control function* $g : \mathcal{X} \times \mathcal{Z} \times \mathbb{N} \to \mathcal{U}$ which defines the agent's controller output as a function of its state, the environment state and the current time. And finally (f) A *probabilistic observation map* $r : \mathcal{X} \times \mathcal{Z} \times \mathbb{N} \to \mathcal{P}(\mathcal{X})$ which selects a noisy state observation for an agent as a function of its actual state, its knowledge of the environment and the current time.

The dynamics functions f and the aggregation function h capture the physical behavior of the system and the coupling between agents—as the control designers, we cannot change them. In this paper, we assume that the controller function g is obtained through existing control theoretic techniques (see Section 2 for a discussion of related work). The only component up for design is the observation map r. In defining the Markov chain below, we will use r to probabilistically update a state component of the agent (called $\tilde{x}_i$ below) which is produced as an observation. This simplifies our model by keeping the observation function η deterministic.

A state of agent i is a point in $\mathcal{X}^2 \times \mathcal{U}$ and its three components are the true agent state (denoted by x_i), the observed agent state ($\tilde{x}_i$), and the control input (u_i), respectively. The state of the environment is $\mathcal{Z}^2$ and the two components are the (true) environment state (z) and the observed environment state ($\tilde{z}$). Thus, the state space of the Markov chain modeling the complete system is $Q \triangleq (\mathcal{X}^2 \times \mathcal{U})^N \times \mathcal{Z}^2$. For each $i \in [N]$ the projection functions $x_i, \tilde{x}_i : Q \to \mathcal{X}$, $u_i : Q \to \mathcal{U}$ give the state, the observed state, and the control input of agent i at system state q. Similarly, $z, \tilde{z} : Q \to \mathcal{Z}$ give the environment state and the observed environment state at q. The space of observations for the Markov chain is $Y \triangleq \mathcal{X}^N \times \mathcal{Z}$. The transition probabilities from a state $q_{t-1} \in Q$ at time $t \in \mathbb{N}$ is defined by the following sequence of equations:

$$u_i(q_t) = g(x_i(q_{t-1}), \tilde{z}(q_{t-1}), t) \tag{1}$$

$$x_i(q_t) = f(x_i(q_{t-1}), u_i(q_t), z(q_{t-1})) \tag{2}$$

$$\tilde{x}_i(q_t) \sim r(x_i(q_t), \tilde{z}(q_{t-1}), t) \tag{3}$$

$$z(q_t) = h(x_1(q_t), \ldots, x_N(q_t)) \tag{4}$$

$$\tilde{z}(q_t) = h(\tilde{x}_1(q_t), \ldots, \tilde{x}_N(q_t)) \tag{5}$$

The first three equations define values of the control input (u_i), the agents state (x_i), and the environment state (z_i), for each $i \in [N]$, in the post state q_t as functions of q_{t-1}. The value of $\tilde{x}_i(q_t)$'s is chosen according to the probability distribution $r(x_i(q_t), t)$ and $\tilde{z}_i(q_t)$.

The observation function η of the Markov chain is defined as follows: for any state $q \in Q$,

$$\eta(q) \triangleq \langle \tilde{x}_1(q), \ldots, \tilde{x}_N(q), \tilde{z}(q) \rangle.$$

In other words, an observation is simply the projection of the state on the $\tilde{x}$ and $\tilde{z}$ components. We sometimes use $x_i(t)$ as $x_i(q_t)$ for short if the execution is clear in the context.

The initial state q_0 is specified by the global preference vector p and the aggregate function h. For each agent, the initial state is defined by the first point of its preference $x_i(q_0) = p_i(0)$. Then the aggregate state is $z(q_0) = h(x_1(q_0), \ldots, x_N(q_0))$. The initial control inputs (u_i) and the initial observed agent states ($\tilde{x}_i$) and initial observed environment state ($\tilde{y}$) are set to 0.

Interpretation of Markov Transitions. From state q_t, the control input $u_i(q_t)$ for agent i is obtained by applying the possibly time-varying control function g to the agent's previous state $x_i(q_{t-1})$ and the observed aggregate $\tilde{z}(q_{t-1})$ at t. The new agent state $x_i(q_t)$ is obtained by applying the dynamics function f to the agent's state at step $t-1$, the state of the environment $z(q_{t-1})$ at $t-1$ and the newly computed control input $u_i(q_t)$. The agent i's observed state $\tilde{x}_i(q_t)$ is updated by choosing a value from the time-varying distribution $r(x_i(q_t), z(q_{t-1}), t)$. This distribution defines how noise is added to the actual value of the state $x_i(q_t)$. The actual environment state and the observed environment state are computed by applying the aggregation function h to the new agent states and the observed agent states. An *execution* of Markov chain $\mathcal{M}(p)$ of length T is a sequence $\alpha = q_0 \ldots q_{T-1}$, where $q_t \in (\mathcal{X}^2 \times \mathcal{U})^N \times \mathcal{Z}^2$. We denote the set $\mathsf{Execs}_{p,T}$ to be the set of all executions up to time T of the distributed system parameterized by p. The observation up to time T $\eta(\alpha)$ is a sequence of $(\tilde{x}_1, \tilde{x}_2, \ldots, \tilde{x}_N, \tilde{z})$ that lives in the space $Y^T = (\mathcal{X}^N \times \mathcal{Z})^T$. The only sources of uncertainty in the behavior of a control system are (a) the preferences of the agents (p) and (b) the randomized observation map (r) which is used to disseminate noisy private information for the sake of better performance. Thus, given a preference vector and an observation sequence, and the

knowledge of the parameters f, g, h, it is possible to infer a unique execution of $\mathcal{M}(p)$. We formalize this notion in Proposition 1.

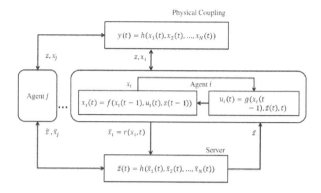

Figure 1: Close-loop distributed system

PROPOSITION 1. *For any randomized control mechanism $\mathcal{M}$, given a preference vector p and an observation sequence β of length k, $\eta^{-1}_{\mathcal{M}(p)}(\beta)$ is a singleton set.*

PROOF. The proof is by induction on the length of β. If β is of length one then $\eta^{-1}(\beta)$ is the single start state θ. As we mentioned previously, the agent i's state matches the first point of p_i, that is $x_i(\theta) = p_i(0)$ which is specified by p. Also, $z(\theta) = h(x_1(\theta), \ldots, x_N(\theta))$. And other variables are initialized as 0. Thus, the start state θ is fixed.

Suppose $\beta = \beta' y$ be an observation of length $k+1$, where $\eta^{-1}(\beta')$ is the unique execution α' ending with last state $q_k = \langle u, x, \tilde{x}, z, \tilde{z} \rangle$. It suffices to show that for the given state q_k and the observation y, there is a unique state q_{k+1} which makes $\alpha' q_{k+1} = \eta^{-1}(\beta)$. From Equation (1), it follows that for each $i \in [N]$, $u_i(q_{k+1})$ is uniquely defined as $g(x_i(q_k), \tilde{z}(q_k), t+1)$. This and Equation (2) implies that $x_i(q_{k+1})$ is uniquely defined. Similarly, the u_i's and the x_i's together with Equation (4) imply that $z(q_{k+1})$ is also uniquely defined. Finally, $\tilde{x}_i(q_{k+1}) = \tilde{x}_i(y)$ and $\tilde{z}(q_{k+1}) = \tilde{z}(y)$ by the definition of the observation function η. $\square$

Thus, given an observation sequence β, there is a one-to-one correspondence between the global preference p and the execution α. Fix an observation sequence, if the adversary has a high confident guess of the preference vector p, then the agents' whole trajectory corresponding to such a p is also of high validity. Otherwise, if the preference vector is protected, the evolution of the agents is hidden. So it suffices to consider privacy of the preference vector p.

4.1 Privacy and Cost in Distributed Control

For formulating privacy of a distributed control system, we first define comparable and adjacent preference vectors. For a pair of preference vectors p and p', the corresponding Markov chains $\mathcal{M}(p)$ and $\mathcal{M}(p')$ are *comparable* if the observable spaces are identical, that is, $Y_{\mathcal{M}(p)} = Y_{\mathcal{M}(p')}$.

DEFINITION 1. *A pair of preference vectors p and p' in $(\mathcal{X}^\omega)^N$ are adjacent up to time T, written as $T\text{-}adj(p, p')$ in short, if there exists a $k \in [N]$, such that for all $t \leq T$, such that (i) $|p_k(t) - p'_k(t)| \leq 1$, and (ii) for all $i \neq k$ $p_i(t) = p'_i(t)$.*

In other words, two preference vectors are T-adjacent if they differ only in the preferences of a single agent upto time T, and the difference in terms of the L^1 norm is at most unity at each time. We adapt the standard definition of differential privacy to this framework of control mechanisms, where the protection of the individual agent's preferences have to be balanced with the benefits of information sharing for control in a shared environment.

DEFINITION 2. *The randomized control mechanism $\mathcal{M}$ is ϵ-differentially private upto time T, if for any two T-adjacent preference vectors p and p' and any set of finite observation sequences Obs, $\mathcal{M}(p)$ and $\mathcal{M}(p')$ are comparable and*

$$\mathbb{P}_{\mathcal{M}(p)}[\eta^{-1}_{\mathcal{M}(p)}(Obs)] \le e^\epsilon \mathbb{P}_{\mathcal{M}(p')}[\eta^{-1}_{\mathcal{M}(p')}(Obs)]. \quad (6)$$

This definition of differential privacy is similar to the one appears in [4] with two technical differences. First, we restrict the preferences to be adjacent upto a time bound. Secondly, owing our choice of the definition of $\mathcal{M}(p)$ which allows all the components of $\mathcal{M}(p)$ to possibly depend on p, for privacy of individual agent's preferences with respect to observation sequences produced from to Markov chains, it is required that the output alphabets of the corresponding chains are same. This requirement is incorporated by making the chains comparable.

Performance of a distributed control system is measured by a cost function. It is standard to consider the following quadratic cost in optimal control theory. Given an execution of length $T+1$, $\alpha = q_0, q_1, \ldots, q_T$, the cost of control for an individual agent i upto T time is the sum of squared distance between the agent's state and its preferred state. That is, $cost_{\mathcal{M}(p),i}(\alpha) \triangleq \sum_{t=1}^{T}(x_i(q_t) - p_i(t))^\top (x_i(q_t) - p_i(t))$. The summation starts with $t=1$ because by definition $x_i(q_0) = p_i(0)$ and no cost is paid at time $t=0$. The cost function of agent i is the expectation of the function $cost_{\mathcal{M}(p),i}(\alpha)$ over the space of executions of length T,

$$cost_{\mathcal{M}(p),i}(T) \triangleq \mathbb{E}\left[\sum_{t=1}^{T}(x_i(q_t) - p_i(t))^\top (x_i(q_t) - p_i(t)) \right]. \quad (7)$$

We introduce an example of a distributed control problem.

Example 1 This example captures the routing of N agents on a 2-D plane whose motion is affected by the center of gravity of all the agents. The agent i's state $x_i \in \mathcal{X} \subseteq \mathbb{R}^2$ has two components, which are the x and y coordinates of agent i. Each agent has a preference which is a path $p_i \in (\mathbb{R}^2)^\omega$. The individual agent's state at time t is affected by three factors: the previous state $x_i(t-1)$, the aggregate state– which is the center of the gravity of the herd–$z(t-1)$ and the individual's control input $u_i(t)$. The update law of the ith agent's state at time $t+1$ follows

$$x_i(t) = 1.5x_i(t-1) + cz(t-1) + u_i(t). \quad (8)$$

The aggregate state $z \in \mathcal{Z} \subset \mathbb{R}^2$ is the center of gravity of the herd.

$$z(t) = \frac{1}{N} \sum_{i \in [N]} x_i(t).$$

Designing a controller for the ith agent, which cancels out the influence of the aggregate state on individual agent and

drives it towards the goal $p_i(t+1)$, needs the actual states of all other agents. With the precise information of others, agent i can achieve its desirable individual cost by using some optimal control technique. For example, the following controller may be used:

$$u_i(t) = -cz(t-1) - 1.3x_i(t-1) + 0.8p_i(t). \quad (9)$$

Combined Equations (9) and (8), we get the update rule for the whole close-loop system

$$x_i(t) = 0.2x_i(t-1) + 0.8p_i(t). \quad (10)$$

The current state $x_i(t)$ is a linear combination of the previous state $x_i(t-1)$ and the current preference $p_i(t)$. If the sequence of preference p_i is fixed for a few rounds, the state x_i converges to it geometrically. Otherwise if the sequence of preference is changing, the state x_i keeps tracking it. The cost of individual agent is defined by the some squared distance between its state x_i and p_i, that is,

$$cost(p,T) = \sum_{t=1}^{T} |x_i(t) - p_i(t)|_2^2.$$

In Section 6, we introduce a mechanism that guarantees differential privacy of individuals for this example. $\quad\square$

4.2 Cost of Privacy

We define the cost of a randomized control mechanism $\mathcal{M}$ as the difference in the cost of two nearly identical Markov chains with observations $\mathcal{M}(p)$ and $\mathcal{M}'(p)$, where $\mathcal{M}(p)$ is the differentially private Markov chain and $\mathcal{M}'(p)$ is identical except that its observation map discloses perfect information about the agents' states. Formally, given $\mathcal{M}(p)$ defined by the parameters f, g, h, and r the perfectly observable version $\mathcal{M}'(p)$ is defined by the parameters f, g, h and r' where

$$r'(x_i(q_t), \tilde{z}(q_t), t) \triangleq \delta_{x_i(q_t)},$$

where δ_a is the Dirac delta distribution at a.

DEFINITION 3. *For any $\epsilon > 0$ and time bound $T \in \mathbb{N}$, and an ϵ-differentially private randomized control mechanism $\mathcal{M}$, the Cost of Privacy (CoP) upto time T, is defined by the supremum of the difference between any individual's cost in $\mathcal{M}(p)$ and the corresponding perfectly observable chain $\mathcal{M}'(p)$ over all preference vector p:*

$$CoP(\epsilon, \mathcal{M}, T) \triangleq \sup_{p,i} \left(cost_{\mathcal{M}'(p),i}(T) - cost_{\mathcal{M}(p),i}(T) \right).$$

We will discuss the cost of privacy of Example 1 in Section 6.2

5. LAPLACE OBSERVATIONS OF DIFFERENTIAL PRIVACY

In this section, we introduce a strategy for creating observation maps that guarantees differential privacy of the agents' preferences. For the remainder of this paper let n be the length of local state x_i. In this design, at time t, each agent reports $\tilde{x}_i(t)$ by adding a noise $\omega_i(t)$ on its actual state $x_i(t)$, that is

$$r(x_i(q_t)) \triangleq x_i(q_t) + \omega_i(t), \quad (11)$$

where $\omega_i(t)$ is a vector consists of n independent random noises drawn from Laplace distribution $Lap(M_t)$.

Before proposing an actual design of M_t, we first define sensitivity of the system. Fix an observation sequence $\beta \in Y^T$ up to time T and a preference vector p. As we mentioned in Proposition 1, $\eta_{\mathcal{M}(p)}^{-1}(\beta)$ is a singleton set. Then, $x(\eta_{\mathcal{M}(p)}^{-1}(\beta)(t))$ is the global state at time t corresponding to the execution $\eta_{\mathcal{M}(p)}^{-1}(\beta)$. To quantify the maximal difference of the system's global states at time t resulted from a pair of adjacent preference vectors p and p', we introduce the sensitivity of the system.

DEFINITION 4. *For a mechanism $\mathcal{M}$, we define the sensitivity of $\mathcal{M}$ at time $t \in \mathbb{N}$ as*

$$\Delta(t) \triangleq \sup_\beta \sup_{adj(p,p')} |x(\eta_{\mathcal{M}(p)}^{-1}(\beta(t))) - x(\eta_{\mathcal{M}(p')}^{-1}(\beta(t)))|,$$

where the norm used is L^1-norm.

We assume that $\Delta(t)$ is bounded for any $t \in \mathbb{N}$ throughout the paper.

THEOREM 2. *At each time $t \in [T]$, if each agent adds a noise vector $\omega_i(t)$ which consists of n independent Laplace noise $Lap(M_t)$ such that $\sum_{t=0}^T \frac{\Delta(t)}{M_t} \leq \epsilon$, then the distributed control system is ϵ-differentially private.*

PROOF. Fix a pair of T-adjacent preference vectors $p, p' \in \mathcal{X}^{TN}$. and a set of observation sequence $Obs \subseteq Y^T$. we will denote the sets of executions $\eta_{\mathcal{M}(p)}^{-1}(Obs)$ and $\eta_{\mathcal{M}(p')}^{-1}(Obs)$ by A and A' respectively. First, we define a correspondence B between the sets A and A'. For $\alpha \in A$ and $\alpha' \in A'$, $B(\alpha) = \alpha'$ if and only if they are the observation sequence up to time T. That is $\eta(\alpha(t)) = \eta(\alpha'(t))$ for all $t \in [T]$. From Proposition 1, for any observation sequence $\beta \in Obs$ there is a unique execution $\alpha \in \mathsf{Execs}_p$ that can produce the observation. Similarly, α' is also unique in $\mathsf{Execs}_{p'}$. So B is indeed a bijection. we relate the probability measures of the sets of executions A and A'.

$$\frac{\mathbb{P}_{\mathcal{M}(p)}[\eta_{\mathcal{M}(p)}^{-1}(Obs)]}{\mathbb{P}_{\mathcal{M}(p')}[\eta_{\mathcal{M}(p')}^{-1}(Obs)]} = \frac{\int_{\alpha \in A} \mathbb{P}_{\mathcal{M}(p)}[\alpha] d\mu}{\int_{\alpha' \in A'} \mathbb{P}_{\mathcal{M}(p')}[\alpha'] d\mu}. \tag{12}$$

Changing the variable using the bijection B we have,

$$\begin{aligned}\int_{\alpha' \in A'} \mathbb{P}_{\mathcal{M}(p')}[\alpha'] d\mu' &= \int_{B(\alpha) \in A'} \mathbb{P}_{\mathcal{M}(p)}[B(\alpha)] d\mu \\ &= \int_{\alpha \in A} \mathbb{P}_{\mathcal{M}(p)}[B(\alpha)] d\mu\end{aligned} \tag{13}$$

From Equations (1)-(5) the definition of r,

$$\int_{\alpha \in A} \mathbb{P}_{\mathcal{M}(p)}[\alpha] d\mu = \int_{\alpha \in A} \mathbb{P}_{\mathcal{M}(p)}[\tilde{x}(\alpha)|x(\alpha)] d\mu$$

where $x(t)$ is the vector of N agent states at t along execution α. Each $x_i(t)$ is a vector of length n. We denote the k state component of $x_i(t)$ by $x_i^{(k)}(t)$. As $\tilde{x}(t)$ is obtained by adding $n \times N$ independent noise values to $x(t)$, from the distribution $Lap(M_t)$, it follows that the probability density of an execution is reduced to

$$\mathbb{P}_{\mathcal{M}(p)}[\tilde{x}(\alpha)|x(\alpha)] = \prod_{\substack{i \in [N] \\ k \in [n] \\ t \in [T]}} p_L(\tilde{x}_i^{(k)}(\alpha(t)) - x_i^{(k)}(\alpha(t))|M_t),$$

$$\tag{14}$$

where $p_L(x|b)$ is the probability density function at x with parameter b. Then, we relate the distance at time t between

the state of α and $B(\alpha)$ with the sensitivity $\Delta(t)$. Let $\beta = \eta(\alpha)$ be the observation sequence corresponding to α.

By the Definition 4, we have

$$|x(\alpha(t)) - x(\alpha'(t))| \leq \Delta(t).$$

The norm in above equation is L^1-norm. The global state $x(t)$ consists of N local state $x_i(t)$, each of which has n component. So $|x(\alpha(t)) - x(\alpha'(t))|$ lives in space $\mathbb{R}^{nN}$. By definition of L^1-norm:

$$\begin{aligned}&\sum_{i=1}^N \sum_{k=1}^n |x_i^{(k)}(\alpha(t)) - x_i^{(k)}(\alpha'(t))| \\ &= |x_i(\alpha(t)) - x_i(\alpha'(t))| \leq \Delta(t).\end{aligned}$$

Recall that by definition of B, the observations of α and $B(\alpha)$ match, that is $\tilde{x}(\alpha(t)) = \tilde{x}(B(\alpha)(t))$. From the property of Laplace distribution,

$$\begin{aligned}&\prod_{i \in [N] k \in [n]} \frac{p_L(\tilde{x}_i^{(k)}(\alpha(t)) - x_i^{(k)}(\alpha(t))|M_t)}{p_L(\tilde{x}_i^{(k)}(B(\alpha)(t)) - x_i^{(k)}(B(\alpha)(t))|M_t)} \\ &\leq \prod_{i \in [N], k \in [n]} e^{\frac{|\tilde{x}(\alpha(t)) - x(\alpha(t)) - \tilde{x}(B(\alpha)(t)) + x(B(\alpha)(t))|}{M_t}} \\ &= \prod_{i \in [N], k \in [n]} e^{\frac{|x(\alpha(t)) - x(B(\alpha)(t))|}{M_t}} \\ &= e^{\sum_{i \in [N], k \in [n]} \frac{|x(\alpha(t)) - x(B(\alpha)(t))|}{M_t}} \\ &\leq e^{\frac{\Delta(t)}{M_t}}.\end{aligned} \tag{15}$$

Combining Equation (12), (13), (14) and (15), we derive

$$\begin{aligned}&\frac{\mathbb{P}_{\mathcal{M}(p)}[\eta_{\mathcal{M}(p)}^{-1}(Obs)]}{\mathbb{P}_{\mathcal{M}(p')}[\eta_{\mathcal{M}(p')}^{-1}(Obs)]} \\ &\leq \frac{\int_{\alpha \in A} \mathbb{P}_{\mathcal{M}(p)}[\tilde{x}(\alpha)|x(\alpha)] d\mu}{\int_{\alpha \in A} \mathbb{P}_{\mathcal{M}(p)}[\tilde{x}(B(\alpha))|x(B(\alpha))] d\mu} \\ &\leq \prod_{t \in [T]} e^{\frac{\Delta(t)}{M_t}} \leq e^{\sum_{t \in [T]} \frac{\Delta(t)}{M_t}}\end{aligned}$$

If M_t satisfy $\sum_{t=0}^T \frac{\Delta_D(t)}{M_t} \leq \epsilon$, then $\prod_{t \in [T]} e^{\frac{\Delta(t)}{M_t}} \leq e^\epsilon$. Thus the theorem holds. □

We can also derive the following corollary from Theorem 2.

COROLLARY 3. *At each time $t \in [T]$ if each agent adds an vector of independent Laplace noise $Lap(M_t)$, where $M_t = \frac{\Delta_D(t)T}{\epsilon}$ to its actual state, then the distributed control system is ϵ-differentially private.*

In this mechanism, the noise added is proportional to the sensitivity of the system and the time bound of the system T. Roughly, an adversary can examine a number of T observations of an individual agent. The parameter of the Laplace noises added is proportional to the length of the observation and the sensitivity of the system.

6. DIFFERENTIALLY PRIVATE LINEAR DISTRIBUTED CONTROL

In this section, we will specialize the general framework of Section 4 to linear control systems. Linear models for the physical dynamics and linear controller functions are the predominant models studied in control theory literature. In this setup, the optimal controller design problem can be formulated and solved effectively using convex optimization. We assume that agent i's state (x_i), its observed state $(\tilde{x}_i)$, its control input (u_i), the environment state (z), and the observed environment state $(\tilde{z})$ are all points in $\mathbb{R}^n$, for some natural number n. Agent i's preference is an infinite (possibly repeated) sequence of points in $\mathbb{R}^n$. Next, we define the remaining four parameters of the control system. The linear dynamics function for the ith agent is:

$$f(x_i, z, t) \triangleq A x_i + c z + u_i,$$

where $A \in \mathbb{R}^{n \times n}$ is the dynamics matrix and $c \in \mathbb{R}$ is a coupling constant. The linear aggregation function h computes the average of the agent states, which is defined as

$$h(x) \triangleq \frac{1}{N} \sum_{i \in [N]} x_i.$$

For this type of dynamics, a linear feedback controller suffices to drive the agent to any fixed preference point. We choose a general linear feedback control function of the form:

$$g(x_i, z, t) \triangleq (K - A) x_i + (I - K) p_i(t) - c \tilde{z},$$

where $K \in \mathbb{R}^{n \times n}$ is a *stable matrix* and I is the identity matrix. Finally, the form of the observation map is

$$r(x_i, t) \triangleq x_i + \omega_i(t),$$

where $\omega_i(t)$ is drawn from a time-dependent probability distribution to be defined below.

As in the general case (Section 4), given a preference vector p, the above parameters define the Markov chain $\mathcal{M}(p)$ which captures the evolution of the system. The system of equations defining the transitions of this Markov chain, corresponding to Equations (1)-(5), can be written as follows: At time $t \in \mathbb{N}$

$$u_i(t) = (K - A) x_i(t-1) + (I - K) p_i(t) - c \tilde{z}(t-1) \quad (16)$$

$$x_i(t) = A x_i(t-1) + c z(t-1) + u_i(t) \quad (17)$$

$$\tilde{x}_i(t) = x_i(t) + \omega_i(t) \quad (18)$$

$$z(t) = \frac{1}{N} \sum_{i \in [N]} x_i(t) \quad (19)$$

$$\tilde{z}(t) = \frac{1}{N} \sum_{i \in [N]} \tilde{x}_i(t). \quad (20)$$

Combining the above equations, the closed-loop dynamics of agent i is:

$$x_i(t) = K x_i(t-1) + (I - K) p_i(t) - \frac{c}{N} \sum_{i \in [N]} \omega_i(t-1). \quad (21)$$

Agent i's state at time t can be written as a function of its preference sequence $\{p_i(s)\}_{s \le t}$ and the sequence $\{\omega_i(s) : i \in [N], s \le t\}$ of noise vectors added in all previous rounds. By iteratively applying Equation (21), we obtain:

$$x_i(t) = K^t p_i(0) + \sum_{s=1}^{t} K^{t-s}(I - K) p_i(s)$$
$$\quad - \frac{c}{N} \sum_{s=0}^{t-1} K^{t-s-1} \sum_{i \in [N]} \omega_i(s). \quad (22)$$

Remark 1. By taking expectation on both side of Equation (21), we can write $x_i(t) - p_i(t) = K(x_i(t-1) - p_i(t))$. Given a stable the matrix K, for agent i, after update at time t, the new state gets closer to the preference $p_i(t)$. The more stable K is, the better tracking $x(t)$ performs towards $p(t)$.

For representing the dynamics of the complete system with N agents, we define two $nN \times nN$ matrices

$$\mathbf{K} \triangleq \begin{bmatrix} K & & \\ & \ddots & \\ & & K \end{bmatrix} \text{ and } \mathbf{C} \triangleq \frac{c}{N} \begin{bmatrix} I & \dots & I \\ \vdots & \ddots & \vdots \\ I & \dots & I \end{bmatrix},$$

where $\mathbf{K}$ is a block diagonal matrix with K matrices as its diagonal blocks and $\mathbf{C}$ is a block matrix with all the blocks set to $\frac{c}{N}$ times the identity matrix I. Combining the Equation (21) for all the N agents we obtain:

$$\begin{aligned} x(t) &= \mathbf{K} x(t-1) + (I - \mathbf{K}) p(t) + \mathbf{C} x(t-1) - \tilde{z}(t-1) \\ &= (\mathbf{K} + \mathbf{C}) x(t-1) + (I - \mathbf{K}) p(t) - \tilde{z}(t-1). \quad (23) \end{aligned}$$

Given a preference vector p and an observation sequence β, by Proposition 1, we know that there is a unique execution $\eta_{\mathcal{M}(p)}^{-1}(\beta)$. The vector of agent states at time $t \ge 0$, along this execution is $x(\eta_{\mathcal{M}(p)}^{-1}(\beta)(t))$. Iteratively applying Equation (23) we obtain:

$$x(\eta_{\mathcal{M}(p)}^{-1}(\beta(t))) = (\mathbf{K} + \mathbf{C})^t p(0) - \sum_{s=0}^{t-1} (\mathbf{K} + \mathbf{C})^{t-s} \tilde{z}(\beta(t))$$
$$+ \sum_{s=1}^{t} (\mathbf{K} + \mathbf{C})^{t-s} (I - \mathbf{K}) p(s).$$

6.1 Sensitivity of Linear Distributed Control

In this section, we state Theorem 4 which establishes bound on the sensitivity $\Delta(t)$. We refer the reader to the full version of the paper for the proof of this nontrivial result [9]. For proving this theorem, we fix two Markov chains of the system (Equations (16) -(20)) with adjacent preference vectors p and p' and compute the difference between two chains. Recall that p and p' are identical except the preference of one agent (i). Then, the difference between the two Markov chains has two components: (1) the change in agent i's state, and (2) the sum of changes in other agents' state. The sensitivity is then computed as a bound of the sum of above two components. With this bound on sensitivity, we introduce a Laplace mechanism defining the observation map (r) in Corollary 5 and then show that the mechanism achieves differential privacy of the linear distributed control system.

THEOREM 4. *For the linear distributed control system, for all $t \in \mathbb{N}$ the sensitivity $\Delta(t)$ is upper bounded by $\kappa(t)$, where*

$$\kappa(t) \triangleq |G^t - K^t| + |K^t| + |H| \sum_{s=0}^{t-1} (|G^s - K^s| + |K^s|),$$

with $G \triangleq cI + K$ and $H \triangleq I - K$.

Remark 2. The upper bound on the sensitivity at time t, $\kappa(t)$ has two components:

(a) $|K^t| + |H| \sum_{s=1}^{t} |K^s|$ overapproximates the change in agent i's state (x_i) if its own preference changes by at most unity at each time upto t, and

(b) $|G^s - K^s| + |H| \sum_{s=0}^{t-1} |G^s - K^s|$ overapproximates the sum of the changes in other agents' state given agent i's preference changes by at most unity upto t.

Remark 3. $\kappa(t)$ is independent to the number of agents (N). It only depends on matrix K, the coupling constant c and time t. K is specified by the individual's control function (Equation (16)), which assumes to be stable. The more stable matrix K is, the faster $|K^t|$ decays to 0. The coupling constant c quantifies the influence of the aggregate on each individual agent. The matrix $G = cI + K$ captures the combined dynamics under the influence of the environment and the dynamics of the individual agents. The weaker physical coupling is, the smaller $|G^t|$ is. Therefore, we conclude that, as the individual agent dynamics becomes more stable or the physical coupling between agents becomes weaker, the sensitivity of the system decreases.

Remark 4. The dependence of $\kappa(t)$ on time t changes based on the stability of the K and G matrices. If G is stable, $\kappa(t)$ converges to a constant as $t \to \infty$. Otherwise if G is unstable, $\kappa(t)$ grows exponentially with t.

Theorems 2 and 4 immediately suggest an observation map (r) which guarantees differential privacy of the distributed linear control system.

COROLLARY 5. *For any time bound T and privacy parameter $\epsilon > 0$, for $M_t \triangleq \frac{T\kappa(t)}{\epsilon}$ and $\omega_i(t)$ chosen as noise vector of length n drawn independently from the distribution $Lap(M_t)$, the resulting observation map makes the linear distributed control system ϵ-differentially private up to time T.*

Example 2 Now we can apply the strategy explained above to Example 1, where $K = \frac{1}{5}I$ is a 2 by 2 matrix. $G = (c+\frac{1}{5})I$ in this case. By Theorem 4, the sensitivity is

$$\Delta(t) \leq \kappa(t) = G^t + (I - K) \sum_{s=0}^{t-1} G^s,$$
$$= \frac{4+20c}{20-25c} + \frac{16-45c}{20-25c}\left(c + \frac{1}{5}\right)^t$$

As stated in Remark 3, the sensitivity is independent of N. If G is stable, that is $|c + \frac{1}{5}| \leq 1$, the sensitivity $\Delta(t)$ is bounded and converges to a constant as $t \to \infty$. Otherwise, if $|c + \frac{1}{5}| > 1$, $\kappa(t)$ diverges. We choose the noise to be $M_t = \frac{\kappa(t)T}{\epsilon}$. By Corollary 5, the system guarantees ϵ-differential privacy upto time T. □

6.2 Cost of Privacy in Linear Distributed Control

The observation map of Corollary 5 adds independently drawn Laplace noise to the state of agent i observation at time t from the distribution $Lap(M_t)$. The noise parameter M_t depends on the individual's dynamics rather than the number of agents. In this section, we discuss the cost of privacy for this mechanism (see, Definition 3) compared to a perfectly observable system using the same controller.

THEOREM 6. *The cost of privacy of the ϵ-differentially private mechanism $\mathcal{M}$ of Corollary 5 is inversely proportional to the number of agents N and the squared privacy*

parameter ϵ^2. *In addition, if matrix G is stable, it is proportional to T^3. Otherwise if G is unstable, the cost of privacy grows exponentially with T.*

PROOF. Given the ϵ-differentially private mechanism $\mathcal{M}$, the perfectly observable system $\mathcal{M}'$ is obtained by setting the noise values to be 0. We denote by $\bar{x}_i(t)$ the state of agent i for $\mathcal{M}'$ at time t. From Equation (22), by fixing $\omega_i(t) \equiv 0$, we get

$$\bar{x}_i(t) = K^t p_i(0) + \sum_{s=1}^{t} K^{t-s}(I - K) p_i(s).$$

We define a $n \times nN$ matrix $\mathbf{B} \triangleq \frac{c}{N}[I, \ldots, I]$. Let $x_i(t)$ be agent i's state corresponding to some execution of $\mathcal{M}(p)$. Again from Equation (22), the state of an individual agent i is

$$x_i(t) = \bar{x}_i(t) - \sum_{s=0}^{t-1} K^{t-s-1} \mathbf{B} \omega(s).$$

The cost of the mechanism $\mathcal{M}$ can be written as

$$cost_{\mathcal{M},i}(T) = \mathbb{E}\left[\sum_{t=1}^{T} |x_i(t) - p_i(t)|_2^2\right]$$
$$= \mathbb{E}\left[\sum_{t=1}^{T} |\bar{x}_i(t) - \sum_{s=0}^{t-1} K^{t-s-1} \mathbf{B}\omega(s) - p_i(t)|_2^2\right]$$
$$= \sum_{t=1}^{T} \mathbb{E}[|\bar{x}_i(t) - p_i(t)|_2^2 + |\sum_{s=0}^{t-1} K^{t-s-1}\mathbf{B}\omega(s)|_2^2$$
$$- 2(\bar{x}_i(t) - p_i(t))^\top \sum_{s=0}^{t-1} K^{t-s-1}\mathbf{B}\omega(s)]$$

The first term on the right hand side is the cost of the system with perfect observations, that is, $cost_{\mathcal{M}',i}(T)$. The last term on the right hand side is the expectation of a linear combination of zero-mean noise terms, and therefore, equals 0. By Definition 3,

$$CoP(\epsilon, \mathcal{M}, T)$$
$$= \sup_{p,i}[cost_{\mathcal{M}(p),i}(T) - cost_{\mathcal{M}'(p),i}(T)] \quad (24)$$
$$= \sum_{t=1}^{T} \mathbb{E}\left[|\sum_{s=0}^{t-1} K^{t-s-1}\mathbf{B}\omega(s)|_2^2\right]$$

In our Laplace mechanism, for different time steps s, τ, $\omega(s)$ and $\omega(\tau)$ are independent. Thus,

$$\mathbb{E}[\omega(s)^\top \omega(\tau)] = \mathbb{E}[\omega(s)]^\top \mathbb{E}[\omega(\tau)] = 0.$$

Then, the right hand side of Equation (24) reduces to

$$\sum_{t=1}^{T} \mathbb{E}\left[\sum_{s=0}^{t-1} \omega(s)^\top \mathbf{B}^\top (K^{t-s-1})^\top K^{t-s-1} \mathbf{B}\omega(s)\right].$$

Recall that each $\omega(s)$ consists of a noise vector $\omega_i(s)$ for each agent $i \in [N]$, and each of these vectors have n independent and identically distributed noise values drawn from $Lap(M_s)$. Each pair of vectors in $\omega(s)$ are independent. Denote $\omega^{(k)}(s)$, $k \in [nN]$, be the kth element of the vector $\omega(s)$.

It follows that (a) for $k \neq j \in [nN]$, $\mathbb{E}\left[\omega^{(k)}(s)\omega^{(j)}(s)\right] = 0$, and (b) for any $k \in [nN]$, $\mathbb{E}\left[\omega^{(k)}(s)\omega^{(k)}(s)\right] = 2M_s^2$.

Thus,the above expression is reduced to

$$\sum_{t=1}^{T}\sum_{s=0}^{t-1} 2M_s^2 \mathrm{Tr}(\mathbf{B}^\top (K^{t-s-1})^\top K^{t-s-1}\mathbf{B}), \qquad (25)$$

where $\mathrm{Tr}(A)$ stands for the trace of matrix A. Recall that $\mathbf{B} \triangleq \frac{c}{N}[I, \ldots, I]$. It follows that

$$\mathrm{Tr}(\mathbf{B}^\top (K^{t-s-1})^\top K^{t-s-1}\mathbf{B})$$
$$=\frac{c^2}{N}\mathrm{Tr}((K^{t-s-1})^\top K^{t-s-1}) = \frac{c^2}{N}|K^{t-s-1}|_2^2.$$

Substituting the above equation into Equation (25) yields

$$CoP(\epsilon, \mathcal{M}, T) = \frac{2c^2}{N}\sum_{t=1}^{T}\sum_{s=0}^{t-1} M_s^2 |K^{t-s-1}|_2^2$$

By interchanging the order of summation we get

$$CoP(\epsilon, \mathcal{M}, T) = \frac{2c^2}{N}\sum_{s=0}^{T-1}\sum_{t=s+1}^{T} M_s^2 |K^{t-s-1}|_2^2$$
$$= \frac{2c^2}{N}\sum_{s=0}^{T-1} M_s^2 \sum_{t=0}^{T-s-1} |K^t|_2^2. \qquad (26)$$

Recall that in Corollary 5, $M_s = \frac{T\kappa(s)}{\epsilon}$. Combining this with Equation (26), we have

$$CoP(\epsilon, \mathcal{M}, T) = \frac{2c^2T^2}{N\epsilon^2}\sum_{s=0}^{T-1}\kappa(s)^2 \sum_{t=0}^{T-s-1} |K^t|_2^2.$$

From the above expression it is clear $CoP(\epsilon, \mathcal{M}, T)$ is inversely proportional to N and ϵ^2. As the matrix K is stable, $\sum_{t=0}^{T-s-1}|K^t|_2^2$ converges to some constant as $T \to \infty$. By Remark 4, if G is stable then $\kappa(s)$ converges to some constant as $s \to \infty$, $\sum_{s=0}^{T-1}\kappa(s)^2$ grows linearly with T and we have $CoP(\epsilon, \mathcal{M}, T) \sim O(T^3)$. Otherwise if G is unstable, $\kappa(s)$ grows exponentially with s and $CoP(\epsilon, \mathcal{M}, T)$ grows exponentially with T. $\square$

Example 3 Continuing with the system described in Example 1, we now establish the cost of privacy associated with the communication strategy of Equation (26). In this example, $K = 0.2I$. We choose the coupling parameter c to be 0.4. Then, the close-loop system is stable. Therefore, the sensitivity is bounded by $\kappa(t) = 1.2 - 0.2 \times 0.6^t$. The cost of privacy of the system with N agents at time T follows $\frac{0.24T^3}{N\epsilon^2} + O(\frac{T^2}{N\epsilon^2})$.

We have explored an alternative communication strategy which also guarantees ϵ-differential privacy while minimizing the cost of privacy (see the Appendix of [9]). By this strategy, the cost of privacy of the system at time T follows $\frac{0.12T^3}{N\epsilon^2} + O(\frac{T^2}{N\epsilon^2})$. $\square$

Example 4 We conclude with a simulation-based analysis of the traffic control Example 1. Consider a linear distributed control system in which each agent is a point on the plane moving towards a randomly chosen destination with dynamics described in Example 3 and control strategies given in Example 3. The cost of each agent is defined by the distance between its position to its destination. The coupling between agents is the repulsive force in the direction of the center of gravity (CM) of the population. Thus,

if the control of an individual fights the force too strongly without the knowledge of the CM then a higher cost is incurred. We numerically simulated the system with different levels of privacy and different distributions of destinations and make the following observations.

Fig 2 shows the relative costs of control with (blue) no communication and (green) private communication, with respect to cost of control with complete (or broadcast) communication. First of all, if both the initial positions and the destinations are chosen with 0 mean, then the CM of the population hovers around the origin and in that case, the contribution of the coupling is small. As a result, there is not much to be gained through communication and we see (Figure 2) that the cost of the system with privacy is comparable to the cost of the system with no communication. When the destination comes from some distributions slightly biased from 0, we start to see that the cost of control with private communication starts to become smaller compared to those of systems with no communications.

Figure 3 shows that for the same distribution of initial positions and destinations the cost of privacy changes as predicted by Theorem 6. First of all, higher level of privacy comes with higher cost (Figure 3a). As ϵ changes from 0.2 to 2, the CoP changes from 10 to 0.1. Secondly, larger number of agents (N) gives lower cost of privacy (Figure 3b). As N changes from 10 to 100, the CoP decreases from 4 to 0.4. And finally a longer time horizon (T) translates to higher costs (Figure 3c). The simulation results suggest that the cost of privacy roughly has the order of $O(\frac{T^3}{N\epsilon^2})$. $\square$

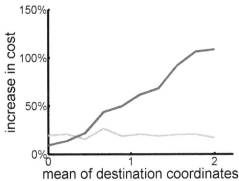

Figure 2: Increase in cost with biased sampled destinations. The blue and green lines capture the relative cost of control with no communication and private communication with respect to the cost of control with broadcast preferences respectively.

7. CONCLUSIONS

We presented a general framework for studying cost of differential privacy for distributed control systems. We proposed a communication strategy by which individual agents can share noisy information about their state which preserves ϵ-differential privacy while aiding the estimation of the aggregate environment and therefore improving control performance. Specializing to linear systems with quadratic costs, we showed that the sensitivity of η^{-1} and therefore the standard deviation of the required noise is independent of the number of participating agents. The sensitivity also decreases with the stability of the dynamics and with the

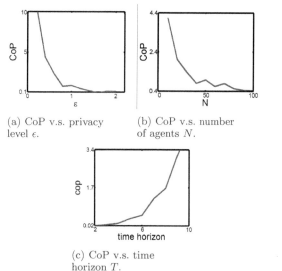

(a) CoP v.s. privacy level ϵ.

(b) CoP v.s. number of agents N.

(c) CoP v.s. time horizon T.

Figure 3: Cost of Privacy for different privacy level, number of agents and time horizon.

weakening the environment's influence on an individual. For stable controllers, for preserving privacy over indefinite time horizons, the variance of the noise to be added is also independent of time. For unstable dynamics, on the other hand, the sensitivity can grow exponentially with time. The cost of ϵ-differential privacy for the proposed communication strategy up to time T for a system with N agents is at most $O(\frac{T^3}{N\epsilon^2})$ for stable systems. This suggests that the proposed communication strategy is best suited for distributed control systems with many short-lived participants.

The proposed framework should enable us to study more sophisticated communication strategies that incur smaller costs for more persistent agents. Another direction for future research will be to establish lower bounds on the best cost of privacy that can be achieved through any communication strategy, not just the form proposed here.

8. REFERENCES

[1] C. Dwork. Differential privacy. In *AUTOMATA, LANGUAGES AND PROGRAMMING*, volume 4052 of *Lecture Notes in Computer Science*, 2006.

[2] C. Dwork. Differential privacy: a survey of results. In *Proceedings of the 5th international conference on Theory and applications of models of computation*, TAMC'08, pages 1–19, Berlin, Heidelberg, 2008. Springer-Verlag.

[3] C. Dwork, K. Kenthapadi, F. McSherry, I. Mironov, and M. Naor. Our data, ourselves: Privacy via distributed noise generation. In S. Vaudenay, editor, *Advances in Cryptology - EUROCRYPT 2006*, volume 4004 of *Lecture Notes in Computer Science*, pages 486–503. Springer Berlin Heidelberg, 2006.

[4] C. Dwork, M. Naor, G. Rothblum, and T. Pitassi. Differential privacy under continual observation. In *Proceedings of the 42nd ACM symposium on Theory of computing*, 2010.

[5] Q. Geng and P. Viswanath. Optimal noise-adding mechanism in differential privacy. *CoRR*, abs/1212.1186, 2012.

[6] M. Hardt and K. Talwar. On the geometry of differential privacy. In *Proceedings of the 42nd ACM symposium on Theory of computing*, STOC '10, pages 705–714, New York, NY, USA, 2010. ACM.

[7] J. Herrera, D. Work, R. Herring, X. Ban, Q. Jacobson, and A. Bayen. Evaluation of traffic data obtained via GPS-enabled mobile phones: The Mobile Century field experiment. *Transportation Research Part C*, 18(4):568–583, August 2010.

[8] Z. Huang, S. Mitra, and G. Dullerud. Differentially private iterative synchronous consensus. In *Proceedings of the 2012 ACM workshop on Privacy in the electronic society*, WPES '12, pages 81–90, New York, NY, USA, 2012. ACM.

[9] Z. Huang, Y. Wang, S. Mitra, and G. Dullerud. On the cost of differential privacy in distributed control systems, 2013. Full version: http://users.crhc.illinois.edu/mitras/research/2013/co

[10] J. Le Ny and G. J. Pappas. Differentially Private Filtering. *ArXiv e-prints*, July 2012.

[11] J. Le Ny and G. J. Pappas. Differentially Private Kalman Filtering. *ArXiv e-prints*, July 2012.

[12] C. Li, M. Hay, V. Rastogi, G. Miklau, and A. McGregor. Optimizing linear counting queries under differential privacy. In *Proceedings of the twenty-ninth ACM SIGMOD-SIGACT-SIGART symposium on Principles of database systems*, PODS '10, pages 123–134, New York, NY, USA, 2010. ACM.

[13] F. McSherry and K. Talwar. Mechanism design via differential privacy. In *Foundations of Computer Science, 2007. FOCS '07. 48th Annual IEEE Symposium on*, pages 94 –103, oct. 2007.

[14] S. Mitra. *A Verification Framework for Hybrid Systems*. PhD thesis, Massachusetts Institute of Technology, Cambridge, MA 02139, September 2007.

[15] J. Reed and B. C. Pierce. Distance makes the types grow stronger: a calculus for differential privacy. In *Proceedings of the 15th ACM SIGPLAN international conference on Functional programming*, ICFP '10, pages 157–168, New York, NY, USA, 2010. ACM.

Energy-Based Attack Detection in Networked Control Systems

Emeka Eyisi
United Technologies Research Center
East Hartford, CT, USA
eyisiep@utrc.utc.com

Xenofon Koutsoukos
Institute for Software Integrated Systems
EECS Department
Vanderbilt University
Nashville, TN, USA
xenofon.koutsoukos@vanderbilt.edu

ABSTRACT

The increased prevalence of attacks on Cyber-Physical Systems (CPS) as well as the safety-critical nature of these systems, has resulted in increased concerns regarding the security of CPS. In an effort towards the security of CPS, we consider the detection of attacks based on the fundamental notion of a system's energy. We propose a discrete-time Energy-Based Attack Detection mechanism for networked cyber-physical systems that are dissipative or passive in nature. We present analytical results to show that the detection mechanism is effective in detecting a class of attack models in networked control systems (NCS). Finally, using simulations we illustrate the effectiveness of the proposed approach in detecting attacks.

Categories and Subject Descriptors

C.2.0 [**Computer-Communication Networks**]: General—*Security and protection (e.g., firewalls)*; H.1.1 [**Models and Principles**]: Systems and Information Theory—*General Systems Theory*

General Terms

Algorithms; Design; Security; Theory

Keywords

Energy-based detection; Networked Control Systems; Attacks

1. INTRODUCTION

The increased autonomy of CPS, together with the introduction of communication networks, has increased the security vulnerabilities of CPS infrastructure to malicious cyber attacks. Within the past few years, there has been a surge in attacks on CPS infrastructures. This increased prevalence of attacks has resulted in increased concerns regarding the security of these systems. Due to the safety-critical nature of CPS, failure or disruption of normal operation can potentially lead to serious harm to the physical system under control and to the people and other infrastructures that depend on

it. Hence, securing these systems in order to ensure resilient operation is of utmost importance. Some of the well-known examples of attacks on CPS include the W32.Stuxnet worm attack that maliciously infected an Iranian Nuclear facility, taking control and heavily disrupting its normal operation according to the attacker's design [6], the cyber attacks on power transmission networks operated by Supervisory Control and Data Acquisition (SCADA) Systems [12], as well as attacks that infiltrated critical systems including medical devices [13] and waste water treatment plants [1].

In securing CPS infrastructures, the reliable detection of attacks is very important and also fundamental to the design of compensation and reconfiguration mechanisms for mitigating the impact of attacks. The presence of the network increases the complexity of the detection of attacks. Hence, effective and yet efficient novel approaches are needed to enable the early detection of attacks in CPS. A majority of the existing detection approaches are typically from the cyber-security community. As highlighted in [3], the traditional approach often used in information/cyber-security neglects the knowledge of the physical process under control in the detection of attacks. Contrary to the traditional cyber-security approach, newer approaches in the CPS community, instead of creating models of network traffic or software behavior, leverage the knowledge of the physical process in designing effective mechanisms in order to facilitate the detection of attacks. The idea is that by understanding the interactions of the control system with the physical world, it would be possible to develop systematic frameworks to detect attacks and secure CPS in general.

In this work, we utilize the energy of physical systems in order to define precise detectability conditions for certain attack models and vulnerabilities. The concept of energy is very important in the behavior of dynamical systems. Compared to traditional detection approaches such as observer-based detection [14], there are only a handful of work whereby the concept of energy or passivity is used in model-based detection. In [7], the authors proposed a fault detection and isolation method for port-Hamiltonian systems to detect variations in the parameters of system components. The work in [4] proposed an energy balance scheme for fault detection for continuous-time passive systems. The author performed fault detection by checking when the energy balance is perturbed indicating the presence of faults. An energy balance fault detection approach was also applied for sensor fault detection in steel galvanizing process [16]. In [18], a passivity-based fault detection method was introduced based on evaluating the traditional passivity-based inequality. In this work, a fault is said to have occurred whenever the inequality is not satisfied. Most of these works in energy-based detection have been focused on reliability as it pertains to the protection of physical components against faults. Additionally, existing work does not consider the introduction of a communication

Permission to make digital or hard copies of all or part of this work for personal or classroom use is granted without fee provided that copies are not made or distributed for profit or commercial advantage and that copies bear this notice and the full citation on the first page. Copyrights for components of this work owned by others than ACM must be honored. Abstracting with credit is permitted. To copy otherwise, or republish, to post on servers or to redistribute to lists, requires prior specific permission and/or a fee. Request permissions from permissions@acm.org.
HiCoNS'14, April 15–17, 2014, Berlin, Germany.
Copyright 2014 ACM 978-1-4503-2652-0/14/04 ...$15.00.
http://dx.doi.org/10.1145/2566468.2566472 .

network and do not address the detection of intentional malicious cyber attacks against CPS.

Using the intuitive notion of energy, we propose an attack detection mechanism for CPS. The proposed approach is complementary to other detection mechanisms such as observer-based detection. The underlying idea is that the presence of attacks disturbs the energy balance of the physical system by dissipating or injecting additional energy. We define the notion of detectability of an attack by its effect on system's energy. The proposed approach provides the additional benefit of detecting when and to what magnitude a system's energy property is impacted due to the occurrence of an attack. In particular, we focus on dissipative CPS, which include a large class of existing systems. We present the use of energy-balance in the detection of attacks in NCS. We present a general characterization of attacks on the energy of a dynamical system. In addition, we demonstrate the impact of specific attack models on the stability guarantees of NCS. Finally, we demonstrate our approach using a case study on the velocity tracking control of a single joint of a robotic arm over a network.

The rest of the paper is organized as follows: Section 2 presents a brief background and underlying definitions used in paper. Section 3 presents the networked control system model, the attack models and formally states the problem that is addressed in this paper. The energy-based attack detection approach, the analytical results on the detection mechanism and the characterization of passive and non-passive attacks are presented in Section 4. Section 5 presents an example case study using simulations to evaluate the proposed approach. The paper is concluded in Section 6.

2. BACKGROUND

We define some fundamental concepts which are important in the description of the proposed approach.

DEFINITION 1. *A dynamic Linear Time-invariant (LTI) system, $\mathcal{H}$, is minimal if it is both controllable and observable.*

The notion of dissipativity and passivity of a system presented in this work follow the behavior-based approach given by Willems in [17] which involves associating the system to a non-negative definite storage function $V(x)$ and a supply function, W. We provide the following definition of dissipativity.

DEFINITION 2. *[2] [9] A discrete-time system, $\mathcal{H}$, is said to be **dissipative** with respect to the **supply function** $W(u(k), y(k))$ if there exists a positive definite function $V(x_k)$ or V_k, called **storage function**, satisfying $V(0) = 0$ such that $\forall x_0 \in X$, $\forall k \geq k_0$, and all $u \in \mathbb{R}^n$ and with, $V_k = \frac{1}{2}x_k^T P x_k$*

$$V_{k+1} - V_0 \leq \sum_{k=0}^{N-1} W(u(k), y(k)) \tag{1}$$

DEFINITION 3. *[10] [17] A dynamic system, $\mathcal{H}$, is said to be **QSR-dissipative** if it is dissipative with respect to the supply rate,W given as*

$$W(u, y) = y^T Q y + 2y^T S u + u^T R u \tag{2}$$

where Q, S, R are matrices of appropriate dimensions with Q and R symmetric. By choosing different values for Q, S, R, special cases of dissipativeness can be derived [8]. Special cases of QSR dissipative systems are as follows. If the system $\mathcal{H}$ is QSR-dissipative then it is

1. Passive *if Q=0, $S=\frac{1}{2}I$, $R = 0$*
2. Strictly input passive (SIP) *if $Q = 0$, $S = \frac{1}{2}I$, $R = -\delta I$*
3. Strictly output passive (SOP) *if $Q = -\epsilon I$, $S=\frac{1}{2}I$, $R = 0$*
4. Very strictly passive (VSP) *if Q=$-\epsilon I$, $S = 0$, $R=-\delta I$*

where ϵ and δ are positive scalars.

LEMMA 1. *[8][**Generalized Positive Real Lemma**] Let $G(z)$ be a transfer function description and $M(z) = R + G^H(z)S + S^T G(z) + G^H(z)QG(z)$, with $G^H(z)$ denoting the hermitian transpose of $G(z)$. Let $\mathcal{H}$ be a minimal realization of $G(z)$. Then $\forall z$ s.t. $\|z\| \geq 1$, $M(z) \geq 0$ if and only if there exist a real symmetric positive definite matrix P and real matrices L and W such that*

$$A^T P A - P = C^T Q C - L^T L \tag{3}$$

$$A^T P B = C^T Q D + C^T S - L W \tag{4}$$

$$B^T P B = R + D^T S + S^T D + D^T Q D + C^T S - W^T W \tag{5}$$

3. SYSTEM MODEL AND PROBLEM

In this section, we describe the components of networked control system and the attack models considered in this work. Subsequently, we formulate the attack detection problem and describe the underlying assumptions. The notations used in the following sections are standard. Let $\mathbb{R}^n$ denote the Euclidean space of dimension n, I denotes the identity matrix of appropriate dimensions. For a matrix $P \in \mathbb{R}^{n \times n}$, its transpose is denoted by P^T. For a symmetric matrix, P, where $P = P^T$, $P > 0$ denotes it is positive definite.

3.1 Networked Control System Model

We consider a networked control system as depicted in Figure 1. The main components of the NCS are the physical plant, the controller, the wave transformation (a static local controller), and the communication network. The data exchange between the plant and the controller is done over a communication network.

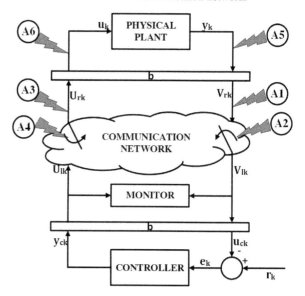

Figure 1: Networked Control System

(a) Physical Plant Model: We model the physical plant as a discrete linear time-invariant system. This version of the plant neglects system nonlinearities and presence of noise in the dynamics and measurement signals. We consider the physical plant which can be represented in the state space form as follows:

$$\mathcal{H}_p : \begin{cases} x_{k+1} = Ax_k + Bu_k \\ y_k = Cx_k + Du_k \end{cases} \tag{6}$$

where $x_k \in \mathcal{X}$ represents the state variables, $u_k \in \mathcal{U}$ represents the control inputs to the plant and $y_k \in \mathcal{Y}$ represents the plant outputs obtained by sensors at sampling instant $k \in \mathbb{Z}$.

(b) Controller Model: The controller modifies the behavior of the physical plant through the application of a control input command in order to achieve a desired objective or satisfy a performance requirement. The controller can be represented in discrete-time state-space form as follows:

$$\mathcal{H}_c : \begin{cases} z_{k+1} = A_c z_k + B_c e_k \\ y_{c_k} = C_c z_k + D_c e_k \end{cases} \tag{7}$$

where $z_k \in \mathbb{R}^q$ represents the controller states, y_{c_k} is the control command, $e_k = r_k - u_{c_k}$ is the error between the reference, r_k and the received plant output, u_{c_k}, with the matrices A_c, B_c, C_c and D_c of appropriate dimensions. It is assumed that the controller is designed under the nominal conditions, i.e. without attacks, to achieve the desired performance objective.

(c) Wave Transformation: In order to preserve the power content of information exchanged over a network, the sensor and control signals are transformed into wave variables which are then sent over the network. From Figure 1, the wave transformation is denoted by the blocks, **b**. The wave variables pair (U_{r_k}, V_{r_k}) on the plant side as well as the pair (U_{l_k}, V_{l_k}) on the controller side of the network can be described by the following expressions:

$$U_{r_k} = \frac{1}{\sqrt{2b}}(y_k + bu_k) \tag{8}$$

$$V_{r_k} = \frac{1}{\sqrt{2b}}(y_k - bu_k) \tag{9}$$

$$U_{l_k} = \frac{1}{\sqrt{2b}}(u_{c_k} + by_{c_k}) \tag{10}$$

$$V_{l_k} = \frac{1}{\sqrt{2b}}(u_{c_k} - by_{c_k}) \tag{11}$$

where $b \in \mathbb{R}_0^+$. From Figure 1, one can observe that under ideal network conditions, $V_{l_k} = V_{r_k}$ and $U_{r_k} = U_{l_k}$.

3.2 Attack Model

Figure 1 depicts the feasible cyber-attacks as a result of the vulnerabilities of the networked control system. While the attacks denoted as **A1**-**A4** model attacks on the information exchanged over the communication network, the attacks denoted as **A5** and **A6** models attacks on sensors and actuators respectively. Similar well-known attack types have be proposed in [15] [11]. For each attack type, $\mathcal{A}_k$, let $\mathcal{T}_a = k_s, ..., k_e$ denote the attack duration with the attack starting from k_s and ending at k_e. We consider two main classes of attacks, integrity attacks and denial-of-service attacks. These attack types are described as follows:

(a) Integrity attacks: In an integrity attack, an adversary deceives a compromised component of the NCS into believing that a received false data is valid or true. The underlying assumption is that all attacks lie within a predetermined range since attacks leading to signals that exceed such a range can be easily detected. The integrity attacks represented as **A1**, **A3**, **A5** and **A6** in Figure 1 can be further categorized into the following:

(i) Min/Max attacks: These attacks involve the adversary modifying the content of compromised signals to their respective minimum or maximum values. We model min/max attacks on the exchanged wave variables as well as the min/max attacks on the sensors and actuators. The attacks on the exchanged variables essentially exploit the vulnerabilities as a result of the communication while the attacks on the sensors and actuators exploit the vulnerabilities of the computing interfaces to these components which may or may not be colocated. We consider them separately since each component's interaction with the overall NCS is different and hence it is important to understand the impact of an attack on each component on the correct operation of the overall NCS.

(1) Min/Max attacks on exchanged wave variables: For attacks on the wave variable, V_{r_k}, sent from the plant we have,

$$\tilde{V}_{r_k}^{min} = \begin{cases} V_{r_k} & \forall k \notin \mathcal{T}_a \\ V_{r_{min}} & \forall k \in \mathcal{T}_a \end{cases} \tag{12}$$

$$\tilde{V}_{r_k}^{max} = \begin{cases} V_{r_k} & \forall k \notin \mathcal{T}_a \\ V_{r_{max}} & \forall k \in \mathcal{T}_a \end{cases} \tag{13}$$

Similar attacks can be launched against the wave variable, U_{r_k}, sent from the controller.

(2) Min/Max attacks on sensors and actuators: For attacks on the sensor signal, y_k, we have,

$$\tilde{y}_k^{min} = \begin{cases} y_k & \forall k \notin \mathcal{T}_a \\ y_{min} & \forall k \in \mathcal{T}_a \end{cases} \tag{14}$$

$$\tilde{y}_k^{max} = \begin{cases} y_k & \forall k \notin \mathcal{T}_a \\ y_{max} & \forall k \in \mathcal{T}_a \end{cases} \tag{15}$$

Similar attacks could be launched against the actuator signal, u_k.

(ii) Additive attacks: This attack involves introducing an additional offset/bias, $\alpha \neq 0$ to the actual exchanged information. We model additive attacks on the exchanged wave variables as well as additive attacks on the sensors and actuators.

(1) Additive attacks on exchanged wave variables: For attacks on the wave variable, V_{r_k}, sent from the plant we have,

$$\tilde{V}_{r_k}^a = \begin{cases} V_{r_k} & \forall k \notin \mathcal{T}_a \\ V_{r_k} + \alpha_k & \forall k \in \mathcal{T}_a \quad and \quad V_{r_k} + \alpha_k \in \mathcal{V} \\ V_{r_{min}} & \forall k \in \mathcal{T}_a \quad and \quad V_{r_k} + \alpha_k < V_{r_{min}} \\ V_{r_{max}} & \forall k \in \mathcal{T}_a \quad and \quad V_{r_k} + \alpha_k > V_{r_{max}} \end{cases} \tag{16}$$

(2) Additive attacks on sensors and actuators: For attacks on the sensor signal, y_k, we have,

$$\tilde{y}_k^a = \begin{cases} y_k & \forall k \notin \mathcal{T}_a \\ y_k + \alpha_k & \forall k \in \mathcal{T}_a \quad and \quad y_k + \alpha_k \in \mathcal{Y} \\ y_{min} & \forall k \in \mathcal{T}_a \quad and \quad y_k + \alpha_k < y_{min} \\ y_{max} & \forall k \in \mathcal{T}_a \quad and \quad y_k + \alpha_k > y_{max} \end{cases} \tag{17}$$

(iii) Min/Max energy attacks: Considering that the proposed approach is based on energy, an attacker's objective could be to apply the largest impact damage on the system based on the knowledge of the system's energy. We model two types of energy-based attacks based on their intended impact on the system.

(1) Max energy attack: In this case, we model attacks that attempt to dissipate maximum amount of energy i.e. the energy of the system becomes positive. This type of attack can be seen as an attacker's attempt to degrade system performance without destabilizing the system in regards to energy. In this attack type, for each time step, the attacker chooses a value for the compromised wave variable such that the total dissipated energy is maximized without exceeding the predetermined limits of the wave variable. The max energy attack can be captured as follows:

$$\begin{aligned} & \underset{V_{r_k}}{\text{maximize}} && E_T \\ & \text{subject to} && V_{r_k} \in [V_{r_{min}}, V_{r_{max}}] \end{aligned}$$

(2) Min Energy Attack: Similar, to the max energy attack, in this case we model attacks that attempts to inject the largest amount of

energy which from the system's perspective portrays the system as generating additional energy i.e. the energy of the system becomes negative. This attack type can be seen as an attacker's attempt to both degrade the performance of the system and potentially destabilize the system. In the model of this attack, at each time step the attacker chooses the compromised wave variable such that the energy is minimized without exceeding the predetermined limits of the wave variable. The min energy attack can be captured as follows:

$$\underset{V_{r_k}}{\text{minimize}} \quad E_T$$

$$\text{subject to} \quad V_{r_k} \in [V_{r_{min}}, V_{r_{max}}]$$

(b) Denial-of-Service (DoS) attacks: DoS attacks, denoted as **A2** and **A4** in Figure 1, prevent signals from reaching the intended destination. In NCS, it involves the disruption of the availability of information exchanged between the plant and the controller. DoS attacks are typically carried out by jamming the communication channel, changing the routing protocol or saturating the receiver with useless signals. The attacker's main objective is usually to degrade the performance of the NCS as well as to potentially destabilize the physical system. The DoS attack can be modeled as a form of the additive attack as follows:

$$\tilde{V}_{r_k}^{DoS} = V_{r_k} + \alpha V_{r_k} \quad \begin{cases} \alpha = 0 & \forall k \notin \mathcal{T}_a \\ \alpha = -1 & \forall k \in \mathcal{T}_a \end{cases} \quad (18)$$

3.3 Problem Statement

Consider the networked control system as shown in Figure 1, under possible cyber attacks as indicated by the attacks **A1-A6** due to the vulnerabilities of NCS. We define what is meant by an energy-based monitor and detectability of attacks in this framework.

DEFINITION 4. *An energy-based monitor is a deterministic algorithm, $\Phi : \Lambda \mapsto \Psi$, with knowledge of the plant dynamics and access to discrete-time measurements and control inputs. The output of a monitor is $\Psi = \{\psi_1, \psi_2\}$, with $\psi_1 \in \{True, False\}$, and $\psi_2 \in \{Passive, Non\text{-}Passive\}$*

DEFINITION 5. *An attack is detectable if in the presence of the attack, $\mathcal{A}_k$, $\psi_1 = True$ and $\psi_2 = Passive$ or Non-Passive.*

The following problem is of interest:
{**1. Detection Problem**} *Design an algorithm, Φ, for an energy-based monitor which can quantify or estimate the energy of the system, E_T, such that in the presence of an attack and with the knowledge of the plant, the controller and exchanged wave variables the following holds:*

$$\Psi = \{\psi_1, \psi_2\} = \begin{cases} \{True, Passive\} & \forall E_T > 0 \\ \{True, Non\text{-}Passive\} & \forall E_T < 0\} \end{cases} \quad (19)$$

In the following sections, we propose a solution to the above problem. We assume the following about the NCS.

Assumption 1: The plant and controller are dissipative by design, both with a sampling period, T_s. The assumption of dissipativity for both the plant and controller is to ensure stability guarantees in the nominal case.

Assumption 2: The components of the NCS including the physical plant, the sensor, actuator, controller and attack monitor are time-synchronized. This ensures that all the components of the NCS are progressing in lock step in regards to time.

Assumption 3: Whenever the input buffers are empty, null packets are processed. This assumption is used to preserve passivity

in the nominal sense in order to avert the typical hold-last sample approach which is known to be non-passive. Other approaches for handling missed packets can be sought in this case as well with no loss of generality.

Assumption 4: It is assumed that the controller and monitoring system for the plant are co-located together. The idea is that the controller is assumed to be trustworthy while the plant's trustworthiness is not known or guaranteed. In the case that the trustworthiness of the controller is not known or guaranteed, an additional monitor can be co-located with the plant.

Assumption 5: The attacker has knowledge of the plant and controller. In this assumption, we consider that the attacker is smart in the sense that he/she can attempt to use knowledge of the system to introduce attacks that cannot be easily detected with a simple bad data detector.

Assumption 6: For our initial analysis, we assume an ideal communication network, hence do not consider the usual communication network effects such as time-delays and packet losses but rather we focus on malicious attacks on the cyber-physical infrastructure. In this regard, we assume that any anomaly in the behavior of the overall system is due to an attack. This assumption will be relaxed later to include network effects in our approach.

4. ENERGY-BASED ATTACK DETECTION

In this section, we derive the energy balance for the networked control system in terms of the input-output wave variables, U_{r_k} and V_{r_k}. Next, we provide a generalized characterization of attacks based on the derived energy balance. We then evaluate the impact of the attack models presented in Section 3.2. Finally, we consider the case where the states of the system are not measurable, in which case we introduce the use of an observer to estimate the states.

4.1 Discrete-Time Energy Balance

We present the energy-based attack detection mechanism for the networked control system in Figure 1. We first present the derivation of general energy balance in terms of the plant's input, u_k and output, y_k, and then we refine the derivation to represent the energy balance system in terms of the wave variables exchanged over the network.

PROPOSITION 1. *Consider the discrete-time physical plant, $\mathcal{H}_p$, with a minimal realization (controllable and observable) defined in (6). If $\mathcal{H}_p$ is QSR dissipative then it satisfies the energy balance, E_T given by*

$$E_T = E_{su} - E_{st} - E_d = 0 \quad (20)$$

where E_{su} is the supplied energy, E_{st} is the stored energy and E_d is the dissipated energy.

PROOF. Recall the storage function, V_k, defined as $\frac{1}{2}x_k^T P x_k$. The change in the storage function, ΔV is given by

$$\Delta V = V_{k+1} - V_k = \frac{1}{2}x_{k+1}^T P x_{k+1} - \frac{1}{2}x_k^T P x_k$$

substituting x_{k+1} from (6), we have

$$\Delta V = \frac{1}{2}((x_k^T A^T + u_k^T B^T)P(Ax_k + Bu_k) - x_k^T P x_k)$$
$$= \frac{1}{2}(x_k^T(A^T P A - P)x_k + x_k^T A^T P B u_k + u_k^T B^T P A x_k$$
$$+ u_k^T B^T P B u_k) \quad (21)$$

From the Generalized KYP lemma described in lemma 1, we can substitute (3), (4) and (5) into equation (21), then we have

$$\Delta V = \frac{1}{2}(x_k^T(C^TQC - LL^T)x_k$$
$$+ x_k^T(C^TQD + C^TS - LW)u_k$$
$$+ u_k^T(D^TQC + S^TC - W^TL^T)x_k$$
$$+ u_k^T(R + D^TS + S^TD + D^TQD - W^TW)u_k) \quad (22)$$

After some manipulation and simplification, we have

$$\Delta V = \frac{1}{2}((Cx_k + Du_k)^TQ(Cx_k + Du_k)$$
$$+ 2(Cx_k + Du_k)^TSu_k + u_k^TRu_k)$$
$$- \frac{1}{2}(x_k^TLL^Tx_k + x_k^TLWu_k + u_k^TW^TL^Tx_k$$
$$+ u_k^TW^TWu_k)$$

From (6), noting that $y_k = Cx_k + Du_k$, we can now write

$$\Delta V = \frac{1}{2}(y_k^TQy_k + 2y_k^TSu_k + u_k^TRu_k)$$
$$- \frac{1}{2}(x_k^TLL^Tx_k + x_k^TLWu_k + u_k^TW^TL^Tx_k$$
$$+ u_k^TW^TWu_k)$$

Summing over the time interval from $k = 0$ to $k = N$ with a sampling time of T_s. The total energy equation becomes

$$\frac{T_s}{2}\sum_{k=0}^{N}(y_k^TQy_k + 2y_k^TSu_k + u_k^TRu_k) - T_s(V_{k+1} - V_{k_0})$$
$$- \frac{T_s}{2}\sum_{k=0}^{N}(x_k^TLL^Tx_k + x_k^TLWu_k + u_k^TW^TL^Tx_k$$
$$+ u_k^TW^TWu_k) = 0 \quad (23)$$

where

$$E_{su} = \frac{T_s}{2}\sum_{k=0}^{N}(y_k^TQy_k + 2y_k^TSu_k + u_k^TRu_k)$$
$$E_{st} = T_s(V_{k+1} - V_{k_0})$$
$$E_d = \frac{T_s}{2}\sum_{k=0}^{N}(x_k^TLL^Tx_k + x_k^TLWu_k + u_k^TW^TL^Tx_k$$
$$+ u_k^TW^TWu_k)$$

Hence, $\quad E_T = E_{su} - E_{st} - E_d = 0 \quad \square$

The system under consideration is a networked system and the components of the system communicate over a packet-switched network. Hence, it is appropriate to directly relate the energy based equation to the transmitted and received components over the network. We now provide the energy balance in terms of the exchanged wave variables.

PROPOSITION 2. *Given the system $\mathcal{H}_p$ with the energy balance as defined in (23) and the wave transformation provided in (8)-(11). The resulting energy balance of the system in wave domain is*

$$E_{T_{wv}} = E_{su_{wv}} - E_{st_{wv}} - E_{d_{wv}} = 0 \quad (24)$$

where $E_{T_{wv}}$ is the total of the system, $E_{su_{wv}}$ is the supplied energy, $E_{st_{wv}}$ is the stored energy and $E_{d_{wv}}$ is the dissipated energy.

PROOF. From equations (9) and (10), and also assuming $\mathbf{b} = 1$, solving for the plant output, y_k and input, u_k, we have

$$y_k = \frac{1}{\sqrt{2}}(U_{r_k} + V_{r_k}) \quad (25)$$

$$u_k = \frac{1}{\sqrt{2}}(U_{r_k} - V_{r_k}) \quad (26)$$

After some manipulations and simplification, the plant dynamics can be expressed in terms of the input wave variable, U_{r_k} and output wave variable, V_{r_k}. The resulting system, $\mathcal{H}_{p_{wv}}$ can be described as

$$\mathcal{H}_{p_{wv}} : \begin{cases} x_{k+1} = \bar{A}x_k + \bar{B}U_{r_k} \\ V_{r_k} = \bar{C}x_k + \bar{D}U_{r_k} \end{cases} \quad (27)$$

with

$$\bar{A} = A - B(D + I)^{-1}C; \bar{B} = \frac{B}{\sqrt{2}}(I - (D + I)^{-1}(D - I))$$

$$\bar{C} = \sqrt{2}(D + I)^{-1}C; \bar{D} = (D + I)^{-1}(D - I)$$

Recall the total energy expression given in (23), by substitution, the energy balance in the wave domain becomes

$$\frac{T_s}{2}\sum_{i=0}^{N}(V_{r_k}^T\bar{Q}V_{r_k} + 2V_{r_k}^T\bar{S}U_{r_k} + U_{r_k}^T\bar{R}U_{r_k}) - T_s(V_{k+1} - V_0)$$
$$- \frac{T_s}{2}\sum_{i=0}^{N}(x_k^T\overline{LL^T}x_k + x_k^T\overline{LW}U_{r_k} + U_{r_k}^T\overline{W^TL^T}x_k$$
$$+ U_{r_k}^T\overline{W^TW}U_{r_k}) = 0 \quad (28)$$

where

$$\bar{Q} = (\frac{Q - 2S + R}{2}); \bar{S} = (\frac{Q - R}{2}); \bar{R} = (\frac{Q + 2S + R}{2}); \quad (29)$$

$$\overline{LL^T} = (LL^T - \frac{LW\bar{C}}{\sqrt{2}} - \frac{\bar{C}W^TL^T}{\sqrt{2}} + \bar{C}^TW^TW\bar{C})$$

$$\overline{LW} = (\frac{LW}{\sqrt{2}} - \frac{LW\bar{D}}{\sqrt{2}} - \frac{\bar{C}^TW^TW}{2} + \frac{\bar{C}^TW^TW\bar{D}}{2})$$

$$\overline{W^TL^T} = (\frac{W^TL^T}{\sqrt{2}} - \frac{\bar{D}^TW^TL^T}{\sqrt{2}} - \frac{W^TW\bar{C}}{2} + \frac{\bar{D}^TW^TW\bar{C}}{2})$$

$$\overline{W^TW} = (\frac{W^TW - W^TW\bar{D} - \bar{D}W^TW + \bar{D}^TW^TW\bar{D}}{2})$$

With

$$E_{su_{wv}} = \frac{T_s}{2}\sum_{i=0}^{N}(V_{r_k}^T\bar{Q}V_{r_k} + 2V_{r_k}^T\bar{S}U_{r_k} + U_{r_k}^T\bar{R}U_{r_k})$$
$$E_{st_{wv}} = T_s(V_{k+1} - V_0)$$
$$E_{d_{wv}} = \frac{T_s}{2}\sum_{i=0}^{N}(x_k^T\overline{LL^T}x_k + x_k^T\overline{LW}U_{r_k} + U_{r_k}^T\overline{W^TL^T}x_k$$
$$+ U_{r_k}^T\overline{W^TW}U_{r_k})$$

Hence, $E_{T_{wv}} = E_{su_{wv}} - E_{st_{wv}} - E_{d_{wv}} = 0 \quad \square$

4.2 Energy Balance in the Presence of Attacks

In this section, we provide a generalized characterization of the total energy in the presence of attacks.

THEOREM 1. *Consider the networked control system depicted in Figure 1, under cyber-attack, $\mathcal{A}_k$, where by the attacker can remove or modify the exchanged wave variables U_{r_k} and V_{r_k}. Since the plant is assumed to be linear and time-invariant, the modified variables due to an attack can be modeled as*

$$\tilde{U}_{r_k} = U_{r_k} + U_{a_k}; \tilde{V}_{r_k} = V_{r_k} + V_{a_k}; \tilde{x}_k = x_k + x_{a_k} \quad (30)$$

The total energy of the plant, $\tilde{E}_{T_{wv}}$, in the presence of attack is

$$\tilde{E}_{T_{wv}} = E_{T_a} \neq 0 \quad (31)$$

PROOF. Based on the attack-modified input-output relations, the energy for the system becomes

$$\tilde{E}_T = \frac{T_s}{2} \sum_{k=0}^{N} (\tilde{V}_{r_k}^T \bar{Q} \tilde{V}_{r_k} + 2\tilde{V}_{r_k}^T \bar{S} \tilde{U}_{r_k} + \tilde{U}_{r_k}^T \bar{R} \tilde{U}_{r_k})$$
$$- \frac{T_s}{2} \sum_{k=0}^{N} (\tilde{x}_k L \bar{L}^T \tilde{x}_k + \tilde{x}_k L \bar{W} \tilde{U}_{r_k} + \tilde{U}_{r_k} W^{\bar{T}} L^T \tilde{x}_k$$
$$+ \tilde{U}_{r_k} W^{\bar{T}} W \tilde{U}_{r_k})$$
$$- T_s(\frac{1}{2} \tilde{x}_{k+1} P \tilde{x}_{k+1} - \frac{1}{2} \tilde{x}_0 P \tilde{x}_0) \quad (32)$$

Next, we simplify the above total energy based on the individual energy components which include supplied, stored and dissipated energies. For the new supplied energy we have,

$$\tilde{E}_{su} = \frac{T_s}{2} \sum_{k=0}^{N} (\tilde{V}_{r_k}^T \bar{Q} \tilde{V}_{r_k} + 2\tilde{V}_{r_k}^T \bar{S} \tilde{U}_{r_k} + \tilde{U}_{r_k}^T \bar{R} \tilde{U}_{r_k}) \quad (33)$$

substituting (30) in (33), we have

$$\tilde{E}_{su} = \frac{T_s}{2} \sum_{k=0}^{N} ((V_{r_k} + V_{a_k})^T \bar{Q}(V_{r_k} + V_{a_k})$$
$$+ 2(V_{r_k} + V_{a_k})^T \bar{S}(U_{r_k} + U_{a_k})$$
$$+ (U_{r_k} + U_{a_k})^T \bar{R}(U_{r_k} + U_{a_k}))$$
$$= \frac{T_s}{2} \sum_{k=0}^{N} (V_{r_k}^T \bar{Q} V_{r_k} + 2V_{r_k}^T \bar{S} U_{r_k} + U_{r_k}^T \bar{R} U_{r_k})$$
$$+ \frac{T_s}{2} \sum_{k=0}^{N} (V_{a_k}^T \bar{Q} V_{a_k} + 2V_{r_k}^T \bar{Q} V_{a_k} + 2V_{r_k}^T \bar{S} U_{a_k})$$
$$+ \frac{T_s}{2} \sum_{k=0}^{N} (2V_{a_k}^T \bar{S} U_{r_k} + 2V_{a_k}^T \bar{S} U_{a_k} + 2U_{r_k}^T \bar{R} U_{a_k}$$
$$+ U_{a_k}^T \bar{R} U_{a_k}) \quad (34)$$

From (34) above, it can be seen that,

$$\tilde{E}_{su} = E_{su_{wv}} + E_{su_a} \quad (35)$$

Next, the new stored energy component becomes,

$$\tilde{E}_{st} = T_s(\frac{1}{2} \tilde{x}_{k+1}^T P \tilde{x}_{k+1} - \frac{1}{2} \tilde{x}_0^T P \tilde{x}_0) \quad (36)$$

substituting (30) in (36), we have

$$\tilde{E}_{st} = T_s(\frac{1}{2}(x_{k+1} + x_{a_{k+1}})^T P(x_{k+1} + x_{a_{k+1}})$$
$$- \frac{1}{2}(x_0 + x_{a_0})^T P(x_0 + x_{a_0}))$$
$$= \frac{T_s}{2}((x_{k+1}^T P x_{k+1} - x_0^T P x_0)$$
$$+ (x_{a_{k+1}}^T P x_{a_{k+1}} - x_{a_0}^T P x_{a_0} + 2x_{k+1}^T P x_{a_{k+1}} - x_0^T P x_{a_0})) \quad (37)$$

From (37) above, it can be seen that,

$$\tilde{E}_{st} = E_{st_{wv}} + E_{st_a} \quad (38)$$

Finally, the new dissipated energy component becomes

$$\tilde{E}_d = \frac{T_s}{2} \sum_{k=0}^{N} (\tilde{x}_k L \bar{L}^T \tilde{x}_k + \tilde{x}_k^T L \bar{W} \tilde{U}_{rk} + \tilde{U}_{rk} W^{\bar{T}} L^T \tilde{x}_k$$
$$+ \tilde{U}_{rk} W^{\bar{T}} W \tilde{U}_{rk}) \quad (39)$$

substituting (30) in (39), we have

$$\tilde{E}_d = \frac{T_s}{2} \sum_{k=0}^{N} (x_k^T L \bar{L}^T x_k + x_k^T L \bar{L}^T x_{a_k} + x_{a_k}^T L \bar{L}^T x_k$$
$$+ x_{a_k}^T L \bar{L}^T x_{a_k} + x_k^T L \bar{W} U_{rk} + x_k^T L \bar{W} U_{a_k} + x_{a_k}^T L \bar{W} U_{rk}$$
$$+ x_{a_k}^T L \bar{W} U_{a_k} + U_{rk}^T W^{\bar{T}} L^T x_k + U_{rk}^T W^{\bar{T}} L^T x_{a_k}$$
$$+ U_{a_k}^T W^{\bar{T}} L^T x_k + U_{a_k}^T W^{\bar{T}} L^T x_{a_k} + U_{rk} W^{\bar{T}} W U_{rk}$$
$$+ U_{rk} W^{\bar{T}} W U_{a_k} + U_{a_k} W^{\bar{T}} W U_{rk} + U_{a_k} W^{\bar{T}} W U_{a_k}) \quad (40)$$

From (40) above, it can be seen that,

$$\tilde{E}_d = E_{d_{wv}} + E_{d_a} \quad (41)$$

Hence, from (35), (38) and (41), the total energy, $\tilde{E}_T$ in the presence of attack(s), then becomes

$$\tilde{E}_T = \tilde{E}_{su} - \tilde{E}_{st} - \tilde{E}_d$$
$$= E_{su_{wv}} + E_{su_a} - E_{st_{wv}} - E_{st_a} - E_{d_{wv}} - E_{d_a}$$
$$= E_{T_{wv}} + E_{T_a} \quad (42)$$

From (24), we have

$$\tilde{E}_T = E_{T_{wv}} + E_{T_a} = E_{T_a} \quad (43)$$

$\square$

COROLLARY 1. *In the absence of any detectable attack, $\mathcal{A}_k$, the total energy of the system, $\tilde{E}_{T_{wv}}$ is*

$$\tilde{E}_{T_{wv}} = E_{T_{wv}} = 0 \quad (44)$$

PROOF. This result follows directly from the system total energy property described in Theorem 2 and the results in Theorem 1 in the presence attacks. $\square$

REMARK 1. *The detection algorithm for the monitor is evaluated based on the information received at the controller. Considering the fact that the controller is considered trustworthy, the effects of attacks on the wave variable, U_{l_k} which is received as U_{r_k} by the plant will be reflected on wave variable V_{l_k}, which is V_{r_k} sent from the plant side of the network. Recall the expression in (9) relating the actuator signal and sensor signal , to the wave variable,*

$$V_{r_k} = \frac{1}{\sqrt{2b}}(y_k - bu_k)$$

It is straight forward to see that attacks on either the sensor or actuator will be reflected on the wave variable V_{r_k}, which is subsequently received at the controller as V_{l_k}.

COROLLARY 2. *An attack, $\mathcal{A}_k$, is characterized as a passive attack if the presence of the attack results in $\tilde{E}_{T_{wv}} > 0$.*

From the definition of passivity in (2), $\tilde{E}_{T_{wv}} > 0$ implies that the supplied energy for the attack system is larger than the dissipated and stored energies.

COROLLARY 3. *An attack, $\mathcal{A}_k$, is characterized as a non-passive attack if the presence of the attack results in $\tilde{E}_{T_{wv}} < 0$.*

This essentially implies that the supplied energy of the attacked system is less than the dissipated and store energies. Therefore, the system generates additional internal energy which results in a non-passive behavior. This implies that the overall stability of the networked control system is no longer guaranteed.

The energy-based attack detector can be summarized by Algorithm 1. Figure 2 also shows the block diagram for the energy based monitor. The inputs to the algorithm, also denoted in Figure 2, are the wave variables, V_{r_k} and U_{r_k} and the plant's state x_k. The output of the algorithm is Ψ, which provides information on whether an attack has occurred and the impact of the attack on the overall system. The blocks supplied energy, stored energy and dissipated energy in Figure 2 corresponds to the computation of the supplied energy, stored energy and dissipated energy respectively as indicated by lines 1-4 in Algorithm 1. Figure 2 shows the block

---

Algorithm 1: Energy-Based Attack Detection

Input: V_{r_k},U_{r_k},x_k
Output: Ψ
1 Compute the supplied energy, $E_{su_{wv}}$
2 Compute the stored energy, $E_{st_{wv}}$
3 Compute the dissipated energy, $E_{d_{wv}}$
4 Compute the total energy, $E_{T_k} = E_{su_{wv}} - E_{st_{wv}} - E_{d_{wv}}$
5 **if** $E_{T_k} \neq 0$ **then**
6   ψ_1 =True
7   **if** $E_{T_k} > 0$ **then**
8   ψ_2 =Passive
9   **else**
10   ψ_2 =Non-Passive
11 **else**
12   ψ_1 =False
13 $\Psi = \{\psi_1,\psi_2\}$
14 **return** Ψ

---

diagram for the designed energy based monitor for attacks in the case of measurable plant states.

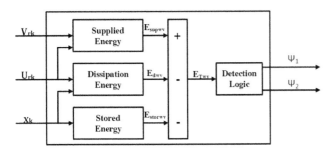

Figure 2: Energy-Based Monitor

REMARK 2. *Thus far, the characterization of attacks are based on the notion that in the absence of attacks, the nominal energy balance of the monitored system should be zero. In a more realistic setting, this assumption can be relaxed in order to integrate the potential effects of the network communication as a result of delays or packet loss. In the presence of network effects and possibly other system uncertainties, instead of the energy balance being zero, a*

notion of a maximal value of energy due to network effects and system uncertainties are considered. Based on this notion, a threshold boundary, E_{th}, is defined. The characterization of attacks are then evaluated based on the impact of the attacks that results in computed energy that lies outside the boundary. This maximal energy value can be obtained empirically through simulations and by imposing worst-case network conditions for the NCS.

4.3 Characterization of Attack Models

In order to illustrate the impact of attack models on the physical system, we evaluate the effect of classical attacks on the total energy of the system. For brevity, we focus on the attacks **A1** and **A2**, although similar approach can be used to evaluate the effects of attacks **A3-A6**. Also, due to space limitations we consider the cases where the dissipative plant is passive. The proofs for the presented results as well as the case for strictly-output passive plant is provided in [5].

Assuming there are no attacks on U_{r_k}, the impact of the attacks on V_{r_k} is reflected on only the supplied energy resulting in the component,

$$\tilde{E}_{T_{wv}} = E_{T_{wva}} = E_{su_{wva}}$$
$$= \frac{T_s}{2} \sum_{k=0}^{N} (2V_{r_k}^T \bar{Q} V_{a_k} + V_{a_k}^T \bar{Q} V_{a_k} + 2V_{a_k}^T \bar{S} U_{r_k}) \quad (45)$$

PROPOSITION 3. *Consider the passivity-based network control system depicted in Figure 1, under a max integrity attack, $\mathcal{A}_k$, if the system dynamics $\mathcal{H}_p$ is passive, then*

$$\mathcal{A}_k : \begin{cases} \text{Passive} & \text{if } \sum_{k=0}^{N} V_{r_{max}}^T V_{r_{max}} < \sum_{k=0}^{N} V_{r_k}^T V_{r_k} \\ \text{Non-Passive} & \text{if } \sum_{k=0}^{N} V_{r_{max}}^T V_{r_{max}} > \sum_{k=0}^{N} V_{r_k}^T V_{r_k} \end{cases} \quad (46)$$

PROPOSITION 4. *Consider the passivity-based network control system depicted in Figure 1, under a min integrity attack, $\mathcal{A}_k$, if the system dynamics $\mathcal{H}_p$ is passive, then*

$$\mathcal{A}_k : \begin{cases} \text{Passive} & \text{if } \sum_{k=0}^{N} V_{r_{min}}^T V_{r_{min}} < \sum_{k=0}^{N} V_{r_k}^T V_{r_k} \\ \text{Non-Passive} & \text{if } \sum_{k=0}^{N} V_{r_{min}}^T V_{r_{min}} > \sum_{k=0}^{N} V_{r_k}^T V_{r_k} \end{cases} \quad (47)$$

PROPOSITION 5. *Consider the passivity-based network control system depicted in Figure 1, under an additive integrity attack, $\mathcal{A}_k$, if the system dynamics $\mathcal{H}_p$ is passive, then*

$$\mathcal{A}_k : \begin{cases} \text{Passive} & \text{if } \sum_{k=0}^{N} 2V_{r_k}^T \alpha_k < -\sum_{k=0}^{N} \alpha_k^T \alpha_k \\ \text{Non-Passive} & \text{if } \sum_{k=0}^{N} 2V_{r_k}^T \alpha_k > -\sum_{k=0}^{N} \alpha_k^T \alpha_k \end{cases} \quad (48)$$

PROPOSITION 6. *Consider the passivity-based network control system depicted in Figure 1, under a denial-of-service attack, $\mathcal{A}_k$, if the system dynamics $\mathcal{H}_p$ is passive, then*

$$\mathcal{A}_k : \text{Passive with } E_{su_{wva}} = \frac{T_s}{2} \sum_{k=0}^{N} \frac{V_{r_k}^T V_{r_k}}{2} > 0 \forall V_{r_k} \neq 0 \quad (49)$$

REMARK 3. *The result obtained for the characterization of DoS attacks is similar to the analysis of packet losses due to unreliability of network in the literature. While packet losses are due to unreliable network, DoS is as a result of intentional and malicious attacks by an adversary.*

4.4 The case of unmeasurable states

In the case unmeasurable plant states, a Luenberger observer of the form in (50) is introduced to reconstruct an estimate of the plant states.

$$\mathcal{H}_{obs} : \begin{cases} \hat{x}_{k+1} = A\hat{x}_k + BU_{r_k} - L(V_{r_k} - C\hat{x}_k - DU_{r_k}) \\ \hat{V}_{r_k} = C\hat{x}_k + DU_{r_k} \end{cases}$$
(50)

where L is the observer gain. Recall that the plant system is assumed to be observable. This means there exists an observability matrix L such that the estimated state $\hat{x}_k$ of the Luenberger observer asymptotically converges to the true state x_k.

PROPOSITION 7. *Given the system $\mathcal{H}_p$ with the energy balance described in Theorem 2. In the case whereby the states are unmeasurable assuming a Luenberger observer, $\mathcal{H}_{obsv}$ as given in (50) is integrated to estimate the states, $\hat{x}_k$. Then, the resulting equivalent total energy of the system in wave domain, in the absence of attacks can be described by*

$$E_{T_{wv}} = E_{T_{wvo}} = -E_{st_{oe}} - E_{d_{oe}}$$
(51)

Due to limited space, the proof is presented in [5].

Similar to Algorithm 1, in the case of unmeasurable states, the energy-based detection with the integration of an observer can be summarized by Algorithm 2 below.

Algorithm 2: Energy-Based Attack Detection in the case of unmeasurable states

Input: V_{r_k}, U_{r_k}
Output: Ψ

1 Estimate the states, $\hat{x}_k$
2 Compute the supplied energy, $E_{su_{wvo}}$
3 Compute the stored energy, $E_{st_{wvo}}$
4 Compute the dissipated energy, $E_{d_{wvo}}$
5 Compute the total energy,
 $E_{T_{wvo}} = E_{su_{wvo}} - E_{st_{wvo}} - E_{d_{wvo}}$
6 **if** $E_{T_{wvo}} \neq 0$ **then**
7   ψ_1 =True
8   **if** $T_{wvo} > 0$ **then**
9   ψ_2 =Passive
10   **else**
11   ψ_2 =Non-Passive
12 **else**
13   ψ_1 =False
14 $\Psi = \{\psi_1, \psi_2\}$
15 **return** Ψ

---

5. EVALUATION

In this section, we evaluate the proposed energy-based detection mechanism using simulations. The system under consideration is a control system composed of a plant and controller that exchange information over a network in order to cooperatively achieve a specified objective.

5.1 Simulation Setup

The case study involves the velocity control of a single joint robotic arm over a communication network. It is assumed that the only information the networked controller receives from the plant is the wave variable, V_{r_k}, which becomes V_{l_k} at the controller side

of the network. Hence the detection mechanism with an integrated observer, as described in Section 4.4, is used in this evaluation. The NCS is considered to passive by design.

The simulation of the NCS is performed in Matlab/Simulink. The plant, controller, energy-based monitor, scattering transformation, attack models and communication are implemented using a combination of Matlab scripts and blocks from the Simulink library. The dynamics of the plant is described by the discrete-time state-space representation as defined in (6) with a sampling time of $T_s = 0.01s$. The parameters for the plant are A=0.9952, B=0.0625, C=0.1214, D=0.0251. The controller for the robot is a Proportional-Integral (PI) controller and similar to the plant is represented by the discrete time state space representation defined in (7) with the sampling time $T_s = 0.01s$. The parameters for the controller are $A_c = 1$, $B_c = 0.0625$, $C_c = 0.1$, $D_c = 0.6385$. The main objective of the controller is to modify the behavior of the plant in order to track a reference velocity trajectory, r_k over a communication network.

5.2 Scenarios

First, we present the control of the plant in the nominal case when there are no attacks. We also present the effects of the network on the system's energy. Next, we evaluate the behavior of the system under attack and the ability of the proposed approach to detect the attacks. In the experiments with attacks, the simulated attacks are injected from the duration, $t = 15s$ to $t = 20s$. Due to space limitations, we only present results for some of the attack models, results for other cases are presented in [5].

(1) Nominal Case: In this scenario, the NCS operates nominally while achieving the tracking objective. Figure 3a depicts the reference velocity of $0.15 rad/s$ as well as the plant velocity clearly showing that the plant is able to track the velocity as desired. Figure 3b shows the energy balance of the monitored plant computed based on the approach described in Section 4.2. In order to illustrate the effect of communication network on the energy-balance, we also co-located the energy-based detector at the plant side of the network to essentially perform the same total energy computation. The only difference being the delay experience by the monitor co-located with the controller. From Figure 3b, the energy-balance computed by the local monitor is essentially zero as expected but the balance computed by the networked monitor has an offset as a result of the communication network. Hence, this offset value or a more conservative value can be used to characterize the threshold energy, E_{th}, which will be non-zero due to network effects.

(2) Integrity Attacks

(a) Min Attack on V_{rk}: In this scenario, we assume the NCS channel from the plant to the controller, transmitting V_{rk}, is compromised and during the attack duration, the attacker replaces the true or actual signal exchanged with the value of $V_{r_{min}}$. Figure 4a shows that the presence of the attack results in the degraded reference tracking performance. Figure 4b depicts the total energy computation clearly indicating the presence of the attack. Additionally, one can observe that the min integrity attack can be characterize as a passive attack as it leads to increase in the computed total energy which indicates the dissipation of energy. Based on the computed energy, passivity of the overall NCS is still guaranteed.

(b) Max Energy Attack on V_{rk}: In this scenario, we again assume the NCS channel from the plant to the controller, transmitting V_{rk}, is compromised and during the attack duration, the attacker replaces the true or actual signal exchanged with the value of V_{r_a} that maximizes the energy dissipated at that time step. Figure 5a shows that the presence of the attack results in the degraded reference tracking performance. Figure 4b depicts the total energy com-

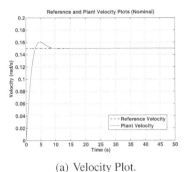

(a) Velocity Plot.

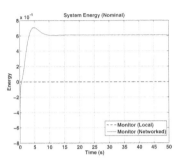

(b) Energy Balance Plot.

Figure 3: Nominal Case.

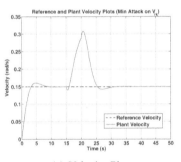

(a) Velocity Plot.

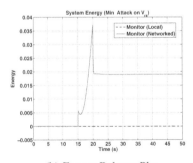

(b) Energy Balance Plot.

Figure 4: Min Attack on V_{rk}.

putation clearly indicating the presence of the attack. Additionally, one can observe that as expected the max energy attack results in an increase in the computed total energy. Based on the computed energy, passivity of the overall NCS is still guaranteed.

(c) Max Attack on the Sensor, y_k: In this scenario, we assume the sensor signal from the plant, y_k, is compromised and during the

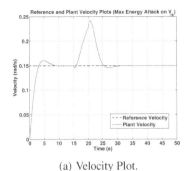

(a) Velocity Plot.

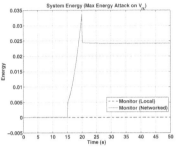

(b) Energy Balance Plot.

Figure 5: Max Energy Attack on V_{rk}.

attack duration, the attacker replaces the true or actual signal exchanged with the value of y_{max}. Figure 6a shows that the presence of the attack results in the degraded reference tracking performance. Figure 6b depicts the total energy computation clearly indicating the presence of the attack. From the energy plots, one can observe that as expected the max integrity attack on the sensor perturbs both the local and networked energy monitors, clearly indicating that the attack is perpetuated locally. From Figure 6b, the max attack on the actuator results in a decrease in the system energy indicating the injection of excess energy and hence can be characterize as a non-passive attack. Based on the computed energy, the injected max attack on the sensor leads to the violation of passivity of the overall NCS, in addition to the observed significant degradation in performance.

(3) Denial-of-service attack on V_{rk}: In this scenario, we introduce a denial-of-service attack on the NCS. During the attack duration, the attacker erases or discard the information exchanged over the network based on a simulated Bernoulli random variable, the probability of erasure for this evaluation was set at 0.2. Figure 7 shows that the presence of the attack clearly degrades the tracking performance. From Figure 7, one can observe that the denial-of-service attack can be characterized as passive attack as it leads to a positive total computed energy and this is in line with the results in Section 4.3 defining DoS attacks as always passive. Hence, passivity is always maintained but the performance in tracking is deteriorated.

6. CONCLUSION

Due to increased attacks on CPS, there is an increased effort towards approaches to detect and secure CPS from cyber attacks. We present an energy-based attack detector for a class of CPS that are considered dissipative. We provided analytical results to show the detector can successfully detect attacks. Using well-known attack models we characterize attacks that can be considered either passive or non-passive based on their impact on the evaluated system

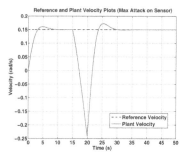

(a) Velocity Plot.

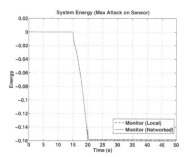

(b) Energy Balance Plot.

Figure 6: Max Attack on Sensor, y_k.

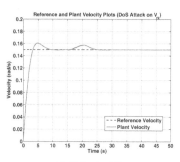

(a) Velocity Plot.

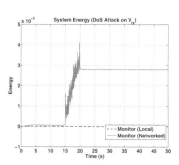

(b) Energy Balance Plot.

Figure 7: DoS Attack on V_{rk}.

energy. We quantitatively evaluate the performance of the proposed mechanism using simulations and experiments on a networked single joint robotic arm with the introduction of artificially simulated attacks. The results show that the proposed detection mechanism is effective in detecting attacks based on the energy balance of a system.

7. ACKNOWLEDGMENTS

This work is supported in part by the National Science Foundation (CNS-1238959, CNS-1035655) and NIST (70NANB13H169).

8. REFERENCES

[1] M. Abrams and J. Weiss. Malicious control system cyber security attack case study: maroochy water services. 2008.

[2] C. I. Byrnes and W. Lin. Losslessness, feedback equivalence, and the global stabilization of discrete-time nonlinear systems. *IEEE Trans. on Aut. Control,*, 39(1):83–98, 1994.

[3] A. A. Cárdenas, S. Amin, and S. Sastry. Research challenges for the security of control systems. In *Proc. of the 3rd Conf. on Hot topics in security*, pages 1–6, 2008.

[4] W. Chen, S. Ding, A. Q. Khan, and M. Abid. Energy based fault detection for dissipative systems. In *Conf. on Control and Fault-Tolerant Systems*, pages 517–521, 2010.

[5] E. Eyisi and X. Koutsoukos. Energy-Based Attack Detection in Networked Control Systems. Technical Report ISIS-13-107.

[6] N. Falliere, L. Murchu, and C. E. W32.stuxnet dossier. 2011.

[7] C. Fantuzzi and C. Secchi. Energetic approach to parametric fault detection and isolation. In *American Control Conf.*, volume 6, pages 5034–5039, 2004.

[8] G. C. Goodwin and K. S. Sin. *Adaptive filtering prediction and control*. Courier Dover Publications, 2013.

[9] W. M. Haddad and V. Chellaboina. *Nonlinear dynamical systems and control: a Lyapunov-based approach*. Princeton University Press, 2011.

[10] D. Hill and P. Moylan. The stability of nonlinear dissipative systems. *IEEE Trans. on Aut. Control*, 21(5):708–711, 1976.

[11] Y.-L. Huang, A. A. Cárdenas, S. Amin, Z.-S. Lin, H.-Y. Tsai, and S. Sastry. Understanding the physical and economic consequences of attacks on control systems. *Int. J. of Critical Infrastructure Protection*, 2(3):73–83, 2009.

[12] T. W. S. Journal. Electricity grid in u.s. penetrated by spies. A1, April 2009.

[13] C. Li, A. Raghunathan, and N. Jha. Hijacking an insulin pump: Security attacks and defenses for a diabetes therapy system. In *Int. Conf. In e-Health Networking Applications and Services*, pages 150 –156, June 2011.

[14] R. Patton and J. Chen. Observer-based fault detection and isolation: Robustness and applications. *Control Engineering Practice*, 5(5):671 – 682, 1997.

[15] A. Teixeira, D. Pérez, H. Sandberg, and K. H. Johansson. Attack models and scenarios for networked control systems. In *Proc. of the 1st Int. Conf. on High Confidence Net. Sys.*, pages 55–64, 2012.

[16] D. Theilliol, H. Noura, D. Sauter, and F. Hamelin. Sensor fault diagnosis based on energy balance evaluation: Application to a metal processing. *ISA Trans.*, 45(4):603–610, 2006.

[17] J. C. Willems. Dissipative dynamical systems part ii: Linear systems with quadratic supply rates. *Arch. for Rat. Mechanics and Analysis*, 45(5):352–393, 1972.

[18] H. Yang, V. Cocquempot, and B. Jiang. Fault tolerance analysis for switched systems via global passivity. *IEEE Trans. on Cir. and Sys. II: Express Briefs*, 55(12):1279–1283, 2008.

From CRCs to Resilient Control Systems: Differentiating Between Reliability and Security for the Protection of Cyber-Physical Systems

Invited Talk

Álvaro A. Cárdenas
Department of Computer Science
University of Texas at Dallas
Richardson, TX75080, USA
alvaro.cardenas@utdallas.edu

ABSTRACT

In this talk I will discuss the need to establish clear differences between reliability and security for protecting cyber-physical systems (CPS).

This is particularly important given the recent interest from researchers in exploring the vulnerability of a CPS when an attacker has partial control of the sensor or actuator signals, which has led to the proposal of several anomaly detection schemes for CPS by using data collected from physical sensors (as opposed to traditional network sensors). In the general setting, data obtained from *normal behavior* of the system is used to create a model and then any outlier is considered an anomaly and a potential failure or attack; however, this line of research is very similar to the fault-detection, and safety mechanisms that have been deployed in control systems for decades. In particular, the protection of control systems has traditionally been enforced by several safety mechanisms, which include bad data detection, protective relays, safety shutdowns, interlock systems, robust control, and fault-tolerant control; however, so far there has not been a systematic study that tries to identify how much these protection mechanisms can help against attacks (as opposed to failures or accidents), and how can they be broken by an attacker and potentially fixed by a system designer that incorporates attack models in the design of their system.

In this talk I describe how current protection mechanisms are analogous to how error correcting codes are used in communications: they protect against a vast majority of random faults and accidents; however they are not secure against attacks—the way cryptographic hash functions are. As a community we need to revisit protection mechanisms available from control theory and then analyze them from a security perspective, giving new guidelines on security metrics and new ways to design attack-resilient CPS. In addition, we also need to avoid falling into the trap of proposing security mechanisms that are evaluated using similar tools from reliability.

Categories and Subject Descriptors

K. 6.5 [**Management of Computing and Information Systems**]: Security and Protection

Keywords

Cyber-physical systems; reliability, security

Permission to make digital or hard copies of part or all of this work for personal or classroom use is granted without fee provided that copies are not made or distributed for profit or commercial advantage, and that copies bear this notice and the full citation on the first page. Copyrights for third-party components of this work must be honored. For all other uses, contact the owner/author(s). Copyright is held by the author/owner(s).

HiCoNS'14, April 15–17, 2014, Berlin, Germany.
ACM 978-1-4503-2652-0/14/04.

Multilateral Trades in Interconnected Power Systems: A Local Public Goods Approach

Erik Miehling
University of Michigan
EECS Department
1301 Beal Avenue
Ann Arbor, MI 48109
miehling@umich.edu

Demosthenis Teneketzis
University of Michigan
EECS Department
1301 Beal Avenue
Ann Arbor, MI 48109
teneket@umich.edu

ABSTRACT

We study the multilateral trade problem in interconnected power systems with asymmetric information and non-strategic regional transmission operators (RTOs).

We consider a physical network with finite capacity lines connecting the buses within and between RTOs. Each RTO knows the network topology, bus angle constraints, and cost functions within its own region. Each RTO also knows the topology of the network connecting its own region to its neighboring regions and the bus angle constraints of the buses of neighboring RTOs that are immediately connected to its own region. The transmission system is modeled by a modified DC approximation where the power flow equations are represented as convex functions of the angle difference between buses; such an approximation considers lossy flows. The objective is to determine multilateral trades that satisfy the network's informational and physical constraints and minimize the sum of costs of all RTOs.

We formulate the above multilateral trade problem as a local public goods problem. We propose a two-layer optimization algorithm that satisfies the problem's informational and physical constraints and results in a sequence of trades that converges to a trade which achieves a local minimum of the corresponding non-convex centralized information multilateral trade problem.

Keywords

Multilateral trades, electricity networks, local public goods, externalities, optimization.

Permission to make digital or hard copies of all or part of this work for personal or classroom use is granted without fee provided that copies are not made or distributed for profit or commercial advantage and that copies bear this notice and the full citation on the first page. Copyrights for components of this work owned by others than ACM must be honored. Abstracting with credit is permitted. To copy otherwise, or republish, to post on servers or to redistribute to lists, requires prior specific permission and/or a fee. Request permissions from Permissions@acm.org.

HiCoNS '14 April 15 - 17 2014, Berlin, Germany
Copyright 2014 ACM 978-1-4503-2652-0/14/04 ...$15.00
http://dx.doi.org/10.1145/2566468.2566479 .

1. INTRODUCTION

Structural changes in the energy sector from a monopolistic, vertically-integrated system to a more competitive, distributed framework has created many interesting new problems. Although diverse in their nature, these problems have the unifying characteristic of asymmetric information. Power companies are not interested in revealing their cost or capacity information and, furthermore, cannot even be assumed to have knowledge of the network topology outside their own localized region. Achieving the most efficient outcome under these informational asymmetries is complicated by the fact that there are losses within the network, limits on power transmission, contingency considerations, the fact that power cannot be efficiently stored, and the underlying, fundamental rule that the flow of power cannot be controlled; power flows through the network by rules that are dictated by the laws of physics (Kirchhoff's laws). Specifically, Kirchhoff's laws create a phenomenon in power systems termed *loop-flow*, in which power can, in general, flow throughout the entire network, including back to the source of the original injection. This loop-flow creates externalities in the markets for electrical energy [4].

In this paper, we consider a network of interconnected power systems, termed regional transmission operators (RTOs), who are involved in energy trading with one another, termed *multilateral energy trading*, under the condition that each RTO possesses only localized knowledge. The existence of such networks of RTOs has been foreseen by reports of both the North-American Electric Reliability Council (NERC) and the U.S. Federal Energy Regulatory Commission (FERC). They predict that all current independent system operators (ISOs) will eventually be encompassed by four or six RTOs [12],[13]. We propose and analyze a negotiation process for energy trading among RTOs which aims to determine the total cost minimizing set of trades while satisfying the system's informational and physical constraints.

1.1 Literature Review

Power flow and multilateral power trading problems with asymmetric information have been investigated in many papers; we cite the most relevant [1, 2, 3, 5, 7, 8, 9, 10, 14, 20, 21] to our work. A large group of these papers use the method of responsive pricing and Lagrange multipliers [1, 3, 5, 7, 8, 14] in which agents react to prices (Lagrange multipliers) by reporting their consumption and generation to a centralized auctioneer who is responsible for price updating. Another class of papers, that aim to improve computational efficiency over the Lagrangian methods, are augmented Lagrangian methods [2, 10, 20]. In [21] trades are made with the help of a broker and the power systems operator (PSO) which ensures that the constraints imposed by the network topology and the physics of the problem (power flow equations) are satisfied.

In our paper we formulate a multilateral energy trading problem with asymmetric information and present a local public goods approach for its solution. Our approach is distinctly different from those appearing in [1, 2, 3, 5, 7, 8, 9, 10, 14, 20, 21].

We note that a local public goods approach to the power flow problem has appeared in [9]. However, externalities in [9] are assumed to arise only because of the presence of a communication system through which messages among the users are exchanged. In our formulation externalities arise because of the physical flow of power in the network.

1.2 Local Public Goods Approach

In this paper, we present a methodology for the solution of the multilateral trade problem with asymmetric information and non-strategic RTOs based on the theory of local public goods [16].

In general, as pointed out earlier, loop flow describes how the power injection of one bus can flow across the entire network, even back to the originating bus, creating externalities for all buses within the network. The issue of loop flow could be managed if it were possible to specify an entire, feasible vector of power injections for the system. However, the RTOs in our problem are assumed to have incomplete knowledge of the power system network, and thus no single RTO is able to propose a system-wide injection vector that satisfies the physical constraints. Instead, as we show in the paper, by specifying voltage angles, rather than power injections, we can manage the externalities created by loop flow and capture the fact that RTOs have localized knowledge. Under our modified DC approximation, the specification of the pair of bus angles corresponding to a particular line completely defines the flow of real power along that line. Under this approach, the total power injection at each bus will then depend on the specifications of its own angle and the angles of its neighboring buses. Since the injection ultimately determines a particular cost or benefit to a bus, the decisions of neighboring buses affects the utility of that bus, and that bus will want to have a say in the bus angles of his neighbors. Thus the decision (bus angle propositions) of each bus localizes the externality effect to the immediate network of neighboring buses, unlike the network-wide effect discussed in the loop flow problem. In our method, each RTO specifies voltage angles of all buses within its own region, as well as the angles of the buses immediately neighboring its region (that is, those buses in other RTOs that are connected to a bus in its own region). Under this approach, RTOs take into account their own cost as well as the induced externalities of their decisions. Through the proposed algorithm, RTOs agree upon the profile of voltage angles that minimize the social cost (defined in Section 4) while obeying both the physical and informational constraints.

We propose a two-layer iterative method where RTOs solve a sequence of convexified localized problems whose aggregated (across regions) solutions converge to a local optimum of the non-convex centralized information problem while satisfying informational constraints. The original non-convex problem is decomposed into localized (regional) subproblems. Each one of these subproblems is convexified by their respective RTO. RTOs negotiate until they each obtain a convergent solution to their localized convexified subproblem. This solution is then used to form the respective RTOs next convexified localized subproblem. This process is repeated, with the sequence of aggregated solutions (across regions) converging to a local minimum of the corresponding non-convex centralized information problem.

We believe that our approach is applicable to very large interconnected power systems as there is no need for a centralized entity in our problem.

1.3 Contributions of the Paper

The main contributions of the paper are:
(1) The formulation of the multilateral trade problem with asymmetric information and non-strategic agents as a local public goods problem. To the best of our knowledge, this is the first time the multilateral trade problem has been approached within the context of local public goods.
(2) The solution of the multilateral trade problem with asymmetric information and non-strategic agents via a two-layer optimization methodology which guarantees convergence to a local minimum of the corresponding non-convex centralized information optimization problem.

1.4 Organization of the Paper

In Section 2 we introduce the notation that is used throughout the paper. In Section 3 we present the model developed in the paper. We state the assumptions we make, and discuss their implications. In Section 4 we formulate both the centralized and decentralized information multilateral trade problems with non-strategic RTOs. In Section 5 we present the solution methodology for the decentralized information multilateral trade problem. We discuss the two layers of the proposed algorithm, the inner layer (Section 5.1) and the outer layer (Section 5.2). We prove convergence of the proposed algorithm to a local minimum of the corresponding non-convex centralized information problem. We conclude in Section 6.

2. NOTATION

Before we discuss our model, we introduce the notation used throughout the paper and provide the definition of the network topology. We assume a set of connected, disjoint RTOs, denoted by $\mathcal{N} := \{1, 2, \ldots, N\}$. Each RTO_k, $k \in \mathcal{N}$, contains $N_k + 1$ buses, denoted by the set $\mathcal{N}^k$. We number the buses sequentially in the network based upon the RTO index, that is, $\mathcal{N}^1 := \{1, \ldots, N_1 + 1\}$, $\mathcal{N}^2 := \{N_1 + 2, \ldots, N_1 + N_2 + 2\}$, and so on, up to $\mathcal{N}^N := \{N_1 + \cdots + N_{N-1} + N, \ldots, N_1 + \cdots + N_N + N\}$. The set of *boundary buses* $\mathcal{N}_b^k \subseteq \mathcal{N}^k$ is defined as the set of buses which have at least one direct connection to another RTO_l, $l \neq k$. We term the *interior buses* of RTO_k as the buses in $\mathcal{N}^k \backslash \mathcal{N}_b^k$. We assume that there is a slack bus within each RTO indexed by $s_1, s_2, \ldots, s_N$, termed *area slack* buses, whose voltage angles are set to zero. The assumption of multiple slack buses has also been seen in (p.165, [17]). The remaining buses within each RTO are not a priori specified as net generation or net consumption buses. The set of neighboring buses to bus i in RTO_k is denoted as $\mathcal{R}_i^k$, with $i \in \mathcal{R}_i^k$. We denote the set of buses in and immediately connected to buses in RTO_k as $\mathcal{R}^k := \cup_{i \in \mathcal{N}^k} \mathcal{R}_i^k$. We define the set of neighboring RTOs to RTO_k as $\mathcal{S}^k$, that is, $\mathcal{S}^k$ is the set of RTOs that contain at least one bus that is connected to a bus in $\mathcal{N}^k$, with $k \notin \mathcal{S}^k$. The set of voltage angles in RTO_k are represented by $\boldsymbol{\theta}^k \in \mathbb{R}^{N_k+1}$ and for notational convenience we denote θ_i^k as bus i in RTO_k. We denote the area slack in RTO_k by $\theta_{s_k}^k$. For notational convenience, we denote pairs of angles as $\theta_{ij}^k := \{\theta_i^k, \theta_j^k\}$ and $\theta_{ij}^{kl} := \{\theta_i^k, \theta_j^l\}$. The vector $\boldsymbol{\theta} \in \mathbb{R}^{N_1+N_2+\cdots+N_N+N}$ is the complete set of bus angles across the network, $\boldsymbol{\theta} := \cup_{k \in \mathcal{N}} \boldsymbol{\theta}^k$. The feasible set of angles is denoted by $\boldsymbol{\Theta}$. We use $\boldsymbol{\theta}_{\mathcal{R}_i^k}$ to represent the set of angles connected to (and including) bus i, that is $\boldsymbol{\theta}_{\mathcal{R}_i^k} := \left(\cup_{j \in \mathcal{R}_i^k} \theta_j^k \right) \cup \left(\cup_{l \in \mathcal{S}^k} \cup_{j \in \mathcal{R}_i^k \cap \mathcal{N}^l} \theta_j^l \right)$. We also define $\boldsymbol{\theta}_{\mathcal{R}^k}$ as the vector of angles of buses in and immediately connected to RTO_k, that is $\boldsymbol{\theta}_{\mathcal{R}^k} := \bigcup_{i \in \mathcal{N}^k} \boldsymbol{\theta}_{\mathcal{R}_i^k}$.

We term the network between buses that connect RTOs as the *inter-RTO* network, where the set of edges between RTO_k and RTO_l are denoted by $\mathcal{E}^{kl}$. We term the network connecting buses within each RTO_k as the *intra-RTO_k* network with set of edges $\mathcal{E}^k$. The edges of the inter-RTO network have physical parameters represented by the complex-valued admittance matrix, Y^{kl}. The admittance, $Y_{ij}^{kl} = G_{ij}^{kl} + jB_{ij}^{kl}$, of line $(i,j) \in \mathcal{E}^{kl}$ for bus i in RTO_k and bus j in RTO_l, is comprised of a conductance term $G_{ij}^{kl} = \frac{r_{ij}^{kl}}{(r_{ij}^{kl})^2+(x_{ij}^{kl})^2}$ and a susceptance term $B_{ij}^{kl} = \frac{x_{ij}^{kl}}{(r_{ij}^{kl})^2+(x_{ij}^{kl})^2}$ where r_{ij}^{kl} and x_{ij}^{kl} are the resistance and the reactance terms, respectively. If the element $Y_{ij}^{kl} = 0$, then there is no connection between buses i in RTO_k and j in RTO_l. There is a similarly defined matrix $Y^k = G^k + jB^k \in \mathbb{C}^{(N_k+1)\times(N_k+1)}$ which specifies the admittance of lines (i,j) in each intra-RTO_k network. All edges in the inter-RTO network and the intra-RTO network have a finite, fixed transmission capacity given by the real-valued symmetric matrices S^{kl} and S^k, respectively. The network topology is defined as $\mathcal{T} = \left\{ \mathcal{N}, \{Y^{kl}, S^{kl}\}_{k \in \mathcal{N}, l \in \mathcal{S}^k}, \{\mathcal{N}^k, Y^k, S^k\}_{k \in \mathcal{N}} \right\}$. Figure 1 represents an instance of an interconnected power system topology.

3. THE MODEL

The key features of our model are characterized by assumptions **(A1)** – **(A6)**.

Assumption 1: *The transmission network is modeled by a modified (defined below) DC approximation with transmission losses.*

In general, the power injected at a particular node i in the network and the power flowing between two nodes i and j are dictated by nonlinear functions of the voltage angles and magnitudes at the respective nodes. The real power flowing between two buses, i and j, in a power system is represented by the following expression [6]

$$P_{ij} = G_{ij}V_i^2 - G_{ij}V_iV_j\cos(\theta_i - \theta_j) + B_{ij}V_iV_j\sin(\theta_i - \theta_j)$$

The DC approximation assumes that the voltage magnitudes can be made constant (set to 1 p.u. in this paper) and that the voltage angle differences, $\theta_i - \theta_j$, are small. Following the approach taken in [4], a small angle difference allows us to use the approximations $\sin(\theta_i - \theta_j) \approx \theta_i - \theta_j$ and $\cos(\theta_i - \theta_j) \approx 1 - \frac{1}{2}(\theta_i - \theta_j)^2$. The power flow equation along

line (i,j) can then be written approximated as a convex function of the angle difference

$$P_{ij} \approx B_{ij}(\theta_i - \theta_j) + \frac{1}{2}G_{ij}(\theta_i - \theta_j)^2 \qquad (1)$$

Notice that this approximation preserves the asymmetry of the power flow equations, that is $P_{ij} \neq -P_{ji}$ and thus losses are considered in the approximation (unlike with the typical DC power flow). Losses along line (i,j) are given by

$$\begin{aligned} L_{ij} = P_{ij} + P_{ji} &\approx B_{ij}(\theta_i - \theta_j) + \frac{1}{2}G_{ij}(\theta_i - \theta_j)^2 \\ &\quad + B_{ji}(\theta_j - \theta_i) + \frac{1}{2}G_{ji}(\theta_j - \theta_i)^2 \\ &= \frac{1}{2}G_{ij}\left[(\theta_i - \theta_j)^2 + (\theta_j - \theta_i)^2\right] \\ &= G_{ij}(\theta_i - \theta_j)^2 \end{aligned}$$

where we have used the fact that $B_{ij} = B_{ji}$ and $G_{ij} = G_{ji}$. Also notice that the steps used to obtain the approximation in Equation (1) did not require that the conductance, G_{ij}, is small compared to the susceptance, B_{ij}, unlike in the classical DC approximation.

A consequence of the modified DC approximation is that the operating point is defined by just the vector of voltage angles. The validity of this approximation is centered around the ability of the buses to adjust their reactive power accordingly to keep the voltage at a nominal value (1 p.u.). This assumption requires that there is enough reactive power generation at each bus in the network (or a generator at a nearby bus, connected via a low impedance line) so that the bus can adjust its reactive power (or have its reactive power easily adjusted by a nearby generator) to keep the voltage at that node at 1 p.u.

Assumption 2: *RTOs have* local *knowledge of the power network topology.*

We assume that each RTO_k has local knowledge of the power network topology, that is, RTO_k is assumed to know its own network $\{\mathcal{N}^k, Y^k, S^k\}$ and the parameters of the connecting lines $Y^{kl}, S^{kl}, l \in \mathcal{S}^k$.

Assumption 3: *Each bus i in each RTO_k is endowed with a cost function $c_i^k : \mathbb{R} \to \mathbb{R}_+$ which is assumed to be strictly convex and increasing and RTO_k's private information.*

All buses, $i \in \mathcal{N}^k$, $k \in \mathcal{N}$, have a corresponding cost function, c_i^k. If bus i's injection p is positive, then $c_i^k(p)$ represents the *generation cost* of producing power p. If bus i's injection is negative, then $c_i^k(p)$ represents the *negative of the benefit* from receiving power p. All of the functions are assumed to be *strictly convex* and *increasing*. A discussion of the validity of the convexity assumption can be found in [19].

Assumption 4: *Each bus i in each RTO_k has voltage angle constraint, Θ_i^k, that is, $\theta_i^k \in \Theta_i^k$.*

We place a lower and upper bound on all bus' angles $\theta_i^k \in [\underline{\theta}_i^k, \overline{\theta}_i^k] = \Theta_i^k$, with $\underline{\theta}_i^k \leq 0$ and $\overline{\theta}_i^k \geq 0$ for all $i \in \mathcal{N}^k$, $k \in \mathcal{N}$. We also impose the condition that for all area slack buses, $\Theta_{s_k}^k = \{0\}$.

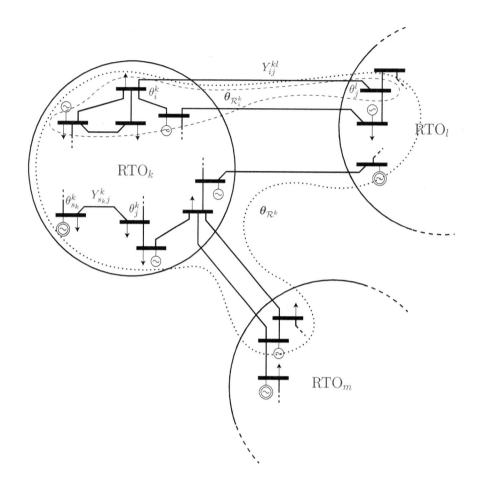

Figure 1: Single-line diagram of a sample network topology for the multilateral trade problem. Consider bus i **in RTO**$_k$ **with voltage angle** θ_i^k. **The set of angles** $\theta_{\mathcal{R}_i^k}$ **are the angles of all neighboring buses (including** i**),** **represented by the outlined region surrounding bus** i **(dashed line). Notice that** $\theta_j^l \in \theta_{\mathcal{R}_i^k}$. **The larger region** **(dotted line) surrounding all of the buses in RTO**$_k$ **and neighboring buses represents the set** $\theta_{\mathcal{R}^k}$. **Slack buses** **are the buses for which there is a double-encircled generators present;** $\theta_{s_k}^k$ **is the angle of the slack bus in** **RTO**$_k$. **The set of neighboring RTOs to RTO**$_k$ **is** $\mathcal{S}^k = \{l, m\}$.

Assumption 5: *The angle constraints of the interior buses of a given RTO are private information of the respective RTO. The angle constraints of the boundary buses are common information of the neighboring RTOs.*

We assume that RTO$_k$ knows each Θ_i^k, for all $i \in \mathcal{N}^k$. Furthermore, each RTO$_k$ knows Θ_j^l, for $j \in \mathcal{R}^k \cap \mathcal{N}^l, l \in \mathcal{S}^k$.

Assumption 6: *RTOs are non-strategic.*

As a consequence of Assumption 6, the RTOs obey the rules of the mechanism/algorithm that is designed for the solution of the multilateral trade problem.

4. THE MULTILATERAL TRADE PROBLEM – FORMULATION

The goal of the multilateral trade problem is to determine the optimal trades among RTOs while ensuring feasibility between and within RTOs and satisfying the informational constraints. To achieve the above goal we proceed as follows. First, we formulate the centralized information multilateral trade problem (termed the centralized problem) where we assume that there is an entity that has complete knowledge of the power network's topology, as well as both the cost functions and angle constraints of all buses in the network. The optimal solution to this problem defines the best possible multilateral trades for the given problem. Second we consider the decentralized information multilateral trade problem (termed the decentralized problem), where we enforce the informational constraints imposed by assumptions (**A2**), (**A3**), and (**A5**). Finally, in Section 5, we present a trade mechanism for the decentralized multilateral trade problem that leads to a locally optimal set of trades for the centralized multilateral trade problem.

4.1 Centralized Problem Formulation

We now formulate the centralized information multilateral trade problem assuming that there is an entity that has complete system knowledge. Recall that each bus in each RTO has an associated cost function which represents their cost or negative benefit for generating or receiving a certain amount of power, respectively. The *social cost*, $C(\boldsymbol{\theta})$, is defined to be the sum of all buses' costs across all RTOs. The optimal multilateral trades are those that achieve the minimum social cost. The centralized information multilateral trade problem (P_C) is

$$\min_{\boldsymbol{\theta}} \quad C(\boldsymbol{\theta}) \qquad (P_C)$$

subject to $\quad \boldsymbol{\theta} \in \boldsymbol{\Theta} := \Big\{ \boldsymbol{\theta} \Big| \theta_i^k \in \Theta_i^k, \, i \in \mathcal{N}^k;$

$$-S_{ij}^k \le g(\theta_{ij}^k) \le S_{ij}^k, \, (i,j) \in \mathcal{E}^k;$$

$$-S_{ij}^{kl} \le h(\theta_{ij}^{kl}) \le S_{ij}^{kl}, \, (i,j) \in \mathcal{E}^{kl}, l \in \mathcal{S}^k; k \in \mathcal{N} \Big\} \quad (2)$$

where $C(\boldsymbol{\theta}) := \sum_{k \in \mathcal{N}} C_k(\boldsymbol{\theta}_{\mathcal{R}^k})$. Each RTO$_k$'s aggregated cost is

$$C_k(\boldsymbol{\theta}_{\mathcal{R}^k}) := \sum_{i \in \mathcal{N}^k \setminus \mathcal{N}_b^k} c_i^k \Big(f_i^k \big(\boldsymbol{\theta}_{\mathcal{R}_i^k} \big) \Big) + \sum_{i \in \mathcal{N}_b^k} c_i^k \Big(f_i \big(\boldsymbol{\theta}_{\mathcal{R}_i^k} \big) \Big)$$

where $f_i^k(\boldsymbol{\theta}_{\mathcal{R}_i^k}) := \sum_{j \in \mathcal{R}_i^k} g(\theta_{ij}^k)$ is the injected power at interior bus i of RTO$_k$ and $f_i(\boldsymbol{\theta}_{\mathcal{R}_i^k}) := \sum_{j \in \mathcal{R}_i^k \cap \mathcal{N}^k} g(\theta_{ij}^k) + \sum_{l \in \mathcal{S}^k} \sum_{j \in \mathcal{R}_i^k \cap \mathcal{N}^l} h(\theta_{ij}^{kl})$ is the injected power at boundary bus i of RTO$_k$. The first set of constraints are the voltage angle constraints. By $(\mathbf{A1})$, flow between buses (i,j) within RTO$_k$ is given by

$$g(\theta_{ij}^k) := B_{ij}^k (\theta_i^k - \theta_j^k) + \frac{1}{2} G_{ij}^k (\theta_i^k - \theta_j^k)^2,$$

whereas the flow between buses (i,j) in adjacent RTOs, k and l, respectively, termed a *trade*, is denoted by

$$h(\theta_{ij}^{kl}) := B_{ij}^{kl} (\theta_i^k - \theta_j^l) + \frac{1}{2} G_{ij}^{kl} (\theta_i^k - \theta_j^l)^2.$$

The remaining set of constraints represent transmission capacity constraints of the intra-RTO and inter-RTO networks, respectively.

We now analyze the convexity of Problem (P_C). The objective function, $C(\boldsymbol{\theta})$, is strictly convex in $\boldsymbol{\theta}$. By assumption $(\mathbf{A4})$, since $\Theta_{s_k}^k = \{0\}$ for each $k \in \mathcal{N}$, $\theta_{s_k}^k = 0$, and thus the function $f_i^k(\boldsymbol{\theta}_{\mathcal{R}_i^k}), i = s_k \in \mathcal{N}^k \setminus \mathcal{N}_b^k$ (or $f_i(\boldsymbol{\theta}_{\mathcal{R}_i^k})$ if $i = s_k \in \mathcal{N}_b^k$) is $f_{s_k}^k(\boldsymbol{\theta}_{\mathcal{R}_{s_k}^k}) = \sum_{j \in \mathcal{R}_{s_k}^k} -B_{s_k,j}^k \theta_j^k + \frac{1}{2} G_{s_k,j}^k (\theta_j^k)^2$ which is a strictly convex function in $\boldsymbol{\theta}^k$. Since all c_i^k functions are assumed to be strictly convex and increasing, by $(\mathbf{A3})$, $C(\boldsymbol{\theta})$ is strictly convex in $\boldsymbol{\theta}$. Notice that the feasible set $\boldsymbol{\Theta}$ is non-convex due to the non-convex inequality constraints. Thus, Problem (P_C) is a non-convex optimization problem.

4.2 Decentralized Problem Formulation

By assumptions $(\mathbf{A2})$, $(\mathbf{A3})$, and $(\mathbf{A5})$, none of the RTOs in the network possess the information required to obtain the optimal solution of Problem (P_C). As a result, we formu-

late the decentralized information counterpart to Problem (P_C), termed Problem (P_D), which imposes the additional restriction that information is localized to each RTO. The decentralized information problem (P_D) is

$$\min_{\boldsymbol{\theta}} \quad \big\{ C(\boldsymbol{\theta}) \big| \boldsymbol{\theta} \in \boldsymbol{\Theta}; (\mathbf{A2}), (\mathbf{A3}), (\mathbf{A5}) \big\} \qquad (P_D)$$

which is the centralized information problem with the added informational constraints imposed by assumptions $(\mathbf{A2})$, $(\mathbf{A3})$, and $(\mathbf{A5})$. The remainder of the paper will focus on the process of obtaining the solution to Problem (P_D).

5. DECENTRALIZED MULTILATERAL TRADE PROBLEM – SOLUTION METHODOLOGY

The proposed solution method for Problem (P_D) consists of a two-layer optimization process which converges to a local minimum of Problem (P_C) while satisfying the problem's informational and physical constraints. Given an initial feasible point $\mathbf{z} \in \boldsymbol{\Theta}$, the inner layer describes an iterative process (where iterations indexed by n), termed the externality algorithm, of how RTOs reach a trade agreement by solving their respective convexified (around $\mathbf{z}$) problems. Once an agreement is reached, each RTO forms a new convexified problem around the agreement. The outer layer, iterations indexed by t, describes how the aggregated (across regions) sequence of agreements converge to a local minimum of Problem (P_C).

Given an initial feasible point $\mathbf{z} \in \boldsymbol{\Theta}$, each RTO forms a convexified set of the constraints in their local network using only its available information. We denote RTO$_k$'s convexified set, around a given point $\mathbf{z}_{\mathcal{R}^k}$ (where the indexing notation for $\mathbf{z}$ is the same as the one used for $\boldsymbol{\theta}$), which is a subvector of $\mathbf{z}$, as $\hat{\boldsymbol{\Theta}}_{\mathcal{R}^k}(\mathbf{z}_{\mathcal{R}^k})$, that is defined by

$$\hat{\boldsymbol{\Theta}}_{\mathcal{R}^k}(\mathbf{z}_{\mathcal{R}^k}) := \Big\{ \boldsymbol{\theta}_{\mathcal{R}^k} \Big| \theta_i^k \in \Theta_i^k, i \in \mathcal{N}^k;$$

$$g(\theta_{ij}^k) \le S_{ij}^k, -\hat{g}(\theta_{ij}^k, z_{ij}^k) \le S_{ij}^k, (i,j) \in \mathcal{E}^k;$$

$$h(\theta_{ij}^{kl}) \le S_{ij}^{kl}, -\hat{h}(\theta_{ij}^{kl}, z_{ij}^{kl}) \le S_{ij}^{kl}, (i,j) \in \mathcal{E}^{kl}, l \in \mathcal{S}^k;$$

$$\theta_j^l \in \Theta_j^l, j \in \mathcal{R}^k \cap \mathcal{N}^l, l \in \mathcal{S}^k \Big\} \qquad (3)$$

where $\hat{g}(\theta_{ij}^k, z_{ij}^k), (i,j) \in \mathcal{E}^k$, and $\hat{h}(\theta_{ij}^{kl}, z_{ij}^{kl}), (i,j) \in \mathcal{E}^{kl}, l \in \mathcal{S}^k$, are first-order (affine) Taylor expansions around $\mathbf{z}_{\mathcal{R}^k}$ defined by

$$\hat{g}(\theta_{ij}^k, z_{ij}^k) = g(z_{ij}^k)$$
$$+ \nabla g(z_{ij}^k)^\top \Big((\theta_i^k - z_i^k)\mathbf{e}_1 + (\theta_j^k - z_j^k)\mathbf{e}_2 \Big), \quad (4)$$

$$\hat{h}(\theta_{ij}^{kl}, z_{ij}^{kl}) = h(z_{ij}^{kl})$$
$$+ \nabla h(z_{ij}^{kl})^\top \Big((\theta_i^k - z_i^k)\mathbf{e}_1 + (\theta_j^l - z_j^l)\mathbf{e}_2 \Big), \quad (5)$$

$$\nabla g(z_{ij}^k) = \Big(B_{ij}^k + G_{ij}^k (z_i^k - z_j^k) \Big) (\mathbf{e}_1 - \mathbf{e}_2), \quad (6)$$

$$\nabla h(z_{ij}^{kl}) = \Big(B_{ij}^{kl} + G_{ij}^{kl} (z_i^k - z_j^l) \Big) (\mathbf{e}_1 - \mathbf{e}_2), \quad (7)$$

$$\mathbf{e}_1 = (1,0), \quad \text{and} \quad \mathbf{e}_2 = (0,1). \quad (8)$$

Notice that if we were to convexify the original non-convex constraint set $\boldsymbol{\Theta}$ around the point $\mathbf{z}$, to generate the convexified set $\hat{\boldsymbol{\Theta}}(\mathbf{z})$, we would obtain the same feasible set as that obtained by the union of the localized convexified feasible sets. That is

$$\hat{\Theta}(\mathbf{z}) = \bigcup_{k \in \mathcal{N}} \hat{\Theta}_{\mathcal{R}^k}(\mathbf{z}_{\mathcal{R}^k}). \tag{9}$$

Thus each agent is able to locally compute their feasible set. The convexified set $\hat{\Theta}(\mathbf{z})$ is an approximation of the true set of feasible solutions and lies *within* the true set of feasible solutions (the first order approximation of a convex function is a lower bound to the function), that is $\hat{\Theta}(\mathbf{z}) \subseteq \Theta$ (an important distinction from the convex hull, which extends the feasible set of solutions beyond the true set). The proposed convexified set approach is desirable, particularly in our application, since reaching a solution which lies outside the true feasible set would violate system security conditions and cause physical damage to the network.

We denote the convexified Problems $(\hat{P}_C^t)$ and $(\hat{P}_D^t)$, linearized around a point $\boldsymbol{\theta}^t \in \Theta$, by

$$\min_{\boldsymbol{\theta}} \; \left\{ C(\boldsymbol{\theta}) \big| \boldsymbol{\theta} \in \hat{\Theta}(\boldsymbol{\theta}^t) \right\}, \tag{$\hat{P}_C^t$}$$

$$\min_{\boldsymbol{\theta}} \; \left\{ C(\boldsymbol{\theta}) \big| \boldsymbol{\theta} \in \hat{\Theta}(\boldsymbol{\theta}^t); (\mathbf{A2}), (\mathbf{A3}), (\mathbf{A5}) \right\}. \tag{$\hat{P}_D^t$}$$

We now analyze the inner layer of the proposed algorithm.

5.1 Inner Layer

Recall the discussion of Section 1.2 where we describe the local public goods aspect of the problem. Each RTO proposes the voltage angles of all buses in its own region as well as the angles of its neighboring buses, that is each RTO proposes $\boldsymbol{\theta}_{\mathcal{R}^k}$. For two neighboring RTOs, the initial proposals of the voltage angles of the shared boundary buses will not, in general, agree. The inner layer consists of an externality algorithm from [16] which describes how RTOs reach a trade agreement by iteratively solving (as described below) their localized convexified problems $(\hat{P}_D^t)$. The solution to Problem $(\hat{P}_D^t)$ achieved by the externality algorithm is the same as the optimal solution to Problem $(\hat{P}_C^t)$.

Algorithm 1 – Externality Algorithm

Step 0: Set $n = 0$. Every RTO$_k$, $k \in \mathcal{N}$, agrees upon:

- An initial angle vector $\hat{\boldsymbol{\theta}}^{(0)} \in \Theta$.

- A sequence of nonincreasing, bounded parameters, $\{\tau^{(n)}\}_{n=1}^{\infty}$, s.t. $0 < \tau^{(n+1)} \leq \tau^{(n)} \leq 1$ for all $n \geq 1$, $\tau^{(m)} \to 0$ as $m \to \infty$; $\sum_{m=1}^{n} \tau^{(m)} \to \infty$ as $n \to \infty$.

Step 1: At the nth iteration, each RTO$_k$, $k \in \mathcal{N}$, solves their own optimization problem to obtain $\tilde{\boldsymbol{\theta}}_{\mathcal{R}^k}^{(n+1)}$, then computes the weighted average, $\boldsymbol{\omega}_{\mathcal{R}^k}^{(n+1)}$, as follows

$$\tilde{\boldsymbol{\theta}}_{\mathcal{R}^k}^{(n+1)} := \underset{\boldsymbol{\theta}_{\mathcal{R}^k} \in \hat{\Theta}_{\mathcal{R}^k}\left(\boldsymbol{\theta}_{\mathcal{R}^k}^t\right)}{\operatorname{argmin}} \left\{ C_k(\boldsymbol{\theta}_{\mathcal{R}^k}) + \frac{\left\| \boldsymbol{\theta}_{\mathcal{R}^k} - \hat{\boldsymbol{\theta}}_{\mathcal{R}^k}^{(n)} \right\|_2^2}{\tau^{(n+1)}} \right\} \tag{10}$$

$$\boldsymbol{\omega}_{\mathcal{R}^k}^{(n+1)} := \frac{1}{\sigma^{(n+1)}} \sum_{m=1}^{n+1} \tau^{(m)} \tilde{\boldsymbol{\theta}}_{\mathcal{R}^k}^{(m)} \tag{11}$$

where $\sigma^{(n+1)} := \sum_{m=1}^{n+1} \tau^{(m)}$. We denote the components of $\tilde{\boldsymbol{\theta}}_{\mathcal{R}^k}^{(n+1)}$ (resp. $\boldsymbol{\omega}_{\mathcal{R}^k}^{(n+1)}$) that are within RTO$_k$ by $\tilde{\theta}_i^{k,(n+1)}$ (resp. $\omega_i^{k,(n+1)}$); for the components of $\tilde{\boldsymbol{\theta}}_{\mathcal{R}^k}^{(n+1)}$ (resp. $\boldsymbol{\omega}_{\mathcal{R}^k}^{(n+1)}$) that are within RTO$_l$, we denote the bus angles by $\tilde{\theta}_i^{k \to l,(n+1)}$

(resp. $\omega_i^{k \to l,(n+1)}$) to specify RTO$_k$'s angle proposal of bus i in RTO$_l$ at the $(n+1)^{\text{st}}$ iteration.

Each RTO$_k$ broadcasts the following angles to its neighbor RTO$_l$, $l \in \mathcal{S}^k$

$$\left(\tilde{\theta}_i^{k \to l,(n+1)} \right)_{i \in \mathcal{R}^k \cap \mathcal{N}^l} \tag{12}$$

Step 2: Upon receiving the angle proposals from each neighbor, each RTO$_k$ computes the following quantities. For interior buses, $i \in \mathcal{N}^k \backslash \mathcal{N}_b^k$, set

$$\hat{\theta}_i^{k,(n+1)} = \tilde{\theta}_i^{k,(n+1)} \tag{13}$$

For boundary buses, $i \in \mathcal{N}_b^k$, set

$$\hat{\theta}_i^{k,(n+1)} = \frac{\tilde{\theta}_i^{k,(n+1)} + \sum_{l \in \mathcal{S}^k} \sum_{j \in \mathcal{R}_i^k \cap \mathcal{N}^l} \tilde{\theta}_j^{l \to k,(n+1)}}{1 + \left| \bigcup_{l \in \mathcal{S}^k} \mathcal{R}_i^k \cap \mathcal{N}^l \right|} \tag{14}$$

Increment the iteration by setting $n = n + 1$ and return to Step 1.

In Step 1 of the externality algorithm, each RTO solves a convex optimization problem described by Equation (10). The additive norm-squared term in (10) penalizes RTO$_k$ for deviating from the previous iteration's average proposal. This term incorporates the externalities created by RTO$_k$'s neighbors, and creates a *force* which pulls RTO$_k$'s decision to the average of the proposals from its neighboring RTOs. The effect of externalities become more significant for each RTO as the algorithm progresses. This can be seen by recalling that $\{\tau^{(n)}\}_{n=1}^{\infty}$ is a nonincreasing, bounded sequence, thus, the norm square term eventually dominates each RTO's objective function. As a result, each RTO's sequence of computed angle profile converges to a stationary profile. Computation of the weighted average, Equation (11), takes into account each RTO's aggregated cost function. Theorem 1 below asserts that the sequences $\boldsymbol{\omega}_{\mathcal{R}^k}^{(n)}$ converge to the minimum of Problem $(\hat{P}_C^t)$.

THEOREM 1. *[16]*
Define the vectors $\mathbf{w}_k^{(n)} \in \mathbb{R}^{(N_1 + N_2 + \cdots + N_N + N) \times 1}$, $k \in \mathcal{N}$ *by*

$$\mathbf{w}_{k_i}^{(n)} = \begin{cases} \omega_i^{k,(n)} & if\ i \in \mathcal{N}^k \\ \omega_i^{k \to l,(n)} & if\ i \in \mathcal{N}^l, l \in \mathcal{S}^k \\ 0 & otherwise \end{cases} \tag{15}$$

and the matrix $\mathbf{W}^{(n)} \in \mathbb{R}^{(N_1 + N_2 + \cdots + N_N + N) \times N}$

$$\mathbf{W}^{(n)} = \begin{bmatrix} | & | & & | \\ \mathbf{w}_1^{(n)} & \mathbf{w}_2^{(n)} & \cdots & \mathbf{w}_N^{(n)} \\ | & | & & | \end{bmatrix} \tag{16}$$

Let $\{\mathbf{W}^{(n)}\}_{n=1}^{\infty}$ *be a sequence of matrices generated by Algorithm 1 and Equations (15) and (16). Then*

i) $\mathbf{W}^{(n)} \to \mathbf{W}^*$ *as* $n \to \infty$.

ii) Let $\mathbf{w}_k^*$ *denote the* k^{th} *column of* $\mathbf{W}^*$. *The vector* $\mathbf{w}^* = (\mathbf{w}_{k_i}^*)_{i \in \mathcal{N}^k, k \in \mathcal{N}} \in \Theta$ *is the solution of Problem* $(\hat{P}_C^t)$.

Given the above result, the externality algorithm finds the optimal solution of the convexified decentralized information problem $(\hat{P}_D^t)$ and this solution is the same as the optimal solution of the convexified centralized information problem $(\hat{P}_C^t)$.

5.2 Outer Layer

We now describe how the sequence of solutions to successive problems $(\hat{P}_D^t)$, $t = 1, 2, \ldots$ converges to a local minimum of the original non-convex problem, Problem (P_C). Consider the following function $\mathcal{A} : \Theta \to \Theta$

$$\mathcal{A}(\mathbf{z}) := \underset{\boldsymbol{\theta}}{\arg\min} \left\{ C(\boldsymbol{\theta}) : \boldsymbol{\theta} \in \hat{\Theta}(\mathbf{z}); (\mathbf{A2}), (\mathbf{A3}), (\mathbf{A5}) \right\} \quad (17)$$

The result of Theorem 1 implies that

$$\mathcal{A}(\mathbf{z}) = \underset{\boldsymbol{\theta}}{\arg\min} \left\{ C(\boldsymbol{\theta}) : \boldsymbol{\theta} \in \hat{\Theta}(\mathbf{z}) \right\} \quad (18)$$

Because of Equations (17) and (18) from this point on we will examine the sequence of solutions of the Problems $(\hat{P}_C^t)$, $t = 1, 2, \ldots$. The process of finding solutions to problems $(\hat{P}_C^t)$, $t = 1, 2, \ldots$, can be described by the iterative process, $\boldsymbol{\theta}^{t+1} = \mathcal{A}(\boldsymbol{\theta}^t)$, initialized by some $\boldsymbol{\theta}^0 \in \Theta$. According to Theorem 1, the solution to each of the minimizations is the aggregation of the RTO's solutions, obtained from the externality algorithm.

We show that the sequence of solutions to Problems $(\hat{P}_C^t)$, $t = 1, 2, \ldots$, converges to a local minimum of Problem (P_C) under the assumption that the set $\hat{\Theta}(z)$, defined by Equations (3)–(9), has an interior point for any $\mathbf{z} \in \Theta$. For that matter, we first prove the following result.

LEMMA 1. *Each of the Problems $(\hat{P}_C^t)$ possesses the following properties*

(i) *$C(\boldsymbol{\theta})$ is strictly convex and g, h are convex.*

(ii) *The function $\mathcal{A}$ is uniformly compact on Θ.*

(iii) *$\mathcal{A}(\mathbf{z})$ is nonempty for any $\mathbf{z} \in \Theta$.*

PROOF. Property (i) is satisfied; $C(\boldsymbol{\theta})$ has already been established to be strictly convex whereas g, h are convex by construction (see the formulation of Problem (P_C)). To prove (ii), we show that Θ is compact [18]. Since Θ is in Euclidean space, we just need to verify that Θ is closed and bounded. It is bounded since $\Theta \subseteq \prod_{i \in \mathcal{N}^k, k \in \mathcal{N}} \Theta_i^k$, a bounded set. To show that Θ is closed, we note that the functions defining the inequality constraints in Θ (see Equation (2)) are differentiable on their entire domain and thus continuous on their entire domain. We apply Theorem 18.1 (p.104, [15]) to conclude that Θ is closed. Thus Θ is compact. To prove property (iii), we first note that $\hat{\Theta}(\mathbf{z})$ is compact for any $\mathbf{z} \in \Theta$ (this can be shown by arguments similar to those that establish property (ii)). Since $C(\boldsymbol{\theta})$ is a continuous function on the compact (finite-dimensional) space $\hat{\Theta}(\mathbf{z})$, $C(\boldsymbol{\theta})$ has a maximum and minimum by the Weierstrass theorem [11], thus $\mathcal{A}(\mathbf{z})$ is nonempty for any $\mathbf{z} \in \Theta$. $\square$

As a result of Lemma 1 and the above assumption on $\hat{\Theta}(\mathbf{z})$ the following theorem holds.

THEOREM 2. *Assume that the set $\hat{\Theta}(\mathbf{z})$, defined by Equations (3) and (9), has an interior point for any $\mathbf{z} \in \Theta$. Let $\{\boldsymbol{\theta}^t\}_{t=0}^{\infty}$ be any sequence generated by $\mathcal{A}$. Then $\boldsymbol{\theta}^t \to \boldsymbol{\theta}^*$ as $t \to \infty$, where $\boldsymbol{\theta}^*$ is a local minimum of Problem (P_C).*

PROOF. By Lemma 1, each Problem $(\hat{P}_C^t)$, $t = 1, 2, \ldots$, possesses properties (i)-(iii). Furthermore, under the assumption that the set $\hat{\Theta}(\mathbf{z})$ has an interior point for any

$\mathbf{z} \in \Theta$, each Problem $(\hat{P}_C^t)$, $t = 1, 2, \ldots$ satisfies a constraint qualification. Therefore, the assertion of the theorem follows directly from Theorem 10 of [18]. $\square$

The reason the proposed two-layer optimization algorithm cannot guarantee convergence to the global minimum of Problem (P_C) for general network topologies is because of the non-convexity of the set Θ. The set Θ may be disconnected; in such a case, if the selection of the initial condition $\boldsymbol{\theta}^{(0)}$ is not in the subset of Θ that contains the globally optimal solution $\boldsymbol{\theta}_{\text{opt}}^*$ of Problem (P_C) the algorithm will converge to a local minimum.

6. CONCLUSION

We formulated the problem of multilateral trades in interconnected power systems with asymmetric information and non-strategic RTOs as a local public goods problem. We presented a two-layer (optimization) algorithm which satisfies the problem's informational and physical constraints and results in a sequence of trades that converges to a local minimum of the corresponding centralized multilateral trade problem.

We plan to illustrate the proposed algorithm through numerical examples. We also plan to investigate the same problem with strategic RTOs.

7. ACKNOWLEDGMENTS

This research was supported in part by NSF grant No.: CNS-1238962. The authors are grateful to M. Rasouli and H. Tavafoghi for useful discussions.

8. REFERENCES

[1] R. Baldick, R. Kaye, and F. Wu. Electricity tariffs under imperfect knowledge of participant benefits. *Power Systems, IEEE Transactions on*, 7(4):1471–1482, 1992.

[2] J. Batut and A. Renaud. Daily generation scheduling optimization with transmission constraints: a new class of algorithms. *Power Systems, IEEE Transactions on*, 7(3):982–989, 1992.

[3] P. Biskas and A. Bakirtzis. Decentralised security constrained dc-opf of interconnected power systems. *Generation, Transmission and Distribution, IEE Proceedings-*, 151(6):747–754, 2004.

[4] H. P. Chao and S. Peck. A market mechanism for electric power transmission. *Journal of Regulatory Economics*, 10:25–59, 1996.

[5] A. Conejo and J. Aguado. Multi-area coordinated decentralized dc optimal power flow. *Power Systems, IEEE Transactions on*, 13(4):1272–1278, 1998.

[6] O. Elgerd. *Electric Energy Systems Theory: An Introduction*. McGraw-Hill, 1973.

[7] F. D. Galiana, A. L. Motto, A. J. Conejo, and M. Huneault. Decentralized nodal-price self-dispatch and unit commitment. In B. F. Hobbs, M. H. Rothkopf, R. P. O'Neill, and H. P. Chao, editors, *The Next Generation of Electric Power Unit Commitment Models*, volume 36 of *International Series in Operations Research and Management Science*, pages 271–292. Springer US, 2002.

[8] G. Hug-Glanzmann and G. Andersson. Decentralized optimal power flow control for overlapping areas in power systems. *Power Systems, IEEE Transactions on*, 24(1):327–336, 2009.

[9] M. Kallitsis, G. Michailidis, and M. Devetsikiotis. Optimal power allocation under communication network externalities. *Smart Grid, IEEE Transactions on*, 3(1):162 –173, March 2012.

[10] B. Kim and R. Baldick. Coarse-grained distributed optimal power flow. *Power Systems, IEEE Transactions on*, 12(2):932–939, 1997.

[11] D. Luenberger. *Optimization by Vector Space Methods*. Professional Series. Wiley, 1968.

[12] North-American Electric Reliability Council. Reliability assessment 2001-2010. http://www.nerc.com/~filez/rasreports.html/, 2001.

[13] US Federal Energy Regulatory Commission. Regional transmission organizations. Order No. 2000, 20 December 1999.

[14] A. Motto, F. Galiana, A. Conejo, and M. Huneault. On walrasian equilibrium for pool-based electricity markets. *Power Systems, IEEE Transactions on*, 17(3):774–781, 2002.

[15] J. R. Munkres. *Elements of algebraic topology*, volume 2. Addison-Wesley Menlo Park, CA, 1984.

[16] S. Sharma. *A mechanism design approach to decentralized resource allocation in wireless and large-scale networks: Realization and implementation*. PhD thesis, University of Michigan, 2009.

[17] Y. Song and X. Wang. *Operation of Market-oriented Power Systems*. Engineering online library. Springer, 2003.

[18] B. Sriperumbudur and G. Lanckriet. On the convergence of the concave-convex procedure. *Advances in neural information processing systems*, 22:1759–1767, 2009.

[19] B. Stott, O. Alsac, and A. Monticelli. Security analysis and optimization. *Proceedings of the IEEE*, 75(12):1623–1644, 1987.

[20] A. Sun and D. Phan. Fully decentralized optimal power flow algorithms. In *to appear in Proceedings of IEEE PES General Meeting*, 2013.

[21] P. Varaiya and F. F. Wu. Coordinated multilateral trades for electric power networks: theory and implementation. In *Electrical Power and Energy Systems 21*, pages 75–102, 1999.

A Network Interdiction Model for Analyzing the Vulnerability of Water Distribution Systems

Lina Perelman[*]
Department of CEE, MIT
Cambridge, MA, US

Saurabh Amin[†]
Department of CEE, MIT
Cambridge, MA, US

ABSTRACT

This article presents a network interdiction model to assess the vulnerabilities of a class of physical flow networks. A flow network is modeled by a potential function defined over the nodes and a flow function defined over arcs (links). In particular, the difference in potential function between two nodes is characterized by a nonlinear flux function of the flow on link between the two nodes. To assess the vulnerability of the network to adversarial attack, the problem is formulated as an attacker-defender network interdiction model. The attacker's objective is to interdict the most *valuable* links of the network given his resource constraints. The defender's objective is to minimize power loss and the unmet demand in the network. A bi-level approach is explored to identify most critical links for network interdiction. The applicability of the proposed approach is demonstrated on a reference water distribution network, and its utility toward developing mitigation plans is discussed.

Categories and Subject Descriptors

G.1.6 [**Mathematics of Computing**]: Numerical analysis—*Optimization*

Keywords

Vulnerability assessment; Cyber-physical systems; Network flow analysis; Network interdiction; Water distribution systems

1. INTRODUCTION

The water sector is one of 18 critical infrastructure sectors established under the authority of Homeland Security Presidential Directive 7 (HSPD-7). 84% of the U.S. population receives their potable water from approximately 160,000 public drinking water systems [14, 33].

[*]Postdoctoral fellow; linasela@mit.edu

[†]Assistant Prof.; amins@mit.edu

Permission to make digital or hard copies of all or part of this work for personal or classroom use is granted without fee provided that copies are not made or distributed for profit or commercial advantage and that copies bear this notice and the full citation on the first page. Copyrights for components of this work owned by others than ACM must be honored. Abstracting with credit is permitted. To copy otherwise, or republish, to post on servers or to redistribute to lists, requires prior specific permission and/or a fee. Request permissions from permissions@acm.org.

HiCoNS'14, April 15–17, 2014, Berlin, Germany.
Copyright 2014 ACM 978-1-4503-2652-0/14/04 ...$15.00.
http://dx.doi.org/10.1145/2566468.2566480.

Drinking water systems are typically comprised of: (1) Water resources and treatment plants, producing a high quality water, e.g., from ground and underground natural water bodies and/or desalination plants. (2) Water transmission system (WTS) delivering water from the treatment plants to water storage reservoirs, through open channels and/or pressurized pipeline transmission mains. (3) Water distribution system (WDS) delivering water from the urban reservoirs to consumers taps through underground pressurized pipeline network. Water transmission and distribution systems additionally comprise of pumping stations, control and pressure release valves, and operational storage tanks to ensure adequate supply of consumers' demands with suitable pressures. As opposed to the water treatment and transmission systems, which are highly monitored and physically secured, the distribution system, which is spatially distributed with many exposed elements (e.g. fire hydrants), is typically monitored only at limited locations, e.g., pumping stations and operational storage tanks. This makes the vulnerability of WDS an essential aspect of assessing the vulnerability of the urban water sector. This work focuses on the vulnerability of (3) – water distribution systems.

Reliability of WDS mainly refers to the ability of the network to provide consumers with adequate and high quality supply under normal and abnormal conditions. The reliability of water systems has been further classified by researchers as mechanical reliability and hydraulic reliability. Mechanical reliability usually refers to failures of system components, such as pipe breakage or pump being out of service. Hydraulic reliability, on the other hand, refers to consequences of uncertainties, such as nodal demand, pipe roughness and reservoir and tank levels [28].

Traditionally, reliability of WDS has been addressed at the design level of the system. Majority of works have focused on hydraulic reliability, i.e., uncertain demands and/or hydraulic parameters. To address this problem, various optimization-based formulations have been developed in the past, including stochastic [34, 7] and robust optimization [25] and heuristic solution techniques [15, 6]. Few works addressed the mechanical reliability of WDS by linking sampling-optimization techniques [23, 38, 35]. Random pipe failure scenarios are sampled under some hydraulic-failure probability function and the system's pipes and / or pumps characteristics are selected as a result of an optimization.

Reliability analysis of WDS has recently attracted more attention adopting graph-theory deterministic network metrics to investigate the topological connectivity of networks

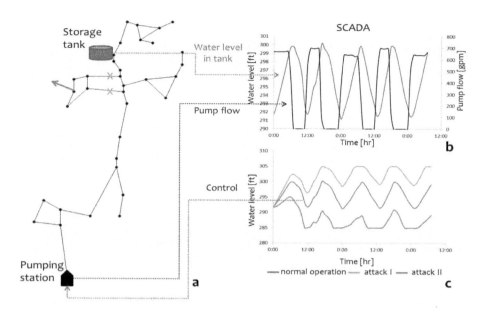

Figure 1: **Qualitative attack on cyber-physical water distribution system.** (a) **Water distribution system.** (b)-(c) **SCADA system: pump operation is controlled based on the measured water level in the storage tank.** (c) **Discrepancies in the sensory data in case of attack I (green line) and attack II (red line).**

[37, 36]. Notably, urban water networks typically have low degree nodes (two or three) due to physical and geographical constraints and lack centrally located critical components with large failure consequences. This is in contrast to social, information, and technological networks. Hence, purely topological connectivity metrics are not sufficient to capture components with critical impact on system performance. Additional distinction between social and physical networks is the non-linearity in water flow dynamics. These characteristics of the physical network, may lead to counter-intuitive notions of most vulnerable links. Furthermore, the set of most vulnerable links may be sensitive to demand patterns, operating conditions, and other fluctuations.

The dependency of the function of complex networks on their structure, particularly of infrastructure systems, has been recently studied in electric power [27, 13], transportation [8, 2], and military supply-chain [1] networks. The vulnerability of a network is formulated as network interdiction or an attacker-defender sequential game model, i.e. Stackelberg game. The attacker's (leader) objective is to maximize system operational cost by interdicting network links. The defender's (follower) objective is to minimize that cost. The defender problem is formulated as a max-flow problem with linear flow cost and linear constraints, and the attacker problem is formulated as an integer program with limited budget constraint. The solution of the network interdiction problem is attained through duality theory [11] or Bender decomposition approach [27, 13, 1]. All of the mentioned interdiction models, are characterized by a topological-connectivity network, flow and cost of the flow defined over network links.

Many similarities exist between the electric power and water distribution systems both in structural and modeling aspects: (1) large-scale spatially distributed infrastructure networks, (2) dynamic supply, (3) dynamic uncertain demands, (4) flow defined over network links, (5) potential defined over network nodes. One of the key differences be-

tween the modeling of the two is that DC approximation of the AC power-flow model, which neglects the reactive power effects and nonlinear losses, is typically used to simulate power networks versus nonlinear relationship between head-loss and flow that is used to simulate water flow networks. Among physical differences are storage capabilities and elevated versus underground infrastructure. However, to the best of our knowledge similar interdiction models have not been developed for water distribution networks. The above implies that consideration of network flow dynamics, governing equations, and characteristics of infrastructure system components is required for a more realistic analysis of vulnerability of WDS.

Specifically, we study the vulnerabilities in physical flow networks with a potential function defined over the nodes and a flow function defined over the arcs. The difference in potential (or flow cost) is characterized by an increasing nonlinear function of the flow on network links. The above mentioned models [27, 13, 8, 2, 1], for electric power, transportation, and supply-chain networks, can be directly modeled using the developed approach by relaxing the nonlinear cost flow functions. The method presented in this work consist of the following main steps: (1) Formulation of the *fixed-demand* network analysis problem as a nonlinear convex optimization problem (Section 3.2), (2) Formulation of the *variable-demand* network analysis problem allowing for demand shortages by relaxing the demand constraints (Section 3.3), (3) Formulation of the *auxiliary network graph* for the efficient solution of the variable-demand model (Section 3.3.1), (4) Assessment of the value of network links based on physical and hydraulic metrics (Section 5.3), (5) Formulation of the network interdiction problem (Section 4), (6) Application of the methodology to an illustrative water distribution network (Section 5). In the next section, we discuss the characteristics of integrated water-sensor network and provide specific examples of relevant security issues.

2. CYBER-PHYSICAL SYSTEMS

In recent years there have been fast developments in wireless/wired sensor networks for various applications such as environmental monitoring, infrastructure security, and water distribution systems monitoring [3]. The *cyber-physical system (CPS)*, integrating the physical and cyber systems, expands the capabilities of physical systems through sensing, computation, communication, and control. The application of sensor-actuator in water supply systems principally focuses on performing temporary data analysis for operational control of the system, e.g. model predictive control, encapsulated in the framework of supervisory control and data acquisition (SCADA) [22, 31]. SCADA systems enable to remotely monitor water levels in tanks and velocities and pressures at some additional locations. Based on the collected information, control actions are automatically generated, such as pumping operation and valve setting. Additional application of sensing and metering of the WDS is utilized for quality control of the system, such as identification of possible hydraulic and/ or quality faults [24, 30] and billing.

The water sector is vulnerable to a variety of physical and cyber attacks. If these attacks were realized, the result could be, for example, a loss of service that would result in social and economic impact. Critical services such as firefighting and healthcare (hospitals), and other dependent and interdependent sectors, such as energy, food and agriculture, and transportation systems, would suffer negative impacts from a los of water sector service [14].

The cyber and the physical water systems are highly dependent in the sense that an attack on one would cause failures in the other. Example of threats to the WDS: (1) Pollution threats - biological or chemical contaminants could be injected to a distribution system, (2) Physical threats - disruption of assets, rapid valve closure creating water hammer effects, water thefts (3) Cyber threats - physical disruption of SCADA system, deception attacks on sensor and control data. The importance of vulnerability and threats assessment of water supply systems has grown tremendously in recent years providing some qualitative measures for risk reduction [20]. However, quantitative measures for estimating realization of attacks and their impacts are lacking. One of the first works conducted in this field investigates the vulnerabilities of SCADA systems of irrigation canal systems [5]. In this work, the authors characterize the effect of adversarial actions on the sensor and control data on the performance of the water canal system, demonstrate the difficulty in the detection of attacks, and conduct field operational test to support their approach.

Figure 1 illustrates simulated attacks on the water distribution CPS and their dependencies. Figure 1a shows an illustration of a water distribution system consisting of one pumping station and one storage tank. The SCADA system observes water levels in the tank and operates the pumping station to deliver water to consumers with adequate quantities and pressures (Figure 1b). The operation of the pump is typically done by estimates of the water demand of the entire system and the changes of the water levels. Figure 1c demonstrates the changes in the measured water level in the tank in case of two attack scenarios:

I) Interdiction - two pipes of the system are interdicted causing part of the system to be disconnected. The

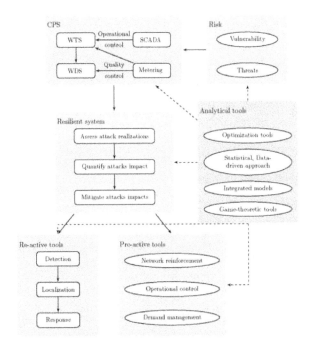

Figure 2: Assessing CPS resilience - schematic chart

total demand of the system is reduced causing the water level in the tank to rise (green line). If appropriate actions are not taken on the operator side this could cause damage to the system, in addition to the loss of service that part of the system is experiencing.

II) Water theft - water is withdrawn from the system at a hydrant connection. System total demand increases causing pressures and water level in the tank to decrease. The operator again should take appropriate actions to maintain functionality of the WDS.

The aforementioned effects on physical flow dynamics can also be realized via *cyber-attacks*. For example, feeding false information about the state of the water level in the tank would cause a response actions by the operator, that in turn, could result in network-wide failures of the physical system.

Figure 2 demonstrates the principal components of the research on security of CPS and their interconnections. The framework is comprised of five main modules: (1) CPS model, (2) Vulnerability, (3) Threats, (4) Realization of attacks, (5) Mitigation of consequences of faults. All of the modules, although, typically are treated separately, are highly dependent. For example, vulnerability analysis requires a profound understanding and modeling of the system. The model, in turn, depends on the type of vulnerability in hand. This is partially addressed by integrated models approach. Similar framework is applicable for security and resilience of electric distribution systems. The principal for a secure resilient CPS is assessing attack realizations. The key for a successful model of a resilient system is the understanding that threats and vulnerabilities are different concepts and must be treated separately and system feature can become a vulnerability only in combination with an attack [19].

This work studies the vulnerabilities of the physical network focusing on more realistic modeling of the system. This model will serve the core of future work for the integrated CPS modeling for vulnerability and threats assessment and mitigation.

3. MODELING

3.1 Water distribution system

Water networks deliver water from its sources to its consumers through connecting pipes. The network is operated and controlled through pumping stations, valves, and storage tanks. The topology of a water distribution network can be represented as a graph $G = G(N, A)$ where N is a set of nodes comprised of a set of supply (source) nodes $N_S \subset N$, intermediate nodes $N_I \subset N$, and demand (consumption) nodes $N_D \subset N$ such that $N_S \cup N_I \cup N_D = N$; and A is a set of directed arcs $j \sim (i, k) \in A$ where i and k are the start and the end nodes of the arc j, respectively. A demand rate $b(i)$ is associated with each node $i \in N$ in the network with positive values for supply and negative for withdraw, i.e., $b(i) > 0$ for $i \in N_S$, $b(i) = 0$ for $i \in N_I$, and $b(i) < 0$ for $i \in N_D$.

The connectivity of the network can be represented using a *node-arc* incidence matrix $E = e(i, j)$ defined as:

$$e(i, j) = \begin{cases} +1 & \text{if } i \text{ is the start node of edge } j, \\ -1 & \text{if } i \text{ is the end node of edge } j, \\ 0 & \text{otherwise.} \end{cases} \quad (1)$$

Every column in the incidence matrix has exactly one $+1$ and one -1. E is $n \times m$ matrix, where $n = |N|$ and $m = |A|$ are the number of nodes and links in the network, respectively.

The state of the system is characterized by hydraulic heads $p(i)$ $[m]$ (potentials) associated with each node $i \in N$ and flows $x(j)$ $[m^3/h]$ associated with each arc $j \in A$. The relationship between the flow and the potential difference between the start and the end nodes is characterized by a nonlinear *cost of a flux* function, i.e. $\Delta p_j = p(i) - p(k) = \phi_j(x_j)$, where the flow is directed from node i to k.

3.2 Fixed-demand model

The problem of finding the distribution of flows and potentials in the network can be formulated as the *fixed-demand* optimal distribution problem over the graph G [26], such that the total cost of the flows in minimized:

$$\begin{aligned} \underset{x}{\text{minimize}} \quad & \sum_{j \in A} \int_0^x \phi_j(t) \, dt \\ \text{subject to} \quad & y(i) = b(i) \qquad \forall i \in N \\ & x(j) \geq 0 \qquad \forall j \in A \end{aligned} \quad (2)$$

where

$$y(i) = \sum_{j \in A} e(i, j) x(j) = b(i), \forall i \in N$$

$$\sum_{i \in N} b(i) = b(N) = 0$$

$y(i)$ is the linear demand/supply mass balance equations, $b(N)$ is total mass conservation in the network, and $\phi_j(t)$ is a real-valued, continuously differentiable convex function.

For pressurized flows, Hazen-Williams or Darcy-Weisbach models can be adopted to describe the potential loss across a link as a function of the characteristics of the link (pipe) and flow passing through it [9]. The head-loss is computed as: $\phi_j(x(j)) = R(j)x(j)^\alpha$, where $R = R(D, L, C)$ can be thought of as the resistance of the pipe, which depends on the diameter, length, and friction of the pipe, respectively. Particularly, head loss (i.e. cost of a flux) for pipe j with flow $x(j)$ is computed as:

$$\phi_j(x(j)) = \frac{aL_j}{C_j^{1.852} D_j^{4.87}} x(j)^{1.852} \quad (3)$$

where a is a unit coefficient.

It can be shown (see Appendix A) that the solution of the network equilibrium model satisfies the the Kuhn-Tucker necessary condition of the nonlinear distribution problem with $\phi_j(x(j))$ representing the hydraulic head loss-flow relationships.

Since the flow in the head-loss equation (3) has to be non-negative, parallel link with same characteristics and opposite flow direction is added to each link in the network graph. This addition allows for water to flow in both direction (See Figure 3a-b). In the optimal solution only one of the flows will have positive value since the objective is to minimize total flux cost, and the direction of the flow will be determined by the combination of the two flows, i.e.:

$$x_{j \sim (i,k)} = x_{(i,k)} + x_{(k,i)} | x_{(i,k)} \geq 0, x_{(k,i)} \geq 0 \quad (4)$$

3.3 Variable-demand model

Next, we introduce a *variable-demand* optimal distribution problem. This formulation allows for a more realistic representation of the flow dynamics in WDS. The fixed-demand or demand-driven approach is widely accepted model simulating the steady-state flow dynamics in flow networks under normal operating conditions, when nodal pressures are above some operational minimum (typically 30 $[m]$ in WDS). The demand-driven approach assumes that all demands will be satisfied (equality constraint in (2)) at the expense of nodal potential. However, the actual nodal demand is dependent on the available pressure at the node. Hence, under abnormal or failure conditions, the system will experience shortages of pressure and consequently shortages in demands. The fixed-demand model is extended to account for these demand-pressure dependencies. This is achieved by adding a dissatisfaction function Ω of shortages in demands to the objective function, by relaxing the equality constraints on nodal demands and supplies, and adding an upper bound on the flow variable:

$$\begin{aligned} \underset{x}{\text{minimize}} \quad & \sum_{j \in A} \Phi_j(x(j)) + \sum_{i \in N} \Omega_i(y(i) - b(i)) \\ \text{subject to} \quad & b(i) \leq y(i) \leq 0 \qquad \forall i \in N_D \cup N_I \quad (5) \\ & 0 \leq y(i) \leq b(i) \qquad \forall i \in N_S \\ & 0 \leq x(j) \leq u(j) \qquad \forall j \in A \end{aligned}$$

where $\Phi_j(x(j)) := \int_0^x \phi_j(t) \, dt$. The first term of the objective function is the power loss and the second term is the cost of not supplying consumers' demands. The solution of this problem satisfies the flow balance and hydraulic energy conservation in the system. If the limits constraints on the flow are not binding, the fixed-demand and the variable-demand models have the same solution.

Pipe	Start Node	End Node	Length [m]	Diameter [mm]	Roughness [ ]	R [ ]	Node	Demand $[\frac{m^3}{h}]$	Elevation [m]
1	1	2	1000	457.2	100	1.52E-05	1	1120	210
2	2	3	1000	254	100	2.66E-04	2	-100	150
3	2	4	1000	406.4	100	2.70E-05	3	-100	160
4	4	5	1000	101.6	100	2.31E-02	4	-120	155
5	4	6	1000	406.4	100	2.70E-05	5	-270	150
6	6	7	1000	254	100	2.66E-04	6	-330	165
7	3	5	1000	254	100	2.66E-04	7	-200	160
8	7	5	1000	25.4	100	1.97E+01			

3.3.1 Auxiliary network graph

The variable-demand problem (5) can be reformulated as the optimal distribution problem (2) on the augmented network $\overline{G} = \overline{G}(\overline{N}, \overline{A})$ defined as follows. A dummy node N_T with zero demand is added to the original network G balancing the unmet demands and the unused supply. A set of corresponding directed dummy links is added: A_{sup} connecting the dummy source node N_T with the demand nodes $i \in N_D$ and a circulation link A_{circ} connecting the source and the storage nodes (see Figure 3c).

The flow cost function $c_j(x(j))$ per unit flow is set according to the dissatisfaction model:

1. For original links:

$$c_j(x(j)) = \phi_j(x(j)) \quad \forall j \in A \quad (6)$$

2. For a set of dummy links A_{sup} connecting the dummy source node to the demand nodes:

$$c_j(x(j)) = \omega_j(x(j)) \quad \forall j \in A_{sup} \quad (7)$$

where $\omega_j(x(j))$ is the cost of the unmet demand or the dissatisfaction level.

3. For the circulation link:

$$c_j(x(j)) = \omega_j(x(j)) \quad \forall j \in A_{circ} \quad (8)$$

where $\omega_j(x(j))$ is the storage cost.

The cost of flow $\omega_j(x(j))$ on the dummy and circulation arcs will be further discussed in Section 5.2.

With the cost functions of augmented graph $\overline{G}$ defined by (6)–(8), the variable demand optimal distribution problem (5) can be re-formulated to problem (2):

$$
\begin{aligned}
\underset{x}{\text{minimize}} \quad & \sum_{j \in \overline{A}} \int_0^x c_j(t)\,dt \\
\text{subject to} \quad & y(i) = b(i) && \forall i \in \overline{N} \\
& 0 \leq x(j) \leq u(j) && \forall j \in \overline{A}
\end{aligned}
\quad (9)
$$

The value of the auxiliary graph is two-folded: the original structure of the optimization problem (as in (2)) is maintained and it can be efficiently solved by standard optimization software.

4. NETWORK INTERDICTION MODEL

The interaction between the operator and the adversary is formulated as a leader-follower (Stackelberg) game. The game is characterized by: (1) network topology, (2) network physical model, (3) two players – adversary and operator, and (4) two stages – in the first stage, the attacker z can disrupt a limited number of edges in the system. In the second stage, the defender attempts to divert flow away from the interdicted links by opening/ closing control valves, i.e. if $z(j) = 1 \Rightarrow x(j) = 0$ and if $z(j) = 0 \Rightarrow x(j) \geq 0$. In this work, it is assumed that control valves are located on every pipe in the system, i.e. each pipe can be isolated without interdicting additional pipes. This assumption can be relaxed by introducing a set of additional constraints. The network interdiction problem can be formulated as:

$$
\underset{z}{\text{maximize}}
\begin{cases}
\underset{x}{\text{minimize}} & \sum_{j \in A} \Phi_j(x(j), z) + \\
& \sum_{i \in N} \Omega_i(y(i) - b(i)) \\
\text{subject to} & \\
& b(i) \leq y(i) \leq 0 & \forall i \in N_D \cup N_I \\
& 0 \leq y(i) \leq b(i) & \forall i \in N_S \\
& 0 \leq x(j) \leq u(j) & \forall j \in A
\end{cases}
$$

$$
\sum_{j \in A} z(j) \leq N_z \quad (10)
$$

$$
z \in \{0, 1\}
$$

The inner problem in the above formulation is the optimal flow distribution problem minimizing the power loss and the unmet demands in the network. In the outer problem, the attacker interdicts links in the network as to maximize the damage to the network. The number of simultaneous attacks is limited by the attackers resources N_Z.

The attacker-defender model can be naturally formulated as a bi-level program, following the concepts of generalized benders decomposition [17]. The master problem (MP) is the outer problem whose decision variables represent the attacker's actions, and the sub-problem (SP) is the inner problem whose decision variables represent flows distribution in the network. The bi-level approach involves successive solutions of the sub and the master problems.

Following the formulation in [27], in each iteration, the variable-demand on the auxiliary graph sub-problem (9) is solved for a given action profile of the attacker:

$$
\begin{aligned}
\text{SP}(z_k): \quad \underset{x}{\text{minimize}} \quad & \sum_{j \in \overline{A}} \int_0^x c_j(t, z_k)\,dt \\
\text{subject to} \quad & y(i) = b(i) && \forall i \in \overline{N} \\
& 0 \leq x(j) \leq u(j) && \forall j \in \overline{A}
\end{aligned}
\quad (11)
$$

where k is an iteration counter.

The solution of the sub-problem, in turn, is used to sequentially update the MP:

$$\text{MP}(k): \quad \underset{z}{\text{maximize}} \quad \sum_{j \in A} \overline{V}^k(j) z(j)$$

$$\text{subject to} \quad \sum_{j \in A} \left(z^0(j) - z(j) \right) \geq 1$$

$$\sum_{j \in A} \left(z^1(j) - z(j) \right) \geq 1$$

$$\vdots \qquad \qquad (12)$$

$$\sum_{j \in A} \left(z^{k-1}(j) - z(j) \right) \geq 1$$

$$\sum_{j \in A} z(j) \leq N_z$$

$$z \in \{0, 1\}$$

where $\overline{V}^k(j)$ the value of link j in iteration k and z^k, $k = 0, \ldots, k-1$ are the solutions in previous iterations. Assessment of the value of network links will be discussed in the application section. The attacker objective is to interdict most valuable links of the network. The growing set of constraints ensures that the action profile of the attacker in iteration k is different from previous iterations.

The main steps of the algorithm are:

1. Initialize: $k = 0$ set iteration counter and initial solution $z_0 = (0, \ldots, 0)$.

2. Solve SP(k): obtain the optimal flows in the system x_k^* for a given interdiction plan z_k.

3. Update MP($k + 1$): evaluate value of links $\overline{V}^k$ based on performance and importance indicators scaled and averaged over previous iterations (Section 5.3), update the objective function, and constraints (Section 5.4).

4. Solve MP($k + 1$): obtain z_{k+1}^*.

5. Check convergence: if $z_{k+1}^* = \emptyset$, then *stop* , otherwise set $k = k + 1$ and return to step 2.

5. CASE STUDY

The developed methodology is demonstrated on an illustrative benchmark WDS first introduced by [4]. This network has been intensively studied in the water management community for the optimal design problem. The system consists of one source node (reservoir), six demand nodes, connected by eight links. Network data and its layout are shown in Table 1 and Figure 3a, respectively. The system was designed to operate under a representative loading condition. The optimal design of the systems was adopted from [29] and is used for vulnerability analysis in this paper.

5.1 Fixed-demand model

Formulating the optimal flow distribution problem following (2) and taking the head loss function as the cost of the flow on each link (3), the objective function of the optimization problem can be explicitly written as:

Table 2: Optimal flow distribution solution

Pipe	Flow x $\left[\frac{m^3}{h}\right]$	Head loss [m]	Node	Demand $\left[\frac{m^3}{h}\right]$	Pressure [m]
1	1120.00	6.75	1	1120	0.00
2	336.87	12.77	2	-100	53.25
3	683.13	4.79	3	-100	30.48
4	32.57	14.62	4	-120	43.46
5	530.56	3.00	5	-270	33.83
6	200.56	4.89	6	-330	30.45
7	236.87	6.65	7	-200	30.57
8	0.56	6.74			

$$\sum_{j \in A} \int_0^x \phi_j(t)\, dt = \frac{1}{\alpha + 1} \sum_{j \in A} R(j) x(j)^\alpha x(j) =$$
$$\frac{1}{\alpha + 1} \sum_{j \in A} \Delta p(j) x(j) \qquad (13)$$

The term $\sum_{j \in A} \Delta p(j) x(j)$ is defined as the *power loss* $[m^4/h]$ of the system and also can be computed as $\sum_{i \in N} p(i) b(i)$ [12]. Intuitively, the interpretation of this model is that flows are distributed in the network such that the total power loss of the system is minimized.

To allow flow in both directions, two edges are drawn for each pipe of the system (see Figure 3b). The fixed-demand flow distribution problem (2) was solved using *fmincon Matlab* solver [21] and the resulted flows and computed nodal hydraulic heads are listed in Table 2. For validation of the model, the results (flows and pressures) are were compared to EPANET [32]. EPANET is an open source software for the simulation of hydraulic state of pressurized WDS developed by the U.S. Environmental Protection Agency and is widely used among water systems practitioners and research community. The results demonstrated zero error with three significant digits (limited to the accuracy of the EPANET software). It can be observed, that during normal operating conditions, the pressures at all nodes is above $30[m]$, which is considered desired operational pressure. Below this pressure, the consumers might experience shortages in demands.

5.2 Variable-demand model

Next, variable-demand model (9) is formulated by adding a *dummy* node and a set of links. The auxiliary graph is depicted in Figure 3c. For continuity, cost of the flow on the dummy links is characterized by the same function as for real links $\omega_j(x(j)) = R(j) x(j)^\alpha$. The resistance parameters R for the dummy links is set to be higher than for real links to avoid using these links during feasible operating conditions. From Table 1, it can be seen that the typical values of R are very small, with the exception of pipes 4 and 8, having very small diameters 101.6 and $25.4[mm]$, respectively. Hence, the resistance for dummy links was set to $R(j) = 1, j \in A_{sup} \cup A_{circ}$. For this small network, the optimization model was not sensitive to these values. The upper limits for the flows on network links u is evaluated based on the realistic maximum head loss in a link, $u = \left(\frac{\Delta p_{max}}{R}\right)^{\frac{1}{\alpha}}$, where $\Delta p_{max} = 15[m]$. For the supplementary links, the upper bounds are set as the demand of the node corresponding

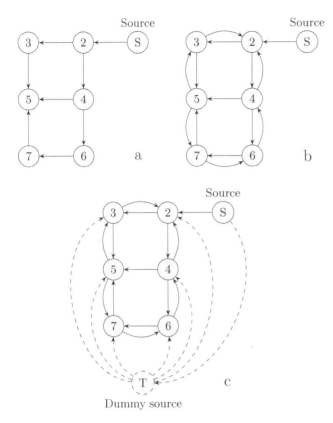

Figure 3: Network graph: (a) directed graph - water can flow in one direction, (b) bi-directed graph - water can flow in both directions, and (c) auxiliary graph - supplementary node and links to allow for shortages in demand and supply

to each link, $u_{j\sim(T,i),j\in A_{sup}} = b(i)$, and the total demand for the circulation link $u_{j\sim(S,T),j\in A_{circ}} = \sum_{i\in N_D} b(i)$. The flow on the dummy links can only be directed as depicted in Figure 3c.

To asses the *value* of the variable-demand model, link 2 connecting nodes 2 and 3, is interdicted. Figure 4a shows the original network graph corresponding to the fixed-demand model and Figure 4b shows the auxiliary network graph corresponding to the variable-demand model. Table 3 lists the results of the optimization problem for the fixed-demand and the variable-demand models designated by G and $\overline{G}$, respectively.

The results in Table 3 demonstrate that the fixed-demand model G is not capable of capturing the dynamics in the interdicted system, resulting in unrealistically high head losses, pipes 4 and 8, and negative pressures, nodes 3 and 5. Whereas, the variable-demand model demonstrates shortage in these nodes while keeping all pressures positive.

It is important to note, that the limitation of fixed demand-driven models have been acknowledged before, and pressure-driven models have been suggested for better simulation of the WDS dynamics [16]. These models introduce stepwise nonlinear pressure-demand curves to account for pressure-dependent demand. Then the modified energy and mass conservation equations (Appendix A) are directly solved using Newton based techniques [18]. This models are, however, non smooth, suffer from convergence issues, and do not

guarantee uniqueness of solution. In contrast, the variable-demand model developed in this paper has the advantage of being continuous, convex, and can be efficiently solved by standard optimization software.

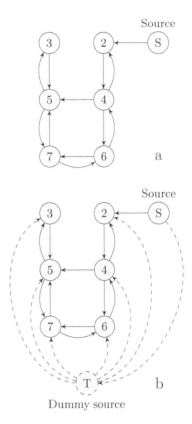

Figure 4: Interdicted network: (a) original network graph and (b) auxiliary network graph

5.3 Assessing value of links

The value of network links depends on flow, head loss, and distance from source. An integrated measure of the value of link is suggested by scaling and weighting these three measures, as follows:

For each loading condition, for each link j:

1. The flow of each link is scaled to the total system demand: $v_1 = \frac{x}{x_{max}}, x_{max} = 1120[\frac{m^3}{h}]$.

2. The remaining available head loss of each link is computed by scaling the head loss to the maximum realistic head loss and deducting that value from 1: $v_2 = 1 - \frac{\Delta p}{\Delta p_{max}}, \Delta p_{max} = 15[m]$.

3. The distance from source is computed as the number of links on the shortest path from the source. This gives an indirect measure of the value of link, as the disruption of a link closer to the source would, generally, result in disruption in service to larger parts of the network. The shortest path between the source and destination link can be efficiently computed using breadth first search algorithm. The measure of distance level v_3 is again scaled to the number of links in the system.

Table 3: Attack on pipe=2 G vs. $\overline{G}$

| | G | | $\overline{G}$ | | | G | | $\overline{G}$ | |
| | Flow x | Head loss | Flow x | Head loss | | Demand | Pressure | Demand | Pressure |
Pipe	$[\frac{m^3}{h}]$	$[m]$	$[\frac{m^3}{h}]$	$[m]$	Node	$[\frac{m^3}{h}]$	$[m]$	$[\frac{m^3}{h}]$	$[m]$
1	1120.00	6.75	783.89	3.49	1	1120	0.00	1120	0.00
2	0.00	0.00	0.00	0.00	2	-100	53.25	-100	56.51
3	1020.00	10.07	683.89	4.80	3	-100	-1223.91	0.00	0.00
4	360.62	1255.74	33.02	15.00	4	-120	38.18	-120	46.71
5	539.38	3.10	530.86	3.01	5	-270	-1212.56	-35	36.71
6	209.38	5.29	200.86	4.90	6	-330	25.08	-330	33.71
7	100.00	1.35	0.00	0.00	7	-200	24.79	-200	33.80
8	9.38	1247.35	0.86	15.00					

4. Additional measure is used to estimate the total value of the network as the fraction of demand shortage, $v_4 = \overline{S} = 1 - S$, which is computed as the weighted sum of the fraction of supplied demand to node i: $S = \sum_i w_i s_i$. Where $\sum_i w_i = 1$ and $0 \leq s_i \leq 1$ depending on the actual delivered demand compared to the desired demand at node i. This measure is averaged over interdicted links, hence when the network is fully operational $\overline{S} = 0$.

5. These values are then weighted to give a single measure: $V = \sum_i w_i v_i$.

Figure 5 shows the values v_1, v_2, v_3 of all links in the network with no interdiction, i.e. $v_4 = 0$. From the figure, it can be seen that there is no strict ordering of the three metrics, hence the *value* of a link should be evaluated by integrating the three metrics. This, in turn, will directly influence the formulation and the result of the network interdiction problem (12). Furthermore, this result emphasizes that purely topological metrics are not sufficient for vulnerability assessment of WDS.

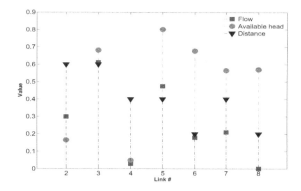

Figure 5: Values of network links: (a) Flow (blue squares), (b) Available head loss (red circles), and (c) Distance level (black triangles).

5.4 Network interdiction

After establishing the variable-demand flow model and assessing the value of links, the bi-level network interdiction problem can be formulated and solved. For this reference network, only one link interdiction problem is demonstrated.

The weights considered for integrating the four measures are: $[w_1, w_2, w_3, w_4] = [1, 0.5, 02, 1]$. The weights of consumers for computing the total satisfaction of delivered demands are assumed equal. The results are compared to enumeration of the attacker's options. It is assumed that all network links can be interdicted, with the exception of link 1 which is directly connected to the source. This assumption is plausible, since water reservoirs and tanks are usually physically protected. Following the main steps of the bi-level approach presented in previous section:

1. Initialize: $k = 0$ set iteration counter and initial solution $z_0 = (0, \ldots, 0)$.

2. Solve SP(0): The variable-demand optimal distribution problem is solved on the auxiliary network $\overline{G}$ with no interdiction.

3. Update MP(1): The values of links are estimated as described in Section (5.3) based on the results of SP(0) (Table 4, second column, V_1). For example, from Figure 5, for link 2:
$[v_1, v_2, v_3, v_4] = [0.3, 0.16, 0.6, 0]$; $[w_1, w_2, w_3, w_4] = [1, 0.5, 02, 1]$; The value of the link is computed as $V = \sum_i w_i v_i = 0.5$.

4. Solve MP(1): The optimal link for interdiction is link 3, i.e. $z_1^* = (0, 1, 0, 0, 0, 0, 0, 0)$.

5. Check convergence: Update $k = k + 1$.

6. Solve SP(1): SP solved on $\overline{G}$ with interdiction z_1^*.

7. Update MP(2): The values of links are estimated based on the results of SP(1) (Table 4, third column, V_2) and averaged over previous iterations (Table 4, fourth column, $\overline{V}_2$. For example, for link 2, $\overline{V}_2 = (V_1 + V_2)/2 = 0.5 + 0.46 = 0.48$.

8. Solve MP(2): $z_2^* = \emptyset$.

9. Check convergence: $z^* = z_1^*$.

Table 5 list the results of all possible interdicted links, where *power loss* is the value of the optimization problem including the cost of flow on the supplementary links, *effective power loss* is the power loss considering only the true network links, S is the fraction of delivered demand, and *minimum pressure* is the lowest pressure in the system. It can be seen that interdiction of link 3 results in the highest impact to the system.

Table 4: Updating value of links

Pipe	V_1	V_2	$\overline{V}_2$
2	0.50	0.46	0.48
3	1.07	0.58	0.83
4	0.13	0.10	0.11
5	0.96	0.56	0.76
6	0.56	0.53	0.55
7	0.57	0.54	0.56
8	0.33	0.07	0.20

Table 5: Attack impact

Attacked pipe	Power loss	Effective power loss	S	Minimum pressure
0	1.96E+04	1.94E+04	1.00	30.54
2	2.24E+07	9.11E+03	0.70	33.71
3	1.22E+08	9.33E+03	0.42	4.25
4	2.06E+04	2.05E+04	1.00	28.46
5	7.73E+07	7.70E+03	0.53	12.63
6	7.23E+06	1.24E+04	0.82	12.78
7	1.17E+07	1.04E+04	0.79	32.84
8	1.96E+04	1.94E+04	1.00	30.55

5.5 Mitigation of vulnerabilities

From a (naive) topological view point, based on the data in Tables 1, it might appear that 4 and 8 are bottlenecks of the system, since their resistance R is relatively high. This can be also supported by the head loss on these pipes, which reaches its upper limit (see Table 2). Common intuition may lead to the hypothesis that reinforcing these pipes by adding parallel pipes or replacing them with larger diameter pipes, will reduce the vulnerability of the system. To check this novice assumption, the diameters of pipes 4 and 8 are increased to 254 [mm] and the optimization problem is solved again for the most critical interdiction plan (pipe 3). The total amount of delivered demands remains the same 0.42, however with higher minimum pressure of 11.85 [m] and different distribution of delivered demands: [1, 0.82, 0, 0.93, 0.1, 0, 0.42] compared to [1, 0, 0, 0, 0.46, 0.56, 0.27] in the un-reinforced network. If the consumers are assigned different weights indicating their importance, the total value of delivered demand will be different in the two cases. Straightforwardly, increasing all diameters to 406.4 [mm] will result in a fully resilient system to one link attack, however at a very high cost. From these results, it is apparent that systems supplied by a single source are highly vulnerable. However, reinforcement should be weighted versus the threats of attacks and the potential impact of these attacks.

6. CONCLUSIONS

The method developed in this work provides a general modeling and vulnerability assessment of physical flow networks, with particular application to water distribution systems. The developed modeling approach allows for a more realistic representation of the flow dynamics in WDS while keeping the convexity properties of the optimization problem.

The results imply that due to the nature of the physics of WDS, maintaining topological connectivity or considering linear cost flow models is not sufficient for assessing system

vulnerabilities. It was also implied that developing strategies to mitigate these vulnerabilities may be counter-intuitive.

Future research needs to: (1) Test the proposed methodology on large networks, (2) Include systems with additional water sources, pumping stations, and pressure reducing valves, (3) Assess the vulnerability under changing loading conditions, (4) Develop structured approach on how to mitigate these vulnerabilities through reinforcement and operational changes.

7. ACKNOWLEDGMENTS

This research was supported by the MIT-Technion fellowship program and NSF grant number: 1239054 CPS Frontiers: Foundations Of Resilient CybEr- physical Systems (FORCES).

8. REFERENCES

[1] D. L. Alderson, G. G. Brown, W. M. Carlyle, and L. A. Cox. Sometimes there is no most-vital arc: assessing and improving the operational resilience of systems. *Military Oper. Res.*, 18(1):21–37, 2013.

[2] D. L. Alderson, G. G. Brown, W. M. Carlyle, and R. K. Wood. Solving defender-attacker-defender models for infrastructure defense. In *12th INFORMS Computing Society Conference*. INFORMS, 2011.

[3] M. Allen, A. Preis, M. Iqbal, S. Srirangarajan, H. B. Lim, L. Girod, and A. J. Whittle. Real-time in-network distribution system monitoring to improve operational efficiency. *J. Amer. Water Work. Assoc.*, 103(7):63–75, July 2011.

[4] E. Alperovits and U. Shamir. Design of optimal water distribution systems. *Water Resources Research*, 13(6):885–900, May-June 1977.

[5] S. Amin, X. Litrico, S. S. Sastry, and A. M. Bayen. Stealthy deception attacks on water scada systems. In *HSCC'10, Stockholm, Sweden*, pages 161–170. ACM, April 2010.

[6] A. Babayan, D. Savic, G. Walters, and Z. Kapelan. Robust least cost design of water distribution networks using redundancy and intergration based methodologies. *J. Water Resour. Plann. Manage.*, 133(1):67–77, 2007.

[7] A. Babayan, G. Walters, Z. Kapelan, and D. Savic. Least cost design of water distribution networks under demand uncertainty. *J. Water Resour. Plann. Manage.*, 131(5):375–382, 2005.

[8] H. Bell, U. Kanturska, D. Schmocker, and A. Fonze. Attacker - defender models and road network vulnerability. *Phil. Trans. R. Soc. A*, 366:1893–1906, 2008.

[9] P. F. Boulos, K. E. Lansey, and B. W. Karney. *Comprehensive water distribution systems analysis handbook for engineers and planners.* MWH Soft, Inc. Publ., Pasadena, CA, 2006.

[10] S. Boyd and L. Vandenberghe. *Convex optimization.* Cambridge university press, The Edinburgh Building, Cambridge, UK, 2004.

[11] G. G. Brown, W. M. Carlyle, J. Salmeron, and K. Wood. Analyzing the vulnerability of critical infrastructure to attack and planning defenses. In *Tutorials in Operations Research*, pages 102–123. INFORMS, 2005.

143

[12] B. Calvert and G. Deady. Braess's paradox and power-law nonlinearities in networks. *J. Austral. Math. Soc. Ser.B*, 35:1–22, 1993.

[13] A. Delgadillo, J. M. Arroyo, and N. Alguacil. Analysis of electric grid interdiction with line switching. *IEEE Trans. Power Syst.*, 25(2):633–641, May 2010.

[14] EPA. Water sector-specific plan, an annex to the national infrastructure protection plan. In *EPA 817-R-10-001*. Water Security Division, 2010.

[15] G. Fu and Z. Kapelan. Fuzzy probabilistic design of water distribution networks. *Water Resour. Res.*, 47:W05538, 2011.

[16] O. Fujiwara and J. Li. Reliability analysis of water distribution networks in consideration of equity, redistribution, and pressure-dependent demand. *Water Resources Research*, 34(7):1843–1850, July 1998.

[17] A. M. Geoffrion. Generalized benders decomposition. *J. Opt. Theor. Appli.*, 10(4):237–260, October 1972.

[18] O. Giustolisi, D. Savic, and Z. Kapelan. Pressure driven demand and leakage simulation for water distribution networks. *J. Hydr. Engi.*, 134(5):626–635, May 2008.

[19] R. Johnson. Being vulnerable to the threat of confusing threats with vulnerabilites. *J. Phys. Secur.*, 4(2):30–34, May 2010.

[20] M. Karamouz, S. Saadati, and A. Ahmadi. Vulnerability assessment and rist reduction of water supply systems. In *World Environmental and Water Resources Congress*, pages 4414–4426. ASCE, October 2010.

[21] MATLAB. *version 8.0.0.783 (R2012b)*. The MathWorks Inc., Natick, Massachusetts, 2010.

[22] C. Ocampo-Martinez, V. Puig, G. Cembrano, and J. Quevedo. Application of predictive control strategies to the management of complex networks in the urban water cycle. *Control Systems, IEEE*, 33(1):15–41, February 2013.

[23] A. Ostfeld. Water distribution systems connectivity analysis. *J. Water Resour. Plann. Manag.*, 131(1):58–66, January 2013.

[24] L. Perelman, J. Arad, M. Housh, and A. Ostfeld. Event detection in water distribution systems from multivariate water quality time series. *Environ. Sci. Technol.*, 46:8212–8219, 2012.

[25] L. Perelman, M. Housh, and A. Ostfeld. Robust optimization for water distribution systems least cost design. *Water Resour. Resear.*, 49(10):6795–6809, 2013.

[26] R. T. Rockafellar. *Network flows and monotropic optimization*. Athena Scientific, Belmont, MA, 1998.

[27] J. Salmeron, K. Wood, and R. Baldick. Analysis of electric grid security under terrorist threat. *IEEE Trans. Power Syst.*, 19(2):905–912, May 2004.

[28] D. A. Savic. Coping with risk and uncertainty in urban water infrastructure rehabilitation planning. In *1st Italian Urban Hydraulics Conference*, pages 28–30, September 2005.

[29] D. A. Savic and G. A. Walters. Genetic algorithms for least cost design of water distribution networks. *Water Resources Planning and Management*, 123(2):67–77, March-April 1999.

[30] S. Srirangarajan, M. Allen, A. Preis, M. Iqbal, H. B. Lim, and A. J. Whittle. Wavelet-based burst event detection and localization in water distribution systems. *J. Sign. Process. Syst.*, 72(1):1–16, July 2013.

[31] C. Sun, V. Puig, and G. Cembrano. Multi-layer model predictive control of regional water networks: Application to the catalunya case study. In *52nd Conference on Decision and Control*. IEEE, December 2013.

[32] USEPA. *EPANET 2.00.12*. U.S. Environmental Protection Agency, Cincinnati, Ohio, 2002.

[33] WSCC-CSWG. Roadmap to secure control systems in the water sector. In *Water Sector Cyber Security Working Group*. Water Sector Coordinating Counsil Cyber Security Working Group, March 2008.

[34] C. Xu and C. Goutler. Reliability based optimal design of water distribution systems. *J. Water Resour. Plann. Manage.*, 125(6):352–362, 1999.

[35] C. Xu and I. C. Goutlter. Probabilistic model for water distribution reliability. *J. Water Resour. Plann. Manag.*, 124(4):218–228, July 1998.

[36] A. Yazdani and P. Jeffrey. Applying network theory to quantify the redundancy and structural robustness of water distribution systems. *J. Water Resour. Plann. Manag.*, 38(2):153–161, March 2012.

[37] A. Yazdani and P. Jeffrey. Water distribution system vulnerability analysis using weighted and directed network models. *Water Resour. Res.*, 48:W06517, 2012.

[38] B. Zhuang, K. Lansey, and D. Kang. Resilience/availability analysis of municipal water distribution system incorporating adaptive pump operation. *J. Hydraul. Eng.*, 139(5):527–537, 2013.

APPENDIX

A. KARUSH-KUHN TUCKER (KKT) CONDITIONS

The KKT conditions to problem (2) can be written as:

$$\nabla \Phi(x) + \sum_{i=1}^{N} \nu_i \nabla \left(\sum_{j \in A} e(i,j)x(j) - b(i) \right) = 0$$

$$\sum_{j \in A} e(i,j)x(j) - b(i) = 0$$

Setting ν to represent nodal potentials, the KKT conditions are precisely the energy and mass conservation equation on every link and node of the network, respectively, i.e.:

Energy conservation for every link:

$$\sum_{i \in N} e(i,j)\nu_i = 0 \quad \forall j \in A$$

Mass conservation for every node:

$$\sum_{j \in A} e(i,j)x(j) - b(i) = 0 \quad \forall i \in N$$

If x^* and ν^* satisfy KKT condition for a convex problem, then they are optimal [10].

Cyber-Insurance Framework
for Large Scale Interdependent Networks[*]

Galina A. Schwartz
University of California at Berkeley
337 Cory Hall, MC 1774
Berkeley, CA 94720-1774
schwartz@eecs.berkeley.edu

S. Shankar Sastry
University of California at Berkeley
717 Sutardja Dai Hall
Berkeley, CA 94720-1776
sastry@eecs.berkeley.edu

ABSTRACT

This article presents a framework for managing cyber-risks in large-scale interdependent networks where cyber insurers are strategic players. In our earlier work, we *imposed* that breach probability of each network node (which we view as a player) is a function of two variables: first, player own security action and second, average security of all players. In this article, we formally *derive* the expression of breach probability from the standard assumptions. For a homogeneous interdependent network (identical users), we provide a solution for optimal security choice of each node in environments without and with cyber insurers present. Then, we introduce a general heterogeneous network (many user types), and derive the expression for network security. Lastly, we consider the network with two user types (normal and malicious), in which we allow one user type (malicious users) to subvert monitoring of the insurers, even if these insurers are able to perfectly enforce security levels of normal users (at zero cost). Our analysis confirms a discrepancy between informal arguments that favor cyber-insurance as a tool to improve network security, and formal models, which tend to view insurance as an instrument of managing risks only. In particular, our results support the case *against* cyber-insurance as the means of improving security. Our framework helps to identify the crucial network parameters for improving incentives to provide secure networks.

[*]This research was supported by NSF grant CNS-1239166, which provides funding for a frontier project FORCES (Foundations of Resilient CybEr-Physical Systems), NSF grant CNS-0910711, and by TRUST (Team for Research in Ubiquitous Secure Technology), which receives support from the NSF (#CCF-0424422) and the following organizations: AFOSR (#FA9550-06-1-0244), BT, Cisco, DoCoMo USA Labs, EADS, ESCHER, HP, IBM, iCAST, Intel, Microsoft, ORNL, Pirelli, Qualcomm, Sun, Symantec, TCS, Telecom Italia, and United Technologies. We thank Saurabh Amin for his comments.

Permission to make digital or hard copies of all or part of this work for personal or classroom use is granted without fee provided that copies are not made or distributed for profit or commercial advantage and that copies bear this notice and the full citation on the first page. Copyrights for components of this work owned by others than ACM must be honored. Abstracting with credit is permitted. To copy otherwise, or republish, to post on servers or to redistribute to lists, requires prior specific permission and/or a fee. Request permissions from permissions@acm.org.
HiCoNS'14, April 15–17, 2014, Berlin, Germany.
Copyright 2014 ACM 978-1-4503-2652-0/14/04 ...$15.00.
http://dx.doi.org/10.1145/2566468.2566481.

1. INTRODUCTION

The question of security incentives and optimal security risks is an integral part of studying the resilience of modern networks. In this article, we are broadly concerned with the question of how to mitigate interdependent risks to which large-scale networks are exposed, mainly due to the present-day ubiquitous connectivity. Our particular contribution is a game theoretic model, which allows to introduce competitive cyber insurers as players. The network security properties are determined as an equilibrium of the game in which players (or networked nodes) make individually optimal strategic choices, and player payoffs depend on player own choices, as well as the choices of other players, which possibly include cyber insurers. This game theoretic framework permits us to study user security choices with and without availability of cyber contracts.

Depending on the context, we will use the terms "node" and "player" and "user" interchangeably. This will also help us to make the exposition more intuitive. Examples of nodes in networked systems include sensors, actuators, computing nodes, etc. In emerging cyber-physical networks, each node can be considered a smart networked device that is capable of making certain decisions; for e.g., a sensor deciding on its measurement strategy, an actuator deciding on a local control strategy, and a computing node choosing to perform computations.

The field of networked and embedded control systems has made promising advances in designing optimal decisions for these smart devices, both in centralized and decentralized context. In this article, we assume that each node has a decision making capability that has direct connotations for the node's failure due to imperfect security of the network, and primarily due to *cyber insecurity.*

From a practical viewpoint, one can imagine numerous security choices for each smart node. Below we list some examples of the choices available to nodes: i) which specific device to install, whether to use encryption, and if so which encryption method to follow; ii) frequency of communications with other nodes, and how powerful should each communication signal, how many channels should be used for transmission; iii) whether computations are local to a node, or rely on data from other nodes; iv) whether the node location is physically secure or security is software based; v) whether node is permanently networked or could be placed off-line for maintenance and patching; vi) how frequently security updates are made, etc.

For the sake of simplicity, we do not consider multidimensional security choices in this article. Instead, we aggregate all these choices and work with one-dimensional security metrics, i.e., we will index the security of each node by a value, a so-called own *security level* of a node. This level ranges between zero and one, with zero level meaning that the node is insecure, i.e., it has certainty (hundred percent chance) of a security breach, and thus, always incurs a loss. At security level of one, the node is fully secure, and no loss could occur. Such a one-dimensional security level assumes that each player optimally allocates his resources among the aforementioned security choices i) – vi). In other words, we assume that each node is capable of making the best security choices for self; i.e., the node's reaches the highest possible security level conditional on total amount of security resources that it expands.

The plan of the paper is as follows. In Section 2, we consider a network consisting of n identical nodes. In Section 3, we solve homogenous network case without cyber insurers present, and in Section 4 – with insurers. We derive an optimal cyber insurer contract. In Section 5, we compare equilibrium network security in different environments. In Section 6, we generalize to a heterogeneous network case. In Section 7, we discuss the extensions and conclude. To improve the exposition, technical details are relegated to Appendix.

1.1 Literature

At present, risk management capabilities for ICT[1] are all but nonexistent [2]. Three factors that hinder cyber risk management via cyber-insurance are identified in [3]: correlations, interdependence and information asymmetries. This article combines the two latter factors and builds a framework for the analysis and comparative evaluation of cyber risk management solutions for large scale networks.

The widely held view among the researchers [2] is that network insecurity primarily caused by misaligned incentives as technology-based solutions are available, but not utilized. [5] emphasizes that information deficiencies contribute to the misaligned incentives and hence, hinder the adoption of improved security practices.

We introduce a modeling framework to investigate the possibilities of mitigating cyber risks in large scale networks. Thus, we consider the network with and without cyber-insurance, and study the effects of insurance. Our framework allows to study both problems that manifest in environments with information asymmetries: *moral hazard* (when insurers are uninformed of user security levels) and *adverse selection* (when insurers cannot distinguish different user types).

In this paper, we focus on formulation of a general framework that allows to study both, adverse selection and moral hazard effects. We combine the model of large scale network, in which individual user security and network security are interdependent with ideas of asymmetric information literature, originated by Akerlof [1], Rothschild and Stiglitz [11].[2]

Due to space restrictions, we will omit technical discussion of existing cyber insurance literature. We refer an interested reader to [3], and the most recent developments will be presented in our forthcoming technical report.

---

[1] Here ICT stands for information and communication technology.

[2] See [1, 15] for the literature review.

2. INTERDEPENDENT NETWORK

To start, we consider a network consisting of n identical nodes (players / users). We will generalize to heterogeneous network in Section 6.

2.1 Homogeneous network

Each player i choice variable is his security level s_i to maximize his expected utility u_i:

$$E[u_i] = B_i \cdot U(W - L) + (1 - B_i) \cdot U(W) - h(s_i), \quad (1)$$

where s_i – user security, $h(\cdot)$ – user security cost function for reaching his chosen security level, which we assume to be twice differentiable, and $h'(x), h'' \geq 0$ for every $x \in [0, 1]$, and $h(0) = 0$, $h'(0) = 0$, and $h(1) = \infty$. The intuition is that user security costs increase with security, and that improving own security level imposes an increasing marginal cost on the player, with $h(1) = \infty$ characterizing a hypothetical "perfectly secure" system. Indeed, it is realistic to assume that marginal benefit from higher security level is decreasing, whereas marginal cost of security improvements is increasing with security. $h(0) = 0$ illustrates the ease of initial security improvement, and $\lim_{x \to 1} h(x) = \infty$ illustrates the prohibitive expense of complete security. [An example of such an h is $h(x) = \frac{x^2}{1-x}$].

Players are risk-averse: $U'(\cdot) > 0$, $U''(\cdot) < 0$, and W denotes user initial wealth, L – his amount of loss, and B_i – the probability of loss (resulting from successful breach) for player i.

The reasons for keeping security costs in (1) separately from monetary wealth are two fold. First, this specification reflects that security costs are in many cases non-monetary. For example, it is hard to put a price tag on one's efforts to remember multiple passwords, and second, in today's world, security budget is frequently determined by the player's efforts to obtain the funds (or manpower) for a given, specific security need, such as performance of security updates, or increasing the frequency of backups (both these tasks require extra resources, such as manpower and equipment).

We will start with an expression for B_i standard for the literature modeling security interdependencies, as in [8, 6, 10, 7, 9, 3], and many others. To be concrete, let us borrow the specification from [10], see p. 21, where breach probability $B_i = B_i(s_1, ... s_n)$ for node i is defined as:

$$B_i(s_1, ... s_n) = 1 - s_i + s_i \prod_{j \neq i}^{n} \{q(1 - s_j)\}, \quad (2)$$

Thus, player i face two types of attack threats, direct and indirect. A direct threat attacks player i directly, while an indirect threat results from attacks on other network nodes, $j \neq i$. Each user i have to chose his security level to mitigate against both these threats. From (2), for player i with security s_i, success probability of direct attack is $(1 - s_i)$; and success probability of indirect attack from others is $q(1 - s_j)$, $j \neq i$, and $q \in (0, 1)$. parameter $q = q(n)$ is assumed to be small; the magnitude of $q(n)$ characterizes the strength of node inderdependencies of the network, with more interdependent networks having higher $g(n)$.

We argue that for large scale networks, the coherent $q(n)$ must decrease with n, because if it does not, by adding sufficiently many extra nodes to the network, B_i will reach, and then exceed 1. Therefore, such specification is unsuitable for analyzing large scale networks. Moreover, we suggest that for such networks, an assumption of $q = q(n) \to 0$ is sensible to assure that q_n remains small for any given n, where $q_n := q(n)n$.

2.2 Breaches in large scale networks

We start with (2), and derive an expression of breach probability for large scale networks with security interdependencies. As we suggested above, we assume that $q(n)n$ decreases with n, and that $g_\infty := q(n)n|_{n \to \infty}$ is small. Then, we can ignore the terms non-linear in q, and re-write (2) as:

$$B_i(s_1, \ldots s_n) = 1 - s_i + s_i q(n) \sum_{j \neq i}^{n} (1 - s_j), \qquad (3)$$

from which we can express as:

$$B_i = 1 - s_i + s_i q_n \left\{ (1 - \bar{s}) - \frac{(1 - s_i)}{n} \right\}, \qquad (4)$$

where $q_n := q(n)n$ and $\bar{s}$ denotes average network security:

$$\bar{s} = \frac{1}{n} \sum_{j=1}^{n} s_j.$$

When n is high, we can ignore the last term in curly brackets:

$$B_i = B(s_i, \tilde{s}) = 1 - s_i [1 - q_n + \tilde{s}], \qquad (5)$$

where $\tilde{s} := g_\infty \bar{s}$. We will call s_i *own security* of player i, and $\tilde{s}$ – *network security*. In the limit $n \to \infty$, user i breach probability is:

$$B_i = 1 - s_i(1 - q_\infty) - s_i \tilde{s},$$

where

$$q_\infty := q(n)n|_{n \to \infty} \text{ and } \tilde{s} := g_\infty \bar{s}.$$

In line with common sense, from (5), no-breach probability $s_i(1 - g_\infty) + s_i \tilde{s}$ increases in both: own security (s_i) of player i, and network security ($\tilde{s} := g_\infty \bar{s}$). Parameter g_∞ is small, For more interdependent networks, the effect of interdependence on breach probability is stronger, and, by the same token, network security is more important.

In contract with our earlier work [13, 14, 12], where we *imposed* that for each player, breach probability is a function of two variables: player own security action, and average security of all players, in this paper we will formally *derive* the expression of breach probability from a standard one (3). The expression (4) is appropriate for large scale networks, and we will especially focus on its limiting case of high n, as given in (5).

This model of interdependence does not account for a possibility of correlated attack probabilities. That is, all attacks are assumed to be independent, and simultaneous attacks are ignored. In Section 7.1, we discuss the possibilities of modifying our assumptions on distribution of network risks to account for correlated (or cascading) risks. To account for correlated breach probabilities at the level of the entire network, we suggest to include an additional term high loss term.

3. HOMOGENOUS NETWORK WITH NO CYBER INSURERS: A SOLUTION

In this section, we will find individually optimal security choices of each player (i.e., Nash equilibrium) when no cyber insurers are present, and insurance contracts are unavailable. Then, each player i choice variable is security level $s_i \in [0, 1]$ which he chooses to maximize (1) with breach probability given by (3). Expected user i utility (1), can be written as:

$$U(W - L) + s_i \left[1 - q(n) \sum_{j \neq 1}^{n} (1 - s_j) \right] \cdot \Delta_0 - h(s_i),$$

where

$$\Delta_0 := [U(W) - U(W - L)].$$

User i optimal action (from FOC wrt s_i) is a solution of:

$$\left[1 - q(n) \sum_{j \neq i}^{n} (1 - s_j) \right] \Delta_0 - h'(s_i) \geq 0. \qquad (6)$$

We rewrite FOC as:

$$\left[1 - q_n(1 - \bar{s}) + \frac{q_n (1 - s_i^*)}{n} \right] \Delta_0 = h'(s_i^*), \qquad (7)$$

where $\Delta_0 > 0$, and we use $q_n \sum_{j \neq i}^{n} (1 - s_j) = q_n(1 - \bar{s}) - \frac{q_n(1 - s_i)}{n}$, and $q_n = \frac{q(n)}{n}$. Since user i SOC is negative, because from the proverties of the function $h''(\cdot) < 0$ for any s_i, and thus, a single interior optimum $s_i^* = s_i^*(\bar{s})$ exists (for any fixed $\bar{s}$), and from the properties of function $h(\cdot)$, the boundaries of $s = 0$ and $s = 1$ cannot be optimal, thus, the interior maximum is indeed the optimal.

Next, let there exists an equilibrium with $\bar{s}^*$, and let there exist two players whose optimal actions $s_i^* \neq s_j^*$. Let wlg $s_i^* > s_j^*$. Then, we can write FOC for player j as:

$$\left[1 - q_n(1 - \bar{s}^*) + \frac{q_n (1 - s_j^*)}{n} \right] \Delta_0 = h'(s_j^*), \qquad (8)$$

and subtracting (8) from (7) (FOCs for players j from FOC for player i) we obtain:

$$\frac{q_n}{n} (s_j^* - s_i^*) \Delta_0 = h'(s_i^*) - h'(s_j^*).$$

Since h' is increasing in s, for $s_i^* > s_j^*$, the right hand side is positive while the right hand side is negative. We conclude that $s_i^* = s_j^*$ and since i and j were arbitrary, player equilibrium security is identical, i.e., only symmetric equilibrium exists. This allows us to compute the equilibrium directly by setting $\bar{s} = s_i = s^*$ and using (7):

$$\Delta_0 = \frac{h'(s)}{\left[1 - \frac{(n-1)}{n} q_n(1 - s) \right]}, \qquad (9)$$

which for the limit of large n can be written as

$$\Delta_0 = R(s), \qquad (10)$$

where

$$R(s) := \frac{h'(s)}{[1 - q_\infty(1 - s)]}.$$

Equilibrium is unique, if the solution of (9) is unique. A sufficient condition for that is $R' > 0$:

$$R' = \frac{h''(s) [1 - q_n(1 - s)]}{[1 - q_n(1 - s)]^2} - \frac{h'(s) q_n}{[1 - q_n(1 - s)]^2} \geq 0,$$

$$h''(s) - q_n [h'(s) + (1 - s) h''(s)] \geq 0.$$

Further, to simplify the exposition, we will impose $R' > 0$ and restrict our attention to the case of a unique Nash equilibrium. For example, imposition of $h'''(\cdot) > 0$ results in $R' > 0$, which guarantees the uniqueness.

4. HOMOGENOUS NETWORK WITH CYBER INSURERS: A SOLUTION

Let us consider security choices of networked players (nodes) in the presence of (perfectly) competitive cyber insurers. We will define a setting following Rothschild-Stiglitz [1976], who examine equilibrium in insurance markets with adverse selection. Each insurer offers a single insurance contract in *a class of admissible contracts*, or does nothing. A Nash equilibrium is defined as a set of admissible contracts such that: i) all contracts offered at least break even; ii) taking as given the contracts offered by incumbent insurers (those offering contracts) there is no additional contract which an entrant-insurer (one not offering a contract) can offer and make a strictly positive profit; and iii) taking as given the set of contracts offered by other incumbent insurers, no incumbent can increase its profits by altering his offered contract.

The literature refers to such contracts as *competitive contracts*, because entry and exit are free, and because no barrier to entry or scale economies are present. We consider risk neutral cyber insurers, who compete with each other. In addition, following to Rothschild-Stiglitz, we assume no individual insurer can affect the network security $\tilde{s}$; thus, take each insurer takes network security as a given parameter.

We assume the following timing of the game: First (ex ante), network nodes (players) observe all contracts offered by cyber insurers; second, each node chooses which contract to accept (if any); third (ex post), the nodes choose their security level(s), (in both cases, with cyber contract or without). We assume that each cyber insurance contract includes a stipulation prohibiting the insured node to buy more than a single cyber security policy (contract).

At this point, some readers perhaps recognize that our formulation of the game does not specify whether ex ante, the players (the nodes and the insurers) have the information about ex post network security $\tilde{s}$. Still, as we demonstrate in Appendix, the game as we stated it could be solved. To proceed we will divide the problem into three steps. In Step 1, we will derive optimal security choices by the nodes under an assumption of buying contract (ρ_c, L_c). In Step 2, we will derive the contracts that are *viable* for cyber insurers. By a viable contract we mean that expected profit is non-negative, given that network nodes security choices are optimal. In Step 3, we derive an equation which solution gives equilibrium contract(s) $(\rho_c^\dagger, L_c^\dagger)$. The derivation employs an argument that only the contracts that maximize user utility will be purchased in equilibrium.

4.1 Step 1: Optimum with the contract (ρ_c, L_c)

Let there exist some given cyber contract (ρ_c, L_c) that is offered, and consider the choices of user i. Each user decides (i) which contract to purchase (in case if other, alternative contracts are offered) and (ii) which security level to choose. Since a decision to buy no insurance can be modeled as purchase of a contract $(0,0)$, we always can phrase user choice as a choice between at least two alternative contracts.

$$E[u_i] = B_i \cdot U(W - L - \rho_c + L_c) + (1 - B_i) \cdot U(W - \rho_c) - h(s_i),$$

where in general, $B_i = B_i(s_1, \ldots s_n)$, but from the derivation in Section 2.2, we have $B_i = B(s_i, \tilde{s})$.

User i expected utility with cyber-insurers present, AND assuming that he entered into a contract (ρ_c, L_c) could be written as:

$$B_i \cdot U(W - L - \rho_c + L_c) + (1 - B_i) \cdot U(W - \rho_c) - h(s_i). \quad (11)$$

From user ex post optimization (conditional on the purchase of a contract), we know that if all users indeed buy insurance, equilibrium is symmetric: the proof follows the same steps as in no-insurance case above, see Section 3. User i FOC is:

$$\Delta_{c0} = R(s, \tilde{s}), \quad (12)$$

where

$$R(s, \tilde{s}) := \frac{h'(s)}{[1 - q + \tilde{s}]} \quad (13)$$

and

$$\Delta_{c0} := [U(W - \rho_c) - U(W - \rho_c - (L - L_c))].$$

We can formulate the following proposition:

PROPOSITION 1. *For a network with a given security $\tilde{s}$, for a user with a contract (ρ_c, L_c), with $L_c > 0$, individually optimal security $s = s^\dagger(\tilde{s}, \rho_c, L_c)$ is strictly lower than his optimal security $s = s^*(\tilde{s}, 0, 0)$ with no insurance coverage $L_c = 0$:*

$$s^\dagger(\tilde{s}, \rho_c, L_c) < s^*(\tilde{s}, 0, 0).$$

We use symmetry of user optimum $\bar{s}^\dagger = s^\dagger = s$, and $\tilde{s} = qs$:

$$\Delta_{c0} = \frac{h'(s)}{[1 - q(1 - s)]}, \quad (14)$$

Differentiating (14) wrt s, with an assumption of $h''' > 0$ we obtain that the right hand side derivative is positive:

$$\frac{h''(s)[1 - q(1 - s)] - h'q}{[1 - q(1 - s)]^2} > 0, \text{ if } h''' > 0. \quad (15)$$

Thus, there exists a unique user symmetric optimum for a given contract.

4.2 Step 2: Properties of viable contracts

We will use the results of Section 4.1, in which we derive optimal user responses to a specific given contract to investigate the properties of viable cyber contracts. We will say that a contract is viable when expected insurer profit is non-negative. To assure non-negative cyber insurer profit, the following constraint has to hold

$$\rho_c = \rho_c(s_1, \ldots s_n, L_c) \geq B_i L_c.$$

With perfect cyber insurer competition, each insurer's expected profit is zero:

$$\rho_c = \rho_c(s_i, \tilde{s}, L_c) = B_i(s_i, \tilde{s})L_c, \text{ with a given } \tilde{s}, \quad (16)$$

where since each insurer is small, he treats network security $\tilde{s}$ as given. A contract (ρ_c, L_c) with a premium given by (16) is called *actuarily fair contract*.

Consider some equilibrium in which $\tilde{s} = \tilde{s}^\dagger$, and assume that in this equilibrium user actions are identical: $\tilde{s}^\dagger = q_n \bar{s}^\dagger$, and $\bar{s}^\dagger = s_i^\dagger = s$. In this case, any given viable contract (ρ_c, L_c) offered for some insurers, will be accepted by all nodes due to the symmetry of their optimal action. A formal proof of symmetric optimal action mimics the proof of Section 3. Let $s_i^\dagger(\rho_c, L_c, \bar{s})$ denote optimal response of user i with contract (ρ_c, L_c) when average security is $\bar{s}^\dagger$. Then,

$$s_i(\rho_c, L_c, \bar{s}) = \bar{s}, \qquad (17)$$

because from zero profit condition (16) and (17) we can express $\rho_c(s_1, ... s_n, L_c) = \rho_c(s, L_c)$.

$$\rho_c^\dagger(s) = \rho_c^\dagger(s, L_c^\dagger) = B(s) L_c^\dagger(s), \qquad (18)$$

where

$$B(s) = \left[1 - s(1-q) - (s)^2 q\right]. \qquad (19)$$

If users buy the same contract $(\rho_c^\dagger(s), L_c^\dagger(s))$, and network security is $\tilde{s} = q_n s$, and (14) holds:

$$R(s) = \Delta_{c0}.$$

Thus allows us to restate insurer problem as a problem of one independent variable, i.e., network security $\tilde{s}$ (or user security s). We will use s as an independent variable, and demonstrate that viable contract is unique, and can be determined from user optimality (14) and insurer zero profit (18). In Appendix, we prove the following result:

PROPOSITION 2. *Due to user optimum choices, for any given network security s, and if user optimal actions are symmetric (identical), there exists a unique corresponding viable contract $(\rho_c, L_c) = (\rho_c^\dagger(s), L_c^\dagger(s))$, and the derivatives $\frac{dL_c^\dagger}{ds}$ and $\frac{d\rho_c^\dagger}{ds}$ are negative.*

In Appendix, we obtain the expressions for $\frac{dL_c^\dagger}{ds}$ and $\frac{d\rho_c^\dagger}{ds}$, see (32) and (31):

$$\frac{dL_c^\dagger}{ds} = \frac{[R' + \Delta_{c1} B' L_c]}{B\Delta_{c1} - U'(W - \rho_c - L + L_c)} < 0, \qquad (20)$$

and

$$\frac{d\rho_c^\dagger}{ds} = B' L_c + B \frac{dL_c^\dagger}{ds}, \text{ and } B' < 0. \qquad (21)$$

Alternatively, one can express the conditions for viable contracts with L_c as an independent variable (instead of s). In some cases, such a formalization could be more intuitive, and also preferable on computational grounds. We will include it into a longer version of this paper (in preparation).

4.3 Step 3: User preferred contract(s)

Next, we derive an interior contract with which users reach maximal utility. We can demonstrate that such a contract exists (by construction). Consider an insurer a choice of a contract, such that if user optimum is symmetric $(\rho_c(s), L_c(s))$, this contract is viable for insurers, and also allows user utility to reach its maximum. Using the results of Section 4.2, to find such user preferred contract is equivalent to finding s that corresponds to this contract:

$$\max_s \left\{ B \cdot U(W - L - \rho_c + L_c) + (1 - B) \cdot U(W - \rho_c) - h(s) \right\}.$$

Then, insurer FOC, will determine equilibrium contract with which user utility is the highest. Let equilibrium be interior

in s and user optimal actions be symmetric. Then,

$$\left\{ \{-s(1-q) - sq\} \Delta_{c0} - h'(s) \right\} - sq\Delta_{c0} \qquad (22)$$
$$+ B\Delta_{c1} \frac{d\rho_c^\dagger}{ds} + B \cdot U'(W - L - \rho_c + L_c) \frac{dL_c^\dagger}{ds}$$
$$= 0,$$

where

$$\Delta_{c1} := \left[U'(W - \rho_c - (L - L_c)) - U'(W - \rho_c) \right] > 0.$$

We can combine (20) or (21) with user optimum and insurer FOC (i.e., user preferred contract), to obtain connection of L_c and s in equilibrium:

$$\frac{B\Delta_{c1} + U'(W - \rho_c - L + L_c)}{B\Delta_{c1} - U'(W - \rho_c - L + L_c)} = \frac{sqR - B\Delta_{c1} B' L_c}{B[R' + \Delta_{c1} B' L_c]}, \quad (23)$$

and we use (13), (19) and (16) for R, B, and ρ_c:

$$R(s) := \frac{h'(s)}{[1 - q(1 - s)]},$$

$$B = \left[1 - s(1-q) - (s)^2 q \right],$$

$$\rho_c = B L_c$$

to derive equilibrium contract(s) explicitly. Notice, that with a simplifying assumption of quadratic U, equilibrium equation (23) is analytically solvable: it is then quadratic in L_c.

Lastly, we have to investigate whether asymmetric user equilibrium could occur in some cases. In a longer version of this paper, we demonstrate that due to perfect insurer competition, no asymmetric user equilibrium exists. In this version, we restrict our attention by symmetric user equilibria only.

5. BENCHMARKS

5.1 Social optimum with no cyber insurers

To find a social optimum, we no longer consider and each individual's best responses, but instead find security level that maximizes cumulative expected payoff of all the users of the network. Let s^{**} denote security in social optimum. As for Nash, one can demonstrate that social optimum is symmetric. Under symmetry, social planner optimization problem becomes:

$$E[u_i] = U(W - L) + s\left[1 - q(1 - s)\frac{(n-1)}{n}\right] \cdot \Delta_0 - h(s),$$

and from FOC, in social optimum, we have

$$\left\{ \left[1 - q(1 - s)\frac{(n-1)}{n}\right] + 2sq\frac{(n-1)}{n} \right\} \cdot \Delta_0 - h'(s) \geq 0,$$

and in interior optimum we:

$$\frac{h'(s)}{\left\{ \left[1 - q(1 - s)\frac{(n-1)}{n}\right] + 2sq\frac{(n-1)}{n} \right\}} = \Delta_0. \qquad (24)$$

Comparison of (9) and (24), gives that social optimum coincides with Nash equilibrium only if $n = 1$. With more then one player, in Nash equilibrium (individual optimum), security is always lower than socially optimal, due to an extra term in the denominator of social planner FOC (24).

PROPOSITION 3. *In equilibrium, individually optimal user security s^* is strictly lower in social optimum:*

$$s^{**} < s^*.$$

From our analysis, Nash Equilibrium security is below socially optimal, and the gap (and thus, inefficiency) increases with network size (number of nodes) and for networks with higher interdependencies.

5.2 Optimum with vs without insurers

From the results of Sections 3 and 4, we infer that for homogenous networks the presence of insurers negatively affects security incentives:

PROPOSITION 4. *Let $s^\dagger$ denote user optimal security choice with a contract (ρ_c, L_c) purchased. In a symmetric interior equilibrium with non-zero coverage, user security $s^\dagger$ is strictly lower than user optimal choice with no insurance coverage $s^\dagger \leq s^*$.*

$$s^\dagger \leq s^*.$$

To prove Proposition 4, we compare (14) with (9) due to the fact that the right hand side of both, (14) with (9) increases with s, and left hand side is smaller with positive insurance coverage than without any coverage:

$$\Delta_{c0} \leq \Delta_0.$$

Notice, that we have not yet considered a (theoretically possible) asymmetric equilibrium where only some fraction of the nodes has positive coverage, while other nodes choose zero coverage. Then, in expectation, users with and without coverage must be indifferent between these two options. In a longer version of this paper, we prove that such configuration never occurs, and thus, equilibrium is always symmetric.

6. HETEROGENEOUS NETWORKS

Next, we consider network with n nodes / players, who can be heterogeneous. For such heterogeneous network, we will say that *two players have the same type* if their objective function (1) is identical, and (ii) both players employ identical equilibrium action(s).[3] We will assume that for each type k, the number of nodes is large. An alternative definition of a *player type* is to require (i). When for players of the same type equilibrium is symmetric, these definitions coincide. Requirement (ii) is especially appropriate for environments with multiple network nodes owned by the same player, which could result in asymmetric equilibria.

In this paper, we are limiting our attention to the case when each node chooses its action as a separate (individual) player. Let n_k be the number of type k nodes. Then:

$$\sum_{k=1}^{m} \alpha_k = 1, \ n = \sum_{k=1}^{m} n_k \ \text{and} \ \alpha_k := \frac{n_k}{n},$$

---

[3] An alternative definition of a type could require that any two nodes of the same type to have identical expected utility function. When in equilibrium players with identical utilities make identical equilibrium choices, i.e., for players of the same type the equilibrium is symmetric, both definitions coincide. But our definition will be especially convenient when multiple network nodes are owned by the same player. In this paper, we will limit our attention to environments in which each node chooses its actions as a separate player.

where $m > 1$ is the number of different types of the network; the network with $m = 1$ is homogeneous network consisting of identical nodes. Each player i of type k players maximizes his expected utility:

$$E(u_{ik}) = B_{ik} \cdot U_k(W_k - L_k - \rho_c + L_c) + \quad (25)$$
$$(1 - B_{ik}) \cdot U_k(W_k - \rho_c) - h_k(s_{i_k}).$$

From (25), users of different types, may vary by their risk aversion (i.e., the shape of function $U = U_k(\cdot)$), security cost function $h = h_k(\cdot)$, initial wealth $W = W_k$, and $L = L_k$. Also, cyber contracts available for different types can differ by type: offered In addition, available cyber insurance contracts $(s_c, \rho_c, L_c) = (s_{ck}, \rho_{ck}, L_{ck})$ could differ with player type, and possibly, be non-zero contracts could be offered to certain user types only, but not for all the types. The types for whom cyber insurance is unavailable can be modeled as constrained to a contract with zero coverage $(0, 0, 0)$. Also, cyber insurance could be mandated for some (or all) types. In heterogeneous network, breach probabilities are defined by (2), and B_{ik} for player i of type k can be simplified (as for homogeneous network (2)), and wlg $B_{ik} = B_k$, and for $i = 1$ and $k = 1$:

$$B_1 = 1 - s_1$$
$$+ s_1 \left[\sum_{k \neq 1}^{m} q_k \sum_{j=1}^{n_k} (1 - s_j) + q_1 \sum_{j \neq 1}^{n_1} (1 - s_j) \right],$$

where q_k denotes indirect effect of node of type k on all other nodes; we assume that type k nodes have the same indirect effect on all others. We rewrite $B_{1k} = B_{i1} = B_1$ as:

$$B_1 = 1 - s_1 + s_1 \left[\sum_{k \neq 1}^{m} q_k(n_k) n_k (1 - \bar{s}_k) \right]$$
$$+ s_1 q(n_1) n_1 \left\{ (1 - \bar{s}_1) - \frac{(1 - s_1)}{n_1} \right\},$$

where $\bar{s}_k = \frac{1}{n_k} \sum_{j=1}^{n_k} s_j$, is average security of type k nodes (i.e., only type k nodes securities are averaged to obtain $\bar{s}_k$).

$$B_1 = 1 - s_1 + s_1 \sum_{k=1}^{n_k} q(n_k) n_k \{ (1 - \bar{s}_k) \}$$
$$- s_1 q(n_1) n_1 \left\{ \frac{(1 - s_1)}{n_1} \right\}.$$

For high n, we ignore the last term in curly brackets:

$$B_1 = 1 - s_1 (1 - q) - s_1 \sum_{k=1}^{n_k} q_k \bar{s}_k,$$

where $\bar{s}_k = \frac{1}{n_k} \sum_{j=1}^{n_k} s_j$, and

$$q_k := q(n_k) n_k, \ q := \sum_{k=1}^{n_k} q_k,$$

and $\tilde{s} := \sum_{k=1}^{n_k} q_k \bar{s}_k$, and we will call $\tilde{s}$ *network security* for heterogeneous network.

$$B_k = 1 - s_k (1 - q) - s_k \tilde{s}. \quad (26)$$

Thus, we have shown that breach probability for the network with heterogeneous users could be expressed very similar to breach probability in the network of identical (homogeneous) users. Interestingly, when interdependence term ($q_k \equiv q$) is the same for all types k, breach probability is identical for homogeneous and heterogeneous networks. This allows remarkable simplification of the analysis for networks with heterogeneous types of nodes.

With identical players, we already derived breach probabilities $B_i = B_i(s_i^*, \bar{s} = s_i^*)$, when players security is optimal $s_{ik}^* = s(u, W, L, h, \bar{s} = s_i^*)$. These choices depend on player i risk-aversion, wealth, cost of security, and the amount of his loss. Similarly, breach probabilities B_i for a network with heterogeneous nodes can be derived from player security and network security, i.e., from player characteristics $U_k(\cdot), h_k(\cdot), W_k, L_k, q_k$, and network security $\tilde{s}$. Superficially (5) and (26) look the same, but for heterogeneous network, network security reflects the effects of different node types, by accounting their influence on others via interdependence (via q_k) and overall frequency of occurrence (via $\bar{s}_k$).

Below we will consider an important extension to two player types. It is straightforward to generalize this analysis to networks with multiple node types. For cases of multiple types of network nodes, computational algorithms based on our initial analysis should be developed. Once these steps are undertaken, these models can be fitted (parametrically) to investigate security of real cyber physical systems. In this case, the parameters of the model should be taken from data, and / or from simulations. Thereafter, with the help of testbeds the recommendations could be made for targeted (optimal) node security.

6.1 Network with two node types: A solution

We consider the network populated by two types of users, and within each type, users are identical, and for each player type, the effect on network security $\tilde{s}$ is negligible. Each user of first type, which we will call normal user type, maximizes (1) with breach probability given by (26):

Users of a second user type, whom we will call malicious, face no damage, even if attacked successfully. An example of a malicious user is a disgruntled employee. Or, malicious user could be criminal, aiming to game the system and milk the insurers. We will assume that type two users have the capabilities of subverting insurer monitoring of their security level, even when insurers could perfectly monitor (at zero cost) security levels of the normal users. Realistically, insurer monitoring is not perfect and costless. Thus, even if insurer requires the insured party to invest in security, she cannot assure that her insurees do maintain the required security level at all times. We assume that normal users are law-obedient. That is, they do not, or cannot subvert the insurer monitoring. For example, the subversion could be too costly for first user type.

Real networks undoubtedly has many users who do not care about security. These users typically have meager (or zero) losses and find it too costly to implement any security measures. We assume that a certain (fixed) fraction $\alpha \geq 0$ of network users belong to second type. Expected utility for type 2 is:

$$B_2 f(W) + (1 - B_2) f(W) - h(s) = f(W) - h(s), \quad (27)$$

where

$$B_2 = 1 - s_2(1 - q) - s_2 \tilde{s},$$

From (27), for type 2, expected utility does not depend on B_2, and zero security is optimal for such users, which entails

$s_2 = 0$ (and $h(0) = 0$):

$$E[U_{ik=2}] = f(W) - h(s) = f(W),$$

and

$$B_2 = 1,$$

and

$$B_1 = 1 - s_1(1 - q) - s_1 \tilde{s},$$

where

$$\tilde{s} := \sum_{k=1}^{n_k} q_k \bar{s}_k = q(1 - \alpha)\bar{s}_1,$$

where to simplify the exposition we let $q_1 = q_2 = q$, which gives

$$B_1 = 1 - s_1(1 - q) - s_1 q(1 - \alpha)\bar{s}_1.$$

For type 1 users optimal security is the same for all i $s_{i1}^m = s_1^m$, in which we use the fact that optimal action is symmetric (as demonstrated in Section 3). Optimal security $s_1^m = \bar{s}_1^m$ can be found as a solution of FOC for type 1 users:

$$\frac{h'(s_1^m)}{[(1 - q + q(1 - \alpha)s_1^m)]} = \Delta_0 \quad (28)$$

From comparison with (10) which gives for s^* for the case of homogeneous network of normal users:

$$\frac{h'(s)}{[1 - q(1 - s)]} = \Delta_0.$$

and (28) we infer

$$s^* < s_1^m,$$

and

$$s^* < s_1^m$$

$$\tilde{s}^m = q(1 - \alpha)s_1^m < \tilde{s}^*.$$

To prove the last equation, consider a model of identical users with different (lower) interdependence parameter equal to $q^d = q(1 - \alpha)$. In this case, optimal security s^{d*} solves

$$\frac{h'(s^{d*})}{[(1 - q(1 - \alpha) + q(1 - \alpha)s^{d*}]} = \Delta_0, \quad (29)$$

and comparison of (10) and (29) gives

$$s^* < s^{d*} \text{ and } \tilde{s}^* = qs^* < qs^{d*}.$$

When no malicious users are present, i.e., $\alpha = 0$, network is populated by identical normal users, (10) and (28) coincide, and $s^m = s^*$, the higher is the fraction α of malicious users, the higher is normal users optimal security investment relative to $\alpha = 0$, but network security $\tilde{s}^m$. Thus, we have shown:

PROPOSITION 5. *With malicious users present $[\alpha \neq 0]$, in equilibrium, network security is lower, and normal users' security s^m – higher than the respective values for $\alpha = 0$.*

Similarly, from comparison with a socially optimal allocation we infer:

PROPOSITION 6. *With malicious users present $[\alpha \neq 0]$, in social optimum, network security is lower, and normal users' security – higher than with $\alpha = 0$.*

From Propositions 5 and 6, we infer that although the presence of malicious users forces higher security of normal users, with malicious users explicitly included into setting, network security decreases.

7. CONCLUDING COMMENTS

Our analysis provides a rigorous derivation of cyber security contracts in a general setting, yet we demonstrated that our derivation requires only a limited amount of information. as we discuss in Section 6, our methodology generalizes to heterogeneous networks. Still, there remain several important issues that our model so far neglects. Below we briefly talk of three important avenues that we are planning to address in our future research.

Our analysis confirms a discrepancy between informal arguments that favor cyber-insurance as a tool to improve network security, rather than merely manage risks. Specifically, we observe that that in presence of cyber insurers, equilibrium network security is lower than if no cyber coverage is available. Thus, our results support that in isolation, availability if cyber-insurance does not allow to improve network security. Our framework helps to identify the crucial network parameters for improving incentives to provide secure networks.

7.1 Modeling correlated risks

Finally, some (or all) types could be subjected to additional loss(es) caused by correlated network risk (for example, risk of natural disasters (earthquakes), or risk or a terroristic attack). Such risks have very low probability $b_r \ll B_i$ of a very high loss $L_r \gg L_c$,.and even $L_r > W$. Such risks are called "catastrophic risks" or "rare events", and typically they are ignored by individual agents. Still, these risks have to be addressed at the societal level. Including these risks in utility allows to design mechanisms improving the management of these risks.

7.2 Modeling more detailed contracts

It is difficult to model multiple strategic insurer choices, and literature is dominated by the models that assume monopolistic insurers, which is not particularly realistic. Another extreme (that we pursuing in this paper) is to assume perfectly competitive market of cyber insurers, that makes insurers non-strategic due to complete lack of market power. Even papers that assume required return (load factor) do not model strategic insurer choices.

We will consider different assumptions on observability of player security and network security. And, we will consider two types of contracts: with (s_c, ρ_c, L_c), and without (ρ_c, L_c), imposition of required user security, where ρ_c – premium, L_c – amount of loss covered, and s_c a minimal security level required by the contract.

7.3 Modeling the causes of breaches

CPS risks can be broadly divided in two categories, strategic (that is driven by intended human actions), and non-strategic (that is driven by natural causes). Security policies, laws and regulations could affect both categories, albeit technical tools for the analysis are somewhat different. Your model permits to introducing attacker(s) as special player types, and examine the effects of various regulatory impositions on attacker incentives.

References

[1] G. A. Akerlof. The market for 'lemons': Quality uncertainty and the market mechanism. *The Quarterly Journal of Economics*, 84(3):488–500, August 1970.

[2] R. Anderson, R. Böhme, R. Clayton, and T. Moore. Security economics and European policy. In *Proceedings of WEIS'08*, Hanover, USA, Jun. 25-28 2008.

[3] R. Böhme and G. Schwartz. Modeling cyber-insurance: Towards a unifying framework. In *Proceedings of WEIS'10*, Cambridge, USA, Jun. 7-10 2010.

[4] G. Dionne, N. Doherty, and N. Fombaron. *Adverse Selection in Insurance Markets*, chapter 7, pages 185–244. Handbook of Insurance. Boston: Kluwer Academic, 2000.

[5] E. Gal-Or and A. Ghose. The economic incentives for sharing security information. Industrial Organization 0503004, EconWPA, Mar. 2005.

[6] G. Heal and H. Kunreuther. Interdependent security: A general model. NBER Working Papers 10706, National Bureau of Economic Research, Inc, Aug. 2004.

[7] A. Hofmann. Internalizing externalities of loss prevention through insurance monopoly: an analysis of interdependent risks. *Geneva Risk and Insurance Review*, 32(1):91–111, 2007.

[8] H. Kunreuther and G. Heal. Interdependent security. *Journal of Risk and Uncertainty*, 26(2-3):231–49, March-May 2003.

[9] M. Lelarge and J. Bolot. Economic incentives to increase security in the internet: The case for insurance. In *INFOCOM 2009, IEEE*, pages 1494–1502, April 2009.

[10] H. Ogut, N. Menon, and S. Raghunathan. Cyber insurance and it security investment: Impact of interdependent risk. In *Proceedings of WEIS'05*, Cambridge, USA, 2005.

[11] M. Rothschild and J. E. Stiglitz. Equilibrium in competitive insurance markets: An essay on the economics of imperfect information. *The Quarterly Journal of Economics*, 90(4):630–49, November 1976.

[12] G. Schwartz, N. Shetty, and J. Walrand. Why cyber-insurance contracts fail to reflect cyber-risks. In *Allerton Conference*, pages XX – XX, 2013.

[13] N. Shetty, G. Schwartz, M. Felegyhazi, and J. Walrand. Competitive Cyber-Insurance and Internet Security. In *Workshop on Economics of Information Security 2009*, University College London, England, June 2009.

[14] N. Shetty, G. Schwartz, and J. Walrand. Can competitive insurers improve network security? In A. Acquisti, S. Smith, and A.-R. Sadeghi, editors, *Trust and Trustworthy Computing*, volume 6101 of *Lecture Notes in Computer Science*, pages 308–322. Springer Berlin Heidelberg, 2010.

[15] R. Winter. *Optimal Insurance under Moral Hazard*, chapter 6, pages 155–183. Handbook of Insurance. Boston: Kluwer Academic, 2000.

APPENDIX

A. DETAILS OF THE PROOFS

Below we present the derivations for for Sections 4.2 and 4.3. To prove Proposition 2, consider user FOC in a symmetric case:

$$\Delta_{c0} = R(s, \tilde{s}) = R(s),$$

where

$$\Delta_{c0} := [U(W - \rho_c) - U(W - \rho_c - (L - L_c))],$$

and we use (13) ,(19) (16) to have R, R', B, B' and ρ_c:

$$R(s) := \frac{h'(s)}{[1 - q(1 - s)]},$$

$$R'(s) = \frac{h''(s)[1 - q(1 - s)] - h'q}{[1 - q(1 - s)]^2},$$

$$B = [1 - s(1 - q) - (s)^2 q], \quad B' = -(1 - q) - 2sq,$$

$$\rho_c = BL_c.$$

We differentiate user FOC (12) wrt s to derive the expression for $\frac{dL_c^\dagger}{ds}$

$$R' = \Delta_{c1}\frac{d\rho_c^\dagger}{ds} - U'(W - \rho_c - L + L_c)\frac{dL_c^\dagger}{ds}, \quad (30)$$

where

$$\Delta_{c1} := [U'(W - \rho_c - (L - L_c)) - U'(W - \rho_c)] > 0,$$

and

$$\frac{d\rho_c^\dagger}{ds} = B'L_c + B\frac{dL_c^\dagger}{ds}, \text{ and } B' < 0, \quad (31)$$

$$R' = \Delta_{c1}\left[B'L_c + B\frac{dL_c^\dagger}{ds}\right] - U'(W - \rho_c - L + L_c)\frac{dL_c^\dagger}{ds}$$

$$R' = \Delta_{c1}B\frac{dL_c}{ds} + U'(W - \rho_c - L + L_c)\frac{dL_c}{ds} + \Delta_{c1}B'L_c$$

$$\Delta_{c1}B - U'(W - \rho_c - L + L_c)$$
$$= (B - 1)\Delta_{c1} - U'(W - \rho_c) < 0$$

$$\Delta_{c1}\left[1 - s(1 - q) - (s)^2 q\right] - U'(W - \rho_c - L + L_c)$$
$$= -s(1 - q) - (s)^2 q\Delta_{c1} - U'(W - \rho_c)$$

$$\underset{[+]}{\left[R' - \Delta_{c1}B'L_c\right]}$$
$$= \Delta_{c1}B\frac{dL_c^\dagger}{ds} - U'(W - \rho_c - L + L_c)\frac{dL_c^\dagger}{ds},$$

and we have

$$\frac{dL_c^\dagger}{ds} = \frac{[R' + \Delta_{c1}B'L_c]}{B\Delta_{c1} - U'(W - \rho_c - L + L_c)} < 0, \quad (32)$$

and combining with (31) provides that Proposition 2 is proven.

For Step 3, we can combine (20) with the best user contract (user preferred), which we find from:

$$\max_s \{ B \cdot U(W - L - \rho_c + L_c)$$
$$+ (1 - B) \cdot U(W - \rho_c) - h(s) \},$$

which gives (under the assumptions of interior solution and symmetry of user equilibrium)

$$\{\{-s(1 - q) - sq\}\Delta_{c0} - h'(s)\} - sq\Delta_{c0}$$
$$+ B\Delta_{c1}\frac{d\rho_c^\dagger}{ds} + B \cdot U'(W - L - \rho_c + L_c)\frac{dL_c^\dagger}{ds}$$
$$= 0$$

where the first curly bracket is zero (due to user optimality), and thus:

$$-sq\Delta_{c0} + B\Delta_{c1}\frac{d\rho_c^\dagger}{ds} + B \cdot U'(W - L - \rho_c + L_c)\frac{dL_c^\dagger}{ds} = 0. \quad (33)$$

Next, we use (31) to get rid of direct dependence on $\frac{d\rho_c^\dagger}{ds}$ in (33).

$$-sq\Delta_{c0} + B\Delta_{c1}\left[B'L_c + B\frac{dL_c^\dagger}{ds}\right]$$
$$+ B \cdot U'(W - \rho_c - L + L_c)\frac{dL_c^\dagger}{ds}$$
$$= 0.$$

$$B^2\Delta_{c1}\frac{dL_c^\dagger}{ds} + B \cdot U'(W - \rho_c - L + L_c)\frac{dL_c^\dagger}{ds}$$
$$= sq\Delta_{c0} - B\Delta_{c1}B'L_c$$

$$B\left[B\Delta_{c1} + U'(W - \rho_c - L + L_c)\right]\frac{dL_c^\dagger}{ds}$$
$$= sqR - B\Delta_{c1}B'L_c$$

And then, substitute an explexsion (20) for $\frac{dL_c^\dagger}{ds}$ into (33) to obtain equation connecting equilibrium $L_c^\dagger$ and $s^\dagger$

$$\frac{[B\Delta_{c1} + U'(W - \rho_c - L + L_c)]}{[B\Delta_{c1} - U'(W - \rho_c - L + L_c)]} \quad (34)$$
$$= \frac{sqR - B\Delta_{c1}B'L_c}{B[R' + \Delta_{c1}B'L_c]},$$

With a simplification to a quadratic U, equilibrium equation (34) is analytically solvable (quadratic in L_c).

Author Index

www.ingramcontent.com/pod-product-compliance
Lightning Source LLC
La Vergne TN
LVHW060142070326
832902LV00018B/2910